# The
# ❖Little Book❖
# of the GREat
# enchäntment

## steve Blamires

SKYLIGHT
PRESS

Published in Great Britain in 2013 by Skylight Press, 210 Brooklyn Road, Cheltenham, Glos GL51 8EA.

First published in the USA in 2008 by R.J. Stewart Books, Arcata, California.

Typeset by Arisha Wenneson
Cover design and landscape photo by Rebsie Fairholm

Skylight Press would like to thank R.J. Stewart and Anastacia Nutt for their kind assistance with this reissue.

www.skylightpress.co.uk

Printed and bound in Great Britain by Lightning Source, Milton Keynes.

British Library Cataloguing in Publication Data.
A catalogue record for this book is available from the British Library.

ISBN 978-1-908011-83-1

# Acknowledgements

*With thanks to Glenn Turner of Ancient Ways and PantheaCon,*
*California, for her sponsorship assistance with publication of this book.*

The research and compilation for this biography would not have been possible without the considerable help I have received from many sources. The staff of the Port Townsend Library assisted me greatly in obtaining obscure publications and magazine articles and to them I am indebted. Similarly the staffs of the National Library of Scotland Edinburgh, the Mitchell Library Glasgow, the New York Public Library, the Bancroft Library Berkeley and Sonoma State University Library have all provided material, suggestions and technical help that moved the whole process along. I am also grateful for the publishers and copyright holders who have allowed me to quote from their various publications – the University of Chicago Press for *"Autobiography of Maud Gonne: A Servant to the Queen"*, Mary K Greer author of *"Women of the Golden Dawn"*, Patrick Benham author of *"The Avalonians"*, Konrad Hopkins editor of *"The Wilfion Scripts"* and Ian Boughton of The Rutland Boughton Music Trust for allowing me to quote from the libretto to *"The Immortal Hour."* My appreciation is extended to The Bancroft Library, Berkeley for permission to publish the photograph of Edith Wingate Rinder, and to the Princeton University Library for permission to publish the photograph of Mary B. Sharp.

My deepest gratitude is extended especially to William F. Halloran who has allowed me such free access to the collected letters of William Sharp, which, at the time of writing, he is still in the process of editing. But his invaluable personal and first-hand knowledge of some of the key-players and events described in the ensuing pages were the most valuable of all. I am eternally in his debt for being so free and accommodating with my many requests and questions.

My wife Helen has been supportive of this project from the start and accepted my long hours in front of a computer, plus frequent visits to the UK and obscure islands, with nothing but encouragement and patience. Thank you. Now that you know about "the other woman" in my life I hope you agree it has all been worthwhile.

Finally I must mention the good people of the Highlands and Islands of Scotland, and especially the Isle of Arran that William Sharp, Fiona Macleod and I all love dearly. It was from my family, friends and acquaintances there that I learned of the mysterious Fiona Macleod when I was still young. Had that seed not been planted by those many anonymous Gaels and Celts of my childhood then this book would never have been written.

Tapadh Leibh agus Moran Taing.

Steve Blamires
Port Townsend, Washington, September 2008

# About This Book

William Sharp (1855-1905) was a prominent figure in the literary and art worlds of the last decades of the 19th century. He was a prolific writer; friend and confidant to the literati of the day; and an active member of the blossoming occult world of the late Victorian period. Sharp was a man who spent his entire life cloaked in ever-increasing layers of secrets. The most important of these secrets was that from 1893 until 1905 he was the pen behind the hugely popular writings of the mysterious Fiona Macleod. William Sharp never fully understood just what the phenomenon of Fiona Macleod really was. He kept her true identity a closely guarded secret to all but a few of his friends and magical co-workers. Here is the first full and detailed biography of William Sharp that strips away the layers of secrets to reveal just what Fiona Macleod was, both in this world and in the magical world.

Many famous people – W.B. Yeats, "AE", MacGregor Mathers, Dante Gabriel Rossetti – were involved in William Sharp's short life; he was a member of the Hermetic Order of the Golden Dawn as well as Yeats' secret Celtic Mystical Order; and he and Fiona Macleod were involved with the mysterious Dr. Goodchild whose ancient bowl was proclaimed by many to be the true Holy Grail. But the enduring legacy of these two fascinating writers is the wealth of Faery magical lore contained in the wonderful writings of Fiona Macleod. For the first time in over a century this book reveals previously unknown secrets from the life of William Sharp and shows clearly how to recover the Faery lore still available to us not only in Fiona Macleod's literary output but also in her intimate relationship to Sharp, his wife Elizabeth, and his secret lover Edith Wingate Rinder. The writings of Fiona Macleod are not only about the Realm of Faery, they are the first authentic first-hand accounts from the Realm of Faery, revealing previously unknown Faery gods and goddesses, Faery belief, lore and magic and how to use this information to safely and successfully access Faery.

Some years after Sharp's death in 1905, The Immortal Hour, a powerful magical drama about the interactions between the human and the other worlds, became a huge stage success in the operatic version scored by Rutland Boughton, bringing profound inspiration to many writers, poets, and visionaries whose work resonates to this day. The early years of the 21st century have seen a renewed interest in all things Faery. The Little Book of the Great Enchantment adds significantly to the corpus of serious writings on this greatly misunderstood subject.

## *Steve Blamires*

Steve Blamires is a Scottish author, now living in the Pacific North West of the USA. He has published a number of acclaimed books on spiritual magical and mythic themes within the broad Celtic tradition.

# Introduction

*I am but an obscure chronicler of obscure things, that old charm and stellar beauty of Celtic thought and imagination, now, alas, like so many other lovely things, growing more and more remote, discoverable seldom in books and elusive amid the sayings and oral legends and fragmentary songs of a passing race.* – Fiona Macleod

William Sharp was, in every sense of the word, a Victorian gentleman. He made his living as an art and literary critic, biographer, novelist and poet, was friend and confidante to many of the writers and artists at the end of the nineteenth century and he loved to travel. He was also wrapped in ever increasing layers of secrets. Some he kept from his public but revealed to colleagues and associates, some he kept from everyone apart from his wife and one or two close friends and a few he kept so well hidden that even his wife did not know of them. The most intense of these secrets was the fact that he was Fiona Macleod. Fiona, like William, was a writer and poet but her subject matter was very different. She wrote of life in the remote Scottish Highlands and Islands where Gaelic was the first language, where people fell in love, some lasted but some parted, where the beauty of nature superceded the tragedies of death and loss, and where the old customs, traditions and sayings were the bedrock of this isolated and ancient society. William Sharp would spend the last twelve years of his life writing prolifically under the name Fiona Macleod while simultaneously strenuously denying that he was she. He did this because he believed, indeed he knew, that Fiona was real, was much more than a pseudonym or literary ploy, and that if her identity was revealed to the world she would die. In the end it was William Sharp who died at the early age of fifty. On his posthumous instructions the Fiona secret was revealed but many of the other secrets of his life remained untold. He hated holding on to so many hidden aspects of his life and past and he hated lying to dear friends and family but, in his mind, it was necessary, there was no other way. This book is an attempt to reveal with honesty and dignity the secrets of the life of William Sharp so that he can finally rest in peace and know that his conscience is clear and that the truth has been told. I believe he always wanted that.

To date the main source of information on the life and writings of William Sharp is *"William Sharp (Fiona Macleod): A Memoir"* written by his widow, Elizabeth Sharp, published several years after his death. Many of his friends and acquaintances were still alive when it was published and this greatly restricted what and how much Elizabeth could say. Whereas it is a detailed account of his public life, writings, travels and inspirations, it tells us almost nothing of one of his better known secrets, his magical interests and pursuits, nor does it tells us anything of one of his deeper secrets, his deep and passionate relationship with another woman, a relationship that caused the phenomenon of Fiona Macleod to occur.

The only other biography that has so far been written is Flavia Alaya's "*William Sharp – 'Fiona Macleod' 1855-1905*" that gives an excellent discussion and interpretation of the literary output of these two writers, especially in relation to the social mores and norms of the day. Being a literary biography it too does not reveal much about William's occult interests nor the Gaelic and Faery lore of Fiona's domain. But, as Ms. Alaya observes, "*With William Sharp, unfortunately, a great deal of this understanding must be conjectural. Past efforts hint of the same difficulty: there is something about William Sharp that nearly defies biography.*"[1] Fortunately a considerable amount of new material has come to light since these two biographies were written and in particular a web site dedicated to publishing the letters of William Sharp has been set up making available a wealth of material that was not available to Elizabeth Sharp or Flavia Alaya. So, with Ms. Alaya's words ringing in my ears, I shall attempt to use all of these sources and resources to fill out the gaps left open deliberately by Elizabeth Sharp and unavoidably by Flavia Alaya. To this end, I have made extensive use of quotations throughout the book, letting the people involved speak for themselves as much as possible.

My main point of divergence from the above biographies is that I treat William Sharp and Fiona Macleod as two individual and separate people. I use 'she' and 'her' when talking about Fiona and 'he' and 'his' for William. This makes the text less clumsy and easier to follow and also helps the reader to understand what was really going on with this whole phenomenon. The comment above that there is something about William Sharp that nearly defies biography is true if an attempt is made to deal with the double literary output and the double social and personal life as that of one individual. By splitting them into the two separate sources that they actually were much of this confusion is removed. But this brings with it a new problem, especially to modern readers. My ideas and suggestions will no doubt be considered controversial to some and down right insane to others. Be that as it may. During his short lifetime not even William Sharp could explain what was really happening to him with regard to the manifestation of Fiona Macleod. I have in essence written two biographies in one, that of William Sharp and that of Fiona Macleod. By reading their words concerning themselves and each other, and by supplementing these with the comments and observations of close family, friends and acquaintances, I shall leave the reader to draw his or her own conclusion as to just what Fiona Macleod really was. Whether or not you agree with my conclusions I hope you will discover that William Sharp led a most remarkable life, was an important person in the art and literary worlds of the *fin-de-siecle* and was a crucial figure in the development of what we now call the Western Magical Tradition.

In all of this Fiona Macleod aided him considerably along her own unique lines. The writings under her name contain an immense amount of detail on a magical system based on Faery tradition and Faery mythology. By that I mean the traditions and mythology known to the Faeries themselves, not the traditions and mythology that we as humans have created in our minds about them. This is important. What Fiona Macleod revealed to the world was her personal, first hand account of her own Faery tradition. As far as I am aware this is unique.

Unfortunately today the word Faery, however you care to spell it, conjures up an image that is very different from that known to William Sharp and the public mind of the late Victorian era. Today we think of gossamer winged little sprites with glittering wand in hand, often dressed in remarkably modern human garb, sitting on pretty flowers or fluffy bunny rabbits - and they are clearly not real. The Faeries as perceived by William Sharp, William Butler Yeats, George Russell and others mentioned in this book, were powerful, dangerous, elusive and undoubtedly real. During my researches for the writing of this book it struck me that nowhere in the many references to Faeries and Faery encounters by these and other writers, was there any hint of ridicule or disbelief in the very notion of the existence of Faeries. They were as real as the animals in the field or the birds of the air. Nor was the belief in Faeries kept secret or discussed only amongst an esoteric few. It was well known that W.B. Yeats spent much of his early life as a member of various magical groups and that he had a keen interest in Faery but nobody thought that he was mad or even a bit odd, indeed he went on to become a well respected Senator for the Irish Free State and received the Nobel Prize for Literature. How many politicians would be elected to senior government office today if it became known that they practiced magical rituals and regularly communicated with Faeries?

The public's perception of Faeries has changed considerably, but the Faeries have not. By employing Coleridge's technique of the temporary suspension of disbelief I hope you, dear reader, can better understand who William Sharp and Fiona Macleod were, and thereby obtain a grasp of the nature of the powers that drove them both to write what they did. In her writings Fiona Macleod laid out how to access these power, powers that are still accessible today. I lay out how to recognise and interpret these important passages in the hope that one day soon the public mind will restore to the realm of Faery the stature it truly deserves and has only recently lost.

A final comment: during my research and writing of this book I experienced so many strange coincidences and odd experiences, all of which were relevant to the specific subject I was researching or writing about at the time, that I have felt compelled to include them at the appropriate places in the text. Make of them what you will. To me they served to reinforce my belief in the beauty, wonder and mystery of the lives of William Sharp and Fiona Macleod.

---

[1] Alaya, William Sharp – "Fiona Macleod," 1855-1905, page 3

# Table of Contents

# Setting the Scene

To understand why the writings of Fiona Macleod so often contain references to the sorrow of women, and why the writings of William Sharp so often don't; and to understand why Fiona displays a great sense of beauty, wonder and mystery at the world around her, while William kept things factual and academic, it is necessary to look at the influences they were both writing under. The world in which William's parents met, courted, married and raised their eight children was a dramatically changing one. During William's short life, 1855-1905, there would be many dramatic changes in all aspects of society, science and the arts that would affect him and Fiona profoundly.

When William was born Queen Victoria had been on the throne for eighteen years. The British Empire was expanding and people were becoming much more aware of foreign countries, cultures and religions than they had ever been in the past. There was a desire for knowledge, learning and exploration that permeated all the sciences. The search for the elusive Northwest Passage had been going on for centuries. In 1845, only ten years before William's birth, Lord John Franklin and all his men had disappeared while searching for this potentially lucrative northern passage to the riches of the Orient. Many attempts were made to find him and as more and more ships sailed north looking for the lost sailors the previously unmapped and unknown frozen north became much better known and understood. In 1853 the tragic fate of Franklin and his men in the great Arctic wilderness was discovered while at the same time Dr. Livingstone was exploring the dark interior of the great African continent. The expanses of Canada and the United States were also being traversed and explored and long distance trading between America, Europe, India and Asia was rapidly expanding. In 1869 the Suez Canal was opened and the face of world trade changed forever.

But it was not just commercial or geographic exploration and expansion that was taking place. Many people were starting to explore the inner person, the spirit, the mind and the very fabric of God and the universe.

This manifested in many ways and on many levels. In New York in 1827 Joseph Smith founded the Mormon religion. He was murdered in 1844 but followers of this new religion headed west and Salt Lake City was founded in 1847 as a place where they could live in their own particular way without discrimination or harassment. It was a new religion for the New World. The following year, also in New York, a young woman called Kate Fox announced she had discovered a method of communicating with the spirits of the dead. The practice of communing with the ancestors had been practiced by many indigenous religions for countless centuries but it was a new thing for respectable Victorian American and European Christians to be exposed to such a concept. Within a decade the spiritualist movement had swept North America and Europe and séances, table-turnings and materializations of the spirits of the dead were happening in the parlours of respectable families in many major cities. 1863 saw the founding of both the Seventh Day Adventist movement in the west and the Baha'i Faith in the east. In 1875, again in New York, Helena Petrovna Blavatsky and Henry Steel Olcott started the Theosophical Society which took the practical study of the spirit and religion to a new level for most westerners by introducing eastern, mainly Hindu, concepts. Four years later Mary Baker Eddy founded the Church of Christ, Scientist. The Mormons, Spiritualists, Theosophical Society and the Church of Christ, Scientist are all still going strong today.

In 1888 the practice of magic and the study of the occult was given new stature and respectability when several Freemasons with a good deal of social standing in Victorian London society founded the Hermetic Order of the Golden Dawn. This became one of the most influential occult organizations in Europe and soon lodges and temples were being formed in many European and American cities. William was briefly a member, if not a very active one. The Golden Dawn was noteworthy at the time for admitting women as members and for giving them an equal standing with the male initiates. Several of William's later acquaintances were members and the new ideas and ceremonies they were experimenting with included a certain amount of Celtic influence. William Butler Yeats, who had been a member of both the Theosophical Society and the Golden Dawn, would invite Fiona Macleod to help form a Celtic Mystical Order performing rituals restored from ancient Celtic lore. Of this, more later.

Note that these major advancements in geographical and spiritual exploration were started while a woman was on the British throne and note that women were involved in many of the more spiritual advancements and innovations. After centuries of repression the feminine side of divinity was starting to assert itself. While still a young man studying at Glasgow University, William took an interest in such things and was heavily influenced by the feminist movement and the thoughts and writings of several close female friends.

However, as is so often the case, there were negative things taking place alongside these positive advances. Today we tend to think that environmental pollution, racial and sexual discrimination, the unequal status of women in society and the unbalanced distribution of wealth are all modern phenomena. They are not. We also tend to have a very romantic and 'warm glow' image of Victorian society. Witness at Christmas time especially how many greetings cards are depicted in a pseudo-Victorian style and show images of a Victorian family, well fed and in a cozy drawing room, standing round a heavily decked Christmas tree. For the vast majority of Victorians this was far from the world they knew and endured.

William Sharp's family was relatively well off due to his father's mercantile business. They had good social standing and connections in the community, but the world around them was a dark and far from pleasant place especially for women and the underprivileged. When William's parents married they set up home in the town of Paisley, Scotland, then some miles west of Glasgow but today more or less absorbed into that ever-expanding city. Paisley features occasionally in Scottish history and is probably best known as being the likely birthplace of Scotland's national hero Sir William Wallace. Despite the romantic scenery shown in the enormously successful movie "*Braveheart*" Paisley and the surrounding area is flat. There are no rough-hewn, majestic peaks or heather-clad river valleys along which the sound of bagpipes can be heard drifting through deer-strewn mists. Paisley lies in the central belt of Scotland known as the Central Lowlands. It has always been part of Lowland Scotland and the people have always been Lowlanders as opposed to Highlanders. This is important. In later life Fiona would enthuse about life in the Gaeltacht, the Gaelic speaking areas of the Highlands and Islands, and more or less ignore the rest of the country.

Prior to William's birth, and long before his parents David and Katherine met, Scotland had been a divided country. These divisions were on several levels – social, political, religious and particularly geographical. In the north were the Gaels, the Gaelic speaking Highlanders and Islanders, while in the south were the English-speaking Lowlanders with ways and customs very different from their northerly neighbours. And never the twain did meet, at least not if they could help it. The Gaels had always had a harder way of life than their southern cousins. Subsistence farming and fishing had been the mainstay for untold generations. A society based on extended family ties, the clan system ('clann' in Gaelic means children or offspring), was the order of the day. Nothing much had changed in centuries. The people were fervently religious, Catholic in some areas, Protestant in others, but with an odd mixture of pre-Christian and early Christian beliefs and practices thrown in. This was the subject of Alexander Carmichael's monumental and still very important work "*Carmina Gadelica,*" a work that Fiona Macleod borrowed from, as we shall see later.

The one uniting factor the Highlanders and Islanders had was the Gaelic language. This was the very bed-rock of Highland and Island society and was the one thing which gave these dispersed and remote people a sense of unity and belonging. It also totally separated them from the monolingual English speaking Scots in the south and thus created a divided country. This was not important to either the Gael or the Scot. The natural topographic boundaries between the Highlands and the Lowlands kept them apart anyway and intercourse between the two peoples was rare. Up until the late 19th century travel between the two regions was physically very difficult with very few roads and very few commercial ferries. Highlander was virtually unknown to Lowlander and vice versa. This remained the situation for a very long time. As late as 1846 the *Scotsman* newspaper was making comments like, "*The people of Skye are an indolent, ignorant and dirty race*" and taking for granted that its readers all subscribed to the belief that Lowland Scots and Anglo-Saxons were innately superior to anyone of Celtic origin. 'Scientific' evidence to prove this belief was touted from time to time such as, "*Ethnologically the Celtic race is an inferior one and, attempt to disguise it as we may, there is no getting rid of the great cosmical fact that it is destined to give way before the higher capabilities of the Anglo-Saxon.*" This was backed up by comparing the skulls of Celtic skeletons which were '*characterised by a low type of cranial formation approximating to that of the Negro races.*"[1]

In the Central Lowlands and Southern Uplands (the hilly area of Scotland along the border with England) the people had generally been more prosperous. Farms tended to be larger affairs than the small subsistence crofts in the north. People sold produce at markets and, in some cases, worked for money paid by an employer, a concept unknown in the Highlands. Religion was important but the older customs had all but disappeared. And the language was English. It is true that many in the central belt spoke a dialect now called Lallans, the language Robert Burns dared to set in print and use for some of his poetry, but even Lallans speakers used English as their first language. These southerners tended to think upon themselves as sophisticated and modern while they regarded the Gaels as backwards, anachronistic and barbaric.

This situation of two people within one country changed completely and forever on April 16th 1746 when the massed armies of Bonnie Prince Charlie and those of the English Crown met at Drumossie Moor, Culloden, near Inverness, in what was to be the last battle fought on British soil. It was Bonnie Prince Charlie and the Highlanders' last stand and final attempt to reclaim the ancient throne of Scotland and England for the Catholic religion. The events of that day and the build up to it have been described in detail in many a history book. Suffice to say that the Highlanders were massacred, Charlie fled Scotland never to return and the break up of the ancient Scottish Clan system could be heard reverberating throughout the blood-filled glens. Not content with the butchery of Culloden the government in England went on in 1747 to pass an act of parliament known as "*The Act of Proscription.*" This was, to use the modern idiom, an act of ethnic cleansing. Within its provisions were the prohibition of wearing the traditional tartan, the right to bear arms, the gathering of Highland people and the teaching of the written Gaelic language.

The penalty for breaking any of these new laws was seven years transportation to "*any of His majesty's plantations beyond the sea.*" The period became known as "the time of grey" because the traditional bright colours of the tartan were no longer to be seen. The Gaels were being forced to give up their native, traditional ways and instead look and behave like civilized southerners.

The Act of Proscription was repealed in 1782 but after thirty-five years of repression the damage had been done. Two generations of Highlanders had been born and raised without access to their traditional culture or way of life. Many of the few remaining clan chieftains had betrayed their clansmen, their children, and headed south, mainly to London to enjoy the bright lights and social whirl far from their cold and miserable lands in the blighted north. To make matters worse, and to put the final nail in the coffin of the Highland and Island way of life, the landowners of the day were all jumping on the bandwagon of "The Improvements." This was a system of new farming methods and land use that greatly improved the value of the land, hence the name. The unfortunate thing about these improvements was that they involved the whole-scale removal of the people, the tenant farmers, to make way for highly profitable and easily managed sheep. The ordinary people came to refer to this time as "The Clearances" for that is exactly what happened to them. They were simply cleared out of the Highlands and Islands to make way for sheep, which soon earned the nickname "the four-footed clansmen."

The cruelty and brutality of some of these Clearances, which lasted from the late 18th century right into the early 20th century, beggar belief. Many of the tens of thousands of Highlanders and Islanders who were forcibly evicted from their ancient homes and farmlands were bundled onto the ships sailing empty for America to pick up cargoes of timber, tobacco and cotton. Prior to William's birth emigrant ships were sailing regularly from Scotland. These vessels soon became known as the coffin ships due to the high number of deaths at sea. Between 1847 and 1853 at least forty-nine ships from Scotland, each carrying between 600 and 1,000 passengers, were lost. The people who survived the crossing were dumped off on the other side of the Atlantic in Canada and the U.S.A. and left to their own devices. Many of those who had not died of disease on the high seas starved to death in these foreign lands where the Gaelic language was useless. Others ended up in slavery alongside the equally displaced Africans who had suffered similar fates. Only a very few managed to make a living and survive. Back in Scotland those who did not end up on the coffin ships found their way out of the glens their families had inhabited for hundreds of years and drifted down to the cities in the Central Lowlands. Overnight thousands of families who had known nothing but a quiet family cottage in the clear Highland air, next to the cool clear waters of the mountain streams, were suddenly pouring into the overcrowded, disease infested cities. Within a very short time, during the first half of the 19th century, Glasgow had produced some of the worst slums in Europe, many of which were close to the Sharp family home.

Soon the old cultural divisions in Scotland between Highlanders and Lowlanders were being replaced by the huge social gap between the haves and the have-nots. Glasgow and Paisley had several rich families. Tobacco, timber, linen and banking had made many families wealthy. This Scottish nouveau riche invested in buildings and expansive public parks to show off their newfound wealth. To this day Glasgow has some of the finest architecture in the United Kingdom and more public parks than any other city in Europe. They built art galleries and museums to house the exhibits that had been casually plundered from all over the burgeoning British Empire. Superficially there was an air of prosperity and well-being but all the time the slums were growing larger, disease and unsanitary conditions were rampant and the poor were becoming poorer.

Then, laying catastrophe upon disaster, between 1845 and about 1850 the potato crops throughout northern Europe were devastated by a previously unknown, and at that time untreatable, blight. Particularly hard hit was the island of Ireland. Soon tens of thousands of Irish families also had to make the choice between the horrors of the coffin ships or facing starvation at home. Many made their way across the Irish Sea to Liverpool and the other industrial cities of the English Midlands. Many more made their way to Scotland, the land of their Celtic cousins. As a result the already bursting-at-the-seams cities and slums grew even larger, even more overcrowded and even more disease infested. But there was paid work for some, especially women and young children, in the hellish working conditions of the 'manufactories' that had changed little since the Industrial Revolution.

In 1755 before the Clearances and the potato failure 51% of the Scottish population lived in the Highlands and Islands and were Gaelic speakers, 19% lived in the Southern Uplands and less than 30% lived in the Central Lowlands. By the 1850s more than 75% of the population of Scotland lived in the urban Central Lowlands with only 10% still in the Highlands and Islands. Over 50% of the entire British population had moved off the land and into the cities. The United Kingdom was the first country in the world to achieve this dubious record.

Paisley was rapidly growing at this time due to the blossoming linen industry for which the town would become famous. The steady influx of Highlanders and Irish meant that an unending supply of workers was available to the mill and factory owners to operate the machines and produce even more wealth for them and their privileged few. To get some perspective on what working conditions were like for women at that time you need only consider that in 1844 the government felt compelled to ease the burden the young girls and mothers were bearing by introducing legislation, "*The Factory Act*," which, very graciously, limited the working day for women to no more than twelve hours.

Sanitary conditions in the poor housing areas were dreadful and infant mortality was very high. Disease and sickness were always present and the notion of family planning non-existent. A young girl in Paisley at that time could look forward to little or no education, chronic sickness and disease, a back-breaking job in a factory from the age of about twelve onwards and then the production of babies, the delivering of which would probably one day kill her. Even the wealthier women who did not need to work in the factories were at great risk during childbirth.

Things got slightly better for mothers-to-be in 1853 when Queen Victoria's eighth child was delivered while she was under chloroform. This immediately popularized the use of anesthetics during labour. However the grip of the church was strong, especially in Scotland where the Church of Scotland and the newly formed Free Church of Scotland condemned anesthetics during childbirth as being contrary to the teachings of the Bible and the will of God who had made women to suffer. This was reflected in the eyes of the law as well. In 1832 *"Bacon's Abridgement of the Law,"* a standard legal text in common use at the time, stated, *"The husband hath by law the power and dominion over the wife and may beat her* [but] *not in a violent or cruel manner."* "Not violent or cruel" was loosely defined as using a stick or rod providing it was no thicker than the man's thumb. Hence the expression we use today *"rule of thumb"* meaning anything that is a mere guideline or suggestion. In short, women were no more than the property of the man, could be legally beaten with a stick and had virtually no rights of their own, their primary duty being to produce off-spring and to suffer in the process.

Almost all babies were born in the home at that time. This was fine if the mother was healthy and lived in a clean, warm and disease-free house but for the women of the factories and slums it was a very dangerous time to go through. In most cases there would be no midwife to help and if things went wrong there was a very good chance that the mother, the baby or both would die. It was not until 1865 that Joseph Lister came up with the practice of using antiseptics in surgery and it would not be until 1902 that the UK government made the licensing of practicing midwives compulsory with the passing of the *"Midwives Act."*

In amongst this doom and gloom, which motivated Fiona's writings so much, there were some people who tried to make a difference, who cared about the poverty stricken Gaels and who tried to bring social change and improve social awareness of the plight of women. But progress was slow. In 1869 women in the UK gained the legal right to possess property of their own but it would not be until 1918 that women over the age of thirty with a university education gained the right to vote. In 1878 the Booths started The Salvation Army and used a military style Christian organization to bring relief to the poor and needy. It helped a great deal, particularly with the emphasis on temperance and the evils of alcohol. However it was not until 1884, twenty-nine years into William Sharp's life and ten years before Fiona Macleod made her first appearance, that the National Society for the Prevention of Cruelty to Children was formed.

In 1890 the world's first documentary photographic book appeared and profoundly affected many of the 'haves' who were oblivious to the suffering of the hoards of 'have nots' in their own home towns. This was Jacob Riis's photo journal called "*How the Other Half Lives*," a graphic and disturbing record of the slum conditions existing them in New York City. People were truly horrified by what they saw in this book but the social divisions remained for a long time and change, when it did come, was slow, difficult and often ineffective. Riis was a Danish immigrant who worked for a while as a reporter and photographer for the New York Police Department and his daily encounters with the 'have nots' of that burgeoning city inspired him to fight for the plight of the poor everywhere. He also published several scathing articles on the destructive effects of gambling on all social classes and levels of society.

The rapid expansion of industry and the demand for consumer products during William's lifetime resulted in pollution and destruction on a scale previously unknown. As early as the 1860s the Brazilian forests were being cleared as fast as possible to make way for coffee plantations. The American bison population stood at around 50 million but by 1890 it had been cut to less than 1 million. Back in Scotland river pollution was becoming so widespread that a Governmental Royal Commission was set up in 1865 to look into the causes and what could be done to improve water quality. To emphasise how bad things were part of the report was written not in ink but in water taken directly from the River Calder, not all that far from Paisley. In 1896 a Swedish scientist called Svante Arrenhius predicted what we would now call global warming caused by the huge amount of coal being burned in the factories, power stations and private homes of Europe. Unfortunately it is easy for us to relate to these things today because little has changed. It is harder, though, for us to imagine this heavily industrialised world with virtually no automobiles. In 1900 horse transportation was still the normal method of getting around. In London alone the authorities were removing 1 million tons of horse manure a year from the city's streets. In 1905 air quality in the cities had become so bad that the word smog, a combination of smoke and fog, first came into use.

This stark situation was the way the world was on December15th 1854 when David Galbreath Sharp married Katherine Brooks in the High Church, Paisley, Scotland.

---

[1] Hunter, "Scottish Exodus", page 251

# Chapter 1
# Early Days and a Faery Baptism

*I write not because I know a mystery, and would reveal it; but because I have known a mystery, and am today as a child before it, and can neither reveal nor interpret it.*

The Sharp family had originally come from the little town of Dunblane on the edge of the Highlands before settling in Paisley in the Lowlands. When David married Katherine he was a partner in a well-established mercantile house in the town. In her memoir, Elizabeth Amelia Sharp, wife of William Sharp, described his father as, "*a genial, observant man, humorous and a finished mimic. Though much of his life was of necessity spent in a city, he had a keen love of the country, and especially of the West Highlands. Every summer he took a house for three or four months on the shores of the Clyde, or on one of the beautiful sea lochs, or on the island of Arran, now so exploited, but then relatively secluded. Very early he initiated his son in the arts of swimming, rowing and line fishing; sailed with him along the beautiful shores of the West Highlands and Inner Hebrides.*"[1] Katherine was the eldest daughter of William Brooks, the Swedish Vice Council in Glasgow, and she herself was of Swedish lineage. In later life William would occasionally write under the name of W.H. Brooks. Of her Elizabeth said, "*Mrs. David Sharp had been brought up by her father to read seriously, and to take an interest in his favourite study of Geology. It was she who watched over her son's work at college, and made facilities for him to follow his special pursuits at home. But the boy was never urged to distinguish himself at college. He was considered too delicate to be subjected to severe mental pressure; and he met with no encouragement from either parent in his wish to throw himself into the study of science or literature as a profession, for such a course seemed to them to offer no prospects for his future.*"[2]

Just over nine months after their marriage William was born in the family home at 4 Garthland Place, Paisley. Elizabeth said of his birth, "*William Sharp was born on Wednesday 12ᵗʰ September 1855. She* [his mother] *cannot tell me the exact time, but thinks it was about midday. She writes that the bells were ringing and she was told it was because Sebastopol was taken. She thinks it was about 12 o'clock. 12 seems to be a number that has some special significance for my husband's life—as it was on the 12th December on which he passed out of this life. Moreover, I went to Iona this summer—to perform a little rite for him myself there—in St Oran's Chapel—and it chanced to be the 12th September, at 12 o'clock. It was pure accident. He had hoped to be buried in Iona—but that was impossible."* [3] The reference to Sebastopol being taken is to an important battle during the Crimean War. Coincidentally this book was started while I was living in another Sebastopol, the one in Northern California, and continued while I worked on a ship whose captain came from the original Sebastopol in Crimea. During the years of researching and writing this book there were so many such coincidences that I have felt compelled to list them throughout the text.

It was from the maternal side of his family that William inherited his Scandinavian physique and appearance being 6'1" with blue eyes and fair hair. He was, in the words of a friend, *"A Viking in build, a Scandinavian in cast of mind and a Celt in heart and spirit."* [4] He was not a typical Viking, however, as he would suffer from chronic ill health throughout his short life. Later accounts from friends of their first meeting with him almost invariably start with a detailed description of his striking appearance and often used the word Viking or Norseman. For example, his friend Ernest Rhys described his first encounter with William in 1885 thus, *"He towered up, a rosy giant, in the low-raftered room. His fine figure and exuberant contours, set forth in unusually resplendent clothes, suggested a stage Norseman. He talked fast and excitedly, his bright yellow hair brushed up from an open brow, under which blue eyes, rosy cheeks full red lips, and a pointed yellow beard suggested a staring picture by some impressionist painter."* [5]

He was the eldest of a family of nine although only eight survived. William was first-born in 1855 followed by Agnes Henderson (24th December 1856), Elizabeth (24th November 1857), Katherine Marie (15th January 1860), Margaret Alice (9th April 1861), David Charles (14th June 1862), Katherine Brooks (10th October 1863), Mary Beatrice (11th September 1865) and Thomas Edward (9th October 1867). The fourth child, Katherine Marie, died while still a baby. All of these births took place in the family home. As a result young William spent his first twelve years repeatedly watching his mother grow with her almost annual pregnancy and display the usual signs of discomfort and tiredness. Then would come the day of sudden rush and confusion as he was hustled out of the way as the delivery time approached. And then, magically, a new brother or sister would be presented to him. Witnessing the physical effects of pregnancy and delivery on his mother from a very young age had a profound and lasting effect on him. One day though, when he was only five years old, his new baby sister Katherine was suddenly no longer there. Infant mortality was not uncommon in those days but the emotional distress was nonetheless as intense as it is today and he must have been aware of his parents' sorrow and grief. Being a close witness to all of these intense events during his formative years shaped his whole being and psyche in ways that later manifested in an intense concern for the suffering and affairs of women. These themes can be found throughout his writing and the later Fiona Macleod stories that both make frequent references to pregnancy, the pain of labour, death during childbirth and infant mortality.

There is one more background factor to this story, and in particular the story of Scotland and the Scots, which it is important to understand. It also has a curious link to a prominent member of the Hermetic Order of the Golden Dawn who we shall meet later. On June 28th 1837 the young Queen Victoria took the British throne. Her reign lasted longer than William Sharp would live. She died on January 22nd 1901 after more than sixty-three years as monarch, much of the latter part in a permanent state of mourning for her beloved Prince Albert. Early in her reign she developed a passion for Scotland, the Scots and all things Scottish. This is in itself noteworthy because the third verse of the British National Anthem says,

> God grant that General Wade*
> May by Thy mighty aid
> Victory bring
> May he sedition hush
> And like a torrent rush
> Rebellious Scots to crush
> God save the Queen

Fortunately for the Scots God appears to have ignored this plea for extermination. Victoria spent a lot of time at Balmoral, the royal estate in Scotland, where she had many of the rooms decked out in a garish combination of tartans that no true Scot would have ever considered. Soon it became fashionable amongst the English gentry to join the Queen and royal court in Scotland and to adopt Scottish habits and customs. At least, what they considered Scottish habits and customs. This was when the "Balmorality" of Scottish culture took place. To use modern parlance, this was the Disneyfication of the original Scottish way of life, particularly that of the Highlander. Soon the descendants of the Clan chiefs who had abandoned their people and lands back in the 18th and early 19th centuries in favour of sheep were now eager to brag of their noble Scottish ancestral background and were desperate to be seen striding the hills and glens in a bastardized form of the kilt, dogs at heel and servants in tow.

Early in Victoria's reign two Polish brothers managed to ingratiate themselves with her and her court and between them they basically reinvented

---

*General Wade had been sent to Scotland in 1715 to put down a rebellion by Highlanders

Scottish history and culture into the popular image most non-Scots still have to this day. These two young men, John and Charles Sobieski-Stuart, claimed to be grandsons of Bonnie Prince Charlie. Prince Charles was a Stuart and he had married a Polish countess called Sobieski, hence their Polish name. History shows us that their claim to royal descent is highly dubious to say the least for as far as we know from contemporary records the last of Bonnie Prince Charlie's line died out in the early 1800s. However they were accepted at face value and made welcome at Victoria's court. They then set about, amongst other things, creating a specific tartan to be associated with each individual clan, and making previously non-existent connections between non-Scottish family names and the ancient Scottish clan names. They did this in such a way that they could 'prove' to any English member of the royal court he or she was in fact connected to this or that Scottish clan and they were therefore entitled to wear a kilt bearing 'their' tartan. The brothers spent much time researching all this material in the British Museum where they were given their own partitioned alcove bedecked with gold crown motifs and samples of their newly created tartans.

A later acquaintance of William's, whom he met through the Golden Dawn, was Samuel Liddell MacGregor Mathers who we shall discuss in a later chapter. He too spent a great deal of time at the British Museum where his interest was not in creating tartan but in researching the occult. It is possible that in his younger days at the museum MacGregor Mathers may have seen one or other of the brothers going about their tartan research but whether he saw them or not he would certainly have heard of them. Mathers also claimed to be a direct descendant of Bonnie Prince Charlie and on occasion he claimed to be a reincarnation of the Prince himself. Whether he was or whether he was not, it is likely that it was the enormous influence of these two Polish confidence tricksters that persuaded Mathers to adopt the MacGregor part of his name and to cycle around Paris, his home for much of his life, in Highland dress. He even gave himself the title of Comte de Glenstrae.

While all these people were having their fun in London at the expense of the true Scottish culture a new form of Clearance started to take place in Scotland. Whereas the people had been cleared before to make way for sheep now much of the already devastated population remaining in the Highlands and Islands was cleared to make way for deer. It had become much more profitable to rent out entire moors and hillsides for deer hunting than it had been to allow the introduced Cheviot sheep to roam over the moor-covered slopes. Victoria and her gentry did not seem to notice that the people she professed to love and admire so much were disappearing and that their homes were being burned down around them.

When William was born this adulteration of the culture and abuse of the people was in full swing. Not only was he raised during a time of abject poverty and hardship for the Highlanders and Islanders who had been left with almost nothing, but even those who had something were being abused in a more subtle way. Their land, tradition, culture, music, dance and very way of life had been taken over as the playthings of royalty and nobility. It is remarkable that young William, under so much unconscious Lowland pressure, developed such a keen, genuine and life-long interest in the ways of the Gael. It took some thirty-eight years of life before it finally broke through and was given free rein under the pen of Fiona Macleod but it is clear from his childhood reminiscences that it had always been there.

He inherited much of this love of the Gaeltacht from his father who arranged every summer for the entire family to holiday for as long as three or four months at a time in the Western Isles. William had always been considered to be a delicate and somewhat weak child but his father nonetheless taught him to sail, fish and swim in the clear but cold lochs and sea inlets of the Highlands. It was during these long summers of total freedom amongst the wilds of the west coast, away from the polluted city and the dreary blandness of the Paisley area, that he quickly developed his love for the "*Green Life*" as he was to call it. Despite his young years he took a keen interest in the changing weather patterns, the moods of the sea, the ways of the birds and animals and the abundance of plant life all around him.

During these long summers his constant companion was his old Highland nurse Barbara. She taught him the Gaelic of the isles and told him the old stories of Celtic and Viking heroes and warriors and filled his young mind with the Gaelic folklore, charms and sayings that later so influenced the writing of Fiona Macleod. We know nothing about this influential character from his early days or even why a Gaelic speaking Highlander should end up as nurse for a Lowland family in Paisley. It is probable that Barbara's family had been cleared from its native Highland home and she, like so many others, had found her way down to the cities of the Central Lowlands in search of employment.

Even at the tender age of six he was naturally drawn to what he would call a pagan outlook. He used the word pagan in the classical sense meaning a Bohemian and adventurous lover of Nature rather than in its contemporary use as a practitioner of a non-Christian, nature-based religion. During the summer stays at Loch Long he often went to a little wood halfway up the heather clad hillside where he played with invisible companions, as many developing children do. He took things a bit further though in a way that is rare amongst even expressive children. He built a little stone altar and laid white flowers on it as an offering not to his unseen companions but to the spirit of the place. He later recalled, "*I thought that belt of firs had a personality as individual as that of any human being, a sanctity not to be disturbed by sport or play.*"[6] His real and life-long fascination though was with the sea. He recalled, "*When I was a child I used to throw offerings—small coins, flowers, shells, even a newly caught trout, once a treasured flint arrow-head—into the sea loch by which we lived. My Hebridean nurse had often told me of Shony, a mysterious sea-god, and I know I spent much time in wasted adoration: a fearful worship, not unmixed with disappointment and some anger. Not once did I see him. I was frightened time after time, but the sudden cry of a heron, or the snort of a Pollack chasing the mackerel, or the abrupt uplifting of a seal's head became over-familiar, and I desired terror and could not find it by the shore. Inland, after dusk, there was always the mysterious multitude of shadow. There, too, I could hear the wind leaping and growling. But by the shore I never knew any dread, even in the darkest night. The sound and company of the sea washed away all fears."* [7] The sea and terror would be common themes in the later writings of Fiona Macleod.

His aunt and three cousins from London would often stay with them on these long holidays. One of these cousins was Elizabeth Amelia Sharp with whom he quickly developed a deep rapport. She later recalled their first meeting, when he was eight, and described him as *"... a merry, mischievous little boy ... with bright brown curly hair, blue gray eyes, and a laughing face... eager, active in his endless invention of games and occupations."* [8] Elizabeth understood his visions of the spirits of places and he felt he could speak freely to her. He soon learned though that the others could not see his invisible playmates or understand him when he spoke of having "been here before" and so he learned to keep silent. Even at such an early age he learned that there were things so personal to him, beliefs he held so strongly that others did not share, that the only way to deal with them was to hold and cherish these beliefs but keep them secret from the rest of the world. His whole life would follow this pattern of keeping secrets, to the point that their burden seriously affected his physical, mental and emotional health. During this early period in his life he was already feeling how heavy secrets could become and he found it necessary to spend much time alone in the Green World so that he could recharge and regenerate. The more important secrets of adulthood were much more difficult to cope with and the technique of running away to the Green World for succor would no longer suffice.

He once wrote of his childhood memories, *"For I, too, have my dream, my memory of one whom as a child I called Star-Eyes and whom later I called 'Baumorair-na-Mara', The Lady of the Sea, and whom at least I knew to be none other than the woman who is in the heart of Women. I was not more than seven when, one day, by a well near a sea loch in Argyll, just as I was stooping to drink, my glancing eyes lit on a tall woman standing amongst a mist of wild hyacinths under three great sycamores. I stood, looking, as a fawn looks, wide-eyed, unafraid. She did not speak, but she smiled and because of the love and beauty in her eyes I ran to her. She stooped and lifted blueness out of the flowers, as one might lift foam out of a pool, and I thought she threw it over me. When I was found lying among the hyacinths dazed, and, as was thought, ill, I asked eagerly after the lady in white and with hair all shiny gold like buttercups, but when I found I was laughed at or at least, when I passionately persisted, was told I was sun dazed and had been dreaming, I said no more - but I did not forget."* [9]

This early encounter with a Faery woman is significant in two ways.

First, much of the lore that Fiona would later relate, many of the gods and goddesses she talked about with such familiarity and even some of the names she used for her characters, cannot be found in Celtic or Gaelic lore or tradition. They are from the Faery realm. This theme will underlie everything to do with Fiona Macleod when we come to her later and will be discussed in depth at the appropriate places. This Faery woman's act of showering him with the blueness of the flowers, which William compared to the foam of a pool, was very significant as it was no less than his baptism into the world of Faery. For the moment it is important to note the name William gave her 'Baumorair-na-Mara' The Lady of the Sea. Although he says the incident took place 'near a sea loch' he does not say that this Faery woman came from the sea or that she was connected to the loch in any way. In fact she seems to be specifically associated with the little grove containing the hyacinths and sycamores. Why did he give a woodland Faery an aquatic name? Fiona would use the themes of the sea, sea-lochs, sea-caves, encounters with seals, lakes, rivers, sailing, fishermen and fishing boats extensively throughout her poems, stories and essays. Even her personal correspondence frequently mentions boating and sailing, usually among the Western Isles. When we come to examine exactly where, how and when Fiona came into being the theme of water will crop up again in a very important way.

Second, this meeting, factual or imagined, is more important than it may at first seem. Today we would probably consider such a childish experience as cute and endearing but certainly not something to be taken seriously. This was not the prevalent attitude amongst Victorians however. To them Faeries, in whatever guise, were a far cry from the sugary little tinsel-winged sprites of today's New Age. As Carole Silver has shown vividly in her book "*Strange & Secret Peoples*" the Victorians considered the Faeries to be real, dangerous, a threat to life and limb and to be avoided at all cost. The newspapers of the day frequently carried serious stories of children being abducted by Faeries, adults being charged with horrendous crimes against children they considered to be changelings, and accounts by people of all social classes of what they considered to be genuine Faery encounters. As Silver says, "*...from the 1840s till the 1920s, the elfin peoples had a surprisingly large impact on the society that witnessed, studied, painted, dramatized and wrote about them. The Victorian study of fairy lore acts as an excellent reflector of both the dominant ideas and concealed anxieties of the era. The specific areas and problems in fairy faith and fairy lore that preoccupied Victorian folklorists and believers are revelations of social and cultural concerns, perhaps shown elsewhere, but never in such sharp relief.*" [10] and later, "*The best thing to do, all agreed, was to avoid the fairies. Meeting them even in innocent encounters was dangerous; doing them injury or insult was bound to be damaging or deadly.*" [11]

Young William's close encounter of the Faery kind no doubt caused a degree of genuine anxiety and concern from his family and certainly from nurse Barbara. It also explains why in later life he was still prepared to recount the tale, knowing it would be met with reactions of shock and relief at his narrow escape rather than ridicule or astonishment at still believing in such childish fantasies. In the foreword to her play "*The Immortal Hour*," written towards the end of the century, Fiona Macleod emphasised this point when she said, "*It should be added that with the ancient Gaels (and with the few today who have not forgotten or do not disdain the old wisdom) the Hidden People (the Sidhe or Shee; or Shee'an or Sheechun of the Isles) were great and potent, not small and insignificant beings. 'Mab' long ago was the terrible 'dark' queen, Maive (Medb, Medbh, Mabh): and the still more ancient Puck was not a frolicsome spirit, but a shadowy and dreadful Power.*" [12]

Amongst these wild and remote places in the Highlands and Islands can still be found powerful and highly charged areas where many people with little or no psychic ability can feel a presence, an unfamiliar 'something.' The young William, encouraged by his kindly Hebridean nurse and with a great deal of natural psychic ability, could clearly feel and communicate with the powerful forces of Nature all around to the extent that these were more real to him than was the physical world in which the rest of his family lived. Even as a young boy he felt himself to be different from his siblings and cousins. He had the same vivid imagination that so many young children do but to him it was all real, absolutely real. Whereas this conviction normally fades and dies during the process of growing from childhood to adolescence to adulthood, it remained with him for the whole of his life. He always felt apart, distant, from his family as if they were no more than kindly people he knew, but not of the same flesh and blood. In later adult life he maintained very little contact with his siblings apart from his sister Mary but even then only because she acted as his secretary. As Elizabeth said of him, " … *he seemed to feel himself different from the other children of his age, and would fly off alone to the hillside or to the woods to his many friends among the birds and the squirrels and the rabbits, with whose ways and habitations he seemed so familiar. About the dream and vision side of his life he learned early to be silent. He soon realised that his playmates understood nothing of the confused memories of previous lives that haunted him … To his surprise he found they saw none of the denizens of the other worlds – tree spirits and nature spirits, great and small – so familiar to him … He found … a curious power of vision unshared by any one about him.*" [13]

He was no doubt aware of the stories concerning changelings, Faery babies substituted for stolen human children. [14] This is a common theme in Faery lore throughout Europe and, even in the mid to late 19th century, there were stories appearing in the Press of parents maltreating a baby or child because they believed it to be a changeling. William never specifically expressed a belief that he may have been such a substitute child but in later life when reflecting on his childhood it may have crossed his mind. It was certainly there unconsciously as both he and Fiona used this theme in several of their works. In Fiona's books "*The Mountain Lovers*" the heroine is a changeling, the hero in *"Green Fire"* is of uncertain parentage and the title character of *"Cathal of the Woods"* is more changeling than human. William often used this device of uncertain parentage too as in, for example, the heroine of *"The Sport of Chance,"* the enslaved daughter in *"Silence Farm"* and Sanpriel in *"The Children of Tomorrow."* It was obviously a subject that he found interesting.

His father discouraged young William's fantastic visions and invisible playmates and instead emphasised the physical side of experiencing Nature—swimming, hiking, boating, fishing and so forth. There was no religious dimension to all this as far as he was concerned. He did not see all this Faery stuff as being something that had to be discouraged in a young Christian boy but he did ensure the family attended the church on Sundays as all good Victorian gentlefolk were expected to do. In later life William would be horrified by the teachings and imagery of the Christian religion that seemed to be so negative and to completely ignore the beauty of God's Creation. It was this aspect of God, the beauties and wonders of Nature, not the written teachings of the Bible and Church, which he felt so strongly, loved so passionately and constantly drew from for solace in times of hardship, a sense of wonder to keep in check the banality of daily life, and inspiration for his writing and his own sanity in a world rapidly divorcing itself from the powers of the Green World.

His formal education had begun at an early age at home under the tutelage of a governess but at the age of eight he was finally *"captured for the sacrifice of school"* and sent to Blair Lodge, Polmont, the chief boarding school of its day in Scotland. Most children who were given a formal education in those days started their schooling at the age of four or five. William was lucky in that he had been given the freedom to explore, experiment and develop his natural abilities and curiosity for three or four years more than other children before the dogma, discipline and the destruction of imagination caused by the formal education system was imposed on him. Whereas he enjoyed the companionship of the other children he could not accept the limitations of the classroom. The first few weeks of school are hard on many children but at least most can go home after lessons and be with family, friends and familiar things but this is not possible in a boarding school. Although he never commented on it, being taken away from his mother after eight years of closeness was probably very hard on him and not having easy access to the wilder places he so loved must have felt very repressive. As a result he was frequently disciplined for unruly and rebellious behaviour. This actually started on his first day at his new school and home. He said when he arrived a rebellion had already broken out and he eagerly joined in, *"I remember the rapture with which I evaded a master's pursuing grip, and was hauled in at a window by exultant rebels ... I insulted a big boy ... and forthwith experienced my first school thrashing. Later in the day I had the satisfaction of coming out victor in an equal combat with the heir of an Indian big-wig ... this was not a bad beginning, and I recollect my exhilaration (despite aching bones and smarting spots) in the thought that school promised to be a more lively experience than I had anticipated."* [15]

He ran away from the school several times, not because he hated the school but because he needed more adventure and action in his young life than the confines of the classroom and dormitory afforded. On the last such occasion he and some comrades successfully stowed away on a cargo ship in Grangemouth, not far from Polmont, where, *"We slept that night amid smells, rats, cockroaches and a mysterious congregation of ballast and cargo."* [16] Fortunately for them a storm blew up and the ship could not leave port. After three days of cold, hunger and misery, the unsuccessful stowaways gave themselves up and were transported back to Polmont where, *" ... the admiration of comrades did not make up for punishment fare and a liberal flogging."* [17] Running away and rebellion, in many forms and shapes, would be the pattern of his life.

Four years later in 1867 things changed for the better when his parents moved to India Street in Glasgow. He was taken out of Blair Lodge and placed in Glasgow Academy to complete his schooling as a normal day-scholar. The next three or four years were uneventful being spent between studying in Glasgow during term time and roaming his beloved Highlands and Islands during holiday time. He was still a weak child and his health took a turn for the worst in 1871 when at the age of sixteen he was struck down with typhoid fever. By way of convalescence he was sent to the isles where he had already struck up a great friendship with an old fisherman called Seumas Macleod whom he had met during earlier summer holidays. It was Seumas who continued his education of things Celtic that his old nurse Barbara had started. Seumas appears in many of Fiona's works sometimes under different names, Ivor being one of them. We do not know exactly where Seumas lived. All William said was he spent the summer of 1871 on a "remote island" with his old friend Seumas Macleod during his convalescence from the typhoid fever. It is clear though that the extended stay in the isles and the friendship of Seumas Macleod contributed significantly to the development of the persona of Fiona Macleod as well as to the content of her later writings. We shall consider Seumas more closely in a later chapter.

He duly finished his education at Glasgow Academy and was accepted as a student at Glasgow University where for the next three years he studied English Literature. He never completed his degree but by all accounts he worked well and was named as a student worthy of special commendation. His real fascination at university though was the extensive library, not for the study of English Literature, but for the deeper study of mysticism, eastern religions, folklore, the occult and magic from anywhere and everywhere. This exposure to new thoughts and to previously unknown religions, confirmed his belief in a common underlying truth that was behind all religions. It also had the effect of driving him further and further away from the Presbyterian teachings of his upbringing. In later life he would recount his horror at some of the teachings of the Christian religion but, especially, the grotesque and often cruel imagery of its paintings, statues and buildings.

Throughout his life William expressed a hatred for cities. His frequent exposure to the idyllic Highlands and Islands of Scotland from such a young age had left him with a strong distaste for cityscapes, city life and city people. In his book "*The Sport of Chance*" he describes Victorian Glasgow through the eyes of the character Mona, "*She was at once submerged in the dense and fast flowing human stream, and even as a broken flower is swept along by some current, so was she carried Eastward in the direction of the Trongate as if she had no volition of her own. What noise there was, what glare of lights, what brutal faces and brutal words, and brutal laughter, what evil and hollow mockery of gaiety, what drunkenness, what loathsome and omnipresent vice. In the midst of this human maelstrom, Mona felt as if she were in some dreadful nightmare.*" [18] During these university years he escaped the dreadful city whenever he could and took every opportunity to visit the Gaeltacht, the Gaelic-speaking areas of Scotland. As he put it, "*From fifteen to eighteen I sailed up every loch, fjord and inlet in the Western Highlands and Islands, from Arran and Colonsay to Skye and the Northern Hebrides, from the Rhinns of Galloway to the Ord of Sutherland. Wherever I went I eagerly associated myself with fishermen, sailors, shepherds, gamekeepers, poachers, gypsies, wandering pipers and other musicians.*" [19]

Normally in these areas an English speaking Lowlander would have been treated with courtesy but also with a great deal of suspicion. However because he spoke the Gaelic language, taught to him by nurse Barbara and Seumas Macleod, he was quickly accepted by the people he met and was often invited to stay for a few days with local crofters and fishermen. From them he continued his education in all the ancient Celtic and Gaelic lore of these remote reaches of Scotland. This informal education, snatched at odd weekends and holidays whenever he could get away from Glasgow and the university, taught him much that would form the background to most of Fiona's stories, poems and plays.

At eighteen he met up with a band of European gypsies camped at Ardentinny in Argyll. He spent the next three months wandering the Highlands with them in a euphoria created by this dream-come-true lifestyle. It was from this normally secretive and closed community that he learned much lore concerning the trees, birds and animals, the stars and the ways of the weather. The gypsy lore, tradition and language are all very different from that of the Celt and Gael and during his three months he picked up some of the language. As late as 1902 he still remembered some of this and used it in the opening greetings of a letter he sent on November 21st 1902 to a friend, "*Shar Shan, Bor! Which, being interpreted, is Romany (Gypsy) for 'How d'ye do, mate!*" [20] The influence of the gypsies manifested in his writings long before Fiona's Celtic and Gaelic did. In some of his early works published under his own name the gypsy inspiration can be found, mainly in "*Children of Tomorrow*" and "*The Gypsy Christ*." He had planned a story called "*The Gypsy Trail*," which he never wrote, which would have been based on his experiences with the gypsies. As Elizabeth said though, " ... *the present was the absorbing actuality for him, and the future a dream to realise; whether in life or in work the past was the past, and he preferred to project himself toward the future and what it might have in store for him.*" [21]

It is possible that he had intended this way of life to be permanent rather than just a diversion for the summer. He had always had a habit of running away as a child, both literally and figuratively, but now as an adult he may have deliberately chosen to run away permanently to a life on the open road rather than face the confines of conventional living. He often referred back to this period throughout his life with great fondness and in private correspondence he frequently spoke of this time. The whole impression one gets is that he had decide to be a wandering itinerant for the rest of his life, to sleep under the stars and to live with the gypsies and the creatures of the field. Many years later he told a tale of this period to William Butler Yeats which not only shows how much it was still in his mind but, as Yeats makes clear, displays his tendency to tell wild, fantastic stories that seem to have been made up as he went along. According to Yeats, as a boy of eighteen William had, "*loved madly and had been madly loved by a beautiful girl. They decided to die together.*

'*We got in a boat and rowed out for miles and miles into the Atlantic. Then we embraced one another, and I put my foot through the bottom of the boat, and the girl was drowned.*'

'*Yes, but what about you, Sharp?*' demanded Yeats.

'*It was terribly sad: the water came rushing in through the hole and she was drowned.*'

'*Yes, yes, Sharp, but what about you?*'

'*Well, you know, when a man goes through an experience like that it makes a great difference to him: it –* '

'*Yes, but Sharp, what happened to YOU?*'

"*... SWUM ASHORE!*'

*He had started his story and entirely forgotten how to end it.*" [22]

However, his concerned parents would have none of this free roaming spirit nonsense as it was abundantly clear to them that he was heading quickly towards a fruitless life with neither income nor career. In an effort to curb his wanderings and to teach him the acceptable way of life for an up and coming Victorian gentleman they secured for him a position in a lawyer's office in Glasgow. He hated it. The captivity and the long hours in the restrictive environment were hard indeed for him to endure. Even though he had to accept that his wandering days were over he was determined to at least carry on with his studies in religion and folklore. As a result from 1874 until 1875 he set himself a grueling routine of twenty hours work and study per day with only a four-hour rest. Needless to say this taxed to the extreme his already weak constitution.

In August of 1875 the family were once again on holiday in the west, this time in Dunoon on the Firth of Clyde where his aunt and cousins joined them from London. Elizabeth had not seen the now twenty year old William for some time as is clear from the second description she gives of him in her memoir, "*I remember vividly the impression he made on me ... He was six feet one inch in height, very thin, with slightly sloping shoulders. He was good looking, with a fair complexion and high colouring: gray-blue eyes, brown hair closely cut, a sensitive mouth, and a winning smile. He looked delicate, but full of vitality. He spoke very rapidly, and when excited his words seemed to tumble one over the other, so that it was not always easy to understand him.*" [23] The following month they met again in Glasgow where William's family now lived and they became engaged to be married. They decided it would be best not to break the news to their families for the time being, at least until he was able to support them both financially. Here was another secret in which he was enveloping himself. He would eventually tell his family of his betrothal but for several years it was another layer of secrecy he carried around with him.

Elizabeth's description of their engagement is telling in its brevity. Engagement is one of those milestones in any young woman's life that brings excitement, dreaming and the wish to share happiness with friends and family. Her only comment on her engagement is, "*In September my sister and I visited our Uncle and Aunt at 16 Rosslyn Terrace, Glasgow, and before the close of that month their son and I were secretly plighted to one another. Then began a friendship that lasted unbrokenly for thirty years.*" [24] It reads more like a newspaper report than the personal revelation of a very romantic and intimate time in her life. It is interesting that she described the next thirty years of life as being no more than a friendship between them. What about love? Was there no tenderness? Was there no joining of hearts and souls for eternity? This was written several years after William had died and with the benefit of hindsight, and with the events that would subsequently unfold during William's lifetime, she seems to have realised that their marriage was best summed up in the word friendship. We shall return to this theme later.

William's elation was displayed by a sudden outpouring of poetry for his new fiancée. Elizabeth never published it, claiming it was not good enough for publication, but she kept these early attempts at poetry and said of them that they, "*... were all very serious, for his mind was absorbed in psychic and metaphysical speculation. And the reason why he chose such serious types of poems to dedicate to the girl to whom he was engaged was that she was the first friend he had found who to some extent understood him, understood the inner hidden side of his nature, sympathized with and believed in his visions, dreams, and aims.*" [25] William and Elizabeth were still living with their respective parents, he in Glasgow and she in London, and soon they were parted once more. Elizabeth spent three months in the spring of 1876 in Italy and on return the two families were once more reunited in holiday homes at Dunoon on the Clyde.

This was a happy time with the lovers enjoying much sailing, rambling and long walks over the hills. However, things took a turn for the worst when William's father, who had been unwell for some time, died on August 20th. William's already poor health had been aggravated by his tortuous work regime but the stress of his father's passing brought on a complete physical and emotional breakdown. Naturally this was of great concern to his mother and family. It was clear that the damp, cold Scottish climate was not going to be conducive to recovery so he was quickly dispatched to the warm and dry climate of Australia for rest and recuperation – and away from his fiancée and new love. This would be the first of many separations from Elizabeth and removals to warmer climates for the sake of his delicate health.

---

[1] Memoir, page 4

[2] Memoir, page 4

[3] Finneran, Letters to William Butler Yeats, Page 176

[4] Memoir, page 5

[5] Rhys, "William Sharp & Fiona Macleod","Century Magazine", LXXIV, page 112

[6] Memoir, page 6

[7] Memoir, page 7

[8] Memoir, page 8

[9] "The Winged Destiny", page 212

[10] Silver, Strange & Secret Peoples, page 57

[11] Silver, Strange & Secret Peoples, page 155

[12] "Poems & Dramas", page 319

[13] Memoir, page 8

[14] According to W.B. Yeats the Faery name for a changeling is either "*Lorgadan*" or "*Larrigadaun*", meaning long-legged. This name was learned during visionary work with the Faeries. (Kalogera, page 155.)

[15] Memoir, page 10

[16] Memoir, page 11

[17] Memoir, page 11

[18] "The Sport of Chance", page 300

[19] Memoir, page 12

[20] Memoir, page 355

[21] Memoir, page 13

[22] Yeats Annual 14, page 201

[23] Memoir, page 17

[24] Memoir, page 17

[25] Memoir, page 18

# Chapter 2
# Australia and Unexpected Checks

*Then there was William Sharp always telling in what Rossetti called 'the unknown tongue' exaggerated and incredible stories which made him laugh uproariously but were never intended to be believed.*

At the age of twenty years William Sharp's world had changed completely. His father who had taught him to swim, sail and love the water, and who had given him so much freedom as a child, had died. His own health had broken down to the point where his family was convinced he probably would not survive the sea voyage to Australia. He had become secretly engaged to his cousin but was now being torn away from her. His ramblings in the Highlands and Islands of Scotland had come to an abrupt end. He had no money, no prospects and his dreams of being a poet and living the wandering Bohemian lifestyle had evaporated. Throughout his life he suffered many hardships and difficulties and often his response was to pack his bags and run away, often very far away. This enormous move to Australia though had not been his own rash decision but had been imposed upon him by his frail health and the concerns of his family.

It must have been an adventure indeed to leave Scotland for the first time and make such a long and hazardous journey. The only means of transport to Australia was by ship and the voyage could be dangerous and unpleasant. Coming from a wealthy family though William's passage would have been much more comfortable, and on a much safer vessel, than that experienced by many of his fellow countrymen who were being forced to emigrate due to the Highland Clearances. In the early 1850s ships leaving Scotland had a poor reputation for survival. Fifty-three of the 701 emigrants on the *Marco Polo* died at sea, eighty-four of the 754 crammed into the *Bourneuf*, ninety-six on the *Ticonderoga*, forty-one on the *Priscilla* and fifty-six of the 742 on the *Hercules* that took almost five months to make the crossing. In an already weakened condition it must have been hard for him to let go of so much he held dear and to look forward with any optimism to a new life in a totally unknown environment. But survive the crossing he did.

He stayed with family friends in New South Wales and the warm, dry air quickly improved his chest condition. Soon he was on horseback and exploring into the vast interior of this newly settled land. The flora and fauna were unfamiliar but thanks to his deep love of nature, in all its wondrous forms, he drank in all he saw and experienced and marveled at the beauty of the landscape, the brightly coloured birds and the unique mammals only to be found on that vast island continent. The sheer size of the land and the enormous open spaces seemed to allow him to expand and grow in a way he could not amongst the confining glens and hills of Scotland. He wrote long, enthusiastic letters to Elizabeth going into great detail of all the wonderful and new things he was seeing and experiencing. A lot of this new vigour and love of life was probably initiated by the fact that this was the first time in his twenty years that his health had been good enough to allow him to roam so freely and unrestricted.

Having the experience of living in and exploring this wonderfully new and intricately varied country was an enlightening experience for him. Until this time he had only ever known Scotland. He was intimate with its remote and scenic Western Highlands and Islands that he loved with a passion, the same passion with which he hated its noisy and polluted cities, but he had no other place with which to compare it. Australia opened his eyes and soul to the fact that there were places other than Scotland that could evoke such an overwhelming sense of awe and wonder at the beauty of nature and the myriad multifaceted forms of life it produced. It is said that to travel is the most instructive experience anyone can have and William learned an enormous amount from his Australian adventures. He also came to realise that in his heart and soul he did not feel particularly Scottish. His passion for the Highlands and Islands of Scotland was not because they were Scottish per se but because they were places where he could be himself, be free, be expressive, where he could recharge his psychic batteries and communicate in depth with the forces of the Green World. This was a valuable learning experience for him. In later life his apparently uncontrollable urge to incessantly travel, roam and wander came from this time and this realisation. He did not need to remain in Scotland in order to feel close to the ethereal things that were so important to him. A notable difference between the writings of William Sharp and those of Fiona Macleod is their setting. William wrote poems, essays, stories and articles set in Scotland, Ireland, Brittany, Australia, Antarctica, Italy, Greece, and Germany whereas Fiona's settings were almost exclusively in Scotland alone. By the end of his life his personal friends and acquaintances were many but strikingly few were from his native Scotland. Whereas he was passionate about the rights of women and the underdog, wherever they may be, his sense of the importance of nationalism was non-existent. This would cause subtle but important difficulties for him and Fiona in later years when they started to get drawn into the fiery political climate of nationalism, so predominant in Victorian politics.

Eventually the novelty and glamour of this new world faded and he was forced to consider the reality of where he was and what his prospects were. Reluctantly he left the bush-country and returned to the city of Melbourne to look for work. Melbourne would crop up again later in his life in two oblique ways. At one point he was employed as a clerk for the London branch of the Bank of Melbourne and a later friend, Frank Rinder, was an adviser to the National Gallery, Melbourne. And here is another coincidence from my own life – the shipping company I worked for under the captain from Sebastopol had its head office in Melbourne, Australia. But back to William: he did not put much effort into his search for employment as he was abhorred by the thought of once again being fettered to a desk in an office whether it was Australian or Scottish. He was probably not too enamored at the thought of living in the growing city of Melbourne either, which had seen its population grow from 77,000 in 1851, nearly all convicts, to almost half a million by 1857. Many of these newer immigrants were victims of the Highland Clearances some of whom, ironically, went on to become successful sheep farmers. An Australian immigration official at this time said, *"I am put to great difficulty with these people because I am unable to communicate with them except by signs … I do not understand one word of Gaelic and they do not understand one word of English."* He then commented on their uncleanliness and added that they are *" … as near an approach to barbarians as any* [emigrants] *I have ever met with."*[1]

Consequently he did not find any gainful employment and his financial situation was worse than it had been when he arrived in Australia. His physical health had improved significantly and in spirits he was feeling at his peak. However it soon became clear to him that life in Australia would not suit his erratic temperament or his restless nature. In the late spring of 1877 he decided that Australia was not the place for him and he made arrangements to return to Scotland. He knew his health would soon fade in the damp Scottish climate but it would be worth it to be back amongst his beloved landscape and closer to his dear Elizabeth.

It is fitting the ship that took him back to Scotland was named the *"Loch Tay,"* one of William's favourite Highland haunts. The journey involved rounding the treacherous Cape Horn where many a ship has been lost. The *Loch Tay* encountered a storm that caused it to be blown far off course to the south. By the time the winds abated the ship was well into the iceberg strewn waters of the Antarctic seas. Very few people at that time had ventured into this remote and freezing part of the world even by choice and the significance of this was not lost on William. In 1884 he wrote of the wonders he briefly encountered in the frozen south. The poem *"Moonrise On The Antarctic"* may well be the first poem about Antarctica that was written by a poet who had actually been there as opposed to the poetic imaginings of some armchair explorer.

*The huge white icebergs silently*
*Voyage with us through this lonely sea,*
*Noiseless and lifeless, yet they seem*
*Like haunted islands in a dream*
*Holding strange secrets that no one*
*May know and live. In the bright sun*
*They shine immeasurable fair,*
*Bluer than bluest summer air,*
*Or clear to the very heart with green*
*Pure light, or amethyst as seen*
*'Mid sunset-clouds—but now they shine*
*With a cold gleam and have no sign*
*Of loveliness. The ship swings on,*
*Plunging 'mid surging seas whereon*
*Few vessels ever sail, and as*
*Slowly the long hours come and pass*
*The late moon rises cold and white,*
*And sends a flood of wintry light*
*Along the sweeping waves and round*
*Our black and sea-worn hull. A sound*
*Far off dies while it grows—some seal*
*Long-drifted, frozen, waking but to feel*
*Death's grip. And now the spectral isles*
*Grow whiter, icier still, and seem*
*More hollow, with a strange weird gleam*
*As though some pale unreal fires*
*Consumed them to their utmost spires*
*Yet without flame or heat. And still*
*The moon doth rise, and seems to fill*
*Each berg anew with life: we sail*
*Upon a strange sad sea, where pale*
*And moonshine isles float all around,*
*Voyaging onward without sound.* [2]

The ship eventually made its way back to England in June of 1877 without loss or damage. He stayed in London for several weeks at his aunt's house where he was reunited with Elizabeth his secret fiancée. The lovers spent many happy days catching up on each other's news, reading their newly composed poems to one another and discussing all the great literary happenings of the day. His aunt was much more practical and made many introductions for her nephew in the hope of finally securing some gainful employment for the twenty-one-year old dreamer and wanderer. Elizabeth was also making introductions for him to her special friends and acquaintances most of which knew the secret of their betrothal. One of these acquaintances was Alice Mona Alison who had been born on the Isle of Wight but now lived in London. She did not use her first name but preferred to be called Mona. In 1877, not long after meeting William, Mona married James Alexander Henryson-Caird. He was eight years older than her, of a Scottish noble family, and owner of a large estate in southwest Scotland. Mona wrote a good deal about the Victorian attitude to women and specifically women in marriage. Her views, even by today's standards, were very radical and free-thinking but then, especially amongst the landed gentry (of whom her new husband was one), they were considered outspoken and outrageous. Obviously her new husband agreed with her radical social views as he allowed her to travel extensively and freely without him and to write profusely and therefore have her own independent income, a rare thing for women in those days. Despite the fact Mona is mentioned many times in Elizabeth's biography of her late husband, and despite the many, many letters that still exist between Mona and the Sharps, James Henryson-Caird is barely mentioned. Later William would model the fictitious life of Fiona Macleod on the real life of Mona Caird claiming that she too was married to a Scottish landowner who allowed her to travel freely and earn an independent income.

This was an important time for William as far as the development of Fiona was concerned. Elizabeth and Mona were both writers of ability and they gave clear and concise comment and criticism on the fledgling writer's work. It was their feminine insights and comments on the whole issue of women in society, however, that was so informative for him. He had always cared about such things and had watched and observed keenly the women in his life, his mother, sisters and cousins and had been deeply affected by the loss of his baby sister Katherine while he was still a young boy. From these observations as an outside male he came up with his own thoughts and beliefs about the Sorrow of Women, as he would so frequently call it. Now he was hearing these things first hand from the hearts and mouths of women he loved and respected. The effect was deep indeed.

By the autumn of 1877 he had failed to secure employment in London so he moved back to Scotland where his mother had taken a house in the little town of Moffat in the Scottish Border country. His poor health soon made itself known again but despite this he still loved to walk the rolling hills of the Borders and expose himself to the Green Life of Scotland that he loved so dearly. Many of the impressions and thoughts of that time were used as the basis for Fiona's "*Where The Forest Murmurs*" written many years later.

The return to Scotland, his rediscovery of the powerful world of nature and the influence of his feminist fiancée and friends were all starting to cause changes in his unconsciousness. On August 21st he wrote to Elizabeth from the Highland village of Braemar where Highland Games were held in 1831 and were continued annually to amuse Queen Victoria, "*I feel another self within me now more than ever; it is as if I were possessed by a spirit who must speak out … I am in no hurry to rush into print; I do not wish to write publicly until I can do so properly.*"[3] This may be the first stirrings of the embryonic Fiona Macleod who would not manifest for another seventeen years and put so successfully into print all of the things that were churning around in his mind – the beauty, mystery and wonder of nature, the sorrow of women, the feminine aspect of Divinity and the deep spiritual ways of the simple people of the Gaeltacht.

However his dreams of becoming a great literary figure were given a severe jolt by the poet Robert Buchanan. William had admired Buchanan's work for some time and had sent him several of his own poems hoping for a favourable comment. The reply he received was discouraging to say the least with Buchanan's final comment being not to even dream of literature as a career. William was shattered and went into a deep depression. His poor health and the miserable weather of the Scottish winter did not help alleviate his gloom. He was also in the situation of having no money, was seriously in debt and had no immediate prospects of improving his situation unless he did something positive soon. He had hoped that his saving would be through writing but that no longer seemed likely.

So in mid 1878, and in characteristic drastic fashion, he made up his mind to leave Scotland once again. This time though, instead of making the long sea voyage back to Australia, he would head for Turkey and enlist in the Turkish army to do his part in the war with Russia! This bizarre and downright stupid idea was characteristic of the way he handled his life. Whereas most people would either grudgingly accept their situation and get on with it, or find conventional means of improving it, William would stroll along oblivious to the desperate straits he was in until some event would suddenly jolt him back to reality. Then his answer was invariably to drop everything, pack up home and go somewhere totally new and often completely unknown. Joining the Turkish army was certainly one of the more extreme such decisions. Fortunately just before he was about to leave for Turkey a friend of his uncle managed to secure a place for him with the City of Melbourne Bank in London. Despite his abhorrence of office work he realised that this was a much more acceptable alternative to fighting with the Turks so he accepted the offer and headed south again.

This is something else that was uncanny about his short life – the frequent and timely intervention of Fate. Several times during periods of crisis, often financial crisis, he would be intent on some rash action or other when Fate supplied a much more acceptable remedy. His life is strewn with occasions when sums of money would arrive out of the blue just when things were at their worst financially; and acquaintances were made at crucial times which led on to important connections and contacts in both the publishing world and the occult world. It seems that William had a very powerful guardian angel that was not prepared to let him stray from his destiny. He himself came to believe this was literally true when he contracted scarlet fever and phlebitis in 1886. He was already weak from a severe chill and this attack of scarlet fever took him to the brink of death. During the days when he was in a near-death condition he became acutely aware of the 'other life' and found he had no desire to get better. He wanted to die and remain fully in the Otherworld. But, as Elizabeth later recalled, " ... *a hand suddenly restrained him: 'Not yet, you must return.' And he believed he had been freshly sensitized as he expressed it; and knew he had – as I had always believed – some special work to do before he could again go free.*"[4]

So, weak and penniless, he left Scotland and headed south to London where he had at least some prospects of improving his lot. He hated London and he hated being away from the world of nature that meant so much to him. His lodgings at 19 Albert Street were within walking distance of the bank but, more importantly, they were near Regents Park where he could be close to trees and birds, albeit those of a public park. The employment in the London bank was no easier than his previous captivity in the lawyer's office in Glasgow but his financial situation was such that he had to keep gainful employment in order to avoid further debt and to pay off, little by little, the money he already owed. The one positive thing about this move to London was that he could now see Elizabeth on a regular basis; indeed he would stay with her at her mother's house from Saturday until Monday mornings.

Still very few people knew of their engagement and this caused some tension between them. Elizabeth found it hard and disliked being dishonest with her mother whereas William, " ... *delighted in the very fact of the secrecy, of the mystery, and, indeed, mystification, which I did not then realise was a marked characteristic of his nature.*"[5] They were nervous about announcing their engagement as they believed that neither parents would agree to them marrying for several reasons. The more important of these were that William had failed miserably to prove himself as a provider and there was no sign he was going to improve in that area. Secondly they thought that there would be concerns raised as he and Elizabeth were first cousins. As it happened their fears were groundless. When they did finally own up to their engagement their parents did indeed express these concerns but also knew that to forbid the marriage would be futile and counter productive. So after the obligatory sermon on marriage and its responsibilities they happily gave their blessings to the young couple.

On his birthday in 1879 he received a gift of a book, an innocent enough gift in itself, but one that proved to be one of those life-changing incidents mentioned above. A friend, Miss Adelaide Elder, sent him a book of poetry by Dante Gabriel Rossetti. Years later he reminded Miss Elder of this modest gift and the significant affect it had on his life when he wrote to her saying, "*For it was you who ... sent me ... a copy of a beautifully bound book by a poet with a strange name and by me quite unknown – Dante Gabriel Rossetti. To that event it is impossible to trace all I owe, but what is fairly certain is that, without it, the whole course of my life might have been different. For the book not only influenced and directed me mentally at a crucial period, but... I came to know Rossetti himself—an event which completely redirected the whole course of my life."* [6]

It was his artist friend Sir Noel Paton who made the introduction to Rossetti who William first visited on September 1st 1881. Through Rossetti he eventually met and befriended many of the talented writers, artists and thinkers of the day who lived in London or who frequently passed through that great city. Now, finally, in 1881 he was having some of his work published and was touching on the Bohemian lifestyle he had desired for so long. He was now socializing with the luminaries he had admired from a distance despite the fact he himself was still no more than a clerk in a bank. Rossetti liked the young Scotsman and their friendship meant a great deal to him. In his autobiography Hall Caine, a friend of Rossetti, recalled those days in London and the visitors who called on Rossetti, *"Then there was William Sharp, a young fellow in his early twenties, very bright, very winsome, very lively, very lovable, very Scotch, always telling in what Rossetti called 'the unknown tongue' exaggerated and incredible stories which made him laugh uproariously but were never intended to be believed."* [7] He at last felt as if he had been admitted to the inner circle of the London artist and Bohemian community where he felt relaxed and was welcomed socially and taken seriously as a writer and poet. This, coupled with his newfound freedom of expression in lifestyle, opened up much in his personality that had been suppressed for so long.

Once again he was pushing himself to the limit as far as his daily routine was concerned in order to live this new lifestyle to the full. He savoured every moment he could with the circle of friends he was making and he took advantage of all invitations to dinners, parties and social events in order to see and to be seen. But he also had to keep up his day job in the bank. Many of the writers and artists he associated with were nocturnal in habit, not having day jobs as such, which meant that by following their lifestyle he was once more depriving himself of sufficient rest and sleep and his energies were being steadily drained. He was also pursuing his interest in the occult and things spiritual and this was draining him on a psychic level as well. In a letter to Mona Caird dated February 23rd 1880, he commented, *"On Wednesday evening next I am going to a Spiritual Séance, by the best mediums—which I am looking forward to with great curiosity..."* [8] We do not know what transpired at this séance or what his impressions of the 'best mediums' were but it is an indicator that he had not abandoned his researches into the psychic side of life despite his absorption into the literary and artistic world of London.

He was writing profusely at this time, much encouraged by Rossetti. Some of these early writings contained themes that Fiona would take up later, particularly those dealing with the suffering of women and the great importance of motherhood. Elizabeth was spending the winter in Italy with her mother and sisters at this time so William could only share these wonderful days with his fiancée by letter. Here is another peculiarity of his strange life. Throughout their lengthy engagement and throughout their entire married life William and Elizabeth frequently spent long periods apart. Sometimes this was because of the health needs of parents, other times because one party was ill and had to remove to warmer climes for a while or occasionally it was because of the demands of work. In her memoir Elizabeth makes no comment whatsoever on how she felt about these extended separations. From reading her biography of her husband you get the impression that separation was no great issue and was just part and parcel of being married to a Bohemian with wandering tendencies. However from the letters and diary entries that survive it is clear that they were deeply in love and genuinely fond of each other and neither enjoyed these times apart. These separations were especially hard on William.

This particular instance with Elizabeth being in Italy was hard though from a purely selfish point of view; his beloved was not there to see him socializing with, and being entertained by, the writers and artists he so adored. This was the pinnacle of his success so far and Elizabeth was not there to praise him or congratulate him for doing so well. The later frequent separations would be hard on both of them and have a negative effect on their relationship. It was during one of these separations William started an affair with a beautiful younger woman that would last until he died. This affair, like the meeting with Rossetti, would drastically alter his life and result in the birth of Fiona Macleod. I wonder if this extra marital affair would ever have happened if William and Elizabeth had spent less time apart and, if so, would Fiona ever have been born?

His slowly increasing health and vigour were dealt a substantial blow during a visit to friends in Kent when he was caught in a heavy thunderstorm and drenched to the skin. Later while on holiday in Portmadoc, Wales, he developed rheumatic fever and was ill for the rest of that year. This attack had a permanent damaging effect on his heart. His chronic ill health was never induced by violent acts such as physical accidents, attacks on his person or warfare for example. It was always aggravated by natural events such as being caught in a rainstorm. It is ironic that it was the natural events of the Green World, the world he loved so much and could relate to most, that were so often the cause of his failing health.

Meantime Elizabeth continued with her plans to visit Italy with her mother and left the invalid at home in London to slowly recuperate. She was in her element in Italy. Although she was a keen writer her real passion was art, especially the Old Masters. In Italy she roamed from gallery to gallery absorbing and studying the masterpieces she had only read about. They continued to communicate frequently by letter in which William enthused about his social circle and the latest offerings of his new writer friends in London and Elizabeth enthused about the wonderful paintings and sculptures she was seeing in Italy. This exchange of letters gave rise to the one negative comment in Elizabeth's memoir about her husband at this time. It is not directed at their being apart as such but at William's total absorption in his own doings and self-importance to the extent of ignoring the things that were important to her. She says, "*In Italy I was making a careful study of the old masters in painting, and found that my correspondent took but lukewarm interest in my enthusiasm… I regretted his indifference and asked him, banteringly, if his dislike extended equally to the early masters of the pen and to those of the brush.*" [9] He seems to have been genuinely taken aback by this mild rebuke. His response was long and rambling but, basically, said that you cannot compare poets and painters – and he then proceeded to spout again about his own doings without any further question as to Elizabeth's activities!

During these important years in London he was keeping up his writing at a steady pace but his output was very stiff, formal and intellectual and seems to have been written in a style meant to please his new literary friends rather than as an outpouring of his own inner feelings. The mental image one builds up of the author from these stoic writings is of a typical respectable Victorian gentleman who knows his place and manners. However all of the contemporary descriptions and later reminiscences of his acquaintances describe him as being a sensitive person with a great sense of humour, mischievous but with a genuine care for the under privileged of the day, and a dreamer and wanderer who was fun to be with. It has to be said that this picture of William Sharp does not come across in his early writings. Elizabeth commented on this when she rather sadly admitted, "*Unfortunately I have very few letters or notes that illustrate the light gay side of his nature – boyish, whimsical, mischievous with rapid changes of mood. Others saw more of it at this period than I; for to me he came for sympathy in his work and difficulties; to others he went for gaiety and diversion, and to them he made light of his constant delicacy; so that the more serious side of his life was usually presented to me.*" [10] The romantic, intuitive, feminine side, so dominant in the later Fiona Macleod writings, was being kept strictly under emotional lock and key at this time. It would be several more years before it was released on the Victorian public.

Inevitably the boring routine of the bank job and the stifling atmosphere of the city made him restless but as Fate would have it this all changed in August 1881 when his employment with the bank was terminated, much to his great relief. This came about because he failed to keep a business appointment with the head of the bank, ironically a meeting that had been meant to discuss his future prospects. When he awoke that morning it occurred to him he had not yet heard a cuckoo call that year so he took an unofficial day off and went to the countryside in search of the elusive cuckoo. Needless to say the head of the bank did not see this as conduct becoming of a respectable banker and he gave the errant young clerk a choice – he could remain with the Bank of Melbourne if he wished, but in one of its more remote branches in Australia, or he could resign. He chose to resign and remain in London.

Luckily he soon found another job that appealed to him much more than the bank could ever have done. He was hired by The Fine Arts Society in its gallery in Bond Street to look after the newly created section dealing with German and English engravings and etchings. This suited him perfectly and helped to introduce him to the subject of art criticism from a professional standpoint, not just from the standpoint of friend of the artist as had been the case up until now. In later years his love of art grew, much to Elizabeth's pleasure, and he secured writing positions for several papers and magazines as art critic. The position in Bond Street did not last long though as the directors of the society changed their minds about the new section and, once again, William was out of a job and without income.

To make matters worse his dear friend Rossetti died in April 1882. In March William had spent a few days with Rossetti away from London, a trip that both men enjoyed. William returned home to London and in early April he learned of his dear friend's passing by reading of it in a newspaper. He was shattered. The emotional effect on him was tremendous but, paradoxically, gave him the push he needed to really start writing seriously. He was asked by the publishing house Messrs. Macmillan to write Rossetti's biography within the year. He accepted the offer immediately and put everything he could into producing the work quickly and in a manner fitting the memory of his lost comrade. Up until this point his writings rarely expressed complex inner feelings and when they did it was in a rather stiff and masculine way. He had always taken his time over these jottings, carefully choosing the correct words and settings, sometimes spending weeks or months before coming up with the finished article. Now he felt a strong need to complete the biography as soon as possible while the memories of Rossetti were still fresh in his mind. He discovered he had a knack at writing biography and over the next several years he would produce several more. His haste in producing the biography of the recently deceased Rossetti, and later biographies of other recently deceased public figures, caused Oscar Wilde to quip, "*When someone dies Sharp and the undertaker are first on the scene.*"

Not only was he obsessive in completing the work quickly and satisfactorily but his writing technique had altered. He realised that once the creative flow started he should let it flow on at its own pace until it finally dried up. Sometimes this resulted in writing sessions in excess of thirty-six continuous hours. This was destructive as far as his delicate health was concerned but it was constructive in that he was producing a higher quantity and quality of work. He had held the belief that once a piece was written and set down in print it should not be changed. He therefore deliberated long and hard over every word and sentence before setting pen to paper. Now with the urge to finish the Rossetti biography quickly he was letting the words pour from his pen as fast as they came to mind. After Fiona arrived he continued with his belief that his writings should not be altered once finished but she would constantly chop, change, edit and amend her own writings. Even after death she left Elizabeth instructions on how the "*Collected Works of Fiona Ma-*

*cleod"* should be edited. Fiona took a long time to write what were usually comparatively short pieces whereas following Rossetti's death William was producing a wealth of material in a short period of time but only because he was working grueling hours in order to do so.

The publication of the *"Life of Rossetti"* brought William to the attention of publishers and the public alike. Consequently much of 1882 and 1883 was taken up with serious writing intended for commercial publication. His poetry and fiction were starting to receive favourable critical acclaim and this spurred him on to produce more. His first book of poetry, *"The Human Inheritance; The New Hope; Motherhood"* was published this year and although it was overshadowed by the Rossetti biography, he was pleased with it and saw it as a significant turning point in his life and ambitions. The themes of the long poems are mainly to do with spiritual progress, womanhood, giving birth (as an allegory) and motherhood, all things he was passionate about and all subjects that Fiona would later put into prose as well as poem. Money was starting to get a little easier because of this but his health was always the real factor in determining how much he wrote, how much he made and even where he and Elizabeth needed to live.

In 1883 another great influence on his life, Ralph Waldo Emerson, passed away. He always referred to Emerson's *"Volume of Selected Essays"* as his Bible and it accompanied him everywhere. Just before his own death in 1905 he was still studying and annotating his copy of Emerson's works. The loss of his friend Rossetti and the loss of his hero Emerson in such a short time probably made him reflect more on death and the passing of companions and fellow travelers. He was saddened by these passings but not depressed by them, however they inevitably made him look anew at his own life and frailty. He took comfort in his spiritualist and occult interests which proved to him that life carried on after death. Death would certainly become a common theme in Fiona's writings.

Although he was writing profusely at a much higher standard than before, the publishing world was a slow place and the length of time between having a manuscript accepted and actually receiving payment for it could be long indeed. By the end of the year he was once again in debt with no immediate source of income. Typically, his immediate response to this latest financial crisis was drastic. He decided to take his only possession, a revolver, and enlist in the army, the British one this time, not the Turkish. Fate though once more stepped into the breach and diverted him from this over-the-top reaction. On the morning he intended to enlist he came downstairs to find two letters waiting for him. He assumed that they were rejection letters from publishers so he stuffed them into his coat pocket without opening them. Later in the day he remembered them and opened one. It contained a letter from *Harper's* magazine accepting several of his poems for publication accompanied by a cheque for forty Pounds, a lot of money in the 1880s. His financial situation was reprieved for the time being at least. The revolver was put away and once more the Gods of War were denied their impulsive hero, William Sharp.

He was so elated by this that he forgot about the other letter, it remaining in his coat for several days before he came across it again. When he did eventually look inside it he found that this envelope also contained a cheque, but for a much more substantial sum - two hundred Pounds! It was from a friend of Sir Noel Paton who had learned of William's interest in the arts and suggested he use the money to study art in Italy. So, after treating his landlady and family to an evening at the theatre, and after clearing his debts, he headed for Italy where he spent February through June travelling from art gallery to art gallery, absorbing all he could of the Old Masters. During this time he obtained the post of art critic for *The Glasgow Herald* newspaper. It was not so long ago that Elizabeth had been doing the same thing and he had written to her from London that painters could never compare with poets. Now these painters were his bread and butter. This time Elizabeth was the one who stayed home until she met him in Florence in June.

---

[1] Hunter, "Scottish Exodus", page 213

[2] "Earth's Voices", 1884

[3] Memoir, Page 25

[4] Memoir, Page 126

[5] Memoir, page 28

[6] Memoir, Page 35

[7] Caine, My Story, Page 158

[8] Memoir, Page 39

[9] Memoir, Page 49

[10] Memoir, page 53

## William Sharp
From a photograph taken in Rome in 1883

# Chapter 3
# Italy, Marriage and Bohemia

*He was at the birth of every new literary journal,*
*and comfortably absent at its death.*

The later public writings and private correspondence of Fiona Macleod contain many references to the feminine aspect of Divinity, especially to St. Bride, the Mary of the Gael. In the fictitious life that William created for her he stated that she belonged to the Roman Catholic Church. In his early days William had a very negative attitude towards the insitutionalised church, especially the Church of Rome. This had developed in his native Scotland where then, as now, there was a social and cultural divide between the followers of the Protestant faith, as his family was, and those of the Catholic Church. His home area of the Lowlands tended to be mainly Protestant whereas many of the Western Isles were predominantly Catholic. Fiona commented on the negative affect the Protestant church had in the Gaeltacht in a later autobiographical essay, "*The Gael and His Heritage,*" in which she said, "*I do not think any one who has not lived intimately in the Highlands can realise the extant to which the blight of Calvinism has fallen upon the people, clouding the spirit, stultifying the mind, taking away all joyousness and light-hearted gaiety, laying a ban upon music even, upon songs, making laughter as rare as a clansman landlord, causing a sad gloom as common as a ruined croft.*"[1] In her short story "*The Wayfarer*" she summed up the negative effect of the church in one paragraph, "*The Rev. James Campbell spoke for an hour with sombre eloquence. Out of the deep darkness of his heart he spoke. In that hour he slew many hopes, chilled many aspirations, dulled many lives. The old, hearing him, grew weary of the burden of years, and yet feared release as a more dreadful evil still. The young lost heart, relinquished hope.*"[2]

Fiona was not alone in commenting on the negative effect some ministers of the church could have in these remote Gaelic communities. Alexander Carmichael found many examples of this and noted them in his work

"*Carmina Gadelica.*" During a conversation with a lady on the Isle of Lewis he recorded the following comments concerning marriage and other celebrations, "*Our weddings are now quiet and becoming, not the foolish things they were in my young days. In my memory weddings were great events, with singing and dancing, piping and amusements, all night through and generally for two and three nights in succession… There were many sad things done then for those were the days of foolish doings and foolish people… It is long since we abandoned those foolish ways in Ness… In my young days there was hardly a house in Ness in which there was not one or two or three who could play the pipe, or the fiddle, or the trump. And I have heard it said there were men, and women too, who could play things they called harps… but I do not know what those things were… A blessed change came over the place and the people, and the good men and good ministers who arose did away with the songs and the stories, the music and the dancing, the sports and the games, that were perverting the minds and ruining the souls of the people, leading them to folly and stumbling… the good ministers went among the people… and made them break and burn their pipes and fiddles.*"[3]

William had grown up in Scotland with this power of the church as a fact of life constantly in the background but now, in Italy, where the Roman Catholic Church was so much more part of daily life, he was suddenly exposed to how it completely dominated the whole social and family life of the villages in a much more up-front fashion than he had ever seen in Scotland. What he saw in the religious art and in the religious observances of the Italian peasantry only served to reinforce his discomfort and distaste with the practices of the Church of Rome. In a letter to Elizabeth from Florence in March he enthused about the wonderful Italian architecture and paintings he was seeing but he commented specifically on the religious artwork he saw, "*What a horrible imagination, poisoned by horrible superstitions, these old fellows* [the artists] *had: Paradise, while in some ways finely imagined, is stiff and unimpressive, and Inferno simply repellent. It is strange that religious art should have in general been so unimaginative.*"[4]

Later he wrote, "*Yesterday being Holy Thursday we went to several churches… I was quite unprepared for the mystery and gloom of the Duomo… when we entered it was like going into a tomb. Absolute darkness… a dark gloom everywhere… and all the crosses and monuments draped in black crape and a great canopy of the same overhead. This and the mystery and gloom and pain (for, strange as it may seem to you, I felt the agony of the pierced hands and feet myself) quite overcame me, and I burst into tears. I think I would have fainted with the strain and excitement if the Agony of the Garden had not come to an end, and the startling crash of the scourging commenced… I was never so impressed before. I left, and wandered shivering with the excitement of almost foretasted death I had experienced, and unable to control the tears that came whenever I thought of Christ's dreadful agony… I don't know if I can enter the Catholic churches again till the Crucifixion is over, as I dread a repetition of last night's suffering. How I wish you were here with me…* [5] Despite these very negative impressions from William, Fiona would be able to mix the Christian and pre-Christian comfortably and naturally in her own writings in a way that he never did.

He had a chance to compare the modern Christian symbolism of Italy with its own pre-Christian roots. After visiting some ancient Etruscan tombs he wrote, "*I was much struck with the symbolism and beauty of the ornamental portions, Death evidently to the ancient Etrurians being but a departure elsewhere. The comparative joyousness (exultation, as in the symbol of the rising sun over the chief entrance) of the Etruscans contrasts greatly with the joylessness of the Christians, who have done their best to make death repellent in its features and horrible in its significance, its possibilities. Only a renaissance of in the Beautiful Being the only sure guide can save modern nations from further spiritual degradation – and not till the gloomy precepts of Christianity yield to something more akin to the Greek sense of beauty will life appear to the majority lovely and wonderful, alike in the present and the future.*" [6]

Fortunately the entire trip was not all gloom and pain. He wrote frequently to Elizabeth and despite the fact that many of his letters spoke at length of the negative feelings and emotions his encounters with the church were causing they also spoke at great length of the wonderful things he was seeing and experiencing in the Italian countryside, the Green Life of Italy, away from the churches and towns. His health had improved greatly thanks to the warm, dry climate and this helped lift his spirits. While he still loved the Highlands and Islands of Scotland he found that the warmth and sunshine of Italy totally captivated him. Every day brought new wonders, sights and sounds. The strong sensations and feelings he was experiencing daily helped him open up more and more emotionally and allowed him to express the feelings and emotions which had been building up for so long without hope of release in the cold dampness of Scotland. He had experienced this rejuvenating effect of the warmth and sunshine during his stay in Australia but in Italy there was no sense of being as far from home as when he was in the Southern Hemisphere. He was more relaxed and not under pressure to find employment as he had been in Melbourne.

In one letter he wrote to Elizabeth, "*Life, joyousness, brightness everywhere – oh, I am so happy! I wish I were a bird, so that I could sing out the joy and delight in my heart. After the oppression of Rome, the ghastliness of Assisi, the heat and dust of Florence – Venice is like Paradise. Summer is everywhere here – on the Lido there were hundreds of butterflies, lizards, bees, birds, and some heavenly larks – a perfect glow and tumult of life – and I shivered with happiness. The cool fresh joyous wind blew across the waves white with foam and gay with the bronze-sailed fisher boats – the long wavy grass was sweet scented and delicious – the acacias were in blossom of white – life – dear, wonderful, changeful, passionate, joyous life everywhere! I shall never forget this day – never, never. Don't despise me when I tell you that once it overcame me, quite; but the tears were only from the excess of happiness, from the passionate delight of getting back again to the Mother whom I love in Nature, with her wind-caresses and her magic breath."* [7]

These sentiments and the words used to express them are very unlike the dry, academic prose that William Sharp presented to the public in his writings. They could easily have come from a piece written by Fiona. The damp greyness of Scotland had nurtured and fed him since boyhood and now the dry brightness of Italy was feeding and nourishing the latent Fiona. His whole life was a series of paradoxes and opposites. He lived for Scotland, the land of his birth and heritage, but it took Italy, a foreign land with a different culture and language, to awaken Fiona. He loved his wife dearly but it took an affair of the heart with another woman to release Fiona fully. His whole life swung from periods of good health to periods of bad health, often bringing him close to death. His finances fluctuated sharply from periods of affluence and stability to times of poverty and uncertainty. This initial trip to Italy was the catalyst that set many of these swings in motion particularly regarding his dual writings, his magical work and, most importantly, his strengthening contact with Faery.

Another contrast and paradox revealed itself during this first trip to Italy that would totally disappear on his second trip. This was a deep realisation of the many differences between the northern lands and the southern lands. Whereas he fell in love with the beauty and serenity of the Italian countryside he still longed for the scenery and open spaces of Scotland. He began to see that each had its own beauty, allure and appeal which he deeply and genuinely appreciated but as he was appreciating one *in situ* it brought up a longing for the other from which he was parted. When he was in the south he enjoyed it immensely but had an underlying longing for the north; when in the colder, damper north he had an underlying desire to be back in the warmth and sunshine of the south. He was aware of this paradox and introduced this theme into some of his writings. He realised he was not alone in this feeling when he encountered a woman in the village of San Gemignano who was originally from Ayrshire, Scotland, not far from where he was born. She had been living in Italy for some years and during their conversation he learned that, *"She yearned to see once more the land she loved better than the alien country in which her lot was cast."* [8] In a piece from *"The Gipsy Christ"* he created a fictional Norwegian lady, Froken Bergliot, who was partly based on the real Scottish woman. She too lived in Italy and continually longed to see once again the mountains and fjords of her native Norway. The common factor between the real and the fictional women was a longing for the cool and temperate climate of the north after so many years of the heat and arid atmosphere of the south. Years later Fiona would address this subject in a letter dated May 23rd 1902 to her friend John Macleay, *"Much of the best imaginative work of the Celtic, certainly the Gaelic peoples, is inspired by longing, and generally by the peculiar and acute longing caused by the pressure of uncongenial circumstances in a foreign atmosphere, or by absence, or by forced exile. That, and the deeper and insatiable spiritual longing that has ever charac- terised our race.*" [9] William never lived long enough in the south to discover if he too would find this unexpected longing for the cold and damp of the north that had always been so detrimental to his health. However on his sec- ond visit to Italy all this became irrelevant when a surprise encounter would permanently change his view of the south in a very positive way.

He left Italy in June 1883 and travelled to France where he met up with Elizabeth and her mother in the Ardennes. They spent that month in France and by July they were back in London where he sent his reports and criti- cisms of the Italian galleries to *The Glasgow Herald*. In August he was once more on the move but without Elizabeth. He went to Scotland where he spent the month travelling amongst the various islands of the Clyde and In- ner Hebrides. On the Isle of Arran he met his old friend and mentor the well respected artist Noel Paton, who had given him the money for his Italian visit, and they sailed through Loch Fyne, onto Mull and ended up in Iona.

It is interesting to note that several times in Elizabeth's memoir, and in the surviving private correspondence, reference is made to his sisters, but never to his brothers David and Thomas. Even then the only sister who is ever referred to by name is Mary who acted as his secretary. Agnes, Elizabeth, Katherine and Margaret become simply the anonymous "sisters." He clearly did not have a close relationship with his own immediate family. There is no hint anywhere of an argument or break-up that may have caused this. It seems to have been more a matter of his personal choice rather than neces- sity. After he died the newspapers were full of obituaries and reminiscences from his colleagues and members of the art and literary worlds but there was only silence from his family.

Here is another paradox. On the one hand he was often described by friends as a man who cared a great deal about his fellow beings but who, on the other hand, seems to have had little or no emotional relationship with his own family, the people who normally matter most and play such a sig- nificant role in the life of most people. This, coupled with his frequent sepa- rations from Elizabeth, leads one to believe that he was a very lonely man. He was clearly self-absorbed most of the time in his writings and travels. He may have unconsciously worked incredibly long hours not just to finish a project but to occupy his mind and keep it from straying onto thoughts of relationships. He rarely allowed himself time to stop for long and reflect upon and enjoy the intimate company of his family and loving wife. Even Fiona, the emotional one in the family, never spoke of family, lovers or close companions in her correspondence with fans and friends. When she did spe- cifically mention someone it was always as the mouthpiece for some snippet of folklore or as the teller of some tale that she was about to relate. Intimacy was not one of Fiona's hot subjects either. This was compounded by her con- stant insistence on complete privacy and her total refusal to give interviews as will be discussed later.

On his way back to London from his Scottish holiday he lost his briefcase containing all of his Italian photographs and essays plus several finished articles for the paper that were intended to provide his income for the following months. He was distraught and retraced his steps as best he could by taking the train back to Scotland, boarding the various ferries he had travelled on, asking rail and ferry employees for any hint or sign of his lost documents but all to no avail. In his determination to track down his valuable briefcase the persistent Scottish rain several times drenched him. Eventually he realised his searching was futile so, despondent and sick, he returned to London. As a result of his low spirits and his soakings he developed a severe bout of rheumatic fever that endangered his already weak heart. This was similar to the drenching he received two years before in Kent and it would be repeated several times throughout his life including one final time just days before he died. His sister Mary travelled to London to help Elizabeth tend to her sick husband while she carried on writing for the newspaper. To his surprise, some weeks after the loss of his briefcase, the railway company returned it in a sodden condition but with all contents intact. This went some way to lifting his spirits and speeding his physical recovery.

When he was able, in early 1884, he left for Dover on the coast of the English Channel, without Elizabeth or Mary, so that he could complete his recuperation in the sea air and concentrate away from the noise and distractions of London. Several male friends joined him on various occasions and his health greatly improved to the extent that he often walked alone for miles along the famous White Cliffs of Dover, taking in the sea breezes and listening to the cry of the gulls.

Dover was a convenient jumping off point for France and he occasionally took the steamer across to Calais in the morning, spent a pleasant afternoon in France and took the late afternoon steamer back to England. In April of 1884 he spent a longer period in France, this time in Paris. The correspondence he sent to Elizabeth is interesting, not for what it says but for what it so clearly leaves out. His main reason for being there was in his capacity as art critic, a task he now thoroughly enjoyed. He also took the opportunity to acquaint himself with the many writers and poets who lived there. He talks in his letters of discussions with several important French writers, dinner engagements, meetings at cafes etc all in a good deal of detail. Tucked away in one of those letters is the single sentence, *"On Sunday, if I can manage it, I will go to Mdme. Blavatsky."*[10] This must have been an important meeting for him but Elizabeth makes no further mention of it in her memoir.

Mdme. Helena Petrovna Blavatsky, along with Henry Steel Olcott, had founded the Theosophical Society in New York in 1875, a society that is still going strong today. The T.S., as it is affectionately known, was responsible for introducing many western people to eastern, especially Hindu, spiritual concepts and beliefs which up until that time had been the domain of the professor and serious student of religions. It set out a form of mysticism that appealed to the scientific, sceptical Victorian mind-set and generally made such things more accessible to the interested lay public. In the mid 1880s Mdme. Blavatsky was quite a celebrity in Europe. It may seem odd that Elizabeth says nothing more on the matter other than her husband was going to meet with Blavatsky but the reasons for her silence will become clear later.

In 1907, two years after William's death and three years before Elizabeth's biography appeared, William Butler Yeats asked Elizabeth if she was going to tell the whole truth with regard not only to the Fiona secret but also concerning her husband's personal and magical life. Elizabeth answered, "*How can I! Other people are so much involved.*"[11] This statement in itself makes it clear that much was left out of her memoir ostensibly to protect friends, family and associates still living who may have been embarrassed by certain revelations. Whatever the reasons for her lack of detail in certain matters the overall effect has been to leave us with a very incomplete picture of William Sharp. Fortunately today there is much to be gleaned from many sources Elizabeth had no access to and what is now considered socially and morally acceptable is far removed from the constraints she was forced to work under. Yeats should have understood her reticence as he was asked a very similar question by a would-be biographer in the early 1930s, particularly regarding his affair with Maud Gonne, to which he replied rather sternly, "*Sir, do you seek to pry into my private life?*"[12]

On return from France William continued his work with *The Glasgow Herald* and carried on with his own poetry and other writings. His second book of poems, "*Earth's Voices,*" was published in 1884 and was met with favourable critical acclaim. It seemed like this phase of his turbulent and unsettled life was bringing some sort of stability and normality to his work and his relationship with Elizabeth. This was confirmed on October 31st when he and Elizabeth finally married after a nine-year engagement. It is no coincidence that they choose this date, it being the Celtic New Year and, by tradition, the time to start things new and fresh. The wedding took place in London and the newly weds spent their honeymoon in Dover. They made a visit from there to Paris but, again, Elizabeth does not divulge if this was a sightseeing trip or if it was an appointment with Mdme. Blavatsky or any of the other fascinating writers, artists, magicians and mystics living in Paris at that time. On return from Dover they settled in a house in London where they would remain for several years. Elizabeth says, "*The end of November found us settled in a little house in Talgarth Road, West Kensington (No. 46): our relatives furnished the house for us and we began our new life with high hopes and a slender purse. My husband had 30 Pounds in his pocket, and I had an income of 35 Pounds a year.*"[13]

This period in Talgarth Road turned out to be the most productive as far as the writings of William Sharp are concerned. Later he would produce an enormous amount of writing in a very short period under the Fiona Macleod pseudonym but the late 1880's were to see some of the best works that William was to produce. He was now fully established as a writer of some note. He was not by any manner or means a great writer but he was consistent, fruitful and generally liked by the Victorian public, critics and fellow writers alike. He had become acquainted with many of the leading writers, poets and artists of the day during his friendship with Rossetti. Then it was always Rossetti that was the focus of their attention and admiration but now he was the centre of attention and admiration in his own right. He had come far in a short period of time. He and his new bride spent a good deal of time socialising with these luminaries and hosting literary soirees at their Talgarth Road home.

Although he was producing more original works of his own his main writing was still in the form of art critique. He became increasingly interested in literary criticism and regarded the whole idea of written criticism as a very precise science that had to be carried out under strict guidelines and with conscientious adherence to detail. To help him better his own standard of critique he started to study the literature of France and that of the new kingdom of Belgium. He believed by having a comparison with a foreign method of expression he could better understand and express what he needed to say in English. He published much of this criticism of contemporary French and Belgian writers in several British magazines and journals. These eventually found their way to the writers in question and over the next several years he struck up lasting friendships and relationships with many of the more important European writers. His affair later with Edith Wingate Rinder may have been helped along by the fact that they had a common interest for she too translated and published foreign language works, particularly Belgian literature and the folk tales of Brittany. Of this, more later.

In the summer of 1885 he and Elizabeth found time to take a month's holiday in the small fishing village of Tarbert in the West of Scotland, the place where they had first met as children. The cottage did not fully match the description they had been given but it was adequate. Elizabeth made a small comment that shows the Sharps' social standing and their attitude as to what they should do themselves and what they expected to be done for them. She commented, "*The only service that the old woman owner would give was to light the fires and wash up the dishes and black our boots. Everything else devolved on me, for help I could get nowhere and though my husband's intentions and efforts in that direction were admirable, their practical qualities ended there!*" [14] William certainly enjoyed being away from London, which despite his frequent residencies there, he never liked. The weather in Tarbert was typical for a Scottish west coast summer – long periods of rain interspersed with glorious, but brief, days of sunshine and warmth. Once again, on return to London he developed rheumatic symptoms which although not life threatening were persistent and debilitating. This, combined with another prolonged spell of wet weather in London over the winter of 1886, and his insistence on spending gruelling hours writing, contributed to a further, more serious, breakdown in his health. By the spring of that year he was bed-ridden by a combination of rheumatic fever, scarlet fever and phlebitis. As Elizabeth put it, for many days his life hung in the balance.

During this time he again felt the desire to give up life in this world altogether and move wholly to the Otherworld where he felt so energised and powerful. His mind mulled over many things in his feverish and oft times delirious state. At first he imagined himself to be a gypsy travelling around his beloved Argyll in a caravan, resting where he wanted and visiting his many gypsy and fisher friends. For a while he believed himself to be dead to the material world and acutely alive on the other side of things. He felt no desire to return to the material world and rejoiced in his imagined freedom from ill health and greater psychic powers. However, it was not to be. His protectors and guardians on the other side had plans for him that had not yet come to fruition. He heard a voice saying, "*Not yet, you must return.*" He knew then he had some special work to do before he could depart this life. However these periods of intensely depleted energy and health in this world were starting to crack open the door to the Faery realm where he would soon be spending a great deal of time in the persona of Fiona Macleod.

After a full ten weeks in bed his health had improved sufficiently for him to be moved away from the damp and polluted London air to Northbrook, Hampshire where their friends Henry and Mona Caird had given them the use of a house for the summer. The warm sunshine and the clear air helped bring him back to strength but it was clear that this latest spell of ill health, combined with his already weak and much overworked constitution, had left permanent damage on his heart. By summer's end he was as fit as could be expected but still too weak to resume the arduous writing schedule he insisted on setting himself. Inevitably, yet again, their finances were reaching a critical level. William had been unable to produce any work for several months and Elizabeth's income from her own writings was not sufficient to meet their financial commitments. Things had turned full circle with regard to good health becoming bad health and steady financial security becoming potential disaster and financial ruin.

Incredibly, for at least the fourth time in his life, when things were at their lowest possible level with no prospect of improvement, another unexpected gift of money literally dropped through the door. This time it was a cheque for a substantial sum of money, Elizabeth does not reveal exactly how much, that came from the poet Alfred Austin who had heard of their desperate situation. A friend while in a similar financial strait had once helped Austin. The condition of this original gift was that it was not to be repaid to the giver but should be passed on to another in need at a later date. So, now, Austin was fulfilling his obligation and helping out the Sharps who had exhausted all other possible sources of funding. These incidents of monetary aid arriving out of the blue, and the several times in his life when he seems to have been brought back from the brink of death, certainly enforced his belief that he had some special task to perform in this life and that he would not be allowed to leave this mortal coil until it had been completed. Was the Faery called Fiona Macleod behind these synchronistic events? Was there some Grand Scheme being worked out in which William would play a crucial role? In light of the influence Fiona's writings would have, and in light of William's connection with the loose group of people in Glastonbury that would come to be known as The Avalonians, I think there was. We shall learn more of this in Chapter 9.

It should be noted here that William did not always rest on his laurels awaiting further spontaneous gifts of money to magically manifest. On occasion when he needed money he actively went out and sought it. His friend Ernest Rhys related two incidents that illustrate his ingenuity when it came to procuring money. The first was when he had agreed to travel to Algiers with a friend but did not have the money for the fare or on which to subsist. He was mulling over what to do about this as he walked down Fleet Street, London. Suddenly, passing an editor's office, he had a brilliant idea. He told the secretary he had to see the editor urgently. As he waited to be seen he made up, on the spot, the plot of a serial romance. When he was duly admitted to the editor's office he described it in such appealing terms that the editor immediately agreed to buy it. William spent the next ten days furiously writing this nonexistent romantic serial and delivered it to the office where he was duly handed a cheque for fifty Pounds. He repeated this feat a second time by walking into a publisher's office and describing in great detail, with no physical manuscript to back him up, a book he had been working on for some time that was now nearing completion. The publisher was so enthralled by his verbal description of this work that he wrote a cheque for one hundred Pounds there and then. Rhys goes on to say that the book in question, which he does not identify, was duly published and justified the publisher's rather rash act. He finished his story by adding that both of these incidents occurred at an early stage in William's career when he was only known as an occasional reviewer with no track record of his own publications.[15]

He learned very quickly though how to successfully 'work the system' when it came to publishers and editors. Arthur Waugh said that he was, *"... a familiar apparition in editorial offices and literary gatherings ... With his Olympian stature, bright complexion, full head of hair, and well-kempt beard, he attracted attention at once, and took good care to retain it. His manner was a mixture of suavity and aggression, and he knew (no man better) how to overcome the hesitation of editors. He was at the birth of every new literary journal, and comfortably absent at its death. He knew whose money was behind every fresh venture, and exactly how much money there was. He was early on the scene with a string of suggestions, and editors found it more convenient to accept two or three of them off-hand than to await the outburst of a fresh barrage."* [16]

Thanks mainly to the relief of his debt the spring of 1887 saw his health greatly improved. Offers of work were pouring in and soon they were back on track, living in London and making their life work. His writings were becoming known in America and he started to correspond with writers and poets from the States. This helped open up his worldview of things even more and gave him yet another literary comparison to set alongside his French and Belgian studies. He was also working for a children's journal, "*The Young Folk's Paper,*" (in which Robert Louis Stevenson's "*Treasure Island*" first appeared) in a section called "*The Literary Olympic*" in which he responded to young readers who submitted their stories and poems for criticism and possible publication. He accepted the position not because of his love for children but in order to have a steady source of income. He wrote serial potboiling stories for *The Young Folk's Paper* to make money. All of these stimuli assisted in developing and expanding his writing techniques, ideas and characters. Once again Elizabeth made a small comment that displays the social changes that have taken place since William's day. She commented on the work that *The Literary Olympic* involved and said, "... *it put us into touch with the youth of all classes...*" [17]

Their renewed financial stability and their optimistic looking long-term prospects encouraged William and Elizabeth to buy a house in a different part of London. This house was at 17a Goldhurst Terrace, South Hampstead. The postman however continually delivered William's mail to the main house at 17 Goldhurst Terrace so he decided to make the address clearer by giving the house a name. The name he came up with was "*Wescam,*" an anagram of the initials of William, Elizabeth, Sharp, Alice, Mona and Caird. This new home was in a better neighbourhood and sat higher on a hill, consequently the air was cleaner and healthier. London, in those days, suffered from chronic bad air due to the huge number of coal-burning fires around the city. In fact the air quality today, even with the thousands of cars, trucks and vans spewing carbon emissions into the atmosphere, is far better than it was then. There was also easy access to nearby fields which William took advantage of whenever he could. The layout of the house was such that it was possible for him to set up an office on the ground floor of the building thus alleviating the need for him to climb stairs. This indicates just how delicate his constitution was at this time. He was only thirty-two years old, diabetic, and already had difficulty in climbing stairs. He constantly had to monitor his activities so as not to strain his heart further. But his weak physical body was more than compensated for by his unusually sensitive psychic state. This though would later bring its own significant health problems.

Everyone knew that his health was frail, it was clear to anyone who met him, but despite this he made great efforts to hide the extent of his pain and suffering from Elizabeth. Details of just how bad his health could be are to be found in some correspondence from the 1880s to Hall Caine, editor, publisher and friend of Rossetti's. It is likely that when Elizabeth was researching and compiling the material and letters for her memoir that she did not have access to these letters. I hope she did not. It would have been a great shock for her to read the chronic agony her husband had been in for such a long time and to read his earnest pleas to friends not to reveal to her his secret of just how sick he was.

Caine was an important figure in the Victorian literary and art scene and it is odd that Elizabeth does not mention him further in her biography where he receives but a fleeting mention in connection with some sonnets William had sent to Rossetti. After Rossetti died both William and Hall Caine set about writing their own memoirs and biographies of the great man. This, at first, caused a certain amount of tension between them. Elizabeth must have been aware of this, which coupled with her lack of knowledge of their later correspondence, may explain his brief mention in her memoir. It is clear though from the letters that have subsequently surfaced that if there had ever been a riff between the two it had been patched up long ago and they remained close friends. To the extent that William frequently stayed overnight at Caine's home on his journeys to and from Scotland and he clearly felt he could confide in Caine the depth of his physical suffering. In a letter dated September 18th 1883 he says, "*On return to London I at once looked for the recipe that you wanted but have been unsuccessful in finding it… The embrocation was good for all kinds of rheumatic cold (stiff necks, strained muscles, effects of draughts etc)… I am greatly better, so much so that I find it difficult to credit the doctor's doleful prognostications: I feel I must take care, but beyond that I have no immediate cause for alarm. The worst of it is that I am one day in exuberant health and the next very much the reverse. The doctors agree that it is valvular disease of the heart, a treacherous form thereof still further complicated by hereditary bias.*" [18] However less than a year later William wrote to Caine asking for accommodation and he signed off by saying, "*Excuse a hideous scrawl, but my hands are so chilled and pained I can hardly hold the pen – and have to write at a distance.*" [19]

His on going relationship with Caine and his ability to confide in him, and his steadily decreasing health, are both revealed in a letter sent from Scotland to Caine in London on September 1st 1887, "*I think you are the only one of my friends who has recognised what a secret enemy my ill-health is. I look so robust, and (often at a great effort) try to be cheerful and sanguine that many think I have little to complain of. You, however, realise something of what I have really to endure. There are perhaps few people who know what 'angina pectoris' really is, … it sometimes attacks the most robust natures, and is then deadliest. The agony of it is sometimes too great for conscious endurance, and over one's head always hangs the shadow of sudden death… This, added to the precariousness of the literary life and its incessant hard work, gives me many a dark hour. Sometimes I awake at night with the dull gripping pain which is ominous of attack, and as I lie by my sleeping wife I do not know if I shall ever see the morning's light… I betray nothing of this to anyone… I never allow it to overcome me… I have no fear of death, which the soul in me knows but to be the gate of life… You are the only one of my friends to whom I have written this… And now having read my words destroy and forget them.*" [20]

During the three years they lived at Wescam he struck up what would become long lasting friendships with George Meredith, W.B. Yeats, George Russell and other writers, poets and mystics, most of whom were active in the Celtic Revival movement at the end of the 19th century. Many of them were members of the Golden Dawn and very active in psychical and magical research and experimentation. William was in many ways perfect for this. He was well versed in Celtic and Gaelic lore, he had a broad knowledge of world religions and esotericism and his peculiar psychic state made him perfect for magical experiments and Otherworldly investigations. The biographies and collected letters of these friends and associates tell us more of this side of his activity than do Elizabeth's memoir or even William's own notebooks and diaries.

They once again started regular Sunday evening socials with their friends where the conversation ranged over a wide spectrum of topics. Many of their guests and visitors were active in the blossoming Suffragette and Women's Rights movements of the day. Elizabeth had always been interested in these fields and after William's death she became very militant and active in the Suffragette movement. One can imagine the discussions that must have taken place in Wescam. Depending on which particular friends had called, the subjects would have ranged from early Celtic mythology to modern magical movements to women's rights to the literature of Belgium. It was certainly varied if nothing else. About this time Maud Gonne was commenting on an identical situation taking place at W.B. Yeats' home in another part of London, "*We had tea in Willie's rooms in Woburn Buildings in the little room over the cobbler's shop with the dark blue hangings and prints of Blake's drawings on the walls. What strange talks that room had listened to! Men of the I.R.B.* [Irish Republican Brotherhood] *had met there. William Sharpe* [sic] *had told us of his spirit love, Fiona McLeod* [sic]. *MacGregor had talked of his Rosicrucian mysteries.*"[21]

In 1888 William wrote a book called "*The Children of To-morrow*" which Elizabeth described as, "*… the author's first attempt to give expression in prose to the more subjective side of his nature, to thoughts, feelings, aspirations he had hitherto suppressed; it is the direct forerunner of the series of romantic tales he afterward wrote as Fiona Macleod; it was also the expression of his attitude of revolt against the limitations of the accepted social system.*"[22] The book met with very mixed reviews. Those of a more open mind and heart liked it a lot while those who could not see past it as anything other than a piece of fiction considered it depressing and out of touch with reality. The Fiona aspect of it was strong. All critics, favourable and not so favourable, agreed that it contained remarkably fine descriptions of nature. It was the William aspect of it, the ideas and comments regarding marriage, love and the accepted social mores of the day, which challenged and tested the personal beliefs of its reviewers.

In that book, and others from the period, he used the vaguely Dutch sounding name H.P. Siwaarmill – an anagram of William Sharp – and would later use it again in the magazine "*The Pagan Review.*" Many years later he would praise the Flemish writers of Belgium with their Dutch connections. In April 1889 he intended to use the name in a piece for the *"Scottish Art Review"* and in a letter to the editor James Mavor he said, *"... be sure and preserve the secret of my identity with H.P. Siwaarmill"* which shows he was using various secret pseudonyms long before the Fiona Macleod name became so important. In an even earlier letter, late 1885, to another publisher's editor, he said, *"...for what I have hitherto done in that way has been under a pseudonym which I particularly wish to stick to without identifying it with my own name. Although I have a story running through a monthly magazine just now no one knows that the author – Mr. 'Blank' – is me, save a few necessary persons – and even my wife has not read my serial – so you can see my secret has been well kept: nor do I intend to let it eke out if I can help it."* [23] Here he seems to be positively boasting not only about keeping his many pseudonyms secret but that he has managed to keep a whole monthly serial hidden from Elizabeth! Secrets were an ever-present facet of his short life, even secrets from his loving wife. The biggest secret though, Fiona Macleod, had not yet come into being and this would be the hardest to keep. This would become the biggest single contributor to his chronic ill health and delicate nervous disposition.

Elizabeth and other friends and acquaintances frequently stated that William was deeply devoted to his native Scotland and to alleviating the suffering and misery of the underdog wherever he or she happened to be. At the time of his writing *"The Children of To-morrow"* the travesty of the Highland Clearances was in full swing in the Highlands and Islands of Scotland. William must have been aware of this. He was a frequent visitor to the area, much more than most people, and the national newspapers were full of stories on the terrible situation in the Highlands. In 1883 on the Isle of Skye the brutal enforced evictions had become so numerous that the remaining tenant farmers rioted. Troops, naval gunboats and the militia were called in and several bloody confrontations took place. By then things had become so bad in the Highlands and Islands that the government was forced to set up a board of enquiry to establish exactly why so many families were being forcibly evicted and left homeless. The report was eventually published in 1886 and, as a result of what they discovered, an act of parliament was passed which for the first time ever gave the Highland and Island crofters some rights of tenure. William may well have discussed this at length during the Sunday evening socials at Wescam but, for some reason, he must have made a deliberate decision not to mention them in writing. It seems unlikely that this was out of fear of the criticism that he was being too political or outspoken as he had no qualms in voicing his opinion on the abuse of Victorian women, for example, a subject which probably would have 'pressed more buttons' among respectable Victorian gentlemen than would the subject of the Clearances.

His silence may have had something to do with his privileged and well off up bringing. His father was wealthy, treated the family to extended holidays, allowed his son a great deal of freedom, sent him to private schools and, basically, provided him with far more than most people in Scotland at that time had. He was, in short, of the upper class of Victorian society. Perhaps the thought of becoming politically vocal for the cause of evicted Highlanders never entered his head. Whatever the reasons for his silence, this today can only be put down to yet another paradox in his very curious life. Fiona would later mention the Clearances but only infrequently and superficially, as will be discussed later.

In 1889 he was urged by his literary friends to apply for election to the Chair of Literature at University College, London that had become vacant. On the one hand he considered this a wise move as it would certainly increase his social and literary status and may even help his precarious financial situation. On the other hand he knew it would mean giving up his wandering inclinations for several years and abiding by a settled way of life. He was not sure what to do. However once again Fate stepped in and the decision was made for him when his doctor advised him to decline the offer for the sake of his health, particularly that of his heart. So, saddened at having to decline the post but gladdened by his still free reins, he instead made plans to visit North America where his work was greatly admired and where he had acquaintances of long standing. Elizabeth meantime left with Mona Caird for a health retreat in Austria.

He arrived in Canada in August 1889 and for the next two months he travelled extensively taking in Nova Scotia, Newfoundland, Prince Edward Island, Cape Breton, New Brunswick and Quebec, all wild places in the late 19th century. He wrote enthusiastically to Elizabeth about his adventures along the way and the wonderful things and places he was seeing. The trip was clearly beneficial for him and his tone shows he was in high spirits and good health. This is interesting. His correspondence, diary entries and work output from this period on reveal a subtle but very clear point. William's chronic ill-health all but disappeared when he was separated from Elizabeth. He does not seem to have been conscious of this or, if he was, he never voiced it. Was there a strain, some tension, in their relationship? They had known each other since early childhood but now that they had been married for a few years was William's erratic way of life, his sudden drastic decisions and financial instability, and his penchant for keeping secrets, becoming a point of tension between them? Elizabeth made a comment on his solo trip to North America that seems to take note of this phenomenon of health improving while separated, *"Going by himself seemed to promise chances of complete recovery of health..."* [24] but gives no indication of why this should be.

Perhaps it had something to do with the fact that they never had any children. Was this a conscious decision or was it due to infertility on one or both parts? In a letter dated January 15th, 1886 William said to his friend Frederick Langbridge, *"I forget whether I was in Italy or Belgium or France when I last heard from you – or where: anyway, I think it is since then that I 'married my old love' and have since been correspondingly happy – neither of us regretting that as yet no children have made their appearance."* [25] The 'as yet' part implies that it was still a possibility but not one either of them looked forward to at that point in their lives. Later, once Fiona arrived on the scene, William would often refer to her as "our child" when discussing her with Elizabeth. In some of his letters he uses this term and then repeats it with a question mark, *"She is our child, isn't she?"* as if needing reassurance that Elizabeth looked on her this way too. Did Elizabeth actually want children but William knew they would never be able to live the free, Bohemian life that he so craved if there were children to be cared for? All this was before the Edith Wingate Rinder affair started (to be discussed shortly). Shortly after starting this affair William wrote three unpublished sonnets to Edith that deal with the subject of their illicit but intense passion producing a spiritual child. Does this mean that he actually wanted children but knew Elizabeth did not or could not? Whatever the reasons it is obvious from the numerous incidents of William's health suddenly improving dramatically when he was separated from his wife that something untoward was going on between them even at this early a stage in their marriage.

By September he had crossed from Canada into the United States. The American authorities did not allow him to give any paid lectures but he nonetheless travelled through Vermont, Connecticut, Massachusetts, New Jersey and New York. He visited the universities, was made an honorary member of several prestigious clubs and managed to meet many of the friends with whom he had been corresponding for some years. One such acquaintance was the New York banker Edmund Stedman. Stedman was also a poet and he and William had been corresponding for some time before this first visit to the States. William stayed with Stedman and his wife in their New York home for ten days and did the whole literary circuit plus the clubs and universities of that rapidly expanding city. Stedman was influential with the American publishers and William was clearly angling to break into the American market. The two became great friends and every year William would send Stedman a telegram and gift on the occasion of his birthday. Stedman came to refer to William as his "English son." He knew perfectly well that William was Scottish but used this nickname to tease him. They kept in regular contact for the rest of his life.

Here another interesting aspect of William's psyche is revealed. His father had been an important figure, taking him on extended summer holidays in the Western Isles, providing his Gaelic-speaking nurse Barbara, teaching him to swim, sail and so forth. William was clearly shattered by his death. But his father never approved of nor encouraged his itinerant way of life, his interest in literature or his desire to become a writer. It is noticeable that following the death of his father William allied himself with older men, often writers and artists - Sir Noel Paton, Dante Gabriel Rossetti, George Meredith, Walter Pater, Edmund Stedman - and looked to them to provide the emotional sup-

port he needed for his literary efforts and to provide the positive feedback he
so desperately craved. In the case of Stedman this long-distance friendship,
sustained mainly by correspondence, grew much more into a father-son relationship with William writing freely on many personal matters, not just on
literary affairs. The loss of his father had certainly created a gap in his life that
he tried to fill with his older male acquaintances. Perhaps the lack of children
created another gap that he was unable to fill as easily.

On return to Europe he travelled to Cologne where he met up with Elizabeth and Mona Caird and the three travelled back to grey, damp London.
There they settled back into their old routine and resumed the Sunday evening gatherings. By early 1890 he was writing for several different newspapers
and magazines as well as producing his own poems, prose and biographies.
His health had improved and he had developed a daily routine that allowed
him to produce the writing he needed to but without the punishing hours he
had committed to his writing up until that time. Their circle of friends was
increasing steadily and he loved the conversations and social intercourse that
his better health and more relaxed frame of mind allowed him.

Inevitably though the steady, comfortable and relaxed way of life they
had developed soon began to make him restless. He started to see his comfort and security as chains that would slowly tighten and eventually squeeze
out all his desire for wandering, experimentation and adventure. Whereas
he knew he was at the stage in life, thirty five years old and married, when
most men would be pleased to have such a pleasant home, steady income
and wide circle of famous and influential friends, he characteristically decide
that it was no more than another dead-end and he had to escape before he
got sucked into the tediousness and formality that inevitably lay ahead. His
recent North American trip no doubt had stirred again his dormant wan-
derlust. Another large contributing factor in making this decision was his
hatred of the city. London at this time was in the grip of fear caused by the
infamous Jack the Ripper and the Whitechapel murders. These gruesome
slayings of innocent women not only highlighted the evil of the city but
the abuse of women that he had rallied against for so long. So, in typical
dramatic style, he announced to all his friends that he and Elizabeth had decided to sell all their possessions, give up their house, and lead the wandering
life of Bohemians.

On June 17th 1890 he wrote to Stedman, *"Most of my acquaintances
think I am very foolish thus to withdraw from the 'thick of the fight' just when
things are going so well with me, and when I am making a good and rapidly
increasing income ... I am buoyant with the belief that it is in me to do something both in prose and verse far beyond any hitherto accomplishment of mine:
but to stay here longer, and let the net close more and more round me, would be
fatal ... My income will at once drop to zero ... I am ready – I should say we are
ready – to live in the utmost economy if need be ... for my wife, with her usual
loving unselfishness and belief in me, is as eager as I am for the change, despite*

*all the risks. Perhaps I should be less light-hearted in the matter if I thought that our coming Bohemian life might involve my wife in hard poverty when my hour comes, but fortunately her future is assured. So henceforth, in a word, I am going to take down the board*

## WILLIAM SHARP
### LITERARY MANUFACTURER
### (ALL KINDS OF JOBS UNDERTAKEN)

and substitute:

## WILLIAM SHARP
### GIVEN UP BUSINESS: MOVED TO BOHEMIA.
### PUBLISHERS AND EDITORS NEED NOT APPLY.
### FRIENDS CAN WRITE TO W.S.
### C/O "DRAMA" "FICTION" OR "POETRY,"
### LIVE-AS-YOU-WILL QUARTER, BOHEMIA."[26]

He gave up his post with *The Young Folk's Paper* but retained his editor's position with the *Canterbury Poets* editions and continued to work on a biography of Joseph Severn, the friend of Keats who had cared for him in Rome through his final days. His position as London art critic for *The Glasgow Herald* newspaper was given over to Elizabeth. He had not completely abandoned his writing or all of his commitments but the little he retained would be manageable from abroad and it would afford them some income although substantially less than they had been enjoying for the past few years. His comment about Elizabeth's future being assured is because she came from a wealthy family and had her own allowance from that estate.

They gave up the house on June 24th 1890 and spent a few weeks back in Scotland saying goodbye to friends. On return to London they stayed for a while with Elizabeth's mother and then, finally, on October 13th they crossed the English Channel to Antwerp and eventually on to Heidelberg in Germany. While in Germany William met the American novelist Blanche Willis Howard through an introduction from their mutual friend Stedman. She had married the King of Wurtenberg's private physician and was now the very grandly named Frau Hof-Arzt von Teuffel. They liked each other, got on well and formulated an idea to write a novel together. This did not fully get underway until September the following year. During that period William made a note to himself advising caution when dealing with Blanche Willis Howard as he felt he was close to falling in love with her despite the fact they had only just met. This highlights again the fact that his marriage to Elizabeth may have been going through an uncertain period. History shows though that nothing came of this infatuation. William had expected Germany to be a place where he could let his hair down, enjoy good food, good company and generally start to live the Bohemian life to the full. However his illusions were shattered by the reality of the place, especially the people whom he considered to be rough and coarse and even more stiff and formal than the Victorian English. By mid December they had had enough of Heidelberg and Germany and headed south to Rome via Verona and Florence.

They took a small apartment in Rome and William set his mind to a formidable programme of new writing. He wrote to his friend Catharine Janvier telling her of the many titles he was working on, or planning to get started, and he added, "*Well, we were glad to leave Germany. Broadly, it is a joyless place for Bohemians. It is all beer, coarse jokes, coarse living, and domestic tyranny on the man's part, subjection on the woman's ... But what a relief it was to be in Italy again...*" [27] Catharine and Thomas Janvier would become close and important friends to the Sharps and Fiona. Catharine was one of the first people in whom William would confide the secret of Fiona Macleod. Fiona's "*The Washer of the Ford*" was dedicated to "*C.A.J.*" and contains the intriguing comment, "*We have meeting-places that none knows of; we understand what few can understand; and we share in common a strange and inexplicable heritage.*" [28] William probably felt so close to her as she truly lived the Bohemian, adventurous, life of travel he so longed for.

Although the Sharps were based in Rome during their stay in Italy they spent a considerable amount of time travelling and exploring the surrounding Italian countryside. Each new place seemed to give William yet another idea for a book, play or poem but, predictably, very few of these ideas or plans ever saw the light of day. From the letter extract above it is clear that his belief in the need for society to accept and treat women as equal was still prominent in his thinking. His need to write and his concern for the rights of women would come to a head in the next few months as they explored Italy. A meeting with another wandering Bohemian would set in motion events that would culminate in the birth of Fiona.

---

[1] "The Nineteenth Century" magazine, November 1900

[2] "Studies in Spiritual History", page 59

[3] "Carmina Gadelica" pages 26-27

[4] Memoir, page 80

[5] Memoir, page 81

[6] Memoir, page 88, emphasis in the original

[7] Memoir, page 92

[8] "Beautiful Towers", page 326

[9] NLS, Edinburgh

[10] Memoir, page 96

[11] Jeffares, The Gonne-Yeats Letters, Page 235

[12] Mikhail, W.B. Yeats: Interviews and Recollections, page 352

[13] Memoir, page 101

[14] Memoir, page 121

[15] Rhys, "William Sharp and Fiona Macleod", "The Century Illustrated Monthly Magazine", May 1907, pages 111-117

[16] Waugh, "Fiona Macleod: A Forgotten Mystery", "Spectator", August 14th 1936, page 277

[17] Memoir, page 128

[18] WS Archives

[19] WS Archives

[20] WS Archives

[21] Jeffares, A Servant of the Queen, page 320

[22] Memoir, page 146

[23] WS Archives

[24] Memoir, page 150

[25] WS Archives

[26] Memoir, page 166

[27] Memoir, page 170

[28] "The Washer of the Ford", page 3

# Chapter 4
# Lady of the Lake and a Review for Pagans

*From Haschisch-den to Haschisch-den I wandered, from strange*
*vaulted rooms of the gorgeously jewelled and splendidly dressed*
*prostitutes to the alcoves where lay or sat or moved to and fro, behind*
*iron bars, the caged 'beauties' whom none could reach save by gold.*

The Italian climate immediately improved William's health and this, coupled with his pleasure at being back in Italy and settled in one place,
prompted a new flurry of writing. His diary entries for this period show he
was producing a substantial amount of writing that, as before, necessitated
long hours be worked. However it was not all toil. The earlier sense of pressure and urgency to meet publishers' deadlines was gone. Now he could
write what he liked whenever he liked and express whatever he needed to say
without censorship or amendment according to someone else's dictate. After
the disappointment of Germany they were now leading the Bohemian life
that they had left England to enjoy.

At that time it was fashionable for wealthy Victorian British ladies and
gentlemen to spend the winter months in warmer climes away from the
killer smog of the cities. Many Mediterranean and Continental resorts had
a sizeable population of ex-patriots who, naturally, stuck together. William
and Elizabeth, now well known and respected by the Victorian public, gravi-
tated towards the British clique and soon had a large circle of friends with
whom they could converse and socialise. Several of the ex-patriots are mentioned in his diaries and Elizabeth names many in her memoir. One of these
companions was Edith Wingate Rinder, wife of the painter and art critic
Frank Rinder. Elizabeth, in her usual non-committal style, simply says, *"Mrs*
*Wingate Rinder joined us for three weeks, and with her my husband greatly en-*
*joyed long walks over the Campagna and expeditions to the little neighbouring*
*towns."* [1] The Sharps and the Rinders had already met several times before in
London at their Sunday soirees and Elizabeth's close friend Mona Caird was

Frank Rinder's cousin. Although she had only been married a few months Edith was in Italy with Mona Caird but without her husband.

Elizabeth is rather vague about exactly what happened in Italy in late 1890 and early 1891 but we do know that William, a man several years married, and Edith, a woman only recently married, managed to spend a considerable amount of time together travelling around the Roman countryside without their respective spouses. William's diary entries refer to "we" a lot but it is not clear exactly who his companion was. Most of the time it was more likely to be Elizabeth but on other occasions it was definitely Edith. As time progressed their relationship would become far more than one of simple friendship or mutual admiration for each other's writing. In later life both he and Elizabeth would acknowledge that had it not been for Edith, the writings of Fiona Macleod would never have come about. He commented, *"To her I owe my development as Fiona Macleod though, in a sense of course, that began long before I knew her, and indeed while I was still a child, without her there would have been no Fiona Macleod."* [2]

The comment about Fiona having started to develop while he was still a child is a reference back to his early encounter with the Faery woman and his Faery baptism near Loch Fyne. (see Chapter 1) However with the benefit of hindsight it is clear that the full power of Faery could not come through to his psyche and consciousness until an upwelling of deep, inner passion stimulated him sufficiently. Despite his love for Elizabeth she failed to so stimulate him. It took his affair with the beautiful Edith to do that. He loved his wife dearly but he always had, that was the problem. They had known each other since early childhood and consequently there had never been that immediate burst of passion, that sudden sensation of falling in love, a moment of meeting when two hearts and souls know they have found each other. William and Elizabeth played together as children, they exchanged letters and poetry during their adolescence, their families took holidays together. They grew to love each other slowly and steadily as the years went by and as they matured into full adulthood. It was inevitable that they would marry, but they never had that experience of an awe-struck, madly, passionately and instantly in love first meeting. There was not even an early rejection by one and then a determined pursuit and wooing by the other. It just happened. It was normal. It was flat. It was very British and very Victorian. And it was identical to the course that Edith and Frank's relationship had taken. Edith Mary Wingate was born in Ludford, Lincolnshire in 1864 and Joseph Francis Rinder was born on October 24th 1863 at Barrogill Cottage, John O'Groats, Caithness, Scotland. While he was still a child the family moved to Lincolnshire, not far from Edith's family. Their families were friends so Edith and Frank had known each other from childhood. They had played together as young children, grown to adolescence together, discovered they shared the same artistic aspirations and eventually married in London on February 27th 1890.

Although William and Edith had previously met on several occasions in London it was only when they were alone together in Italy that William suddenly fell completely head over heels in love with her. We can pinpoint the exact place and time this happened and, from his description of this incident, understand why. Elizabeth states in her memoir, *"Mrs. Wingate Rinder joined us for three weeks, and with her my husband greatly enjoyed long walks over the Campagna and expeditions to the little neighbouring hill towns."* [3] She then fills out the chapter with extensive quotations from William's diary for the time they were in Italy. The excerpt for January 3rd is by far the longest. In this entry William talks about 'we' travelling to Lake Nemi and the implication is that he was referring to himself and Elizabeth. Further reading into his diary, and subsequent comments he made independently to friends and in magazine articles, indicate that 'we' actually referred to him and Edith, not Elizabeth. Despite the length of the extract there is one place where Elizabeth has left out some information. William wrote in great detail about every stage of their entire wonderful day. When it comes to the part dealing with their arrival at Lake Nemi, Elizabeth extracted the following, *"... and in due time*

*Edith Wingate Rinder*

*reached the high ground, with its olive orchards, looking down upon the Lake of Nemi. It looked lovely in its grey-blue stillness, with all the sunlit but yet sombre winterliness around. Nemi, itself, lay apparently silent and lifeless, 'a city of dream,' on a height across the lake. One could imagine that Nemi and Genzano had once been the same town, and had been riven asunder by a volcano. The lake-filled crater now divides the two little hill-set towns ... Walked through Albano to the N.W. gate, past the ancient tomb, ..."* [4] The whole section detailing what 'we' did at Lake Nemi is missing; Elizabeth's selected quotation jumps from their arrival there to suddenly walking through the nearby town of Alabano.

Fortunately William later described what happened that day to his friend Ernest Rhys. In this highly personal confession he substituted the name Fiona for Edith and said that this was the first time he had met Fiona Macleod who was, "*on the banks of Lake Nemi, when she was enjoying a sun-bath in what she deemed was a virgin solitude, after swimming the lake. 'That moment began,' he declared, 'my spiritual regeneration. I was a New Man, a mystic, where before I had been only a mechanic-in-art. Carried away by my passion, my pen wrote as if dipped in fire, and when I sat down to write prose, a spirit-hand would seize my pen and guide it into inspired verse. We found we had many common friends: we travelled on through Italy, and went to Rome, and then I wrote my haunting 'Sospiri di Roma'...Ah, hers was the divine gift, beauty, and everything she wore impressed her; but her first emanation, clad only in the golden light of Nemi, was the loveliest'.*" [5] He was clearly not with his wife Elizabeth that day. The changing of identities of his true companion from Edith to Fiona was to protect the married Mrs. Wingate Rinder's re-spectability but it turned out to be somewhat prophetic in that Edith would later play the role of Fiona when the occasion demanded.

William's statement that this was his first meeting with Fiona Macleod was rather odd. Later William would claim that Fiona was his cousin, if this had been the case then surely he must have physically met her before 1891? If not, is it not a stretch of the imagination, to say the least, that he should just happen to run into her, lying naked at an Italian lakeside, before discovering that they were actually cousins? It does not matter why he chose this peculiar framework upon which to hang the story. What is important is that William was confiding to his friend Ernest Rhys that the inspiration for all of Fiona's writings had come from this one incident, and that part of the story was certainly true. From the above it is now obvious why Elizabeth chose to edit his diary for publication in her memoir.

The fact is that this was no chance meeting. Edith and William had left Rome together with the intention of taking a day trip to Lake Nemi. Some-time during their day beside the lake Edith decided to take a swim. Although they had known each other for some time already in cold, foggy London this was the first time the thirty-five year old William had been with the twenty-six year old Edith in the idyllic surroundings of Lake Nemi, and she unashamedly allowing him to see her naked beauty. He was instantly in love, and in a way more powerful than he had ever felt for Elizabeth. The book he mentioned above, "*Sospiri di Roma*" (Sighs of Rome, or, as William preferred, Breaths of Rome) was published privately shortly after this incident at Lake Nemi and shows a noticeable change in style and expression from his earlier poetry. Elizabeth acknowledged Edith's positive influence on her husband when she said, "*The 'Sospiri di Roma' was the turning point... There, at last, he found the desired incentive towards a true expression of himself, in the stimulus and sympathetic understanding of the friend to whom he dedicated the first of the books published under his pseudonym. This friendship began in Rome and lasted throughout the remainder of his life.*" [6] One of the poems in the book is "*The Swimmer of Nemi*" which he wrote on February 8th while still with Edith,

*White through the azure,*
*The purple blueness,*
*Of Nemi's waters*
*The swimmer goeth.*
*Ivory-white, or wan white as roses*
*Yellowed and tanned by the suns of the Orient,*
*His strong limbs sever the violet hollows;*
*A shimmer of white fantastic motions*
*Wavering deep through the lake as he swimmeth.*
*Like gorse in the sunlight the gold of his yellow hair,*
*Yellow with sunshine and bright as with dew-drops,*
*Spray of the waters flung back as he tosseth*
*His head i' the sunlight in the midst of his laughter:*
*Red o'er his body, blossom-white mid the blueness,*
*And trailing behind him in glory of scarlet,*
*A branch of the red-berried ash of the mountains.*
*White as a moonbeam*
*Drifting athwart*
*The purple twilight,*
*The swimmer goeth –*
*Joyously laughing,*
*With o'er his shoulders,*
*Agleam in the sunshine*
*The trailing branch*
*With the scarlet berries.*
*Green are the leaves, and scarlet the berries,*
*White are the limbs of the swimmer beyond them,*
*Blue the deep heart of the still, brooding lakelet,*
*Pale-blue the hills in the haze of September,*
*The high Alban hills in their silence and beauty,*
*Purple the depths of the windless heaven*
*Curv'd like a flower o'er the waters of Nemi.* [7]

Here the swimmer is not Edith but is himself, newly alive, strong, physically beautiful and making his way forward surely and steadily. This transposing of genders is not just poetic license but a factor he would struggle with constantly from this time on. Since his early days he had been acutely aware of his feminine side. He was fascinated by it but tried to keep it under some sort of control. From now on though it would become a factor he could no longer control, which would dominate his life and which would drive him to the brink of madness. The imagery of the swimmer with the rowan, or mountain ash, bough in his mouth as he crosses a lake is identical to a passage in the Old Irish legend "*Tain Bo Fraoch*" (The Cattle Raid of Heather) with which William may have been familiar. It crops up again in several of Fiona's writings, particularly in "*Green Branches*" where it is a central motif.[8] In his monumental work "*The Golden Bough*" Sir James Frazer identified Lake Nemi as the location for the grove where the sacred golden bough was kept in safety by a mystical priesthood.

There is another poem in *Sospiri di Roma* that deals with the motif of swimming, "*The Bather*," but in this one the subject is a beautiful woman swimming in the ocean. Clearly the whole Lake Nemi incident had left a strong visual memory with him. The "*Prelude*" to *Sospiri di Roma* and the "*Epilogue: Il Bosco Sacro*" (The Sacred Wood) both bear the dedication, "*To --------.*" The unnamed dedicatee is clearly Edith as both verses are passionate love poems set in the Italian countryside. Another poem "*A Winter Evening*" is specifically dedicated to "*E.W.R.*" Although it would still be some three years before any of the writings under the name of Fiona Macleod would be seen, William believed that Fiona had been born on that day, January 3rd 1891, at Lake Nemi.

That this wonderful turning point in his life happened at Lake Nemi is interesting. In modern times Lake Nemi has become famous for two ancient Roman ships that were recovered from the bottom of the lake in the 1920s and 30s. These vessels were of enormous proportions, some 230 feet long and 60 feet across, being the largest vessels known from that period. They had been commissioned and used by the Emperor Caligula two thousand years ago and when recovered were in remarkably good shape. Their purpose though was not for pleasure sailing. One was permanently moored in the middle of the lake and was a floating temple to the goddess Diana. It was extremely elaborate and sophisticated with under floor heating, fresh water delivered through a complex piping system, open fires, clay ovens for baking, plus the spectacularly ornate inner sanctum of the temple of Diana itself. The other vessel was used to transfer Caligula and his entourage from the shore to the temple. Why these vessels were so large we do not know. Since Medieval times many attempts had been made to raise them but with no success.

In 1827 Annesio Fusconi used a large diving bell and managed to recover many artefacts that confirmed the date and importance of the ships but he was unable to raise them. In 1895, just four years after William and Edith's visit, another attempt was made by Eliseo Borghi who was also unsuccessful but realised the ships were too large to be raised by conventional means so, instead of bringing them to the surface they needed to lower the surface to them! It would not be until October 20th 1928 that the pumps started. Borghi's idea proved to be successful. The level of the water was lowered sufficiently to expose them and they were recovered with very little damage. Unfortunately the retreating Nazi forces during World War 2 destroyed them and they are no more. It is believed that although the temple was dedicated to Diana, significant in itself, Caligula also practiced the Egyptian Rites of Isis there. This gives the lake a special significance in magical history.

A more important fact about Lake Nemi, however, is its association with the Arthurian tradition. The tales of King Arthur and his knights, and the later Grail legends, are found all over Europe and into the Middle East, not just in Britain. Local Italian tradition claims that the stream that feeds Nemi is the home of a water Faery called Egeria. The sacred grove from where this stream emanates is the home of "Rex Nemorensis" (Ruler of the Woodlands) a Green Man type of being. In the Italian Arthurian tradition Egeria is equivalent to the Lady of the Lake found in the British tradition, and the Italian Rex Nemorensis equates in function to the British Fisher King. The Lake, which in the British tradition is unnamed, is the entrance to the Faery world and is where Arthur and Lancelot were both raised and educated by the Ladies of the Lake. This clearly gives Lake Nemi not only a strong Arthurian connection but a strong Faery connection as well. William's intuitive belief that Lake Nemi was Fiona's birthplace is a lot more accurate than even he realised.

There is one more Arthurian and Faery connection worth noting at this point involving a figure that would play an important although periphery role in the future events of William's life. At exactly the same time William, Elizabeth and Edith were in Italy the Scottish artist John Duncan (1866-1945) was also there, travelling from city to city studying Italian art. The main subject for his art at that time was Arthurian legend. Soon after returning to Scotland in 1891 he started to paint some of the most powerful and striking images of Faeries that were produced during the end of the 19th century. He would become involved in the business venture detailed in Chapter 6 and end up marrying one of the important women involved in the strange events detailed in Chapter 9. There is no evidence that John Duncan and William Sharp met during this period in Italy, although they certainly did meet later back in Scotland, but the many coincidental incidents in their lives lend more weight to my theory that there was some extraordinary power guiding the events of the *fin-de-siecle* which involved many important although now mainly forgotten people. But of John Duncan, more later.

Such was the influence Edith had that as well as William dedicating much of his *"Sospiri di Roma"* to her, four years later Fiona dedicated her first book, *"Pharais: A Romance of the Isles,"* to *"E.W.R."* This dedication runs to a full five pages and mentions various bits and pieces of Gaelic lore as well as expressing thanks and appreciation to E.W.R. William's notebooks however indicate that the dedication Fiona had originally intended to use was much shorter –

*To Edith Wingate Rinder*

  *Dear Friend, there is another Paras, the Domhan Toir of friendship. The Tir-na-h'Oighe of the Soul, wherein we two have seen beautiful visions and dreamed dreams. Take then, out of my heart, this book of Vision and Dream.* [9]

Note that this version gives her name in full whereas the published version only gives her initials. This original dedication does appear in *"Pharais"* but only as the last paragraph, and somewhat altered, *"There is another Paras than that seen of Alastair of Innisron – the Tir-Nan-Oigh of friendship. Therein we both have seen beautiful visions and dreamed dreams. Take, then, out of my heart, this book of vision and dream. Fiona Macleod.*"[10] The Alastair of Innisron mentioned here is the main character in the story. At almost the same time that "*Pharais*" came out under Fiona's name, "*Vistas*" came out under William's name. The dedication in "*Vistas*" is to 'Madame Elspeth H Barzia.' This is an anagram of 'Elizabeth Sharp.' Did he try to alleviate guilt feelings about dedicating one book to his lover by dedicating the next to his wife albeit in a form few would recognise? Later in 1897 Edith returned the compliment in her book "*Poems and Lyrics of Nature*" (Canterbury Poets series, London 1897) with the dedication, "*To W.S.*"

In 1895 Fiona dedicated another book, "*The Silence of Amor*," to Edith but again did not give her real name. Here she is called "*Esclarmoundo.*" This dedication is much shorter, one page, but is much more passionate and personal than the longer one in "*Pharais*" which focussed on her as a source of literary inspiration. It is clearly written from the heart of a lover to a lover. As early as 1892 however, within a year of falling in love with her and long before either of these veiled dedications appeared in print, he had written three sonnets inspired by this powerful new love affair. These focus very specifically on the theme of he and Edith having a mystical, spiritual relationship the result of which would be the manifestation of a spiritual child. The idea of a physical child was out of the question. They were both married and even amongst the more liberal sections of Victorian society such an act was unacceptable and would have been social suicide, although we shall need to come back to this topic later. The first of these three sonnets is;

*This child that we shall not have, yet doth live,*
*Where doth it dwell, O blossom of our joy!*
*Will that fair dream know all, and knowing forgive?*
*Will rainbow-rapture never, never cloy?*
*O exquisite dream, dear child of our desire,*
*On mounting wings flitt'st thou afar from here?*
*We cannot reach thee who dost never tire –*
*Sweet phantom of delight, appear, appear!*
*How lovely must thou be wrought of her flesh,*
*With eyes as proud of hers and face as fair,*
*With voice like hers and as the dawn-wind fresh,*
*And with the waving magic of her hair,*
*And all the love and passion of thy sire*
*With hers re-wed in thy white heart of fire!*[11]

Four years later Fiona would rework this sonnet somewhat and give it the name "*The Unborn Child*" and then, once more in 1901, rework and retitle it yet again to become "*An Immortal.*"[12] There were not many William Sharp originals that Fiona later adapted but the fact she tackled this one twice over a period of many years shows it had a deep meaning to her. Perhaps she saw it as autobiographical, she being the spiritual child of William and Edith, and perhaps it reveals something of the mystery of Faery and human interaction that she felt we ought to know. Neither this nor the other two sonnets were ever published.

On a different topic it raises an interesting legal question – can a writer plagiarise him or herself? When Fiona published "*The Unborn Child*" and "*An Immortal*" she gave no credit to William Sharp as the original author. Is this, therefore, an example of the plagiarism (to be discussed later) that Fiona displayed in several of her other works? I wonder if William could have successfully sued her!

Fiona used this theme of a child or children of unknown or uncertain parentage many times throughout her writings and it is something we should take note of. One such poem, "*The Moon-Child*," uses this motif to point out that you do not always realise who you are actually talking to. The child in this poem is the product of a liaison between a male seal and a female woman. The lonely little child spends each day at sea and at evening time she returns to rest on the shore of Iona. St. Columba is at first hostile to this half-seal half-human creature but when he hears her mournful song his heart softens and he apologises for his harshness and takes pity on her. Thanks to St. Columba's change of heart the little girl becomes a little boy and reveals He is the Christ child. (The Washer of the Ford, 1896) This is another common theme in her writing; through a series of events a pre-Christian person or deity suddenly reveals their true identity to be that of Christ or St. Brigid for example. See in particular the short story "*A Dream*" from "*Studies in Spiritual History*" Collected Works Volume 4 page 407 et seq as discussed in Appendix 4.

But back to Edith Wingate Rinder. In 1907, two years after William died, William Butler Yeats met Elizabeth and their conversation touched on the subject of what was the inspiration behind Fiona and her beautiful writings. Yeats recorded part of this conversation in a letter to his own inspiration, Maud Gonne, "*I saw Mrs Sharpe* [sic] *the other day and know a great deal more about the Fiona MacLeod* [sic] *mystery. It is as I thought. Fiona MacLeod was so far as external perception could say a secondary personality induced by the presence of a very beautiful unknown woman whom he fell in love with. She, alas! has disappeared from everyone's sight, no one having set eyes on her except George Meredith who says she was the most beautiful woman he ever saw … poor Mrs Sharpe, though generous and self-sacrificing as I can see does not want to enlarge that unknown woman's share … I noticed that each time she said this personality was awakened in him by a beautiful person she would add as if to lessen the effect, 'and by beautiful scenery'. She was evidently very fond of him …*" [13]

Elizabeth, despite severely limiting any references to Edith in her memoir, was generous when she said, "*Because of her beauty, her strong sense of life and of the joy of life; because of her keen intuitions and mental alertness, her personality stood for him as a symbol of the heroic women of Greek and Celtic days, a symbol that, as he expressed it, unlocked new doors in his mind and put him 'in touch with ancestral memories' of his race."* [14] Many of the later references in the memoir refer only to her as an unnamed friend or correspondent and she is not even listed in the index. This was not as Yeats assumed to avoid enlarging *'that unknown woman's share'* but was to protect her identity because at that time Edith and Frank were still married and well-known London socialites and it would have been a scandal had Elizabeth revealed the whole truth. However the fact of the matter is that there was never any animosity or bad-feeling between the two women and Edith and Elizabeth remained close friends after William's death and right up until Elizabeth's own passing in 1932.

Yeats' reference to George Meredith having set eyes on her is interesting. From the context of his letter the 'her' that Meredith claimed to have met was the beautiful 'unknown woman.' However after the secret of the true identity of Fiona Macleod was made known following William's death Meredith flatly refused to believe that Fiona and William were one and the same person on the grounds that he had met Miss Macleod on several occasions. Meredith mentioned one such meeting in a letter written to Alice Meynell. This letter was written while William was still alive and therefore prior to the revelation of the secret. He stated, *"Miss Fiona Macleod was here on a day of last week: a handsome person, who would not give me her eyes for a time. One fears she was not playing at abashment. Even after I had brought her to laugh, the eyelids drooped."* [15] The rest of the letter says in part, *"She spoke of your beautiful long letters. I repressed my start and moderated my stare."* The reason Meredith had to repress a start and moderate his stare is that Alice Meynell was famous for her <u>short</u> letters. If this woman claiming to be Fiona Macleod had actually received any letters from Meynell she would have known this and would not have commented on the <u>long</u> letters. [16] I have in my possession a copy of a letter Edith sent to Alice Meynell, dated February 19th 1894, thanking her for granting permission to quote from some of her work that Edith was using in a forthcoming anthology so, by that time, Edith may have discovered for herself the brevity of Alice Meynell's correspondence.

Several other reliable witnesses also claimed to have met Miss Macleod in the flesh. As she became more and more popular William was under considerable pressure to produce her, with more and more people demanding, "Where is she? Why can we not meet her?" From the number of accounts of people claiming to have met Fiona Macleod, always in the company of William Sharp, it is clear William had prompted someone to play the role as and when necessity demanded. That person was Edith. The impression we get from Fiona's letters, of which there are many, is not of a shrinking violet but of an educated, well-spoken and socially adept woman. This was not the impression that Meredith had but his comment on her abashment is understandable. If the 'Fiona' he met was actually Edith then it would make sense, not because Edith was a shy person either, but because she was playing a very important and very difficult role. It was crucial that she played this role well and without faltering. Her one big difficulty would have been her voice. Edith was born and raised in rural Lincolnshire, England but Fiona was born and raised in the Gaelic speaking Western Isles of Scotland. It must have been exceedingly difficult to convincingly maintain the fake accent. What if someone asked about her use of the Gaelic language or, worse still, what if she met someone who was fluent in that tongue?

Invariably her meetings were with people who were great fans of her work who would naturally expect her to be able to answer every question on the details of every book and poem she had written. She would need to be completely familiar with all of Fiona's writings in order to field such questions. Not only that but at times she would also need to be familiar with a good deal of private correspondence that Fiona had already exchanged with these same people. It must have taken a good deal of priming on William's part and nerves of steel on Edith's part to even attempt such a ruse. If it had failed then the secret would be revealed and, as William knew, Fiona would die. However, judging from the many people who were taken in by Edith's performance, she managed to pull it off successfully every time. Although there were many comments about the real identity of the author from students of her writing, I have been unable to find any comments from the several people who met "Fiona" in the flesh that they felt she was an impostor. The fact that Edith could play the role of Fiona so successfully must have been a great relief to William. Inevitably though it only led to deeper confusion in his mind as to who was human and who was Faery, a problem he would struggle with for the rest of his life.

But back to Italy: William and Elizabeth were staying briefly in a hotel outside of Rome when the building across the street collapsed, killing one man and severely injuring seven others. The king of Italy happened to be near by, came along and assisted in the rescue, pulling the startled survivors from the rubble. The dramatic image on the Tarot card "The Tower" comes to mind. The imagery of this card, a tower or building tumbling down with people falling from it, symbolises the breaking down of old structures and the removing of old and outworn ideas and habits to make way for new powers and energies that are now ready to manifest physically, emotionally and spiritually. This describes perfectly what was happening with the old William Sharp making way for the new Fiona Macleod, albeit unconsciously. The symbolism would not have been lost on William who was no doubt aware of the Tarot cards thanks to his occult and esoteric studies. Great forces were being unleashed on many levels. On the physical level an earthquake; on the emotional level a passionate love affair; and on the spiritual level the incarnation of a Faery spirit who the world would come to know as Fiona Macleod. I wonder if the king of Italy realised he was partaking in such a significant event?

On the world scene in the early 1890s similar great upheavals and changes were taking place in many fields. Many of these significant events involved women. Sigmund Freud had just published "*The Interpretation of Dreams*" which publicly raised, amongst other things, the whole question of sex and sexuality. Motion pictures started to be screened, giving respectability to the glamorous film star whereas up until then to be an actress on the stage was synonymous with being a prostitute. Emily Dickinson's passionate but secret poetry started to be published. The Royal Geographic Society admitted its first woman member, Isabella Bird Bishop. New Zealand became the first country in the world to give women the vote. The US Geological Survey hired its first woman geologist, Florence Bascom. However in Paris, as if to counter this upsurge in feminism, that great phallic symbol the Eiffel Tower was being erected!

In mid-March of 1891 Elizabeth left her husband and the ex-patriots in Rome and went to Florence to visit her aunt who was living there. This gave William and Edith even more time alone. From her later conversation with Yeats quoted above it is clear that she knew the real depth of the relationship between her husband and Mrs. Wingate Rinder. As this relationship grew and developed over the next couple of years Elizabeth came to see and understand just how crucial it was to the Fiona Macleod phenomenon. She would come to accept Edith as a close friend and together over the years they would collaborate in looking after William as his physical and emotional health deteriorated. But it is important to note that at this early stage of their love affair Fiona had not yet manifested. Why then did Elizabeth give William even more opportunity to be unfaithful to her by leaving for Florence? It is true that Elizabeth, William, Mona Caird who was with them in Rome, and their circle of close friends in London all espoused what were then considered radical views on the institution of marriage and the liberation of women from the shackles of Victorian attitudes and social mores. Did Elizabeth now find herself having to face up to her radical ideals and choose between the new, liberated attitude to marriage and let William carry on as he wished, or slip back into the role of either the angry and jealous wife or the weak, ineffective woman who stands in the background and says nothing as her husband is unfaithful to her? This is what society at that time would have expected her to do.

Elizabeth was struggling with facing the challenge of not just advocating marital change as an intellectual concept but now actually having to live it in the real world of her day-to-day life. She needed a break to give herself time to deal with her emotions that must have been in turmoil and confusion. As has been previously noted, their marriage was already under some strain before Edith came along and this new development between her husband and a younger woman would have forced her to look seriously at where she stood in this newly formed triangle. Whatever the reason, Elizabeth left Rome and later William joined her in Florence, minus Edith. From there they made their way to Provence to visit their friends the Janviers and, eventually, back to England. They spent some time in the Yorkshire seaside town of Whitby but inevitably ended up back in London. But it was not the London of the tedium and regularity they had left the year before. They were still free of the shackles that they had felt binding them so tightly prior to their departure. This spell back in the city was necessary but voluntary. William had various writing commitments to attend to, meetings with publishers etc and he took it all in his new Bohemian stride. His writings were, after all, a substantial part of the income needed to maintain their wandering ways.

In September he returned to Germany to collaborate with Blanche Willis Howard, who was now living in Stuttgart, on the joint writing project they had discussed the previous year. This work, *"A Fellowe and His Wife,"* was eventually published in 1892. The story is a very unusual one and mirrors in some striking ways the events that took place between Edith and William in 1891. The plot centres on a newly married woman – as Edith was – who travelled alone to Rome – as Edith had – where she met and fell in love with another man – as William and Edith had. Here the story changes in that she discovers her new lover has been unfaithful to her, she confesses all in a series of letters to her husband back home and gallantly offers to separate from him. His response is to forgive her and she returns home. However, it being a joint collaboration with Howard, and the story having been started before William and Edith met in Rome, the similarities must all be coincidental. Interestingly though the collaboration involved William writing the part of the remorseful wife while Blanche wrote the part of the forgiving husband. This was the first time that William had written as a woman and from a woman's point of view. He clearly felt that it had been a successful experiment and it was likely a major deciding factor two years later when he revealed the female writer Fiona Macleod to the Victorian public. He later adapted the novel into a five act play for the stage although it was never performed.

It is interesting to note how much his feelings and impressions of Germany had changed since his meeting with Edith. The effect that Germany had on him this time was the opposite of his experiences on his last visit only one-year prior. He wrote to Catherine Janvier from Stuttgart, *"Altogether I feel electrified in mind and body... But the beauty of the world is always bracing – all beauty is. I seemed to inhale it – to drink it in – to absorb it at every pore – to become it – to become the heart and soul within it..."* [17] His diary entries for that time repeat much of the sentiments above and read like the emotions and feelings of a man refreshed from a long sleep or, more likely, invigorated by a passionate love affair and sexual satisfaction. He also started to make more mystical and magical comments both in his public correspondence and in his personal diary. For example the diary entry dated Wednesday September 2nd 1891 reads in part, *"This afternoon was a holiday of the soul. And yet how absolutely on such a day one realises the savage in one. I suppose I was a gipsy once: a wild man before: a wilder beast of prey before that... Today*

*I seemed to remember much ... What a year this has been for me: the richest and most wonderful I have known."* [18]

This of course may have simply been his normal poetic style of expression or he may genuinely have been referring to memories of past incarnations when he <u>was</u> a gipsy, a wild man o' the woods (the Rex Nemorensis of Lake Nemi?) or even a wild beast of prey. It is interesting just how much he was expressing these inner feelings. His comment on that year, the year he met Edith, being the 'richest and most wonderful' he had known are especially interesting. What these letters and diary entries contain are the fledgling feelings and emotions of Fiona Macleod who would soon burst forth into his consciousness and so dominate his writing, his relationships with Elizabeth and Edith, and eventually utterly destroy his already delicate health.

His opinions of Italy had changed as well since Lake Nemi. On his first visit he had become aware of his emotional north–south divide and the longing for one while in the other. This had now gone. Germany was no longer a place of coarse jokes and strong beer but was a refined and intellectually advanced nation. Italy was no longer a place of oppressive religion and unbearable heat but was now a haven, a source of inspiration on all levels and a refuge to which he would turn frequently. Edith was truly causing deep changes within him on many inner levels.

Despite his optimism for the future and his determination to continue the wandering lifestyle he soon found himself settled back in London and churning out articles for newspapers and magazines, but managing to produce his own literature as well. He and Elizabeth gradually slipped unintentionally, unnoticeably, back into the rut they had escaped from the year before. His diary entries for September and October show a great deal of writing taking place, often right through the night and into the following day. The entry for October 2nd 1891 says, *"... when I issue the 'Dramatic Interludes' (five in all) I shall send them forth under my anagram, H.P. Siwaarmill. The volume will be a small one. The longest pieces will be the 'Northern Night,' and 'The Experiment of Melchior van Hoek': the others will be 'The Confessor,' 'The Birth of a Soul' and 'The Black Madonna.'"* [19] These five volumes, *"Dramatic Interludes"* never appeared but became the short-lived *"Pagan Review"*, discussed below, which did go out under his anagram.

The winter that year in London was particularly bad. This affected William physically and mentally. He became very depressed and felt not only his physical strength weakening but also all his creative energy seeping away into the swirling, murky London smog. In an effort to improve his health, and to attend to mounting business commitments on the other side of the Atlantic, he decided to spend some time in New York. Once again he was separated from Elizabeth and making a long sea voyage. He left Britain aboard the "Teutonic" on January 6th 1892 and arrived in New York on the 13th. He stayed with his friends the Stedmans in the city but on the 15th left for Philadelphia. During this U.S. trip he also visited New Jersey and Boston. All of his visits resulted in new contacts being made in the literary and publishing worlds, including a much enjoyed meeting with Walt Whitman, as well as introductions to the important New England socialites of the day. The fact that his financial situation was going through one of its better phases is shown by the fact he declined an offer from a leading figure in the New York theatrical world, Mr. Palmer, to buy the rights to his dramatic version of *"A Fellowe and his Wife."* He had intended to stay in the States longer but while in Boston he received news that his younger brother Edward had died suddenly. He left New York aboard the "Majestic" and headed back across the Atlantic. The voyage was particularly rough and he took ill during the crossing. Although the ship arrived in the UK on February 10th it was not until the 14th that he felt well enough to travel to his mother's home in Edinburgh to deal with the trauma of losing his youngest sibling.

At this time he was attempting to have another book, *"Dramatic Vistas,"* accepted for publication. There was a lot of correspondence between William and various publishers and editors but the interesting point is that he wanted the book to be printed in two editions. The first would be a small, private printing under the H.P. Siwaarmill pseudonym. This edition was to be sent to friends and reviewers without the true identity of the author being revealed. Then, shortly after, a full public edition would be printed under his own name. This rather complicated and bizarre scheme never materialised but his intention was to check the critical acclaim for this new work by people who did not know it was by William Sharp. His reason for doing this was that reviews of his earlier works, particularly his poetry, had been mediocre. He was sure it was not the standard of his work that was at fault. He was convinced that because he had ruffled a few feathers and upset a few egos in his professional role as literary critic his own critics were now being harsh on him. He would never find out if this scheme would work or not as it never came to fruition.

A very plain-spoken article by his friend Richard Le Gallienne, published after William's death, deals with the quality of William's writings, especially after Fiona started publishing. He said in part, *"To speak faithfully, it was the comparative mediocrity, and occasional even positive badness, of the works done over his own name that formed one of the stumbling blocks to the acceptance of the theory that William Sharp could be 'Fiona Macleod.' ... for the most part it had lacked any personal force or savor, and was entirely devoid of that magnetism with which William Sharp was so generously endowed. In fact its disappointing inadequacy was a secret source of distress to the innumerable friends who loved him ... In himself William Sharp was so prodigiously a personality, so conquering in the romantic flamboyance of his sun-like vitality, so overflowing with the charm of a finely sensitive, richly nurtured temperament, so a poet in all he felt and said and did, that it was impossible to patiently accept his writings as any fair expression of himself. He was so much more than his books ... and one was inclined to say of him ... , 'What a pity he troubles to write at all! Why not be sat-*

*isfied with being William Sharp? Why spoil 'William Sharp' by this inadequate and misleading translation?' The curious thing, too, was that the work he did over his own name, after 'Fiona Macleod' had escaped... , showed no improvement in quality, no marks as having sprung from the same mental womb where it had lain side by side with so fair a sister... Indeed, it is doubtful whether if he had published the 'Fiona Macleod' writings under his own name, they would have received fair critical treatment. I am very sure that they would not.*"[20]

Many of other people who knew him commented on his exuberant personality. Catherine Janvier said, "*During his second stay with us... he was William Sharp, and William Sharp in his blithest mood. Though Fiona might smile, it is impossible to imagine her as bursting into a hearty laugh; while her creator could be the gayest of companions, full of fun and frolic, displaying at times a Pucklike impishness worthy of a twelve-year-old boy. He left our town in joyous trim, waving his blue beret from the carriage window until the train was out of sight.*" [21] She is right when she says one cannot imagine Fiona bursting into hearty laughter. Her writings are almost completely devoid of humour. Perhaps this too tells us something of the nature of Faery?

"*Vistas*," as it was finally called, was eventually published by Frank Murray in 1894 in one edition bearing William's own name. Almost simultaneously he published Fiona's "*Pharais*" and the publication of the two works by the same publisher at the same time was a deliberate ploy to divert any suspicion that they were in fact by the same author. In a letter dated December 27th 1893, to Murray he said, "*You will be interested to hear that last week I wrote 'finis' to 'Pharais': and have not only finished it but think it is the strongest and most individual thing I have done. For several reasons, however, I wish to adhere rigidly to the 'Fiona Macleod' authorship. I think the book will attract a good deal of notice, on account of the remarkable Celtic renaissance which has set in and will inevitably gather weight: it touches, too, new ground – and, I think, in a new way. What is best of all is that it is written literally out of my heart – and indeed, though the critical incident has nothing to do with me, most else is reminiscent. It is, in fact, your agreement to accept my two most paramount conditions – pseudonymity and publication by the end of March – that weighed with me against a letter from the Editor of one of the leading magazines in America... I don't know if you are interested in Celtic matters. If so, you will find a good deal in 'Pharais' that will interest you – particularly the strange chants and weird superstitious women in the romance.*" [22] This shows how intent William was in maintaining his own credentials as William Sharp while simultaneously writing in the totally different style of Fiona Macleod, and keeping the two as far apart as possible. As had been the case throughout his whole life so far, he once was more cloaking himself in yet another layer of secrets.

He returned to London in early 1892 and by April they had caught up enough with their commitments to give up their London accommodation and prepare to travel again. In correspondence between giving up their own home and heading for the Continent, William gave his return address as

16 Winchester Road, Swiss Cottage, London. This was the home of Frank and Edith Rinder. In a letter to Stedman he said he was about to leave for France, Elizabeth was going to the Isle of Wight and they would meet up in about three weeks in Paris. So, once more, Elizabeth was leaving William and Edith alone for several weeks. It has never been established what Frank Rinder thought of all this or where he was during the times William and Edith were together, but together they certainly were. Others knew of their intimate relationships. In the same letter to Stedman William wrote, *"My love to Mrs Stedman – but do not let her know that I am a backslider, as she already has but an indifferent opinion of my much tried virtue. I really am going to reform – but 'owing to unavoidable circumstances' must not begin all at once or too hurriedly!"* The 'unavoidable circumstances' were his too-good-to-be-true opportunity to spend three weeks in France alone with Edith.

He wrote to Thomas Janvier from the Grand Hotel in Paris and commented on trying to keep down his too cosmopolitan acquaintanceships in Paris and that after May 2nd when Elizabeth would join him, he would reform and remain reformed. But at the same time he wrote *"we shall be happy at our gipsy encampment in the Forest of Fontaineblue."* [23] The 'we' must have been himself and Edith. The 'too cosmopolitan acquaintanceships' in Paris were the regular weekly gatherings at the Café du Soleil d'Or where artists, writers and mystics of all nationalities and beliefs met to talk, discuss and debate. Maud Gonne, the Irish activist and close friend of Yeats, was living in France at this time and it is likely that they had mutual friends and acquaintances in the Paris mystical and magical circles although they did not personally meet until some years later.

Their plans for the rest of the year involved Elizabeth going to Bayreuth in July while William would wander the Highlands and Islands of Scotland until August when she would join him there. Winter would be spent first in London and then Sicily and Rome. However these plans had to be altered in June when Elizabeth suffered from a recurrence of malaria while they were staying with their friends the Cairds in England. While she was recuperating William negotiated the purchase of a cottage in Rudgwick, Sussex, which was in the countryside but close enough to London for them to take care of business in the city when necessary. William not only loved making up anagrams and names for people but also giving names to houses, e.g. Wescam. The Rudgwick cottage at first was to be *"The Laurels"* then *"Kingscroft"* but finally he settled on *"Phenice Croft."*

They only lived in Phenice Croft for two years but it was during those two years that he thought out, wrote, published and distributed the one and only issue of *"The Pagan Review."* This was a magazine style publication containing several articles all under the genre of what he called "The New Paganism." Some of the articles were based on classical Greek and Roman themes, some were modern and original, but all expressed an exuberance for life, love and nature. By modern standards some of it is quite turgid and long-winded but in the light of the times in which it was written it was new and groundbreaking. The contents were given as:

| | |
|---|---|
| Foreword | W.H. Brooks |
| The Black Madonna | W.S. Fanshawe |
| The Coming of Love | George Gascoign |
| The Pagans: a Romance | Willand Dreeme |
| An Untold Story | Lionel Wingrave |
| The Rape of the Sabines | James Marazion |
| The Oread | Charles Verlayne |
| Dionysos in India | William Windover |
| Contemporary Record | |
| Editorial | |

The editorial also mentioned an article on "*The New Paganism*" by H.P. Siwaarmill and the editor was said to be W.H. Brooks, two names he had used in the past. In fact it was William alone who wrote all of the articles under pseudonyms created from his fertile imagination. The first one, W.S. Fanshawe, bears his own initials; the third one, Will(and) Dreeme, bears his personal name and a word, in its common spelling, Fiona would use frequently; two of the others, Lionel Wingrave and William Windover, contain elements of Edith Wingate's name. In a sly move he did manage to get his own name in there after the fashion of Alfred Hitchcock appearing in his own films. On the back cover of the magazine is an advertisement for a forthcoming volume on "*Living Scottish Poets*" that includes Mr. William Sharp.

He sent it out unsolicited to friends, acquaintances, colleagues in the publishing and literary world, in fact anyone he thought might be interested in it. He had calculated that he would need to sell five hundred subscriptions just to cover his costs. From his notes it is clear he had planned at least three issues of *The Pagan Review*. The proposed contents for issue Number 2, to be dated September 15th 1892, were given as:

| | |
|---|---|
| H.P. Siwaarmill | The New Paganism |
| William Sharp | Oceanides |
| W.H. Brooks | Madge o' The Pool |
| Maurice Campion | Star of my Life |
| Willand Dreeme | The Pagans |
| R.C. Macfie | Alas |
| R. le Gallienne | Poem |
| James Marazion | Last of the Mystics Or V Leander or The Papadia or The Nomad Prince or The Paranymph |
| Charles Verlayne | The Hamadryad |
| Wm. Windover Dionysius in India | |
| Reviews etc | |

This note was clearly written before August 15th 1892 when the first and only copy came out as two of the above suggestions, "*The Pagans*" and "*Dionysius in India*," appeared in that issue. "*Madge o' The Pool*" would later be published under his own name. There is no record of what, if anything, he had planned for the third issue. It is interesting to note that the proposed date of issue for the second magazine, September 15th 1892, was only one month after the first, which would make the magazine a monthly serial despite his notes to the effect it should be a quarterly.

This first edition contained a call for the submission of articles for future reviews. He soon received several articles from readers, plus many monetary subscriptions, but by then he had already decided not to issue any more. He realised that he would not be able to devote the considerable amount of time it would take to operate a quarterly, let alone a monthly, publication and that for the first few issues especially he would still need to produce most of the articles. It is clear that even on the day he posted out the first issue he had already decided there would be no more. It had served its purpose. As Elizabeth put it, "*... by means of it he had exhausted a transition phase that had passed to give way to the expression of his more permanent self.*"[24]

"*The Pagan Review*" appeared almost exactly one year before he would settle upon the name and style of Fiona Macleod but, as Elizabeth said, he was already feeling the great need to write other than as William Sharp. The names were clearly important but his real push with the review was not so much to hide his identity in fictitious names and anagrams but to bring to the world a new style of writing and an awakening to the theme of the New Paganism. The editorial says in part, "*The new paganism is a potent leaven in the yeast of the younger generation ... The religion of our forefathers has not only ceased for us personally, but is no longer in any vital and general sense a sovereign power in the realm ... The ideals of our forefathers are not our ideals ... A new epoch is about to be inaugurated ... The long half-acknowledged, half-denied dual between Man and Woman is to cease ... through a frank recognition of copartnery ... Far from wishing to disintegrate, degrade, abolish marriage, the new paganism would fain see that sexual union become the flower of human life ... and women no longer have to look upon men as usurpers, and men no longer to regard women as spiritual foreigners ... We are concerned here with the new presentment of things rather than with the phenomena of change and growth themselves.*"

The comments in what is a very lengthy editorial and the contents of some of the articles reveal a strong focus on sexuality and physical union. His affair with Edith had stirred him significantly in this direction and had brought him so much physical joy and release that it had become the single most important focus of his thoughts and written expressions at this time. It also strongly implies that he did not have, and had never had, the same powerful sexual relationship with Elizabeth.

But "*The Pagan Review*" had breathed its first and last. Cheques were sent back to all the subscribers along with a little card saying, "*On the 15ᵗʰ September, still-born The Pagan Review. Regretted by none, save the affectionate parents and a few forlorn friends, The Pagan Review has returned to the void whence it came. The progenitors, more hopeful than reasonable, look for an unglorious but robust resurrection at some more fortunate date. 'For such is the Kingdom of Paganism.' W.H. Brooks*" To finalise this brief-lived venture William, Elizabeth, sister Mary and a friend Stanley Little, on September 15ᵗʰ (the date the second magazine would have been issued) solemnly buried a copy of the review in the garden at Phenice Croft, placing a framed inscription on the grave. It is interesting to note that his sister Mary was present. Her name crops up several times when Elizabeth proudly lists the famous and not so famous visitors they had at their soirees throughout the 1890s. Mary was the only one of his many siblings with whom he kept in regular contact and although her permanent address was that of his mother in Edinburgh she spent a good deal of time in England with her brother. Later Mary would be crucial in creating the illusion of Fiona Macleod being a real person.

Among the letters sent to subscribers telling them of the cancellation of the review is one to his friend Thomas Janvier. He knew that William was the sole author of the contents yet William wrote to him under his W.H. Brooks pseudonym and referred to himself in the Third Person, "*Talking of W.S. what an admirable fellow he is! I take the greatest possible interest in his career … though I cannot say that I hold quite so high a view of his poetic powers as you do, I may say that perusal of your remarks gave me as much pleasure as, I have good reason for knowing, they gave him.*" And in a P.S. he confirmed his true identity by adding, "*Elizabeth A. Brooks was so pleased to receive your letter.*" [25] This may be the first example of what would by necessity become a lifelong habit of writing about himself in the Third Person to maintain the belief in the existence of Fiona Macleod. Several times in such cases he also wrote to friends who knew the secret but spoke of himself as if he was not the writer and signed the letters with Fiona's name. This may have been for no other reason than he enjoyed the mystery of being two people but on other occasions he was clearly confused between his own identity and that of Fiona.

An important contact was made at this time by one of the people who had submitted an article for consideration. This was from a young man called Murray Gilchrist who had earlier submitted a proposal to "*The Young Folk's Paper*" when William was working there. He had now submitted an article, "*The Noble Courtesan,*" that William enjoyed but could not be used due to the demise of the review. He sent Gilchrist a letter under the W.H. Brooks signature explaining why he could not accept the article but added a P.S. saying, "*It is possible that you may surmise – or that a common friend may tell you – who the editor of the P/R is: if so, may I ask you to be reticent on the matter.*" A few days later William wrote to him again and said, "*Although I do not wish the matter to go further I do not mind so sympathetic and kindly a critic knowing that 'W.S.' and 'W.H. Brooks' are synonymous … I look to you as*

*one of the younger men of notable talent to give a helping hand with your pen.
I suppose you come to London occasionally. I hope when you are next south, you
will come and give me the pleasure of your personal acquaintance. I can offer
you a lovely country home, country fare, a bed, and a cordial welcome."* [26] The
confession of his true identity seems surprising considering he did not know
his young correspondent and the offer of accommodation seems remarkably
hospitable for the same reason. Gilchrist would later take him up on his offer and he would become an invaluable confidant to the extent that William
would reveal the secret of Fiona Macleod to him. We shall learn more of
Gilchrist later.

A personal aside: at the time I was compiling this section on *"The Pagan Review"* and William's use of the many pseudonyms, including that of
his grandfather W.H. Brooks, I had been involved in a large scale DNA
sampling experiment that had been going on for some time. One of the
compensations for volunteering a DNA sample was that if any close matches
should be found between my DNA and that of any of the other volunteers
we would be put in touch with each other. Periodically I would be sent an
e-mail of just such matches. The day I finished writing the above section I
took a look at a DNA e-mail that had just come in. There were twelve names
on it. The first name was "W. H. Brooks."

The birth and simultaneous death of one child, *"The Pagan Review,"*
helped to usher in the birth of the next child, Fiona Macleod. It is clear he
needed the permanence and stability of a settled life in order for Fiona to
manifest fully in consciousness and to make her mark on the world. The
mental and emotional stimulation of his wanderings, the stresses of the constant financial and health related ups and downs and, not least, the spiritual
and emotional jolt caused by his affair with Edith, were all the catalysts he
needed to nourish the embryonic Fiona. Although William claimed that
Fiona had been born on that day at Lake Nemi I would say that it is more accurate to say she had been conceived that day. If any place on this earth can
be called the birthplace of Fiona Macleod it was Phenice Croft in England,
not, as she would later claim, Iona, Arran or some other remote island off
the west coast of Scotland.

There are a few references in his correspondence from this period that
other commentators have interpreted as meaning William occasionally
drank too much. Elizabeth does not comment on this, which is not surprising if it was true, yet neither does she state he abstained from alcohol. In
light of what we now know regarding his affair with Edith these ambiguous
statements deserve to be reinterpreted. For example, when William wrote
as W.H. Brooks to Thomas Janvier to tell him that the review had breathed
its last, he continued in the Third Person, and said, *"By the way, he's settling
down to a serious tussle. He has been a 'bad boy' of late: but about a week previous to the death of the Pagan/Review [sic] he definitively reformed – on September 11ᵗʰ in the early forenoon, I believe. I hope earnestly that he may be able to*

*live on the straight henceforth: but I regret to say I see signs of backsliding.*" [27] On August 13th 1892, he sent two letters. One was to Stedman and the other was to Bliss Carman. In the Stedman letter he says, "*By the time you get this – no, a week later – I shall be in Scotland, I hope. My wife cannot go north this year. If all goes well – this ought to be one of the happiest experiences of a happy life. I cannot be more explicit: but perhaps you will understand.... Then I am going to reform, and work hard all winter.*" [28] To Carman he wrote, "*Think of me in early September (from August 30th) in the loveliest of the West Highlands - & in one of the happiest experiences of my life. I can't be more explicit – but you will understand! Thereafter I am going to reform – definitely.*" [29] These are clearly not the promises of a drunkard to go on the wagon but the boasts of a man in the throes of a passionate but secret love affair.

As we now know Elizabeth knew and tolerated this relationship, it certainly helped both William and Fiona blossom, but she did on occasion have other causes for jealousy. In a rather amusing letter to Ford Madox Brown sent from London on January 1st 1890, William describes their New Year celebrations the night before and says, "*But we had a jolly evening, and the only little cloud since was my dear wife's catching me kissing our handsome house maid Kate under the mistletoe. I explained that I felt full of fatherly love, but somehow Mrs S. did not see it. As somebody says in Dickens, 'women is rum's devils.'*"

Although Phenice Croft was a haven for them this was an unstable time in several subtle ways. Elizabeth comments in her memoir of her husband's happiness during their time there but she also talks of his ailing physical and mental health causing her concern. It was certainly a time of much productivity and accomplishment but it was also a time of great stress. He had given up his lifelong desire to wander; he was dealing with the enormous psychological pressure of Fiona coming through and he was coping with the emotional strain of being separated from Edith. In the winter of 1892-93 Elizabeth's health, which was also delicate, took a turn for the worst when she had yet another recurring bout of malaria. It was once again necessary for them to seek warmer climes. They had no money to sustain them away from home for any length of time so William gave up his plans for future serious writing and, instead, turned out a couple of serial adventure stories for children, "*The Red Rider*" and "*The Last of the Vikings,*" for the "*Young Folk's Paper.*" This gave them the money they needed to leave Phenice Croft to improve Elizabeth's health abroad. However instead of going to their beloved and familiar Italy they decided that what they really needed was a trip through Algeria and Tunisia and on into the Sahara Desert!

They had certainly established a pattern of making radical decisions in the past but this one is really baffling. Compared to the well-worn route south to Italy this was a long, dangerous and arduous journey to make in Victorian times. Africa was still the Dark Continent and European visitors, especially women, were uncommon and susceptible to unwanted attention. If the sole purpose of the journey was Elizabeth's health why place her in what would certainly be a dangerous and stressful situation? It may have been on Elizabeth's insistence that they avoid Italy as the memories of her husband's waywardness there last time were still too fresh in her mind. Or it may have been a good chance for William to experience first hand and experiment with Eastern mysticism and magical techniques, a subject that had fascinated him since his student days in the library of Glasgow University. Whatever their reasons they left England on January 7th 1893 and sailed to the Mediterranean. They arrived in Algiers on January 14th and spent the next few weeks travelling mostly by train in Algiers and Morocco, stopping at Constantine, Tunis and Carthage amongst other places. Elizabeth's health started to improve although she was still weak and no doubt fatigued by the travelling. But the excitement of this new place and the sense of danger fired their imaginations and they enjoyed the whole adventure tremendously. Her diary entries for the time they were in Africa show no signs of fear or trepidation. She was clearly enjoying the whole trip as much as William was.

William wrote long letters home describing in detail all the wonderful and new things they were experiencing. While in the city of Constantine one of his wandering fits came on him. As Elizabeth lay resting in their hotel room he slipped out and headed straight for the Casbah. A solitary European wandering the streets after dark must have caused some stares from the local population but he was so enthralled by all the new sights, sounds and smells that he threw all caution to the wind and wandered deeper and deeper into the dark, narrow streets of the ancient marketplace. At one point he did encounter some danger, or at least unpleasantness, but it did not deter him from exploring further, *"I went at last where I saw not one single European: and though at some risk, I met with no active unpleasantness, save in one Haschisch place where by a sudden impulse some forty or fifty Moors suddenly swung round... and with outstretched hands and arms cursed the 'dog of an infidel'... I plunged right into the midst of the whole extraordinary vision ... From Haschisch-den to Haschisch-den I wandered, from strange vaulted rooms of the gorgeously jewelled and splendidly dressed prostitutes to the alcoves where lay or sat or moved to and fro, behind iron bars, the caged 'beauties' whom none could reach save by gold, and even then at risk; from there to the dark, low rooms or open pillared places where semi-nude dancing girls moved to and fro to a wild, barbaric music... I wandered to and fro in that bewildering Moorish maze, till at last I could stand no more impressions. So I found my way to the western ramparts, and looked out upon the marvellous nocturnal landscapes of mountain and valley - and thought of all that Constantine had been."* [30] The above extract implies that he was not only wandering through the 'haschisch-dens' but also actively sampling their wares. A few years later his friends and magical co-workers Yeats, Maud Gonne and MacGregor Mathers would experiment with hashish in an effort to induce visions. William was already ahead of them in the experimentation game.

From North Africa they went directly to Sicily where they stayed in the town of Taormina close to Mount Etna for the duration of the winter. They would return to Sicily several times over the following years. They returned from their great North African and Sicilian adventure in February 1893 and settled back in Phenice Croft, Elizabeth's health being much improved. Elizabeth lists many of the friends who called on them during that summer, Edith being one of them. Elizabeth's brother Robert Farquharson Sharp visited, as did William's sister and secretary Mary. Elizabeth comments that Mary was also known as "Marik." [31] I have never seen this name used in any correspondence or diary entries but in 1909 Elizabeth collected together many short paragraphs and passages of Fiona's work that she published together in a slim volume called "*A Little Book of Nature*" (T.N. Foulis, Edinburgh) which she dedicated to Marik. This is the only reference, if it can be called that, I have been able to find from Elizabeth by way of thanks to Mary for her years of work and years of silence regarding the secret of Fiona Macleod.

In April Elizabeth went to Paris to review the salons for *The Glasgow Herald*. William took a short break in the Isle of Wight and on return to Phenice Croft he became very productive, writing mainly about his North African adventure. Much of this material was published in various magazines. In July they spent several weeks on holiday in Scotland. Yet again they parted company part way through the trip with Elizabeth going off to visit friends and he staying for a while on the Isle of Arran before going to Edinburgh to visit his mother.

Elizabeth commented that, "*... once again he saw visions and dreamed dreams; the psychic subjective side of his dual nature predominated. He was in an acutely creative condition; and, moreover, he was passing from one phase of literary work to another, deeper, more intimate, more permanent. So far, he had found no adequate method for the expression of his 'second self' though the way was led thereto by Sospiri di Roma and Vistas.*" [32] This is about as close as Elizabeth ever got in her memoir to admitting William was actively practicing magic and it was producing results. By the close of 1893 he had produced an enormous amount of work under his own name but the milestone was to be Fiona's "*Pharais.*"

[1] Memoir, page 173

[2] Memoir, page 222

[3] Memoir, page 173

[4] Memoir, page 174

[5] Yeats Annual 13, page 68

[6] Memoir, page 222

[7] Collected Works of Wm Sharp, Vol. 1, page 159

[8] "Under the Dark Star", Collected Works Vol. 3, page 345

[9] NLS, Edinburgh

[10] "Pharais", page 8

[11] NLS, Edinburgh

[12] "Poems and Dramas", page 32

[13] Jeffares, The Gonne-Yeats Letters, page 235

[14] Memoir, page 222

[15] Meredith, Letters of George Meredith to Alice Meynell, page 47

[16] Meynell, Alice Meynell, A Memoir, page 145

[17] Memoir, page 187

[18] Memoir, page 188

[19] Memoir, page 190

[20] Le Gallienne, "The Mystery of Fiona Macleod", "The Forum", February 1911, pages 175-6

[21] Janvier, "Fiona Macleod and her Creator", "The North American Review", April 19
     page 723

[22] NLS, Edinburgh

[23] Memoir, page 196

[24] Memoir, page 204

[25] Memoir, page 205

[26] Memoir, page 207

[27] Memoir, page 205

[28] WS Archives

[29] WS Archives

[30] Memoir, page 213

[31] Memoir, page 215

[32] Memoir, page 221

# Chapter 5
# Fiona, Her Name and Her Influence

*At times he was to all intents and purposes a different being. He would come and sit down by my fireside and talk, and I believe that when 'Fiona Macleod' left the house he would have no recollection of what he had been saying to me.*

There is a very important detail that must be examined here. During the planning and writing stage of "*Pharais*" it was clearly a William Sharp work. In his diaries and notebooks there are references to the general plot of the story and several comments on the main characters but no mention is made of the decision to change the name of its author. One diary entry says, "*In all, I have actually on hand eight books, and innumerable stories, articles, etc. The things first to be done now are*

*Books   1 Finish new Life of Rossetti*
*2 Finish Pharais*
*3 Write Nostalgia…. "*[1]

In a letter dated August 12th 1893 to Catharine Janvier he spoke of it as a book 'he' was writing. He made no mention of Fiona Macleod or the intention to publish under any other pseudonym. Exactly when and why did William decide to change authorship from William Sharp to Fiona Macleod? We do know he had already written several pieces under various pseudonyms and that he had used this device to hopefully elicit honest criticism from those who did not realise it was his own work. However, these early writings under pseudonym were all relatively small, one-off pieces. The Fiona Macleod pseudonym would become a virtual industry. Richard Whiteing, a friend, writer and attendee at the Sharps' soirees, and who would later become one of the few people to know the secret, commented after William's death, "*Mr Sharp was always getting ready to throw off the mask* [of Fiona], *which was assumed solely to enable the critics to judge his work impartially.*"[2] Nobody other than Mr. Whiteing is on record as saying William was ready at any time to reveal his authorship of the Fiona Macleod library and his subsequent determination to protect the secret at all costs show that this was not the case.

It is likely he had already decided to use this name by September of 1893, probably on his birthday, when he visited the publisher Frank Murray in Derby. It was Murray who published "*Vistas*" by William Sharp in his Regent Series (the first of which was "*Frangipani*" by Murray Gilchrist) and "*Pharais*" by Fiona Macleod. In a letter dated December 27th 1893, William said to him that, "*I wish to adhere rigidly to the 'Fiona Macleod' authorship ...*" and that pseudonymity was paramount to publication. This implies that during their September meeting he had already decided on the Fiona authorship and this letter was simply stressing the importance of what had already been agreed in September. On this subject Elizabeth simply says, "*During the writing of Pharais the author began to realize how much the feminine element dominated in the book, that it grew out of the subjective or feminine side of his nature. He, therefore, decided to issue the book under the name of Fiona Macleod, that 'flashed ready made' into his mind.*"[3] It is interesting to note that Elizabeth says 'the author' and not 'my husband' – did she understand that her husband was merely the vehicle through which the story was transmitted by the 'real' author, Fiona Macleod?

The claim that the entire name flashed ready made into his mind is highly unlikely if looked upon solely from a practical point of view. The "Macleod" part he took from his old fisherman friend Seumas Macleod and is more appropriate than it may appear. William was part Scandinavian through his mother's side of the family and he was proud of his Viking heritage, indeed Fiona would write several Viking stories. The name Macleod – Son of Leod - is from the Viking tradition, not the Celtic. Leod comes from the Old Norse word 'Ljotr' which means 'unattractive' and there was such an historical person. This unfortunately named man was son of Olaf the Black, King of the Isle of Man and the Northern Isles. He was descended from the oddly named King Halfdan the Stingy who, by tradition, was descended from the Viking god Frey. The historical Scandinavian source of the name is therefore appropriate to William and the supposed descent from Frey links nicely with Fiona's Faery connections.

But the "Fiona" part is a bit more problematic. The name Fiona had not existed prior to his use of it in 1893. Later William would claim, "*It, Fiona, is very rare now. Most Highlanders would tell you it was extinct – even as a diminutive of Fionaghal (Flora). But it is not. It is an old Celtic name (meaning 'a fair maid') still occasionally to be found. I know a little girl, the daughter of a Highland clergyman, who is called Fiona.*"[4] The old Gaelic name Fionaghal means 'fair shoulder' and is occasionally to be found in the old legends, in particular the Irish legends, but it would never be contracted to Fiona. There is no record of this having happened and, even if it had been, it could not mean 'a fair maid' under that spelling in the Gaelic language. Concerning his claim to know a little girl of that name I believe his memory was playing tricks and his chronology is slightly out of sync. He may well have known a clergyman with a daughter called Fiona but that was <u>after</u> Fiona started to be published and the clergyman in question took his daughter's name from Fiona Macleod, not vice versa. In my own researches I have not been able to find any occurrence of the personal name Fiona prior to 1893. In the West of Scotland, where William and Fiona are remembered more than in most other places, there has long been an oral tradition, one which I first heard many years ago, that he made up the word by combining the name of his favourite island, Iona, with the name of the great Gaelic hero, Fionn, the result being Fiona. The correct form of her full name in Gaelic would be Fhiona nic Leoid but he never used this spelling for the simple reason it is easier for the non-Gaelic speaker to pronounce the phonetic Anglicised form.

However I have uncovered evidence that he had planned to use yet a different pseudonym for this work. It was his habit of using large, grey, stiff paper sleeves or file folders to house his various manuscripts and notes. In the William Sharp Collection in the National Library, Edinburgh, there is such a folder labelled "Husbands-in-Law" containing a fragment of this piece he was planning to publish under the pseudonym Ambrose Moir. This pseudonym crops up several times in the unpublished material. More importantly though is what is on the reverse of this folder. Turn it over and there, yellowed as if it had been lying in the sun for a while, and upside down as if he had originally used this side of the folder and then turned it over to use the other side, is written in ink "'Pharais', by Catriona Macleod." This has been scored over in pencil and "see other side" written over it. It is clear from this that his original intention had been to publish "Pharais" under the name of Catriona Macleod. The name Catriona was and still is a common girl's name in the Gaelic speaking areas and would have been familiar to many people at that time. In English it is Catherine. But there is nothing to say why he had considered that name either. Nor, indeed, is there anything to say why he turned this folder over and abandoned the name Catriona in favour of Fiona.

One possibility is that in 1893, when he started work on "*Pharais*," his friend and correspondent Robert Louis Stevenson published the sequel to his highly successful book "*Kidnapped*." This sequel was called simply "*Catriona*." Did William feel that the novelty had been taken from this name, or did he fear that perhaps when people started to look for the fictitious Catriona Macleod they would guess that her real identity was that of Robert Louis Stevenson? Another possibility is that Catriona/Katherine was the name of his little sister who died while still a baby. Perhaps this brought back painful, unconscious, memories and he simply felt uncomfortable using a name with so much negative emotion attached to it.

Whatever the reason, it must have been a good one. It was the most important decision he made in his life, although he was unaware of it at the time, the ramifications of which are still being felt to this day. Why is it not mentioned in his extensive notebooks and diaries? What was the trigger that made him move from William Sharp to Catriona Macleod to finally Fiona Macleod? It may have been related to his group magical work. Members of the Golden Dawn and similarly structured occult lodges would take a "magical name" as an important part of the occult work they were expected to complete. Usually such a name was a motto or phrase describing the magical aspirations of the initiate and was used during ceremony and ritual in order to distinguish the higher personality of the members from their everyday personality. In formal lodges it was often given in Latin and the member was known as Frater, or Soror, followed by the initials of the magical name. For example William Butler Yeats was initiated into Golden Dawn in March 1889 and later took the magical name Fr. D.E.D.I. (*Daemon Est Deus Inversus*); Maud Gonne was initiated on November 2nd 1891 and eventually took the name Sr. P.I.A.L. (*Per Ignem Ad Lucem*); Moina Mathers was Sr. V.N.R. (*Vestigia Nulla Retrorsum*). The use of Latin was not compulsory. William's friend and magical co-worker MacGregor Mathers had two magical names, one Latin, Fr. D.D.C.F (*Deo Duce Comite Ferro*) and one Gaelic, Fr. S.R.M.D. (*'S Rioghail Mo Dhream* – meaning 'of royalty is my race', Mathers claimed to be descended from or a reincarnation of Bonnie Prince Charlie).

All of these acquaintances were members of the Isis-Urania Temple Number 3 of the Golden Dawn in London. The member list identifies them along with their magical names. William Sharp is on the list but there is no magical name given for him. This simply means that at the time the list was compiled he had not advanced far enough through the grade system to adopt a magical name.[5] Assuming that William later worked his way through the various degrees of the lodge he would have adopted his own magical name but all the indications are that his membership of the Golden Dawn was brief and superficial and it is likely he never got to the stage of composing a magical name. It is interesting to note that there was a Golden Dawn Temple in Edinburgh, Amen-Ra No. 6, that was chartered in 1893 and formally consecrated in 1894, exactly the same period when William started to write "*Pharais*" under his own name, 1893, and by the time it had been published, 1894, the authorship had been changed to Fiona. He also spent some time in Edinburgh during both of these years but as of yet no documentary evidence has come to light that he was a member of the Edinburgh lodge as well as the Isis-Urania lodge.

The Golden Dawn became plagued with in-fighting and schisms and William, Yeats, Gonne and others all eventually resigned, at different times, from the lodge. Maud Gonne in particular was not impressed by the group members and commented, "*I passed four initiations and learned a number of Hebrew words, but there also I was oppressed by the drab appearance and mediocrity of my fellow mystics. Mrs MacGregor and Florence Farr, the actress, were exceptions ... The fratre and sorore who so kindly made me welcome among them seemed to me the very essence of British middle-class dullness. They looked so incongruous in their cloaks and badges at initiation ceremonies; their mysterious titles, "Guardians of the Gates of the East and of the West", "Commanders of the Temple" etc fitted them even less well..."* [6] But she had another more sinister belief that prompted her to quickly resign, she thought, *"...perhaps the Golden Dawn was an esoteric side of Masonry... Free Masonry as we Irish know it is a British institution and has always been used politically to support the British Empire... I would have no connection with it, even to learn its secrets."* [7] Certainly many of the founder members of the Golden Dawn were also senior Masons.

Eventually this group of disenchanted ex-Golden Dawners formed their own occult lodge called the Celtic Mystical Order. They had located an old castle in Ireland, which they referred to as the "Castle of Heroes," that one day they hoped would become their magical lodge. This was Castle Rock, set on an island in Lough Key, Co. Roscommon, and surrounded by woods. It was in a good state of repair as it was not as old as it seemed being a folly only seventy years old. This place fitted the ideas they had formulated for the Castle of Heroes, *"It was to be in the middle of a lake, a shrine of Irish tradition where only those who had dedicated their lives to Ireland might penetrate; they were to be brought there in a painted boat across the lake and might only stay for short periods of rest and inspiration. The castle would be built of native stone and decorated with the Four Jewels of the Tuatha de Danann – the Lia Fail, the Cauldron of the Dagda, the Spear of Lugh and the Sword of Light – and a statue of Ireland, if any artist could be found great enough to make one, which they doubted. All trivialities would be excluded from the Castle of Heroes. In austere surroundings, those dedicated to Ireland might through meditation harmonise their individual efforts with national endeavour as Yeats himself had done. Though as Maud said the Castle of Heroes was to remain a castle in the air, Yeats would remark on the occasion of their last meeting before his death, ""Maud, we should have gone on with our Castle of the Heroes, we might still do it.'"* [8] We shall learn more of the Celtic Mystical Order in Chapter 8.

The purpose of this new Celtic order was to concentrate exclusively on reconstructing what they referred to as the Celtic Rite. They would all have taken new magical names in order to show that their specifically Celtic work was separate from any previous work with the Golden Dawn or any other lodge. William would have been well aware that often heroes and heroines in the ancient Celtic legends deliberately changed their name or were given a new name by some important third party. Such renaming symbolised an initiation to a higher level of spiritual and magical study which itself signalled the beginning of some new important work about to unfold. This was exactly what was happening in William's life where a veritable flood of new writing was on the brink of being unleashed. Deciding to change his pen name at this stage may well have been an unconscious magical act synchronistic with this impending and important new magical work. It furthermore proved to be an essential factor behind adopting his new magical persona. Fiona Macleod would very quickly become much more than just a magical or pen name. William was soon to discover that she had a unique and strong personality of her own that within a very short time almost completely dominated his life.

But all this discussion of magical names and possible identification with other authors is too intellectual and scholarly. There is a much simpler explanation to the Fiona Macleod name. The only motivating factor in all this was Fiona herself. Accepting for a moment that this was the case, the next question that arises is then who, or what, was Fiona Macleod? She could be described in psychological terms as a distinct aspect of William's own personality or as separate part of his psyche caused by, say, schizophrenia. She could be written up in magical terminology as an Inner Plane adept that needed a body to communicate through. She may have been a memory of some previous incarnation, a subject William hinted at in letters and diaries. She could also be described as no more than a deliberate marketing ploy designed to enable him to sell books in a style totally different from his usual, as his friend Mr. Whiteing asserted. It could, of course, have been a combination of any or all of these factors.

I personally lean towards a different belief altogether. Fiona Macleod was a real, individual being from the Faery realms whose name was Fiona Macleod. This would explain how the name could flash ready-made to mind as Elizabeth asserts. It also explains why the name Fiona was unknown in our world before this time, having only ever been used before in the world of Faery. This would also account for some of the other unknown names that she used in her writings asserting confidently they were ancient and common. The highly sensitive and psychic William, with his knowledge of Gaelic and Celtic lore and culture, was a perfectly suitable vehicle for her to use to express the great spiritual beliefs and lore of Faerydom that it was her purpose to reveal to the inquisitive Victorian mind. William was entering a period magically in his life that would have made him very noticeable to those of the Otherworld, Inner Planes or realm of Faery depending on your particular nomenclature. In short, just as William Sharp was about to use the name Catriona Macleod for purely marketing reasons, the real Fiona Macleod popped up and hijacked the whole plan for very different reasons.

Of her birthplace and parentage she once wrote, "*I was born more than a thousand years ago, in the remote region of Gaeldom known as the Hills of Dream. There I have lived the better part of my life, my father's name was Romance, and that of my mother was Dream. I have no photograph of their abode, which is just under the quicken-arch immediately west of the sunset rainbow. You will easily find it. Nor can I send you a photograph of myself. My last fell among the dew-wet heather, and is now doubtless lining the cells of the wild bees. All this authentic information I gladly send you!*" [9] Authentic information, yes, but from the Faery world, not this world. If the writings of Fiona Macleod are looked at from this point of view then they make much more sense and reveal much hidden and valuable Faery lore that is otherwise lost to the romantic, casual reader. Often she herself would become confused between the reality of her own world and the reality of this world, the world in which William and all of her readers lived and had their consciousness. This would cause frequent problems for William in later years.

An example of her use of unfamiliar names is that of the peculiarly named Gloom Achanna who, along with his father and brothers, crops up in several of her stories. John Macleay (1870 –1955), editor of *The Highland News*, Inverness, until 1924 and thereafter at the *Liverpool Daily Post*, wished to know the origin of this peculiar name. He wrote to Fiona to find out and in a reply dated February 18<sup>th</sup> 1896 William, not Fiona, said, "*I don't know where Miss M got the name of "Gloom" from. It is probably her own imagining. Certainly I never heard the word used as a name. She told me once, though, I remember, that in her list of strange names that she compiled and often draws upon, she has one as strange as "Gloom" – and this within her own knowledge, I am almost sure – namely Mulad, meaning I think is much the same as Bron (grief) though possibly rather sadness than grief. The name Achanna I think she owes to me. I knew a man of that name: and indeed Miss M's "Gloom Achanna" is one of her most near-to-life characters – for he is founded on one who is a close relative of Miss M's mother. (A kinsman of my own, a very undesirable one!) The man I knew was Stephen Achanna, and his son changed the name to its better known form Hannay. He is now, I think settled in Glasgow.*"[10] Note the little comment about Gloom Achanna being a relative of Miss M's mother thereby reinforcing the whole legend of Fiona Macleod being a real person. Gloom may well have been a relative of her mother, but not in this world.

Some years later Fiona herself would comment on this particular name. In 1902 the German publisher Tauchnitz published several volumes of Fiona's work. In the one entitled "*Wind and Wave*" there is a new preface to her tale "*Dan-Nan-Ron*" in which she says, "*As to my use of the forename 'Gloom' (in this story, in its sequel 'Green Branches,' in 'The Anointed Man,' and in 'Children of the Dark Star' in The Dominion of Dreams), I should explain that the designation is not a baptismal name. At the same time, I have actual warrant for its use; for I knew a Uist man who, in the bitterness of his sorrow, after his wife's death in childbirth, named his son Mulad (i.e. the gloom of sorrow: grief).*" This reiterates what William said in his letter several years earlier but in a more specific form.

In the lengthy dedication to "*Pharais*" she introduces three names allegedly from Gaelic mythology which, again, have no authenticity in this world. She says, "*In the mythology of the Gael there are three forgotten deities, children of Delbaith-Dana. These are Seithoir, Teithoir and Keithoir. One dwells throughout the sea, and beneath the soles of the feet of another are the highest clouds; and these two may be held sacred for the beauty they weave for the joy of eye and ear. But now that, as surely none may gainsay, Keithoir is blind and weary, let us worship at his fame rather than give all our homage to the others.*

*For Keithoir is the god of the earth: dark-eyed, shadowy brother of Pan:... It is because you and I are of the children of Keithoir that I wished to grace my book with your name."* In a short tale entitled *"The Snow Sleep of Angus Ogue"* which appeared in *"The Evergreen: Book of Winter"* (Patrick Geddes, Edinburgh, 1896) she again refers to Keithoir and describes him as an ancient god of the earth. This is a good example of how she occasionally confused which gods came from which tradition. In this tale the Faery god Keithoir, is accompanied by the authentic Irish god Manannan and the equally authentic Breton god Hesus.

As with the name Gloom I have been unable to find any independent references to Seithoir, Teithoir or Keithoir. Seithoir and Teithoir, are not Gaelic names and do not bear close or distant resemblance to any Gaelic words that I know of or can find in any Gaelic dictionary. The name Keithoir cannot be Gaelic as written because there is no letter 'k' in the Gaelic alphabet. It would more likely be Ceithoir, which is still not a Gaelic word, but it is very close to "ceithir," the Gaelic for the number four. This does not make any sense and is probably no more than coincidental. MacGregor Mathers, the knowledgeable magician of the Golden Dawn, was also unable to recognise or find any references to this mysterious deity and asked the same question regarding the validity of Keithoir. He wrote to Yeats on March 28th 1898 asking *"And do you think that the Keithoir of Fiona Macleod is the same as the ancient Goddess Cessair. Keithoir is called by Fiona the God of the Green World."* [11] It is curious that nobody seems to have thought of asking Fiona about this! The goddess Cessair to whom Mathers refers is mentioned in *"The Book of the Invasions of Ireland"* where she is described as a grand daughter of the Biblical Noah and was the first settler in Ireland. Clearly not the male figure connected with the Green World of Fiona's description.

Yet despite the clear lack of references to these alleged deities from any other independent source Fiona states as a matter of fact that they are forgotten Gaelic gods. If they are 'forgotten' gods by what means did Fiona remember them? The phrase from the *"Pharais"* dedication to E.W.R., *"... because you and I are of the children of Keithoir..."* is interesting. Why did she believe that she, a Faery, and Edith Wingate Rinder, a human being, were both children of this totally Faery realm deity? Was this William's consciousness intruding into Fiona's thought patterns while writing and unintentionally causing her to experience the confusion that plagued him throughout his life regarding Fiona and Edith? Whatever the truth of the origin of these names it is safe to say that they are not three forgotten Celtic gods despite the positive statements from Fiona to this effect.

As well as inadvertently using personal names from the Faery realm Fiona also managed to introduce us to a couple of books that come from there. It was common practice with writers of literature in those days to preface books or individual chapters with short quotations from various sources, usually the classical Greek and Latin writers, Shakespeare or other noteworthy poets and so forth. William and Fiona both followed this tradition and many of their writings have little quotations from Pindar, Sophocles, Coleridge, Nietzsche, the Kalevala etc as headers to chapters. In amongst Fiona's copious output there are several quotations from a book she calls "*The Little Book of the Great Enchantment.*" Of this book she once wrote, "*I read often in this book. It is to me as the sea is, or the wind: for like that unseen and homeless creature, which in the beginning God breathed between the lips of Heat and Cold, it is full of unbidden meanings and has sighs and laughters: and, like the sea, it has limits and shallow, but holds the stars, and has depths where light is dim and only the still, breathless soul listens; and has a sudden voice that is old as day and night, and is fed with dews and rains, and is salt and bitter.*" [12]

A quotation from this book is the preface to "*The Lynn of Dreams*" in "*The Winged Destiny*" which says "*Ah, son of water, daughter of fire, how can ye twain be one?*" This is hardly of major significance but the fore piece to "*The Dirge of the Four Cities*" from "*Poems and Dramas*" gives away a lot more. It says, "*There are four cities that no mortal eye has seen but that the soul knows; these are Gorias, that is in the east; and Finias, that is in the south; and Murias, that is in the west; and Falias, that is in the north. And the symbol of Falias is the stone of death, which is crowned with pale fire. And the symbol of Gorias is the dividing sword. And the symbol of Finias is a spear. And the symbol of Murias is a hollow that is filled with water and fading light.*" These four cities originally appeared in the ancient Irish legends "*Lebor Gaballa Erin*" (The Book of Invasions of Ireland) and "*Cath Maig Tuired*" (The Battle of Moytura)[13] where they are specifically identified as the dwelling places of the Faery people before they came to Ireland. The Battle of Moytura goes on to expand on the cities, their guardians and much symbolism connected with them. All of this is from the Faery realm.

Also in "*Poems and Dramas,*" as a preface to the section called "*Through The Ivory Gate,*" there is another piece taken from "*The Little Book of the Great Enchantment*" that says, "*Love is a vapour that is licked up of the wind. Let whoso longeth after this lovely mist – that as a breath is, and is not – beware of this wind. There is no sorrow like unto the sorrow of this wind.*" This is much more cryptic but interestingly Fiona gives the name of its source in Gaelic, "*Leabhran Mhor-Gheasadaireachd*" which translates literally from the Gaelic as "a small book of great enchantment, or charms." This raises the question what is the language of the Faeries? Is it English, or Gaelic, or something completely outwith our ken? Again in "*Poems and Dramas*" there is a six-page dedication to W.B. Yeats as the preface to the section called "*Foam of the Past.*" Fiona starts this dedication to her fellow poet and mystic saying, "*In a small book in a greater, "The Little Book of the Great Enchantment" in 'The Book of White Magic (or Wisdom)'... the "Leabhran Mhor-Gheasadaireachd" to give the Gaelic name... it is said: 'When you have a memory out of darkness, tell to a seer, to a poet, and to a friend that which you remember: and if the seer say, I see it – and if the poet say, I hear it – and if the friend say, I believe it: then know of a surety that your remembrance is a true remembrance.'"*

This seems to tell us that *The Little Book of the Great Enchantment* is divided into smaller books or sections one of which is *The Book of White Magic* named above. "*Poems and Dramas*" opens with a quotation from "*The Book of White Magic*" that says, "*Was it because I desired thee darkly, that thou could'st not know the white spell? Or was it that the white spell could not reach thy darkness? One god debateth this: and another god answereth this: but one god knoweth it. With him be the issue.*" Fiona again gives the Gaelic name for her source – *An Leabhar Ban* – saying this means "*The Book of White Magic*" but the literal translation of her Gaelic is "*The White Book*" with no mention or implication of magic. Putting aside her Gaelic the important point to note is that Fiona not only gave away much Faery lore and wisdom in her books, not only gave us authentic Faery names in her characters but also gave us the name of a Faery book, The Little Book of the Great Enchantment, which she felt worthy of quoting. I know several Fiona fans who have searched antiquarian bookshops far and wide in an effort to find a dusty old copy of this important tome but to no avail. Not only were they looking in the wrong place but they were looking in the wrong world! It occurred to me some years ago that maybe, just maybe, this book *did* exist in this world – but only in the Gaelic language, which might explain its absence in most bookshops. I therefore spent a considerable amount of time searching in antiquarian and second-hand bookshops in Scotland, on-line and, not least, in the Gaelic manuscripts department of the National Library of Scotland, Edinburgh but I too found nothing.

So when Fiona said a thing was authentic, or that such and such a piece of lore was ancient and forgotten, she was being sincere but sometimes forgot that it was only ancient and authentic in her world, not necessarily so in this world. This is an important point. Students of her writings should keep this in mind when she claims authenticity for a name, place, event or even a book. It may not be the type of authenticity you are used to, but that in itself may lead to other possibilities!

Once again we need to take note of significant events that were taking place elsewhere on the planet at this time. On September 12th 1893, William's thirty eighth birthday, the "*Council for a Parliament of the World's Religions*" was being opened in the city of Chicago. This was a gathering of spiritual leaders from most of the world's religions and was the first time ever that east had met west to discuss and listen to each others religious and spiritual views in an atmosphere not of debate but of openness and acceptance. It was the first important step forward towards worldwide religious tolerance and understanding. It was also the first time that the main orthodox religions of the world sat down and actually listened to and had dialogue with spiritual leaders from many of the world's indigenous pagan and nature based faiths. Amongst these were spiritual leaders from the Native American peoples who were being listened to and treated with respect and dignity as important contributors to the Parliament. Yet only three years earlier, in 1890, Chief Sitting Bull had been killed and the slaughter of Wounded Knee had shocked and horrified the more enlightened members of American society.

As Jabez T. Sunderland, who attended both the 1893 Parliament and the *"Assembly of the World Fellowship of Faiths"* in 1933, said, *"Few persons today realize how great a thing that first Chicago Parliament of Religions was, and fewer still how wide reaching and important have been the results following it. It is probably not an exaggeration to represent it as marking an epoch, if not in the religious history, at least in the religious progress of the world. It was something absolutely new, unique, unprecedented; mankind had never seen anything like it ... In that great Chicago Parliament, for absolutely the first time in human history, eminent representatives of all the important religious faiths of mankind came together in a great world assemblage, and what was more, came in the spirit of equality and mutual respect; came not to antagonize or criticise but to fellowship; came not even for debate, but for thoughtful and brotherly conference over the great worldwide problems and interests of religion, each to represent for the consideration of the rest of the world, an affirmative statement, a constructive interpretation of the central truths, aims, and ideals of the faith which he represented, as understood not by its enemies but by its friends."* [14]

In a letter dated March 4th 1898 to her friend Dr. John Goodchild Fiona expressed the ideals of the Chicago parliament when she said, " ... *more and more I am impressed by the strangeness of the fundamentally identical spiritual ideas which come to many minds. Race, temperament and, perhaps, conditions modify or affect these ideas, but below the accident lies the same spiritual reality."* [15] I was privileged to be invited to speak at the second Parliament in Chicago, held in 1993 on the centenary of the first, where I gave a paper on Celtic spirituality and mentioned the importance of the writings of Fiona Macleod to the assembled international delegates.

Although this significant event opened in Chicago on William's birthday we can say for sure that back in the United Kingdom nobody would be singing *"Happy Birthday To You"* to him as the song had not yet been written – at least not in the form we are familiar with today. But at that same time in 1893 two sisters, Mildred and Patty Hill, composed a little tune and a few words, *"Good Morning To You,"* that they started to sing to their pupils in the school at which they taught. Later the refrain was changed to "happy birthday to you" and what has become the most sung and most well known song throughout the world was born. The song is still under copyright and earns substantial royalties every year. This is just another example of the world changing and world influencing events that took place in that magical year.

Meantime, in another corner of the planet in 1893, an unknown law student in South Africa called Mahatma Ghandi was being stirred on a much deeper level to campaign against racism and human injustices worldwide. This too was the start of something momentous and world changing. Clearly great forces were at work attempting to bring some sanity and unity to the people of the world, a world where fighting over spiritual truths was (and still is) a common problem. Perhaps Fiona Macleod was another manifestation of this campaign for spiritual awareness and enlightenment that was sweeping across the planet. Some may argue that the obscure Gaelic and Celtic lore and culture she wrote about can hardly be compared with the events in Chicago or the subsequent actions of Gandhi. However, considering that the United States, Canada, Australia and New Zealand today, as then, have literally millions of people of Celtic descent, to ignore this enormous body of people with a common spiritual heritage would have left an enormous gap in the worldwide spiritual movements that were taking place.

But as history has shown repeatedly, great strides forward are often met with resistance and a desire to hold onto the familiar. As if to counter the tolerance of the Council for a Parliament of the World's Religions, Queen Victoria was simultaneously actively trying to convert the Muslims and Hindus of India, then part of her enormous empire, to Christianity. By using her German family connections, she arranged for two German missionaries, Marx and Francke, to be sent to Kashmir to see what could be done to introduce Christianity to this corner of her empire. In Kashmir they discovered an account from 1887 by a Russian scholar, Nicolai Notovich, who had come across a biography of a Buddhist prophet called Isa who had raised the dead and performed other miracles. Notovich believed that this was none other than Jesus Christ. Marx and Francke read the biography, accepted Notovich's conclusions and sent word back to Europe that they had proof that Jesus had been to Asia. The Dalai Lama was not too pleased about this hijacking of a Buddhist prophet for Christian propaganda reasons and Victoria was persuaded to drop this line of pursuit. However the seed had been planted and Marx and Francke were soon off looking for other evidence of Christianity being taken to the region at a very early date. They duly found a tomb in Srinagar that was dedicated to a Muslim prophet called Yuza Asaf. They declared that this was a corruption of the name Jesus and, as this particular prophet was not Buddhist and would not upset the Dalai Lama, they broadcast that the tomb of Jesus had been found in the Indian sub-Continent. Nobody seemed to pick up on the theological problem with this that according to the Bible Jesus had been physically taken up to Heaven and therefore had no tomb for His earthly remains. It did not matter. Victoria had been given her proof that Christ had taken his ministry to Asia and, for this reason, her Indian subjects should now convert to Christianity. Many did and soon Christian pilgrims were travelling to the tomb of Yuza Asaf. This opened a floodgate of alleged Christian-related finds including the tomb of Moses at a mountain in Kashmir called Muqam-I-Musa and the tomb of the Virgin Mary in a town called Muree.

Back in Britain however things were moving along at a pace for William and Fiona. The name and personality of Fiona Macleod was a perfect one for William to adopt as a magical persona and likewise William Sharp was a perfect vehicle for Fiona Macleod to choose as the means of telling her authentic Faery stories. His obsession that the secret of her identity had to be kept from the public or else she would die also showed that William realised that she was much more than just a convenient literary ploy. He knew that she was indeed a real person, albeit a Faery person, and that she would literally die to this world if this was made known. It was however a considerable risk to have taken from a purely business point of view. The name of William Sharp was by now well known to the literary world, his books and articles sold reasonably well and all his new writings were examined and criticised by the leading magazines and newspapers of the day. To publish highly romantic and at times horrifying books based on obscure Gaelic lore was in itself a risk but to use a name that literally nobody had ever heard before when things were going so well for the well-known William Sharp could have been a terrible failure. As it turned out the Victorian public loved the Fiona Macleod stories and eventually she became more popular than William had ever been, this would bring more problems for William as we shall see later.

The fact that today the personal name Fiona is so common throughout the English speaking peoples of the world is solely because Fiona Macleod books were so popular that Victorian and Edwardian parents started to give their daughters this new name and it spread like wild fire. It was not only little girls who were being given this new name. To William's delight, not long after the launch of Fiona Macleod, he came across a boat that had been named Fiona. He was sailing with Catharine Janvier at the time and she recounted what transpired, "*As we rounded the point, we saw lying at anchor a fishing boat painted white; and as we neared her I made out what looked like Fiona lettered on her bow. I did not think this possible, and concluded it must be Flora; but on closer view we saw plainly the unusual name 'Fiona.' ... we were a little surprised by the slow uprising above the rail of a man ... Mr Sharp said to him, 'That's a pretty name of your boat. For sure, it's a real name?' The man answered, 'Oh yes; for sure it's a real name.'*

*'And will it be the name of some one you know?'*

*'Ay, I've heard that the daughter of Mr McLane – the minister out Iona way – is called Fiona.'*

*'Ah then it will be after her?'*

*'No, no; for sure, it wasn't after her.'*

*'Then it will be after your wife or sweetheart?'*

*'Ah no, it will only be after a writing lady, a great Highland lady.'*

*'Oh, a writing lady. Who will that be?'*

*'Well, she will be called Miss Fiona Macleod.'*

*'Oh, then you know Miss Macleod?'*

*'No, but I read a story of hers in the Oban Times, or in some other paper; and, after, I read one of her books about Iona – and so I just called my new boat for her.'*

*And, well content, we rowed to shore.*" [16]

Nowadays in the many books available on the origins of Celtic names Fiona is often described as an ancient Scottish or Irish name. It is surprising how quickly a popular writer like Fiona Macleod was forgotten, and amazing how quickly a name created in 1893 has found its way into modern folklore as being ancient. It seems quite appropriate that the name itself has developed a mythology all of its own; that is often the way of Faery things.

## HER INFLUENCE

To get the full picture on how and why Fiona came through right at the moment she did we need to take a closer look at William's personal life and activities and examine what was going on in Phenice Croft during his time there. His physical health had improved during this time, he felt settled, at peace, able to concentrate and work steadily, not only on his writings but also on his magical practices. As Elizabeth states, "*Once again, he saw visions and dreamed dreams; the psychic subjective side of his dual nature predominated.*"[17] It is interesting that she says 'once again' he saw visions as, up until this point in her memoir, there had been no previous references to him having visions other than those induced by illness and fever. We do know from other sources he was capable of voluntarily inducing visions and occasionally experienced involuntary visions of significance even during periods of good health. His passionate affair with Edith had clearly opened up his emotions and feelings to new levels of expression. This, coupled with being settled in a place where he really felt he could relax, enabled him to write more freely and expressively than ever before. His on-going magical studies and practices were bringing about changes in his consciousness, no doubt also stimulated by his love affair. All of these factors, combining as they did in this place and at this time, created the necessary conditions to allow the Faery being called Fiona Macleod to fully become an integral part of the psyche and consciousness of William Sharp.

Right from the start he and Elizabeth agreed that it was vital to talk about her as if she was a unique, separate being with a body, mind and feelings of her own. This was ostensibly to help prevent a careless slip of the tongue giving away the secret when in mixed company but he believed that to explain the phenomenon in psychological or pseudo-scientific terminology would have resulted in the 'death' of the Fiona Macleod energy. It was this conscious decision that led, in later life, to his vehement denials that he, or any other party, was Fiona Macleod. Not only did he wish to protect himself from further scrutiny but he also needed to protect Fiona from being harassed and pursued.

This became the public face of it all but at the same time in private, in his personal diaries and notebooks which were never intended for public scrutiny, he frequently expressed curiosity as to what Fiona was going to do next or how she was going to finish some story or other, thus verifying his belief that she really was a separate being. In a letter dated January 14th

1907, Yeats related to Maud Gonne a conversation he had recently had with Elizabeth, *"A great deal, however, which Sharp used to give in letters as an account of Fiona's doings were she* [Elizabeth] *insists a kind of semi-allegorical description of the adventures of his own secondary personality and its relation with the primary self. For instance in one letter to me he had said 'I will leave your letter where Fiona will find it when she wakes', and by this he meant that the secondary personality when it awoke in him would answer the letter which it certainly did in a much more impassioned way than that of the rest of the letter."* [18] That same year Yeats gave a lecture to the Franco-Scottish Society in Aberdeen, Scotland. In that presentation he said that William really believed that, *"Fiona Macleod was a secondary personality – as distinct a secondary personality as those one reads about in books on psychical research. At times he was to all intents and purposes a different being. He would come and sit down by my fireside and talk, and I believe that when 'Fiona Macleod' left the house he would have no recollection of what he had been saying to me."* [19]

After William's death Yeats recognised what an incredible man he had been but compare that acknowledgement to the remarks he made on his first impressions of William Sharp which he gave in a letter to Katherine Tynan on July 1st 1897, *"I was introduced to Sharp … and hated his red British face of flacid contentment."* Also to Katherine Tynan, in 1890, he passed on a remark by Oscar Wilde, who did not like William, saying, *"Have you heard Oscar's last good thing? He says that Sharp's motto should be 'Acutis decensus averni' ('sharp' is the descent into Hell) The phrase as you know begins in the orthodox way 'Facilis' (easy)"*. [20] Lady Gregory similarly commented on their first meeting that she was greatly annoyed when William took the best seat in the dog-cart and let Yeats mount behind. It seems the Faery in him eventually won their hearts.

Later in his life there would be times when his behaviour was clearly verging on outright madness; times when he sincerely believed that Fiona was a completely separate, physical woman with whom he could travel the Highlands and Islands, converse and enjoy a cup of tea with, and share criticisms on each others work. More disturbingly, there were times when he could not distinguish between the Faery Fiona Macleod and the human Edith Wingate Rinder. His practice of presenting Edith to his friends and acquaintances as the real Fiona Macleod contributed considerably to his confusion. A further contributing factor to this confusion was designed to be a safeguard against making mistakes and errors as to where the fictitious Fiona was supposed to be at any given time. This was the simple ploy of keeping track of where Edith happened to be and using those real places as Fiona's current location or intended destination when discussing her with third parties. It was certainly a good idea to have some consistency in where Fiona was alleged to be but by using the movements of the real Edith it simply led to even more blurring in William's mind between the two women.

At times early in his relationship with Edith he was like someone who has been told a great secret in confidence but who cannot resist dropping hints and suggestions as to what they know. This often manifested in letters where he would relate real events with Edith as if they had been those of Fiona. An example of this was in a letter to Herbert Stone, publisher, where he concluded with, "*Did I ever tell you that she* [Edith] *is Miss Macleod's most intimate woman friend, and that she is the dedicatee of 'Pharais'? They have been staying together recently, and (I believe) writing or planning something to do together – though that, from what I know of Miss F.M., will never come off, as she is far too essentially F.M. to work in harness with anyone.*"[21] This letter was sent at a time when we know William and Edith had been staying at their "House of Dreams," the Pettycur Inn not far from Edinburgh. William often claimed that he could only fully become Fiona when he was with Edith so his comment here about her being Fiona's most intimate friend, and that they were staying together recently, was a veiled reference to a real event that he and Edith had recently shared.

What all this emotional turmoil led to on one level was a great outpouring of new prose, poems and short stories by Fiona but on another level it created a tremendous psychological and emotional strain that would eventually severely affect William's already fragile physical and mental health. These stresses and strains were further heightened by the fact that while they lived in Phenice Croft he continued to delve more and more deeply into his magical experimentations and explorations. The combined affects of all of these things soon began to manifest not only in William's behaviour and emotions but also in the very atmosphere of the Sharp home. Elizabeth noticed this psychic phenomenon and did not like it. In her memoir she states, "*During those two years at Phenice Croft... he was the dreamer – he was testing his new powers, living his new life, and delighting in the opportunity for psychic experimentation. And for such experimentation the place seemed to him to be peculiarly suited. To me it seemed 'uncanny' and to have a haunted atmosphere – created unquestionably by him – that I found difficult to live in, unless the sun was shining. This uncanny effect was felt by more than one friend; Mr Murray Gilchrist, for instance, whose impressions were described by his host in one of the short 'Tragic Landscapes.'*"[22]

Murray Gilchrist was the young writer who had submitted articles for *The Young Folk's Paper* and *The Pagan Review* that had so impressed William. Over the intervening period they had become friends and occasionally William stayed at his home on his many journeys from north to south and back again. In turn Gilchrist had stayed with the Sharps at their various other addresses but it was only in Phenice Croft he too noted and commented on the unsettling psychic atmosphere that disturbed Elizabeth so much. In a letter dated September 26th 1895 William referred back to this time at Phenice Croft when he told Gilchrist, "*Fiona Macleod's new book 'The Sin Eater' will soon be out... there is a small section called 'Tragic Landscapes'... You will read* the third piece, 'Summersleep', with mingled feelings, when you know that it is an exact transcript of – Phenice Croft at Rudgwick, and that the three men are – you, Garfitt and myself. I cannot explain aright: you must read into what you read. The most tragic and momentous epoch of my life followed that visit of yours to Phenice Croft, and is, so far, indissolubly linked with that day I met you, and that time." [23]

In this short piece the three men are not named but, as said above, they are William Sharp, Murray Gilchrist and his partner Garfitt. As they approach the house they speak thus, "... the taller of the two strangers said in his heart:- 'There is something of awe, of terror, about that house: nay, the whole land here is under gloom. I should die here, stifled. I am glad I go on the morrow.'... the smaller and darker of the two strangers said in his heart:- 'It may all be beautiful and peaceful, but something tragic hides behind this flooding sunlight, behind these dark woodlands, down by the water-course there, past the water-mill, up by that house among the orchard-trees.'... the tallest of the three men, he who lived in that square cottage by the pleasant hamlet, said in his heart:- 'It may be that the gate of hell is hidden there among the grass, or beneath the foundations of my house. Would God I were free! O my God, madness and death!'" [24] From this it is clear that even William knew that things were not right with the psychic atmosphere at Phenice Croft and he knew perfectly well within himself that it was all his doing, albeit unwittingly.

William clearly valued Gilchrist's friendship in a way that was much more intimate than with his other many male friends and correspondents. Gilchrist was homosexual, a crime in those days in Britain and, naturally he kept this aspect of his life a close secret. The Garfitt named above was his lover. William was interested in him not because he desired a male sexual partner but because here was someone who could understand the difficulties and torments that living two secret and separate lives brought with it. For obvious reasons they did not speak of this directly in their correspondence but from the many desperate letters that survive from William saying he "must speak" with him and that "he needed to stay" with him for a day or so we get the impression that they spoke freely on these identity issues and that Gilchrist was the only man William could trust to not only keep their conversations secret but who could also truly relate to the problems William needed to discuss so urgently. It was fortunate that William had such a close friend at this very trying period in his life. It is also noticeable that the forms of address William used in his letters to Gilchrist are much more intimate than were those used to other male correspondents – "My dear Boy," "My dear friend and comrade," "My love, sympathy and affectionate heed."

But back to Fiona: "Pharais" was well received and she immediately set to work on her next book "The Mountain Lovers." Both of these initial outpourings set the tone for almost all of the rest of the Fiona Macleod catalogue for the next five or six years. As previously noted many of her writings deal in one way or another with the sea and drownings. In 1892 William published a poem called "*The Coves of Crail*" that deals with the subject of drowning,

*The moon-white waters wash and leap,*
*The dark tide floods the Coves of Crail;*
*Sound, sound he lies in dreamless sleep,*
*Nor hears the sea-wind wail.*

*The pale gold of his oozy locks,*
*Doth hither drift and thither wave;*
*His thin hands splash against the rocks,*
*His white lips nothing crave.*

*Afar away she laughs and sings –*
*A song he loved, a wild sea-strain –*
*Of how the mermen weave their rings*
*Upon the reef-set main.*

*Sound, sound he lies in dreamless sleep,*
*Nor hears the sea-winds wail,*
*Though with the tide his white hands creep*
*Amid the Coves of Crail.* [25]

This incident actually occurred while William was in the early stages of writing what would become Fiona's *"Pharais."* He had taken a short break to the east coast Scottish town of St. Andrews, not far from the little fishing village of Crail, where he liked to sit on the beach and write down the ideas and thoughts that came to him. One morning, as he was mulling over ideas concerning the sea and drowning as part of the plot for the book, the corpse of a drowned fisherman was washed up on the beach in front of him. He was deeply moved by the synchronicity of this and composed the poem above. It had a traumatic affect on him and for a long time he could no longer look on the sea with the same feelings of wonder and love that he had before.

Even at this early stage in her career people were beginning to guess that Fiona Macleod was actually William Sharp. For example his close friend Sir George Douglas had written to him stating he was convinced that all the works of Fiona Macleod had come from William's pen. As Fiona's fame grew and as more and more people started to draw the same conclusion William became quite vehement in his denials but at this early stage, before he realised how successful Fiona was going to become, he admitted to his friend that he was indeed Fiona Macleod. He trusted that Sir George would keep the secret but in his reply dated December 21st 1895 he added an interesting reflective comment, "*I wonder why the strangeness and horror of madness, and the lust of blood, are so potent factors in my imagination – when I know also the wells of tenderness and love for men, women and children, for beasts and all living things, out of which 'Fiona' draws her draught of tears and tragic joy.*" [26] This makes it clear that he really did not know what Fiona would write next and he certainly did not understand her as a person yet. She, being Faery, did not have an emotional self as we would understand it and to her blood, death and tragedy were no different than health, life or joy. They were all equal facts of life with none being any better or any worse than the other. This lack of emotion as we understand it also explains why Fiona cold-heartedly and without remorse drove William to his death with her relentless need to write, write, write. Students of Faery and the Faery realm in general need to take note of this. Do not expect Faery sympathy and understanding to be as we know them.

About these first two books Fiona once said, "*You will find more of me in Pharais than in anything I have written. Let me add that you will find The Mountain Lovers, more elemental still, while simpler... By blood I am part Celt, and partly so by upbringing, by Spirit wholly so ... One day I will tell you of the strange old mysteries of earlier days I have part learned, part divined, and other things of the spirit... I resent too close identification with the so-called Celtic renaissance. If my work is to depend solely on its Gaelic connection, then let it go, as go it must. My work must be beautiful in itself – Beauty is a Queen and must be served as a Queen.*" [27] The comment concerning learning and divining strange old mysteries refers to Faery mysteries and is a big clue as to the importance of the entire Fiona Macleod corpus. It is interesting to note her resentment, strong word, at being labelled 'Celtic.' She was not Celtic, she was Faery and Faeries do not have cultural or racial subdivisions. She and William were clearly linked into something higher than just a national or racial trait or energy. Their real inspirations were beauty, mystery and wonder – inspirations that are not the exclusive domain of the Celt or anyone else. This resentment at being labelled Celtic would cause friction later with the prominent Irish writers of the day who were spearheading the Celtic Revival movement. She also reveals in this short quotation her sole purpose for coming into this world, "*One day I will tell you of the strange old mysteries of earlier days I have part learned, part divined, and other things of the spirit...*" This was her mission from the Faery world, to reveal the Faery Mysteries to the human world. She would spend the next twelve years doing just that. Some would argue that she has never stopped, but that is the matter for another book.

Note that she is careful to point out that she is only part Celt by blood and partly so by upbringing. The other part is Faery. But can this mean she was a half-human, half-faery being? Certainly the tales of many peoples from many lands contain stories of humans and Faeries successfully mating and producing offspring. Often these children spend their upbringing in the Faery realm where they are educated in the ways of Faery and magic and then returned to the human world and their human family to learn the ways of this world. The Arthurian romances contain several examples of this. If this is indeed what she was hinting at then yet another big question concerning Fiona Macleod pops to mind – who were her parents? Was one Faery and one human?

William often commented that Seumas Macleod, the old fisherman he befriended in his childhood, was her real father. This has understandably been taken to mean no more than he was her father in the sense that his knowledge of Gaelic and Faery lore was the inspiration for her later writings. Perhaps though he was being deliberately accurate in his words – Seumas Macleod <u>was</u> her father. If this is so, the next question must be who was her mother and which one, father or mother, was the Faery and which the human? The answers to these apparently obscure and metaphysical questions are actually laid out quite clearly in the combined writings of William and Fiona.

First, let us look more closely at Seumas the father. William often mentioned him when he talked of his childhood and early travels in the Western Isles. Occasionally he named a specific place where they had met, such as Tarbert, the Isle of Eigg, Loch Fyne, but usually the locations were unidentified islands and villages on the west coast of Scotland. However it seems it was never the same place, it was always different. Neither William nor Fiona ever stated exactly where Seumas had his home or specifically where he was born. As noted earlier William was sent to stay with him to recuperate from a childhood illness but all he says of the location is that it was a remote island. In later life, when William or Fiona wrote of encounters with Seumas, it was as if they just happened to run into him unexpectedly at some location or other. They never commented on taking an intentional trip to visit Seumas in his home village or on his home island. It seems odd that they should keep bumping into each other on a regular basis over such a large and sparsely populated geographic area. Certainly as a fisherman he would have travelled more than a farmer or blacksmith would, but to crop up so frequently in the same places that William or Fiona just happened to be is strange indeed. Strange, that is, if he was no more than a fisherman of this world, but not so strange if he was of the Faery and had his home in the Faery realm.

The references to him and his teachings are scattered throughout William's letters, Elizabeth's memoir and Fiona's writings. These are usually fragmentary bits and pieces but Fiona did write one short piece, entitled "*Seumas: A Memory,*" where she once more acknowledged his great influence on her. She described him as, "… *so shrewd and genial and worldly-wise, for all his lonely life; so blithe in spirit and swiftly humorous; himself a poet, and remembering countless songs and tales of old; strong and daring, on occasion; good with the pipes, as with the nets; seldom angered, but then with a fierce anger, barbaric in its vehemence; a loyal clansman; in all things, good and not so good, a Gael of the Isles.*" She related asking him a question regarding the elements by which she meant Earth, Water, Fire and Air. He replied, "*Fire is God's touch … and light is God Himself: and water is the mother of life.*" Note that he only refers to three, Fire, Light and Water, certainly not the elements we are used to dealing with. This is to be expected though as the four solid building blocks of this physical world are of no importance in the ethereal Faery realm.

Fiona went on to ask him if he thought all the old gods were dead and in response he said, "*No, they are not all dead. They think we are. They do not change. They are very patient, the old ancient gods. Perhaps it is because they do not care at all, no, not a whistle of the wind, for what we think or what we do. But some have died. And some are very old, and are sleeping, till they get their youth again.*" Fiona asked about the sea-god Manannan and if he lived. Seumas's reply was, "*Ay, for sure. He was here before Christ came. He will see the end of all endings. They say he sleeps in the hollows of great oceans, and sits on mountain bergs of ice at the Pole, chanting an old ancient chant.*" [28]

This brief conversation reveals a great deal of Faery lore concerning the nature of Faery gods. His comment that the old gods think we are the ones who are dead is interesting. This same notion has cropped up many times in independent Faery communications over the decades since Fiona wrote this down. Seumas also specifically says that some of the old gods have died and that others are sleeping in order to regain their youth. This makes it clear that youth, aging, the passage of time and death itself, are very different in the Faery realm than they are in our solid world. His comment on the nature of Manannan displays the peculiar mixing of the old gods with the Christ that is unique to the Gael of Scotland and Ireland and which weaves a thread through much of Fiona's writing.

To me the comment we really need to take notice of is, "*... they do not care at all ... for what we think or what we do.*" This is a far cry from the modern popular notion of playful little sprites with glittering wands granting us three wishes. Fiona certainly did not behave so beneficently. As we have seen already, and as will be shown in the following chapters, her treatment of William went beyond abusive, it was downright destructive. In her early writings she frequently used other writers' material as if it was her own with no acknowledgement or credit of its true source and we have examples of where she falsified events and deliberately misled colleagues in order to gain approval or recognition. (see Chapter 7 for further discussion on this) The Faery realm and the Faeries do have a great deal to teach us but the student must be constantly on his or her guard and must be constantly questioning and checking all information closely and carefully. This is not because the Faeries are liars, malicious or deliberately deceitful, far from it, but their ways of doing things are far, far different from ours.

To return to Fiona's lineage - if, then, her father was Seumas Macleod of the Faery folk, her mother must have been the human half of the partnership. We know that William and Elizabeth both considered Edith Wingate Rinder to be the power and influence behind Fiona, and we know that William considered Fiona's birth date and place to be Lake Nemi on the day he fell in love with Edith. This indicates that Edith was Fiona's human mother. The date of Fiona's simultaneous conception and birth is not significant but the location certainly is. It was explained in Chapter 4 that Lake Nemi is 'the Lake', or strictly speaking one of the lakes, that appears in the Arthurian tradition. These lakes, wherever they may be in this world, are portals or gateways to and from the Faery world. Seumas Macleod, the Faery fisherman, could as easily slip through this gateway in Italy as he could through any of the myriad doorways that are scattered throughout the Scottish Western Isles. Remembering that Lake Nemi has a connection with another fisherman, the Fisher King, it is possible that Seumas Macleod, the wise old Hebridean fisherman, is nothing less than a manifestation of the archetypical Fisher King of Grail legend. Edith Wingate Rinder, the beautiful young maiden, was 'impregnated' by him as she swam in the sacred waters of Lake Nemi. Note how constantly lakes, rivers, the sea occur in Fiona's writings. When William was suffering a mental collapse while living at Phenice Croft he could not sleep for the sound of waves crashing on the shore yet their home was far inland away from the sea. Water, in all of its many manifestations, was of great significance to Fiona. This makes sense considering she was born of water.

Faery lineage is of great importance but this particular one is especially so. Fiona Macleod was a direct descendant of the Fisher King of the Grail tradition. William Sharp would play an important role in a modern Grail phenomenon when he and Fiona came into contact with Dr. John Goodchild as will be discussed in Chapter 9. Since the start of the 21st century there has been a growing interest in this whole subject of human and Faery mating and much is starting to be written on this obscure and controversial subject. This is another manifestation of the desire of Faeries to become part of our world and to live and develop amongst us, as well as their hope we shall learn about and share their world. There is a great deal more work needing to be done on this fascinating subject. Those interested in learning more can learn much from Mr. Sharp and Miss Macleod.

In 1900, six years after "*Pharais*" and "*The Mountain Lovers*" had been published, her attitude to these books had changed significantly. In a letter to Ernest Rhys dated May 4th 1900, she said, "*They are books at which I look sometimes with dread … Can you understand that when 'Pharais' was published I would have given anything to recall it, partly because of the too much suffering there expressed, but mainly because of that 'Cry of Women,' which nevertheless had brought so many strange and sorrowful letters, and made many unexpected friends.*" [29] It is clear from this intimate remark that Fiona was surprised by the long-term and substantial negative affect this book had on many of her readers. It is true that the lovers in these books, Lora and Alistair in "*Pharais*" and Sorcha and Alan in "*The Mountain Lovers*" all come to a sad end. In several of her shorter stories other pairs of lovers are also separated by death or madness. It is a common theme in her earlier work and it is easy to see how some people would be affected in a very negative way from such unhappy endings. Her reason for repeatedly broaching this subject though was to show again and again that the bonds of love can endure death and are strong enough to survive the grave and continue at a fuller, deeper and more intimate level, in the Otherworld, the afterlife or however you care to label it. From the Faery perspective this is a simple and obvious matter of fact but to us such a notion only exists in the minds of poets and artists. When your lover dies or goes mad it is a tragedy beyond comparison. There is no life in this world let alone in the other world worth living after such a terrible loss. If we pay attention to this valuable Faery lore we may at least see a glimmer of light at the end of the long tunnel of darkness, death and madness.

One of those who was thus affected by the negativity of Fiona's writings was Katharine Tynan who said, "*There is much that is darkening and dreadful in Fiona Macleod's work even when it is most remarkable from a literary point of view. 'The Dan-na-Ron', 'The Ninth Wave', 'The Sin-Eater', have all to my mind a dreadful power of depressing the reader... That they should have the power to depress is a tribute to their literary quality. I may say that my first experience with 'Pharais' left me with a sense of dislike and fear for the work of Fiona Macleod. I felt that it was not good reading for the sensitive and imaginative... Neither William Sharp nor Fiona Macleod brought into their work any hint of the saving sense of humour. To be sure Fiona was always writing at the top of her voice, in a passion which had no room for the ludicrous. I believe William Sharp did write one or two novels which had an intention of humour, but I do not think they amused anybody.*"[30] The world of Faery is devoid of humour as we know it. How many fairy stories can be considered funny or amusing?

Fiona's revelation that she regretted writing '*Pharais*' and '*The Mountain Lovers*' is because by 1900 she had started to better understand the ways of this world that were unknown and totally unfamiliar to her in 1893 when she wrote those books. She seems to have made a conscious decision to move away from the subject of human emotions and interaction, as there is a definite change of emphasis in her work from the late 1890s onwards. Her initial burst of output, from 1894 until around 1897-98, was these first two novels and a flood of short stories and narratives dealing with the life, trials and tribulations of the Gaelic Highlander. By 1898 it is noticeable that she had started to move away from short stories and novels dealing with human subjects. Instead she started to express her Faery lore in essays, poems and commentaries on the beauty and powers of the Green World, on spirituality, on the bigger picture as opposed to the complications of the lives of her individual characters. After four or five years of writing and experiencing our world she began to understand how better to put across to her readers what she was so desperate to reveal in a way that was not so threatening or depressing. This is what she meant in 1899 when she commented to Catharine Janvier, "*I am going through a new birth.*"[31] She was beginning to understand our human way of doing and saying things.

From a literary point of view some critics have seen this change of emphasis as a drying-up of her initial creative ability. Others have commented that the quality of the early work is just not there in the later essays. Whereas this may be true from the purely literary stance these later pieces are still invaluable from a magical and Faery lore point of view. In many ways they are stronger as they reveal more of the workings of nature. It is by understanding this esoteric subject better that we can come to a fuller understanding of Faery and our relationship with them and the later writings of Fiona Macleod, often neglected by the lover of literature, are a treasure trove of valuable information.

William himself undoubtedly had a wealth of information on all things Gaelic and Celtic, personally gathered and garnered from many and frequent excursions to the remote Western Isles. However, following William's death in 1905 a Mr. Alan Northman, writing in the *"Sunday School Chronicle"*, said, *"Miss Carmichael* [daughter of Alexander Carmichael] *gave the interesting information that her father had lent a great deal of his collected material to Mr William Sharp for his private perusal. Mr Sharp kept the manuscript longer than its owner had bargained for, and they had some difficulty in getting it back. No remark was made as to any use ever having been made of the material, which was designed to form part of a great Highland anthology that Mr Carmichael was preparing. Shortly afterwards 'Fiona Macleod' published Pharais, and, to the astonishment of Mr Carmichael and his daughter, the book contained verse and material which could only have been got from the manuscript lent to Mr Sharp. Mr Sharp was of course communicated with. He repudiated his identity with Fiona Macleod but gave no satisfactory explanation of how Mr Carmichael's material had found its way into his book."* Alexander Carmichael (1832–1912) was a government Excise Officer who travelled the Highlands and Islands extensively during the course of his employment. He spoke Gaelic and, like William, collected stories, songs, charms, folk customs etc from the ordinary people wherever he went. These were eventually published as a two volume set entitled *"Carmina Gadelica"* (Songs of the Gaels) in 1900. His daughter and grandson published four more volumes after his death in 1912.

Fiona would quote again from this great corpus of Gaelic lore in the notes to *"The Divine Adventure"* published in 1900 by Messrs. Chapman and Hall. This time though she acknowledged her sources. On this she said, *"The characteristic Gaelic passage quoted is … from a Hebridean source: excerpted from one of the many treasures-trove rescued from extant or recently extant Gaelic lore by Mr Alexander Carmichael, all soon to be published … under the title 'Or agus Ob'* and later *"No one has collected so much material on the subject as Mr Alexander Carmichael has done. Some of his lore, in sheiling-hymns and fishing-hymns, he has already made widely known, directly and indirectly … in his forthcoming 'Or agus Orb'"* Note that she states Carmichael's work had not yet been published so she clearly did have access to the unpublished manuscript. She also refers to it as "Or agus Orb" (Gold and Refuse) which was Carmichael's working title for the book. In a later essay, *"The Gael and His Heritage"* (from The Winged Destiny), she does give full and ample credit to Carmichael and the great value of his collected material. It seems by that time she was becoming aware of copyright and, if nothing else, the courtesy of acknowledging her sources.

This same essay concludes with Fiona quoting again from "*Carmina Gadelica*" but this time it is not a rune or saying but an excerpt concerning a woman, Mary Macrae. Mr. Carmichael gave the names of many of the contributors to his book but Mary Macrae is the only one that Fiona specifically mentioned. Her actions and sayings struck a chord with Fiona and I believe this was because she recognised a fellow Faery in Carmichael's description of Mary Macrae. This is what Fiona said, "*There was another woman, Mary Macrae of Harris, from whom Mr. Carmichael learned much… Let me finish this article by quoting what Mr. Carmichael has to say of her, for indeed I think she also is a type of the half forlorn and weird, half wildly gay and young spirit of her ancient, disappearing race, ever ready to dance to its own shadow if nothing else be available, yet so sad with a sadness that must live and pass in silence.*

'*She often walked with companions, after the work of the day was done, distances of ten and fifteen miles to a dance, and after dancing all night walked back again to the work of the morning fresh and vigorous as if nothing unusual had occurred. She was a faithful servant and an admirable worker, and danced at her leisure and caroled at her work like 'Fosgay Mhoire', our Lady's lark, above her. The people of Harris had been greatly given to old lore and to the old ways of their fathers, reciting and singing and dancing and merry-making; but a reaction occurred, and Mary Macrae's old-world ways were adjured and condemned. But Mary Macrae heeded not, and went on in her own way, singing her songs, and ballads, intoning her hymns and incantations, and chanting her own 'port-a-bial' (mouth-music), and dancing to her own shadow when nothing better was available.*'

*Truly Mary Macrae stands for her people, who, poor and ignored remnant as they are, heed little the loud ways of a world that is not for them, but go their own way, singing their songs and ballads, intoning hymns or incantations, chanting their own wild, sea-smitten music, and dancing to their own shadow, to the shadow of their ancestral thought and dream, whether in blithe waywardness or in an unforgetting sorrow.*"[32] The final sentence adequately sums up the essence of the Faeries and the whole quotation shows that the Faery Fiona Macleod was not alone in this world, there were, and are, others.

A small aside: in her notes to "*The Divine Adventure*" Fiona makes the following interesting comment, "*This section, slightly adapted, is from an unpublished book, in gradual preparation, entitled 'The Chronicles of the Sidhe'.*" Both William and Fiona left notes on many poems, books, plays and essays that never materialised but it is interesting that Fiona had conceived the idea of a book dedicated completely to the Sidhe, the Faery folk. She clearly felt the need to get as much of her Faery lore out into the public mind as was possible. Throughout the centuries many peoples in this world have written their own chronicles, why not also the Sidhe? It is possible that this book, like "*The Little Book of the Great Enchantment*," existed then and still exists today in the realm of Faery but Fiona never got round to transcribing it into our world. It is a pity that this particular project never saw the light of day but, if I am correct that it still exists in Faery, then perhaps someone else will one day complete the task for her.

William was settled, contented, active on both the writing and magical fronts and more productive than he had been for a long time despite his poor physical health and at times his precarious mental health. The quietness and the peculiar atmosphere of Phenice Croft allowed him a freedom of expression without distraction in which Fiona could nurture and grow. However things were quite different for Elizabeth. Not only did she feel the place to be uncanny and unsettling because of William's psychic experimentation, but her physical health once again started to deteriorate. At first she put this down to the damp weather and the cold clay soil on which Phenice Croft was built. Disregarding her own symptoms, she allowed her husband to carry on with his writing and magical work by taking upon herself the task of writing the art criticism column for *The Glasgow Herald* which was still appearing under William's name. This regular newspaper column was really their bread and butter and despite her illness Elizabeth worked hard at maintaining the output. This often necessitated her travelling to London and back by train and she took to staying there with her family for three or four days at a time. Often during these absences from home Edith would stay with William at Phenice Croft.

Elizabeth was aware of this arrangement and knew that it was she who was the inspiration for the works of Fiona Macleod and that it was her presence that greatly improved William's health. But it was very hard emotionally for Elizabeth. All of these things – the dampness, the hard work, the frequent travelling and time away from home, and knowing that another younger, beautiful woman was staying with her husband - combined to further weaken her fragile health. Elizabeth Amelia Sharp was a truly remarkable woman. Had she not tolerated and suffered as she had then the world would never have met Fiona Macleod. It is true, as both she and her husband acknowledged, that it was Edith who was the inspiration for Fiona, but it was Elizabeth who allowed Edith the free rein to so dominate the lives of all three of them.

At first William was so wrapped up in his own magical and literary works that he was oblivious to Elizabeth's deteriorating health. She eventually managed to convince him that they could no longer live in Phenice Croft and that they had to move. He was greatly disappointed by this but understood they had no choice. Elizabeth had suggested finding another quiet cottage in the countryside to allow him to continue writing in peace but one nearer a railway line so she could continue to travel to London when necessary. William however opted for safety and familiarity and decided they should move back to London proper - but not until mid summer. Despite acknowledging Elizabeth's serious health situation he left her to carry on travelling to London to do his work for *The Glasgow Herald* while he took a brief holiday to

Rouen and Dieppe in France. Edith may have accompanied him. In a letter to Murray Gilchrist from Phenice Croft, dated March 27th 1894, he said, *"My wife's health has long been troubling me: and we have just decided that... we must return to Hampstead to live. Personally, I regret the return to town more than I can say: but the matter is one of paramount importance... As for me, one of my wander-fits has come upon me... Before the week is out I hope to be in Normandy – and after a day or two by the sea at Dieppe, and then at beautiful and romantic Rouen..."* [33] At times his actions with regard to his devoted wife seem positively callous.

On June 21st 1894, the Summer Solstice, while Elizabeth was on holiday in the South of France (good for her!), William closed the door of Phenice Croft for the last time. Note that again he and Elizabeth were separated during an important event in their lives. On leaving he performed a little ceremony. He took up a handful of turf, kissed it three times and distributed it to the Four Quarters; he kissed and said goodbye to a chestnut tree in the garden under which Fiona had had visions and heard the surge of the sea as she wrote *"Pharais."* In final commemoration of the place he had loved so dearly he wrote a poem called *"The White Peace."* This is a Gaelic expression meaning death and shows how deeply sad he felt about leaving the little cottage.

### The White Peace

*It lies not on the sunlit hill*
*Nor in the sunlit gleam*
*Nor even in any falling wave*
*Nor even in running stream –*

*But sometimes in the soul of man*
*Slow moving through his pain*
*The moonlight of a perfect peace*
*Floods heart and brain.* [34]

The move back to London took them to South Hampstead. Despite his loathing of the city the move was not as detrimental to his writing and magical work as he had feared it would be.

In early August William travelled alone to Scotland to visit his mother and sisters who were on holiday in Kilcreggan on the Firth of Clyde. It was probably at this time that Mary, William's younger sister, agreed not only to act as his secretary but to take on the important role of writing all the Fiona Macleod letters, at his direction, to be sent to the public and publishers alike. This would prove to be very important in maintaining the illusion of Fiona being a real, live, flesh-and-blood woman in her own right. It was also pretty far thinking on William's part. So far only one book had appeared under that name and it was too early to guess if it was going to be a success or not. Over the next decade Miss Mary Beatrice Sharp would play a crucial role in the development of Fiona Macleod's public personality. Her greatest contribution was her silence. It is interesting to note that all of the influential and crucially important people in William's life were women – Elizabeth, Edith, Mary, Mona and, of course, Fiona. He relied on all of them completely. Had any one of them been removed from his life then the whole charade would have collapsed. It is true there were many important men in his life – Rossetti, Yeats, Meredith, Stedman, Paton, Gilchrist and others – but none of them played the vital, background roles that the women did so well, allowing Fiona to live and breath and have her being. His women friends saw to the welfare of Fiona and his male friends saw to the welfare of William.

In mid August William went to Edinburgh where he met Elizabeth who was now joining him from London and they spent the next six weeks exploring the Western Isles. Part of their holiday was spent on the Isle of Iona. William had been there many times before but this was Elizabeth's first visit. Earlier, while still in Kilcreggan, he had made friends with a man originally from Iona. He learned a great deal of lore and many magical runes from this unnamed friend and he was also given an, " ... *ancient MS. Map of Iona with all its fields, divisions, bays capes, isles etc.*" [35] William made copious notes on the island, inspired no doubt by his gift of the old map, and jotted down ideas and impressions many of which would eventually materialise in various forms in later Fiona Macleod stories. Iona is a tiny island, so small that modern maps show the position and give the names of every one of the few houses on the island. In the 1890s there would have been even fewer. One house, west of the present ferry slipway, is the one the Sharps rented during their stay. Christine Allen and John Duncan rented this same house some thirty years later. Christine had been deeply involved with Dr. John Goodchild, whom we shall meet later with his mysterious bowl. John Duncan was a well-known artist of the day and worked with William and Patrick Geddes in the planned college in Edinburgh as discussed in the next chapter. Not long after the Duncans had stayed there the place cropped up again in magical history when Netta Fornario, friend and magical acquaintance of Dion Fortune, took rooms there during the winter of 1929. Her dead, naked body, lying with a knife out on the turf of an Iona hillside, caused national headlines and remains a mystery to this day. Perhaps this unobtrusive little cottage on the shore is some sort of gateway to Faery, maybe even one used by Seumas Macleod?

He also said of the man who gave him the old map, "*He says my pronunciation of Gaelic is not only surprisingly good, but is distinctively that of the Isles. I have learned the rune also of the reading of the spirit. The 'influence' seems to me purely hypnotic... Last night I got the rune of the 'Knitting of the Knots' and some information about the Dalt and Cho-Alt about which I was not clear. He has seen the Light of the Dead, and his mother saw (before her marriage, and before she even saw the man himself) her husband crossing a dark stream followed by his four unborn children, and two in his arms whom afterwards she bore still-born.*" [36] This is exactly the sort of stuff William went to the Gaeltacht to seek and he positively thrived on it when he found it. Fiona too would make good use of it in her tales of the Isles. I have no idea what either of these two runes are about and I am unfamiliar with the words *Dalt* and *Cho-Alt* but from the wording of this letter to Elizabeth it is clear that they meant something to both of them.

The rest of 1894 rounded out with William writing a great deal under his own name and with their finances becoming steady again. The move to London proved to have been a wise one and soon Elizabeth was back to a better state of health and she too was in good spirits and very productive. That Christmas William gave Elizabeth a little book of woodcut illustrations he had picked up while they were in Iona. In it he inscribed the following words:

### Credo

*The Universe is eternally, omnipresently and continuously
filled with the breath of God.
Every breath of God creates a new convolution in the brain of Nature:
and with every moment of change in the brain of Nature, new loveliness
is wrought upon the earth.
Every breath of God creates a new convolution in the brain of the
Human Spirit, and with every moment of change in the brain of the
Human Spirit, new hopes, aspirations, dreams, are wrought within the
Soul of the Living.
And there is no Evil anywhere in the Light of this creative Breath: but
only, everywhere, a redeeming from Evil,
a winning towards Good.* [37]

But, alas, the pattern of his life kept true to its predictable unpredictable course. After just over a year back in London things began to go awry. He and Fiona were both productive, Elizabeth's health was stable and from a purely practical point of view things were going well. However, now William's health was again deteriorating rapidly especially on the mental level. Early in 1895 he wrote to a friend, "*London I do not like... I suffer here. The gloom, the streets, the obtrusion and intrusion of people, all conspire against thought, dream, true living. It is a vast reservoir of all the evils of civilised life with a climate which makes me inclined to believe that Dante came here instead of to Hades.*" [38] But there was much more going on than just a strong dislike for living in the city. He was working hard, spending long hours writing and getting very little sleep and putting in as much extra time as he could on his magical pursuits. All of these pressures and stresses combined to push him to the brink of insanity, although, as is often the case, the patient did not realise it. Elizabeth did and she was more concerned for his health and sanity than she had ever been before. His thoughts and physical sensations were becoming obsessed with the sea, drowning, the image of the drowned fisherman, the eternal surge of the waves, all themes common to Fiona's writings. As he later put it, "*One night I awoke hearing a rushing sound in the street, the sound of water. I would have thought no more of it had I not recognised the troubled sound of the tide, and the sucking and lapsing of the flow in muddy hollows. I rose and looked out. It was moonlight, and there was no water. When after sleepless hours I arose in the grey morning I heard the splash of waves, I could not write or read and at last I could not rest. On the afternoon of that day the waves dashed up against the house.*"[39] His home at this time was in suburban Hampstead many miles from the ocean.

One morning a telegram arrived for him and Elizabeth took it to his study. Despite her repeated knocking and calling there was no response. Eventually he opened the door and, looking dazed and confused, he said, "*I could not hear you for the sound of the waves!*"[40] She knew he had to stop working immediately and take a break away from writing, magic and Hampstead. She promptly packed his bags and sent him off to one of his favourite haunts, the Isle of Arran in Scotland. This brought about a sudden and dramatic return to improved health – again the usual pattern when separated from Elizabeth – and he later wrote home from Arran to tell Elizabeth he was safe and well. In his first letter he said, "*The following morning we (for a kinswoman was with me) stood on the Greenock pier waiting for the Hebridean steamer ... That night, with the sea breaking less than a score of yards from where I lay, I slept, though for three nights I had not been able to sleep. When I woke the trouble was gone.*"[41] Although he may have felt the trouble was gone the general content of the letter does not display this. He was clearly still confused. The letter is from William Sharp to his wife yet the signature is that of Fiona Macleod. According to Elizabeth the "we" referred to his dual personality and the "kinswoman" referred to Fiona, his other self. The other possibility, and the more probable one, is that the "we" referred to him and Edith. This would explain the unconscious but very clear sense of sexual relief imbedded in the last two sentences.

A few days later he wrote at length to Elizabeth from his hotel in the village of Corrie, Isle of Arran. The letter is full of peace and contentment, lengthy descriptions of the beauty of the island in winter, the quiet and solitude of the hills and glens and the soft sound of the sea all helping to calm and heal him. It reads like the words of a man who has finally found contentment after a long struggle. The last paragraph however still displays a certain amount of confusion, "*There is something of a strange excitement in the knowledge that two people are here: so intimate and yet so far off. For it is with me as though Fiona were asleep in another room. I catch myself listening for her step sometimes, for the sudden opening of a door. It is unawaredly that she whispers to me. I am eager to see what she will do – particularly in 'The Mountain Lovers'. It seems passing strange to be here with her alone at last.*"[42] Part of this reads as if he knew Fiona was not physically there on Arran with him but other parts imply he did believe she was there.

His comment on not knowing what Fiona was going to do in her story "*The Mountain Lovers*" is noteworthy considering that it was he, William Sharp, who was physically putting pen to paper and writing the words of that tale. For the rest of his short life he would often make such comments, never knowing what Fiona was planning, anxious to see how she was going to develop a plot or character and curious as to where she had got certain ideas and snippets of old lore from. Again though, if Edith was with him, it would explain his assertion 'that two people are here: so intimate and yet so far off' and 'it seems passing strange to be here with her alone at last.' Despite his happier, clearer tone in his letters he was still having problems differentiating between himself and Fiona, and between the physical Edith Wingate Rinder and the Faery Fiona Macleod.

This state of confusion and identity crisis was caused by the results of his magical work producing results greater than he was capable of handling. Fiona's personality was growing at a rate much faster than he could keep up with. He was regaining his health and mental stability in Arran but only by allowing Fiona to exist within him as a completely separate personality. It was indeed madness but of the kind that in more enlightened times was considered divine and inspired. Unbeknown to him at the time, this was causing his psychic links with his magical co-workers to become heightened and strengthened as well. In Paris two of the more famous Golden Dawn initiates were psychically picking up on what was happening to their brother initiate in Scotland.

MacGregor Mathers was entertaining Yeats and Mathers related to him, "*I saw a man standing in an archway last night, and he wore a kilt with the MacLeod and another tartan.*" Yeats reacted to this physically and began to shiver at intervals for several hours. Mathers went into a trance and said William was in need, "*It is madness, but it is like the madness of a god.*" Mathers and his wife, Moina, performed a magical ceremony with Yeats in which they successfully sent his soul on an astral visit to William. Years later Yeats recalled receiving, "*... an unbelievable letter from a seaside hotel about the beautiful Fiona and himself. He had been very ill, terrible mental suffering.*" In this letter William related that Yeats' soul had come to him in Arran in the form of a great white bird to heal him. William had then "found" Fiona and told her that he was healed. Yeats commented "*I learned however from Mrs Sharp years afterwards that at the time of my experience he was certainly alone, but mad. He had gone away to struggle on with madness.*"[43] This was not the only such joint psychic experience William, Yeats and others were to share, as we shall see in Chapter 7.

Before leaving Arran he decided to spend a night at the huge standing stone complex on Machrie Moor situated on the west side of the island. He went with the intention of enjoying a last night on Arran in the solitude and silence of the great open moor that is dotted with dozens of standing stones and ancient stone circles. He may or may not have attempted to induce visions but whether it was self-induced or spontaneous the vision he had that night greatly shaped and influenced his future thoughts and beliefs particularly with regard to the druids and the whole idea of resurrecting ancient Celtic practices. He saw in the misty hours of the cold dawn, with the shadowy shapes of the enormous standing stones looming all around him, a vision of the sacrificial slaying of a young girl by men he believed to be ancient Celtic druids. Despite his Celtic and pagan leanings he could not accept this horrific aspect of human sacrifice played out so bloodily before him, albeit that the girl had appeared to go willingly, and the vision haunted him for the rest of his life. However this was not his first visionary experience of druidic sacrifice. Many years before in 1884, he described a similar incident in the poem entitled "*A Record*" part of which says,

> *And dreaming so I live my dream:*
> *I see a flood of moonlight gleam*
> *Between vast ancient oaks, and round*
> *A rough-hewn altar on the ground*
> *Weird druid priests are gathered*
> *While through their midst a man is led*
> *With face that is already dead:*
>
> *A low chant swells throughout the wood,*
> *Then comes a solemn interlude*
> *Ere loudlier rings dim aisles along*
> *Some ancient sacrificial song;*
> *Before the fane the victim kneels*
> *And without sound he forward reels*
> *When the priest's knife the death-blow deals:*
> *The moonlight falls upon his face,*
> *His blood is spatter'd o'er the place,*
> *But now he is ev'n as a flow'r*
> *Uprooted in some tempest hour,*
> *Dead, but whose seed shall elsewhere grow:*
> *And as I look upon him, lo,*
> *Some old ancestral-self I know.* [44]

This poem makes it clear that it was not so much a vision but more a memory of a past incarnation. Maybe this is why he found the Machrie vision so appalling – he could personally relate to the experience of the young girl.

One final contemporary event is worth noting. When "*Pharais*" came out in 1894 there was a poor French priest by the name of Fr. Berenger Sauniere in a small Languedoc village called Rennes-le-Chateau who found something in his little chapel while making repairs. Exactly what he found remains the subject of much speculation in several books to this day but, whatever it was, he quickly became very wealthy. One possible suggestion as to the nature of his find was some sort of documentation or other evidence concerning a possible blood-line traceable back to Jesus Christ. This all ties in with various esoteric lore concerning the Holy Grail and as we shall see in Chapter 9 a close friend of Fiona's would soon become involved in a Grail Mystery of his own. William would also spend a good deal of time over the next twelve years travelling in the Languedoc and Provence regions of France. The final decade of the 19th century was a remarkable time for the spiritual development of humankind.

---

[1] Memoir, page 217

[2] NLS Edinburgh

[3] Memoir, page 227

[4] Memoir, page 226

[5] Colquhoun, Sword of Wisdom: MacGregor Mathers and the Golden Dawn, page 135

[6] Jeffares, A Servant of the Queen, page 211

[7] Jeffares, A Servant of the Queen, page 259

[8] Kalogera, pages 41-42

[9] Memoir, page 279

[10] NLS, Edinburgh

[11] Finneran, page 34

[12] "The Silence of Amor," limited edition, T. Mosher 1902, page 39

[13] see Blamires "Irish Celtic Magical Tradition" for a full examination of this legend

[14] Beversluis, A Source Book for Earth's Community of Religions, page 102

[15] NLS, Edinburgh

[16] "The North American Review", April 1907, page 723

[17] Memoir, page 221

[18] Jeffares, The Gonne-Yeats Letters

[19] Hopkins, The Wilfion Scripts, page 102

[20] Yeats Annual 13, page 104

[21] WS Archives

[22] Memoir, page 223

[23] WS Archives

[24] "The Sin-Eater", pages 143-4

[25] "Poems of Phantasy", 1892

26 WS Archives

[27] Memoir, page 226

[28] "Winged Destiny", Volume 5 Collected Works, page 261

[29] "The Century Illustrated Monthly Magazine", May 1907, page 115

[30] "Fortnightly Review", March 1906, page 574

[31] Memoir, page 423

[32] "The Gael and His Heritage", page 259

[33] Memoir, page 234

[34] Memoir, page 236

[35] Memoir, page 236

[36] Memoir, page 237

[37] Memoir, page 241

[38] Memoir, page 242

[39] Memoir, page 242

[40] Memoir, page 243

[41] Memoir, page 243

[42] Memoir, page 244

[43] Greer, Women of the Golden Dawn, page 203

[44] "Collected Works of William Sharp, Volume 1, Poems", page 67

William Sharp
After an Etching by William Strang, A.R.A.

# Chapter 6
# Outlook Tower and Denials, Denials, Denials

*It is amusing – when a thing is very simple –*
*how it can be made into a mystery.*

During the 1890s William became acquainted with the Scottish bota-
nist, sociologist and town-planner Patrick Geddes (1854–1932), later
Sir Patrick Geddes. Geddes had many grand ideas and schemes involving
the arts and sciences. He wished to use them to show the interconnectedness
of humankind and all things, the need to live in symbiosis with all creatures
and with the very planet itself. For this reason he is often referred to as the
father of environmentalism. In 1886 he married Anna Morton, a gifted musician, and they founded the Edinburgh Social Union. Moving into a workers' tenement, they personally cleaned up many of the worst slum dwellings
along Edinburgh's ancient High Street, commonly referred to as the Royal
Mile. The theme of repairing and cleaning up slum areas as opposed to de-
molishing them in order to rebuild would be prevalent in much of his later
work involving town planning, especially in India.

He was born in Ballater but had been brought up in Perth, still very
much a rural part of the southern Highlands in those days, and not far from
Dunblane where the Sharp family originated. There, like William, he became
interested in his Celtic heritage and the great importance the early Celts
placed on the world of nature. He soon recognised the great contribution
that could be made to his environmental ideals by promoting and preserving
the rapidly disappearing Celtic and Gaelic traditions of his native Scotland.
He believed that the peasant Gael had lived much closer to the Green World
and intuitively knew how to live in harmony with the environment. He also
believed that his scientific knowledge of the Green World as a biologist would
be complimented by William's mystical and magical approach to the same
subject. He wished to cover as many disciplines as possible not only to reach
a wider audience but also to show by example the interconnected nature of
all things.

To this end, in the 1890s, he had purchased land and buildings in Edinburgh known as Ramsay Lodge and Ramsay Garden with the view of setting up a permanent college there. This property sits high on the Castle Rock, adjoining the Edinburgh Castle esplanade, and has commanding views to the north of the city and far into the Kingdom of Fife. He then constructed six entirely new flats on Ramsay Garden. He had already converted a nearby tenement block into student accommodation, which he called University Hall, and the newly constructed flats became known as University Hall Extension. In total he provided accommodation for some two hundred students and teachers.

During his alterations to the original Georgian buildings of Ramsay Lodge he employed the Scottish artist John Duncan to decorate the interior with murals depicting appropriate scenes for the new venture. Duncan had completed seven of these murals by 1898; *The Awakening of Cuchullin*, *The Combat of Fionn*, *The Taking of Excalibur*, *The Journey of St. Mungo*, *The Vision of Johannes Scotus Erigena*, *Michael Scot* and *The Admirable Crichton*. The first two were based on early Celtic mythology, the third on Arthurian lore, the fourth depicted a scene from the life of the Apostle of Strathclyde and Cumbria, the next showed a scene from a vision of the ninth century philosopher and theologian, the next showed the Scottish scholar working on translations of Arabic texts at the court of Frederick II, and the final mural was a scene from the life of James Crichton, son of Lord Advocate Robert Crichton and a scholar and adventurer of note. Thirty years later, Duncan brought the total of murals up to twelve with the addition of *John Napier of Merchiston* the creator of logarithms, astronomer and occult scientist; *James Watt* inventor and refiner of the steam engine; *Sir Walter Scott* writer and creator of much popular Scottish history; *Charles Darwin* accompanied by a pipe-playing Pan; and the final image was *Lord Lister* the pioneer of antiseptic surgery. These images, all chosen by Geddes, depicted the ideals of his proposed new educational establishment. As mentioned briefly in an earlier chapter, Duncan would go on to produce some highly original paintings and drawings of Faery. His most famous is "*The Riders of the Sidhe*" which may have been inspired by discussions with William and W.B. Yeats as to the nature and symbolism of the Sidhe or Faeries. The painting as a whole is striking but there is much symbolism in the colourful scene – the first rider is carrying the Tree of Life and has a wise and scholar appearance; the second carries The Grail and is turning and looking at the viewer with a soft, loving expression; the third carries the Sword of Nuada and appears eager to use it; while the final rider carries a scrying crystal which shows equally the past and the future, her expression is strong and determined. This painting sums up visually Geddes' hopes and ideals.

Immediately behind Ramsay Lodge and Ramsay Garden, sitting directly on the Royal Mile leading straight to the castle, is a building originally known as Short's Observatory. This building had belonged to an optician with an interest in optics of all kinds. He constructed a tower above the dwelling part of the building in which he housed a camera obscura. This is an ingenious optical device that uses a rotating mirror and a system of lenses housed in what looks like a submarine's periscope sticking through the roof of the building. The whole system is used to project onto a white table in a darkened room images of the scenes outside the building. Geddes was fascinated by this device and saw it as symbolic of much of what he was trying to achieve. In 1892 Geddes took over the lease of this building and renamed it "Outlook Tower," a name being more symbolic of his hopes and aspirations. He described it as *the world's first sociological laboratory.* Later, in 1924, he built a small-scale Outlook Tower and University Hall near Montpellier in France where he lived up until his death in 1932.

The Edinburgh Outlook Tower and its camera obscura are still open to the public today as a tourist attraction but Geddes' connections with the buildings and his grand plans have been forgotten. Today visitors enter the building on the ground floor off the Royal Mile, go through the inevitable gift shop and eventually make their way to the top of the tower where they can view Edinburgh city and its surroundings in the images projected onto the table. Geddes however made his visitors go first straight to the top of the building and into the projection room by climbing a steep outside staircase at rapid speed. Once at the top, gasping for breath and peering into the gloom, they could marvel at this optical phenomenon. Next they would be taken on a tour of the floors while descending from the tower on their way back to street level. Each floor had displays and images from the arts and sciences all designed to impress ideas and concepts on the conscious and unconscious mind in what was quite an overpowering manner. There was a sphere you could walk inside which was painted with the stars and constellations of the Zodiac and enabled you to experience the heavens from within; there was a globe of the Earth which was transparent and gave views right through the planet to the countries on the other side; the walls of each room and stairwell were covered in diagrams, maps, plans and schematics of all types displaying a dazzling array of information. Thoughtfully, there was a darkened, quiet room where one person at a time could sit in meditation and try to absorb all that their senses had been bombarded with during their tour of the Outlook Tower.

Earlier, in 1887, Geddes had started a series of what he called Summer Meetings that were basically vacation courses for students of literature, the arts, the sciences and music, many on a Celtic and Gaelic theme. He had a team of teachers, writers, artists, painters and sculptors involved in the project including James Cadenhead, Robert Burns, Pittendrigh MacGillivray, Charles Mackie, Dr. Douglas Hyde, Nora Hopper, Rosa Mulholland, A. Percival Graves, Alexander Carmichael, Geddes himself and eventually William Sharp and Fiona Macleod. Many of them would later contribute to various publications by Geddes. William had been aware of Geddes and the

Outlook Tower before they met in 1894. When they did eventually meet they discovered they shared the same dreams of a revival of the ancient Celtic traditions and spiritual beliefs. Over the ensuing years they became good friends as the surviving correspondence shows. William became godfather to Geddes' son Arthur Allhallow Geddes, so called because he was born on Hallowe'en, coincidentally the Sharps' wedding anniversary.

In January 1895 William wrote to Geddes from London and outlined detailed plans he had formulated for the development of the schemes they had discussed in general terms the previous year. Included in these plans was the idea for a publishing house. William suggested that his connections to the large London publishing houses and his experience as a writer and editor in his own right made him an excellent candidate for the role of editor for the new company.

Geddes liked the idea and a publishing company, Patrick Geddes, Colleagues and Company, was set up, the purpose of which was to publish books that reflected the views and aspirations of Geddes and the other associates connected with Outlook Tower. Not surprisingly William was made managing director of the new publishing company. The annual payment of one hundred guineas went some way to alleviating his financial instability and, in a sense, it was easy money as the records show that William's total involvement in the publishing company as manager was initially minimal. The real benefit for him in taking this position was that he could use the new Geddes imprint to publish future Fiona Macleod books without fear of her true identity being revealed. The possibility that a publisher or publisher's editor might deliberately or accidentally reveal the secret had always been a concern of his but now this potential problem had been removed. William could publish Fiona's writings in confidence and in confidentiality with the full backing of Geddes who had been made privy to the secret. William also clearly saw himself, or, to be accurate, saw Fiona as the emerging foremost figure in the Scottish side of the Celtic Revival. Ireland had Yeats and company doing sterling work for that country and now here was a perfect opportunity for Fiona to do the same for Scotland. Geddes also employed his group of artists to illustrate many of the Geddes imprint books that the company published. John Duncan designed the distinctive multi-spi-

*John Duncan's multi-spiral symbol*

ral symbol that appeared on the covers of the Fiona Macleod books as well as the stylised thistle that appeared on the books' spines. He incorporated a version of his multi-spiral symbol in his 1923 painting "*Ivory, Apes and Pea-cocks*" (it is on the queen's throne on the back of the elephant).

William and Elizabeth took a flat in Edinburgh to be nearer Geddes and the Outlook Tower and they all set to work in making this dream of a Celtic college in the heart of Scotland's ancient capital come true. Part of the plan was for members of the group to give public lectures on relevant topics. William agreed to start the series on the subject of "*Art & Life.*" He divided this into ten lectures and, in typical thorough fashion, prepared far more information for each lecture than the time allowed would permit. The topics he had planned were,

1. Life & Art: Art & Nature: Nature
2. Disintegration: Degeneration: Regeneration
3. The Return to Nature: In Art, In Literature. The Literary Outlook in England & America
4. The Celtic Renascence, Ossian, Matthew Arnold, The Ancient Celtic Writers
5. The Celtic Renascence. Contemporary. The School of Celtic Ornament
6. The Science of Criticism: What it is, what it is not. The Critical Ideal
7. Ernest Hello
8. The Drama of Life, and Dramatists
9. The Ideals of Art – Pagan, Medieval, Modern
10. The Literary Ideal – Pagan, Medieval. The Modern Ideal [1]

Unfortunately his health was not as robust as his enthusiasm led him to believe. Part way through this first lecture his notes fell to the floor as he suffered a heart attack. Amazingly he managed to finish his presentation before collapsing off stage. It was more likely to have been an attack of angina aggravated by his fear of public speaking than a full heart attack but whatever it actually was turned out not to be life threatening. It was clear though that he was in no fit condition to give any more public lectures. In a note to a friend he commented that his " ... *lectures here have been a marked success – but they have told on me heavily.*" Note his use of the plural despite the fact he only managed to give one lecture.

Elizabeth stayed in Edinburgh to carry on the work with Geddes while William went alone across the Firth of Forth to the small village of Kinghorn to recuperate and recover in the little Pettycur Inn. He would return later to this little hideaway several times over the next few years with Edith. In typical flowery fashion and in keeping with his love of naming things he came to call the Pettycur Inn his "*House of Dreams.*" By September he was sufficiently recuperated to make his way to Argyll on the West coast of Scotland where he, Elizabeth, his mother and sisters had taken a holiday cottage for the month.

Geddes published a series of books called "*The Evergreen: A Northern Seasonal*" timed to coincide with the changing of the seasons. He chose the name '*The Evergreen*' in commemoration of a 1724 publication of the same name by Allan Ramsay, the writer who had given his name to the Lodge and Gardens. This had also been an attempt to encourage interest in the Scottish culture and tradition and the importance of the Green World. Geddes had originally planned at least five such volumes but only four ever appeared. These were collections of short pieces of prose, poetry and scientific discussion contributed by several of the writers connected with Outlook Tower and illustrated by its artists. William was able to publish pieces under both of his names in these volumes and thereby maintain the impression of there being two writers at work at the same time.

At about this same period Edith was studying the literature of the contemporary Belgian writers of the day. William developed a similar interest, no doubt fostered by his closeness to Edith, and both he and Edith produced several articles and books on this rather obscure genre. The political importance of this is mainly lost to people today. The independent country of Belgium only came into being in 1830. The following year it became a monarchy when the newly created position of King of Belgium was given to an unemployed member of the royal Saxe-Coburg family in Germany, the same family from which the present British monarch is descended. Immediately the artists, writers and social activists of the country set about establishing a cultural identity that could rightfully be called Belgian; not French, not Dutch, but Belgian. The writers had two languages, French and Flemish, with which to work and this was recognised by William and Edith as a parallel to the English and Gaelic linguistic divisions in Ireland and Scotland. To the political activists in Scotland and Ireland the success of the Belgians in gaining full independence from France and the Netherlands was an encouraging and motivating event that could not be ignored. In the political and cultural worlds of Europe at that time the successful development of this new country was very important. It was also seen as being very threatening to the establishment in the many other European countries with similar linguistic and cultural divides.

William confidently started to describe himself as the only person qualified to comment on the Belgian writers and he became an unofficial spokesman for their cause. He said, "*Obviously, the primary and almost overwhelming handicap lay in the fact that the official and literary language of this small country... was that of its most powerful neighbour, a neighbour upon whose amity its very existence depended. The young Belgian had, like the young Celt of Western Ireland or the Scottish Highlander, no alternative. He had either to use the dominant official and literary language, or be content to have no audience, no reader... Critics, students, general readers, and poets and novelists themselves, saw that Flemish was a steadily narrowing and inevitably doomed language...*"[2] The work of Patrick Geddes and Colleagues, the planned college and "*The Evergreen*" publication were all focussed on the Scottish Celt and Gael but it was also to be used as vehicles for all nationalities who saw themselves in similar cultural and linguistic dilemma. It was nationalistic in some sense but at the same time, paradoxically cosmopolitan.

Despite its strong focus on the Scottish Celt and Gael, there are no articles in "*The Evergreen*" in the Gaelic language. They are all in the English language apart from six in French spread across the four volumes. In "*The Book of Autumn*" issue, (Autumn 1895) there is one piece called "*The Night-Comers*" by the Belgian writer Charles Van Lerberghe that had been translated into English by William who wrote the prologue. The fact there is no Gaelic content is simply because none of the contributors, including William and Fiona, were fluent enough to compose a piece of literature in that language that was worthy of inclusion.

Amongst the Geddes' papers in the National Library, Edinburgh are plans for another publication for 1895 which would have been very similar to "*The Evergreen*." The title "*The Celtic World*" was William's suggestion and although never adopted the framework for the later publication is clear:-

**Plans and outlines for "The Celtic World",**
**Vol. 1 No. 1., July-Sept 1895:-**

| | |
|---|---|
| **Frontispice** | John Duncan |
| 1. The Celtic Renaissance | A Prologue (editorial |
| 2. The Word Anglo-Celtic | A Note (editorial) |
| 3. Anglo-Celtic Magazine | (editorial) |
| 4. The Late Prof. Blackie | by Prof. [ILLEGIBLE] |
| 5. The Hill of God | by Fiona Macleod |
| 6. A Poem | by W.B. Yeats |
| 7. The Hill Way | by Ernest Rhys |
| 8. The House of Rest. | A Forecast by Patrick Geddes |
| 9. A Poem | by Moira O'Nell or Katherine Tynan |
| 10. Three Hebridean Folk-Hymns | by A. Carmichael |
| 11. Celtic Ornament | by J. Duncan? |
| 12. Standish O'Grady's Historical Romance by – | |
| 13. Anima Celtica | by "A.E." |
| Notes | |

Despite Geddes' grand plans and ideas, and despite the considerable amount of work put into the venture by many of its associates, it never materialised into the permanent, stable and expanding school of Celtic vision and dream that had been planned. To a great extent bad management in Edinburgh caused this with too many people not knowing what they should really be doing. One commentator of the day, Louis G. Irvine author of "*Nerves and Brains*," was so frustrated by the company's lack of business acumen that he wrote in April 1897 to Geddes saying, "*P.G. and Colleagues are like the East-India Company. You can't get at anybody in particular to come down upon, the Company perpetually eludes all attempts to fix responsibility...*"[3] Its demise was also due to adverse criticism of "*The Evergreen*" by many critics, including an attack on its worth by H.G. Wells. After four volumes the series was cancelled. Elizabeth states in her memoir that there were five volumes but this is erroneous. Many years later Geddes would say about the publishing company, "*Here is another of my as yet disastrous yet not ill-conceived endeavours...*"[4]

Meantime, independently, Fiona was making a favourable impression with the critics. Several titles appeared under the Geddes imprint - "*The Sin-Eater and Other Tales*" (1895), "*The Washer of the Ford and other Legendary Moralities*" (1895), "*From the Hills of Dream: Mountain Songs and Island Runes*" (1896), and in 1897 a three volume set – "*Spiritual Tales,*" "*Barbaric Tales*" and "*Tragic Romances*" – was issued being a collection of previously published works, some expanded, and with a few new pieces added. William, in collaboration with Elizabeth, also published an important collection of Celtic poems entitled "*Lyra Celtica*" (1896) and prepared an edition of the great collection of old tales known as "*Ossian*" (1896) originally collected in the 18th century by James MacPherson. When MacPherson's Ossianic collection of tales first appeared he was accused by many critics of having fabricated the whole thing as clearly, to their minds, such a substantial body of indigenous Gaelic folk tales never existed. Rather cruelly a few of the Victorian critics accused Fiona Macleod of being yet another Gaelic fraud just like MacPherson.

Very soon the Patrick Geddes imprint was in financial trouble. William frequently did not receive his remuneration as editor and Fiona either didn't get paid her book royalties at all or they were considerably late in arriving. The financial inconvenience of this was offset in some ways by the books receiving favourable critical acclaim. The correspondence between William and Patrick Geddes and Colleagues at that time and for long after is full of demands for payment and excuses why it had not been forthcoming. It was a mess. Geddes was simultaneously using John Duncan to train students to become teachers in his planned School of Art that was to be opened as soon as suitable premises became available. A letter from Duncan to Geddes as early as 1895 shows that even this idea was falling apart, "*You gave me to understand that you were eager to form a School of Art. That this School was not to consist primarily of a great band of students, but a body of artists and their assistants working together with common ideals. The work of this school was not to be the making of mere studies, but to be directed towards the execution of actual work for public and other purposes. You assured me that there was an abundance of work... and not to bother my head about financial matters... I was successful... in getting together four ladies able and willing to work sympathetically... and the decorations of 'The Evergreen' show that they are now thoroughly competent designers. Then... you tell me you have no work for them to do!!... What am I to think?*"[5] The plan for the school collapsed in 1897 and the following year Duncan returned to Dundee although he would continue to undertake occasional commissions from Geddes for the rest of his life.

An interesting letter survives from this period. The letter bears William's signature but the bulk of the letter is not in his handwriting, nor that of his sister-secretary Mary. It reads, "*I have no binding arrangements with any one, save Mrs. Wingate Rinder, who is to have an advance upon her 'Shadow of Arvor,' and Miss Macleod for 'Ossian Retold.' But these are matters for Autumn consideration.*" There then follows a Post Script which is in William's handwriting and says, "*In case I forget, please note that when due Miss Macleod's cheque is to be crossed 'National Provincial Bank' Piccadily Branch, and is to be sent to her c/o Frank Rinder Esq., 7 Kensington Court Gardens, London W.*" [6] This shows that William was acting as agent for both Fiona and Edith, the only person, he says, with whom he had any binding arrangement. This implies that William was giving Fiona's royalty payments to Edith who must have had a bank account with the National Provincial Bank in the name of Fiona Macleod in order to cash the cheques. It is true that on several occasions she played the role of Fiona when William was forced to produce her in the flesh in order to satisfy public curiosity but that hardly seems sufficient reason to donate Fiona's income to her, small though it obviously was. We have to assume that Elizabeth was aware of this financial arrangement, which hopefully, was only a temporary one. This must have made tolerating her husband's affair with Edith even harder to bear, especially during their frequent periods of financial hardship.

Elizabeth was also involved in the Geddes' business plans in her own right. In a reply to a letter from Geddes she commented on a job offer he made to her and, importantly, asked him to consider William's poor health before discussing any more business with him. The letter says in part, "*I wish my Poet were half as well. He met me at Venice, so weak and feeble I was very much alarmed. He had long fainting fits which at first I thought were heart attacks. As soon as I got home I summoned the doctor. He told me that Will has so greatly overworked that he has reduced himself to a dangerous point of weakness that the danger to be avoided is heart failure. He is a little better again, but not strong enough to take the journey from London to Edinburgh without a break. Had I known he was in this state I would never have consented to his going to Venice... – and now I am going to ask you a favour; and that is not to allow him – when you see him – to discuss business matters for any length of time at one sitting. He needs all his time and strength to get well. Each Spring he grows worse – and I can see that if he works at the present speed, and with the present complications he will not see many more Springs. The dual work of F.M. and W.S. is a great drain on his strength, at the present moment too great a drain, and his state at present is unsatisfactory. With regard to your kind proposal which is very seductive (only I should bid for the post of under-gardener!) it, too, alack! must regretfully be refused. For, I cannot get away until about the end of July. I have taken up my Herald work again and must stick to it until the end of summer.*[7] Oddly she concludes the letter with a Post Script saying, "*I have forwarded your note to Fiona to Petticur.* [sic]*"* She had already stated that William was not strong enough to take the journey from London to Edinburgh without a break, meaning that he was not yet in Edinburgh, Geddes knew the secret regarding Fiona's identity, so to whom was she forwarding his note? The only person who could already be at Pettycur that she would call 'Fiona' would have been Edith. Does this mean Geddes also knew the secret of William and Edith's love affair? I doubt this as although their relationship was close and convivial they were not so intimate as to discuss such highly personal, and potentially scandalous, matters. However the circumstances do indicate that the only person who could have been at Pettycur was Edith so perhaps Geddes knew that Edith played the role of Fiona when circumstances demanded.

In a later letter Elizabeth stated in part, "*I cannot express to you how grateful I feel for your loving friendship for my husband and for all the care and thought you and Mrs. Geddes have given him. I am thankful that there is someone else than myself who sees how he is expending health and strength – and encroaching on his reserve – in work of a kind he ought not to do. Like you I have a great believe [sic] in the future of WS and of Fiona M; and I am equally persuaded that he must give up the petty hack-work in order to give his real work its chance. But it is so difficult to do so; he grows nervous, and, I regret to say, chiefly on my account. But I feel sure, that now, your kind interest in him, will do more than any thing else to make him, not only feel, but act on our advice – which coincides. You are indeed a most valuable ally.*"[8]   From these exchanges between Elizabeth and Geddes it is clear that they both saw the work of Fiona Macleod as being of great importance. But they both also saw all too clearly how the production of this work was literally killing William Sharp. I have quoted from these letters at length to show Elizabeth's consistent display of deep love for her ailing husband. She was a remarkable woman.

An undated letter from William to Geddes described how ill he actually was. He asked for the help of Miss Rea, a secretary with the Columbia Literary Agency, and stated that without her help he would be forced to sever all connections with Patrick Geddes and Colleagues. It is a desperate letter that says in part, "*... And one thing is certain: if I find myself unable to do FM's work – & it is imperative that for the next six weeks FM's work should prevail – I must sever my connections with the firm. At all hazards, FM must not be 'killed'. But this is sure: she cannot live under present conditions. Leaving aside then the Doctor's and E's urgent requests as to my not being alone (partly because of my heart and partly because of a passing mental strain of suffering and weakness) it comes to this: (1) I have help (& mind you an 'outsider' is absolutely worthless to me now, & probably at any time) & stay here, and do both FM & WS & PG & Co – each in proportion and harmony: or else I definitely sever my connection – at any rate pro: tem: – before all correspondence: & go away somewhere where FM's funeral would not be so imminent, and WS's nervous health could not be* *so drained. My plans all hang upon … how much I can get done before the end of March (2) and at what mental cost."* He added in a PS, *"God need not send poets to Hell: London is nearer and worse to endure."* [9] This letter may have been sent in early 1897 because in a letter dated March 5th 1897 he stated he no longer had any connections with Patrick Geddes and Colleagues. This was premature though as his association with the company carried on for a few more years although at a more superficial level. He had already revealed to Geddes that he was suffering from depression and that his doctor had ordered him not only to obtain help but to have someone with him at all times. He explained this as meaning his creative ability dried up when he was alone but from exchanges between the doctor, Elizabeth and Edith it is clear the real fear was that his depression was so severe he may attempt suicide. It is obvious that the pressure Fiona was putting on him was becoming unbearable; but she did not relent.

The third Fiona Macleod book, *"The Sin-Eater,"* earned many approving comments from the general public and the literary world alike. The name of Fiona Macleod started to be mentioned in Ireland by members of the Irish Literary Society and what would become the Irish National Theatre. Well-known and well-respected Irish writers such as Dr. Douglas Hyde, Standish O'Grady, Lady Gregory, George Russell (better known as "AE") and William Butler Yeats took a great interest in the writing style of this new Scotswoman on the scene and particularly in what she had to say in her stories and poems about life in the Scottish Gaeltacht. Soon she was being applauded as a great champion of the downtrodden Irish and Scottish Gael and announced as a herald for the new Celtic revival, which everyone believed was just around the corner. The rapid rise to fame and respect was far more than William had imagined and was far in excess of anything he had achieved to date under his own name. The public became curious. People wanted to know more about the author of these mystical Celtic tales. Where did she live? Was she married? What did she look like? When would she be available for interview? Photographs?

This brought with it some unexpected troubles. William revealed in a letter to his friend Sir George Douglas on December 21st 1895, *"A matter that amused me at first has assumed a more tragic hue. A man (a Scottish clergyman – and Highlander) has read & reread F.M.'s books till – he has fallen passionately in love with her! He created an ideal 'Fiona', poor chap, and has "pinned all to his passionate hope." I thought I had definitely prevented all further idea of anything of the kind, or even any correspondence – but I have had a letter from his mother, saying that her son is desperate because of my rebuff, and is dying for love of me; and she begs me to be merciful, & even if I cannot become his wife, at least to see him. She warns me, too, that she fears he will take his life, 'as he has become almost distraught by his mad love for you.'… It may seem only amusing to you – as it did to me at first – but upon my soul I am very uncomfortable about it. After the first definite proposal of marriage (by the way, this is the second Fiona has had!) … I am damnably put out by the whole affair."* [10]

Because everything she had produced so far could be linked or traced in one way or another to William Sharp people started to put two and two together. Very soon William was being frequently asked outright if he was Fiona. His answer was always an emphatic denial. Detailed arguments as to why they were clearly one and the same person started to appear in the Press and literary journals of the day. Many of these were written by literary enthusiasts who had carefully studied and compared William and Fiona's works but others were from newspaper hacks who were just looking for a sensational story. Again denials were forthcoming from William, some of them strongly worded and very indignant. He was obsessed with keeping the secret and maintaining the illusion of a second writer but it was becoming harder and harder, especially when such enquiries and accusations were starting to come from close friends. Reading carefully into the events of 1895 onwards it is clear that William was not prepared for all this attention despite the fact he had had the foresight to employ his sister Mary to write the Fiona Macleod letters. It never occurred to him that Fiona would be so popular so quickly. It took him completely by surprise and he was not prepared to deal with the sudden influx of curiosity and enquiry. In a letter to his confidant Murray Gilchrist he said, "*Fiona Macleod has suddenly begun to attract a great deal of attention. There have been leaders as well as long and important reviews: and now the chief North of Scotland paper, The Highland News, is printing two long articles devoted in a most eulogistic way to F.M. and her influence... There is, also, I hear, to be a Magazine article on her. This last week there have been long and favourable reviews in the Academy and The New Age.*" [11]

He took the stance that the fewer people who knew the secret the safer the secret would be. He trusted the few people already in the know never to reveal the secret and, as time has shown, none of them ever did. As her popularity continued to grow more and more people became very interested in Fiona Macleod. Many of these people were William's own close friends and he soon found himself in the uncomfortable position of having to lie, and continue to lie, to friends and colleagues, including some of his closest magical allies, whom he respected dearly. His cloak of secrets was becoming heavier and heavier. For example, in 1896 he wrote to John Thomson Macleay, editor of "*The Highland News*" in Inverness and also one of the contributors to "*The Evergreen.*" He was a supporter and promoter of Fiona Macleod but did not know the secret. In this letter William says, "*I confess I share to some degree in Miss Macleod's annoyance in the persistent disbelief in her personality to which you allude... She has ever been willing to meet the few persons who have any right to expect an interview... Did you not see the explicit statement I caused to be inserted in the 'Glasgow Evening News', and elsewhere (because of one of these perverse statements) to the effect that 'Miss Fiona Macleod is not Mr William Sharp; Miss Fiona Macleod is not Mrs William Sharp and that Miss Fiona Macleod is - Miss Fiona Macleod.' Surely that ought to have settled the matter; for it is scarcely likely, I imagine, that I should put forth so explicit a statement were it not literally true."* [12] This was, as he said, <u>literally</u> true but he knew that nonetheless it was deceptive and only partly true. William must have felt dreadful about deliberately deceiving a person who was a supporter, ally and fellow Celtophile.

Some months later he was forced to deal with the issue again with Macleay and said, "*Yes, Fiona Macleod is a very tangible reality indeed. She and my sister Mary were here yesterday... and I had to pay for their luncheon etc. ... and one does not pay for phantoms! Apart from her dislike of publicity, she does not wish to have her freedom of movements affected in any way: and it is not too much to say that anyone who once saw her photograph would recognise her in a moment anywhere, for her beauty is of a very stirring kind.*" [13] This comment on her stirring beauty is a reference to Edith with whom he and Mary no doubt did have lunch.

Later that same year though things took an unexpected turn when he had cause to deal with this subject yet again with Macleay who had published in his newspaper a disturbing article entitled, "*Mystery! Mystery! All in a Celtic Haze!*" This was a collection of some of the more vigorous speculation by others as to the true identity of Fiona Macleod. It is likely that he composed this article for no reason other than to boost sales of his newspaper. However as far as William could see it was clearly getting too near the truth for comfort and had to be stopped. In a letter dated August 17th 1896 William's tone had changed remarkably from his correspondence earlier that year, "*I can only say that I regret the ill-bred impertinence of the Glasgow busybodies in question, and the personalities & tone of the said article. They seem to me in very bad taste. I think a paper that respects public and private right should not lend itself to unwarrantable personalities – favourable or unfavourable... Fortunately, all this rather vulgar prying can not have any result: for, as a matter of fact, Miss Macleod's privacy is now so-well safeguarded by her & her friends that she is as 'safe' either in Edinburgh or Glasgow as Prince Charlie in 'the heather.' It is amusing – when a thing is very simple – how it can be made into a mystery.*" [14]

There was quite a flurry of letters between them at this period. The very next day he wrote again, "*The last post has brought me a line from Miss Macleod apropos of the article 'Mystery.' She writes in deep resentment against what she considers its altogether unwarrantable personalities, and against 'the insulting opening, the note of which is more fully emphasized in the cruel and inexcusable phrase: 'I hear again and again that she is a greater fraud than Macpherson of Ossianic fame.' ... I admit I am glad she writes as she does: for I should deeply regret to see her yield to the vulgar temptation to a public controversy concerning herself – whether 'a rather peculiar' one or any other.*" [15] This flood of denials and rebuffs continued for some days, bordering on threatened legal action on William's part, when suddenly he changed tone completely and made great efforts to make it clear to Macleay that he did not blame him personally and that, after all, what else could one expect in the circumstances of her extreme desire for total privacy? It seems he realised the old adage that 'no publicity is bad publicity' and was happy to let the *Highland News* article runs its natural course.

This had been an awkward situation for William as Macleay was not just a newspaper man but a friend and ally of Fiona. Dealing with the rest of the Press was easier as it usually only involved a letter of denial to some publication or other. His diary entry for January 7th 1896 says, "*The British Weekly has a paragraph given under all reserve that Fiona Macleod is Mrs William Sharp. Have written – as W.S. – to Dr R Nicoll and to Mrs Macdonnell of 'The Bookman' to deny this authoratively.*"[16] This parrying and thrusting with the Press carried on for many years. On May 13th 1899 Fiona Macleod wrote an indignant letter to the literary magazine "*The Athenaeum*," saying, "*I am much annoyed at this identification of myself with this or that man or woman of letters – in one or two instances with people I have never seen and do not even know by correspondence. For, what seems to myself not only good, but imperative private reasons, I wish to preserve absolutely my privacy. It is not only that temperamentally I shrink from and dislike the publicity of reputation, but that my very writing depends upon this privacy. But in one respect, to satisfy those who will not be content to take or leave, to read or ignore my writings, I give you authority to say definitely that 'Fiona Macleod' is NOT any of those with whom she had been 'identified', that she writes only under the name of "Fiona Macleod": that her name IS her own; and that all she asks is the courtesy both of good breeding and commonsense – a courtesy which is the right of all, and surely imperatively of a woman acting for and by herself.*"[17]

In correspondence with friends though Fiona did sometimes show some humour and realise the funny side of all this name-guessing. In a private letter to Katharine Tynan she mentioned some of the latest Fiona rumours, "*I am now well aware of much of the mystery that has grown up about my unfortunate self. I have even heard that Fleet Street journalist rumour to which you allude – with the addition that the said unhappy scribe was bald and old and addicted to drink. Heaven knows who and what I am according to some wiseacres! A recent cutting said I was Irish, a Mr. Chas. O'Connor, whom I know not... That I was Miss Nora Hopper and Mr. Yeats in unison – at which I felt flattered... Latterly I became the daughter of the late Dr. Norman Macleod. The latest is that I am Maud Gonne... She is Irish and lives in Paris; and is, I hear, very beautiful so I prefer to be Miss Gonne rather than that Fleet Street journalist!*" Later in the same letter she unusually gave away some personal information, "*I am not an unmarried girl, as commonly supposed, but am married. The name I write under is my maiden name... I come of an old Catholic family, that I am a Macleod, that I was born in the Southern Hebrides, and that my heart still lies where the cradle rocked.*"[18]

The fact that William was somewhat taken by surprise by all the interest in the physical Fiona Macleod whose biography he had not yet fully thought out is further demonstrated by a letter that appeared after his death in the

"*British Weekly.*" Someone, allegedly a friend of William, wrote a piece under the name "Man of Kent" in response to William's obituary notice and the revelation that he was Fiona Macleod. This anonymous correspondent recalled a conversation with William in which, "*He replied, with great frankness, that the authoress was a friend of his own, that she was the wife of a Highland laird, that she had been obliged to separate from her husband, and that she was most anxious to conceal her name, as if it were made known, it would lead to the renewal of her domestic troubles. He told me this, as I say, quite frankly, and asked me to keep it a secret, and so I have kept it.*" [19] The mysterious "Man of Kent" seems to have been given this story at an early date by William who had not yet settled upon the one story to stick with. Most other accounts refer to Fiona as simply being his cousin although there are few other vague comments scattered throughout the correspondence about her being married to a very understanding and tolerant husband who allowed her to roam as she willed. This version was based on the real life circumstances of his friend Mona Caird.

There is some evidence that William led Yeats to believe that he and Fiona were lovers. This of course would be true if by Fiona he actually meant Edith. He may have been inspired to drop such a hint by the relationship Yeats had with Maud Gonne. William's friend Richard Le Gallienne commented, "*On one occasion, when I was sitting with him in his study, he pointed to the framed portrait of a beautiful woman which stood on top of a revolving book-case, and said, 'That is Fiona!' I affected belief, but, rightly or wrongly, it was my strong impression that the portrait thus labelled was that of a well-known Irish lady prominently identified with Home Rule politics, and I smiled to myself at the audacious white lie.*" [20] This photograph was almost certainly of Edith and the 'well-known Irish lady' to whom Le Gallienne refers must have been Maud Gonne. This was at a time when photographic images were not as prevalent or common as they are today and although many people would have heard of Maud Gonne not many would have been able to identify her with certainty in a photograph. There is a photograph of Edith from this period, in profile, where she does bear a resemblance to Maud Gonne. Note that Le Gallienne only had a 'strong impression' that this photograph was of Maud. Another similarity is that they both shared the same name, Maud Gonne's full name being Edith Maud Gonne.

However it seems William may indeed also have had a picture of Maud. On December 13th 1897 Lady Gregory called on the Sharps and wrote in her diary, "*... rather interested as Sharp showed me a portrait of Miss Gonne – a very lovely face – & a drawing by AE & some new poems of his.*" [21] It is not clear if by portrait she meant a photograph or if it was one of AE's drawings. Whichever it was she had not seen Maud Gonne in the flesh at this time and had no previous image in her mind with which to compare this portrait. He definitely had several photographs of Edith, some of which still survive in the various William Sharp collections in libraries in the UK and USA, and it is possible that William did have a photograph of Maud from his visit to Yeats in Paris the previous year. The above quotations serve to show not only the physical similarities between the two women but also the similarities between William and Edith's affair and the attempted affair by Yeats with Maud Gonne. As with the whole of William Sharp's life though this detail only adds to the already considerable confusion!

William's sister Mary had been acting as his secretary, dealing with his business affairs and correspondence for some years. Now that Fiona was generating so much business and interest in her own right Mary also took on her workload. Most of the correspondence was originally done by hand although later letters were produced on a typewriter. William instructed Mary to reply in her own handwriting to letters addressed to Fiona Macleod and he would deal with letters to and from William Sharp. He did not want to risk anyone being able to compare William Sharp's handwriting with that of Fiona Macleod and discover that they were identical. Usually the reply address given on the Fiona Macleod letters was either care of her publisher, the Outlook Tower or care of a private address in Edinburgh that was William's mother's house where Mary lived. Early in his business relationship with Patrick Geddes he had revealed the secret and Geddes had said it would be all right to reveal the secret to his wife Anna. Mary had previously sent a Fiona letter to Anna Geddes so she had already seen the supposed Fiona handwriting. Now William sent a letter to Anna in his own handwriting emphasising the need for secrecy. Curiously he signed the letter, "Fiona Macleod and William Sharp." This is a unique letter bearing the Fiona Macleod signature in William Sharp's handwriting and is yet another example of his frequent confusion of identity.

Many of these letters comment on her being en-route from one location to another and are signed *"in haste"* or *"in great haste,"* a convenient way of avoiding a reply address altogether. However after reading several such letters in sequence, all talking about being here but on her way there, or just about to leave this place in order to get to that place, it is surprising that nobody ever asked the simple question - why? Why was she constantly moving from one place to another? With whom did she stay at all of these various locations? Nobody ever asked the basic question – what does she live on? Where does her money come from? It is astonishing that the very vagueness of her correspondence and the elusive statements by William as to the nature of his cousin did not in themselves raise many more questions and suspicions. Many of her shorter pieces start with comments about travelling on small fishing boats with local fishermen who told her some tale or other, or of some personal acquaintance who goes mad, commits suicide or some other unusual act. What was a seemingly respectable Victorian lady doing spending so much time on small boats with men unrelated to her and how did she come to know so many people of such an unstable disposition? These statements on her constant moving and frequent travelling with others contradict her vehement assertions that she needed peace, quiet and solitude in order to write. It is as well that nobody ever seemed to ask these fundamental questions as William would have had a very hard time indeed inventing an entire life for Fiona with sufficient details to satisfy the enquirer but at the same time retain sufficient vagueness to avoid verification.

He did slip up on his intentional vagueness on a couple of occasions when he claimed that she was either born on the Isle of Iona, had lived there for a period during her early childhood or she had been there on some specific date. Iona is a very small island with a resident population at that time of no more than two hundred people. The local Church of Scotland minister on the island, aware of the Fiona Macleod phenomenon, made enquiries of the older residents but nobody could remember a Fiona Macleod ever residing there. He checked with his own Parish Church records of births on the island but could find no reference to anyone of that name having been born there either. On one occasion Sharp unwittingly gave a specific time when Fiona was supposed to have been in Iona and this same minister made an immediate census of the island's population. He found, of course, no trace of her being there at that specific moment or even being expected by anybody at some later date. The puzzle became so great that his mother's Edinburgh home started to be watched by some zealous members of the Press but nobody ever managed to get a glimpse of Miss Macleod let alone secure an interview with her.

Another basic question that was never asked, and a fact William never gave out, is how old is Fiona? Whenever I ask someone familiar with her writings this question the usual reply is 'in her twenties.' Nowhere though does she or William ever say anything that can help pin down her age. She may indeed have been in her twenties but she could equally have been in her forties or even sixties. She travelled a lot implying a younger, fitter person but on many occasions she complained of lumbago, nervous headaches and various aches and pains that imply she may have been older. This adds to the mystery and helps make it harder to pin down the exact details of her life but the truth is of course that being Faery she has no age as we would understand it.

A personal aside: while staying in Edinburgh during my researches I took the opportunity to visit and photograph the various addresses where William and his family had lived. At one of these houses I knocked on the door to ask the owner if I could photograph his home. As I knocked I heard the phone ringing inside so I waited. A gentleman suddenly opened the door, phone in hand, who motioned me in and pointed to the lounge. I went in, sat down and waited for him to finish his conversation on the phone. I was rather surprised that he had admitted me, a total stranger, at all. He duly reappeared, sat down and asked how I was. There then followed a rather odd conversation consisting of the usual pleasantries about the weather and so forth until I finally managed to explain why I was there. I told him about

William and Fiona, my book, her connection with the house and, finally asked if he had ever heard of Fiona Macleod. For a while he just stared at me, which was even more off-putting, but then he seemed to 'come to' and apologised for his obviously odd behaviour. He said he had never heard of Fiona Macleod but he had heard of Iona, in fact he had been the Church of Scotland minister on the island until only six months prior to my visit. This explained his ease at allowing a stranger into his home; he thought I was a parishioner there on church business. Then he added that his name was Rev. M-------- and that his daughter, Fiona M-------, now lived in this house with him. Now it was my turn to stare, mouth open and heart racing! Fiona M------- from Iona was now living in Fiona Macleod's old home. Hardly daring to ask the question I said, "*Is Fiona at home?*" She was not, being away at college. I have detailed several of the odd and strange occurrences and coincidences that happened to me during the writing of this book but that visit was the strangest and most unsettling of all. I shall never forget it. I do not think the Rev. M------ will either!

But back to the original Fiona. As has already been made clear, the complication of keeping alive the belief in Fiona as a separate being, the deceiving of dear friends, dealing with two lots of correspondence and the constant hoping and praying that none of his friends in the know would ever let slip the secret, placed considerable strain on the already overstressed William Sharp. It is clear however that this was not one of those horrible situations where a person unwittingly starts a lie and soon finds that they cannot stop it even when it has got completely out of control. William maintained the lie, no matter how difficult it became, because he knew that Fiona really did exist in the Faery realm, but to explain to the Victorian public the true nature of her existence would have been impossible. He also knew that to reveal any of this would result in her death. The lying and deceiving was very hard for him, but it was completely necessary.

In May of 1896 he took a break in France to see his friends the Janviers. Elizabeth was already in Italy and William was conscious of the fact that their finances were again in a precarious position, thanks mainly to the unreliability of Patrick Geddes and Co. when it came to making payments. In the past during such times of financial concern various cheques had landed in his lap and provided financial relief just when it was most needed. Once again the 'money fairy' looked down on him, not with a cheque this time but, as he wrote to his friend Murray Gilchrist, with a win of forty Pounds at the gaming tables in Provence, almost half his annual salary with Geddes! How many times in one person's life can such financial windfalls be expected to occur at such opportune times?

[1] Memoir, page 251

[2] "A Note on the Belgian Renascence," Chap-Book IV, December 1895, page 151

[3] Kitchen, A Most Unsettling Person, page 153

[4] Kitchen, A Most Unsettling Person, page 267

[5] Kemply, The Paintings of John Duncan, page 19

[6] Geddes Papers, NLS, Edinburgh

[7] Geddes Papers, NLS, Edinburgh

[8] Geddes Papers, NLS, Edinburgh

[9] WS Archives

[10] WS Archives

[11] Memoir, page 261

[12] NLS, Edinburgh, emphasis in the original

[13] NLS, Edinburgh

[14] NLS, Edinburgh

[15] NLS, Edinburgh

[16] NLS, Edinburgh

[17] NLS, Edinburgh

[18] "Fortnightly Review", March 1906, page 578

[19] Obituary Notices, William Sharp Collection, NLS, Edinburgh

[20] "The Forum", February 1911, page 172

[21] Pethica, Lady Gregory's Diaries, Page 160

# Chapter 7
# The Archer Vision

*There were three that saw; three will attain a wisdom older than the serpent, but the child will die*

From 1894 until the end of the century Fiona was producing a steady flow of writing, dealing with an ever-increasing amount of correspondence and, consequently, impinging more and more on the emotions and thoughts of William. This was not unwanted nor unwelcomed on his part, indeed it was necessary, but it only added to the already tremendous mental and emotional strain with which he struggled. As a result he was forced to seriously take note of his frail health. If he wished to continue living and writing he would need to pay more attention to his physical, emotional and spiritual health than he had done in the past. Until now he had accepted his frequent bouts of ill health and nervous exhaustion as if they were no more than temporary phases that would soon pass. Now he was beginning to understand that ill health and emotional instability would be the norm for him if he was to continue working with Fiona. Despite this, and despite their erratic income and the considerable demands on him to continue writing under both names, he and Elizabeth continued to travel for much of the year. It is astonishing that in such disruptive and unfavourable circumstances he was able to produce anything at all as William Sharp let alone cope with the double output created by Fiona Macleod. From time to time now he did take a break to let his body, mind and spirit recuperate. It was during these quiet times that he was able to draw closer to Fiona and let her come through strongly and clearly. These were the personal, intimate moments alone that they both needed so badly; he to understand what she was trying to achieve and she to let him know what needed to be done next. The constant moving, writing, planning, and dealing with two separate lots of correspondence occupied so much of his time that he rarely had a chance to stop and listen to what Fiona was trying to say. When he did the results were often dramatic.

In 1896, after much travelling in other parts of Scotland, he and Elizabeth arrived at Tarbert, where Frank and Edith Rinder had taken a house for the summer. Mary joined them and they all looked forward to a peaceful and relaxed vacation. Not too long after arriving however Elizabeth decided to return to London to get on with her work for *The Glasgow Herald* newspaper. Whether this was for purely conscientious reasons or whether it was to allow William time alone with Edith she does not say. It may seem odd that Elizabeth would deliberately allow her husband the freedom to be alone with his lover but by this time she, Edith and William had all noticed and come to accept that an important pattern had emerged. When William was alone with Elizabeth he could write freely as William Sharp but he found it very difficult to write as Fiona Macleod. When he was alone with Edith the reverse was the case; Fiona came through in full force and William took a back seat as far as writing was concerned. The fact that both of these women recognised, understood and actually encouraged this phenomenon is astonishing. There is no doubt that there was a physical sexual aspect to William and Edith's relationship but Elizabeth was able to see past this to the greater need for the writings of Fiona Macleod to continue. Edith's husband Frank was also on vacation with them in Tarbert but we do not know if he too graciously left or not to allow them time alone. The little correspondence that survives between William and Frank is clearly that of two good friends. Frank must have known of his wife's affair with William so we can only conclude that he too realised the profound effect it had on Fiona and was willing for it to continue. Very soon after William died, Frank wrote a very touching obituary that was published in the *"Art Journal"* the tone of which implies a deep and sincere friendship existed between the two men. I quote it in part in Chapter 10. William's sister Mary was also there but unfortunately we know nothing of her feelings or impressions of what was going on between her brother and Edith or even how she understood the whole Fiona Macleod phenomenon. I have in my possession a photograph of Mary taken in 1906, the year after her brother died. On the back she has written,

To the Rev. R. Wilkins Rees.

Fiona Macleod's sister, who did all the writing etc. of the Fiona Macleod work and carried on the correspondence connected with it.

Yours Sincerely
Mary B. Sharp
1906

The Rev. Rees wrote about the history of the church with particular reference to folklore and customs. He was very interested in ghosts and spirits. I have no indication of why Mary sent him the photograph but it was after the secret had been revealed, perhaps the Rev. Rees had written to Mary as he was interested in the whole Fiona Macleod phenomenon. Her wording is rather ambiguous – deliberately? Other than this little sentence I have been unable to find any other comment from Mary on her brother, Fiona or even her own part in this whole affair.

But back to Tarbert: Edith's affect on William clearly had not weakened any. During this time in Tarbert Fiona wrote a number of new and important pieces, several dealing with the plight of woman. These pieces, "*The Prayer of Women*," "*The Rune of the Passion of Woman*," "*The Rune of the Sorrow of Women*" and "*The Shepherd*" appeared in various publications and were eventually assembled together by Elizabeth in the Collected Works of Fiona Macleod where they appear under the heading "*From the Heart of a Woman*." Note Elizabeth's use of the indefinite article, missing from Fiona's titles. I wonder if she meant the 'heart of a woman' to be that of Fiona or Edith?

It is clear that Edith was aware of her affect on Fiona and was actively inspiring and encouraging her. She did not passively wait for Fiona to finish writing so she could have her lover back but consciously and knowingly encouraged the ongoing evolution and development of Fiona as a separate female being within William's male body and psyche. This was crucial and something William could never have achieved alone. He was not a woman and had therefore never felt or experienced first hand what it was like to be a woman. Fiona, being Faery, had never had a woman's body nor felt the human emotions of a woman either. She was in the same position as William. They both needed Edith's presence in order to learn, understand and subsequently express these issues so succinctly in their respective writings.

William wrote to Elizabeth from Tarbert on September 23rd 1896, saying, "*Two days ago I wrote the long-awaited 'Rune of the Passion of Woman', the companion piece in a sense to the 'Chant of Woman in Pharais – and have also done the Savoy story 'The Archer'… I am not built for mixed companies, and like them less and less in proportion as the imperative need of F.M. and W.S. for greater isolation grows. I realise more and more the literal truth of what George Meredith told me – that renunciation of ordinary social pleasures (namely of the ordinary kind in the ordinary way) is a necessity to any worker on the high levels: and unless I work that way I shall not work at all.*"[1] Three days later he wrote, "*… I went alone for an hour or so to revise what had stirred me so unspeakably, namely the third and concluding 'Rune of the Sorrow of Women.' This last Rune tired me in preliminary excitement and in the strange semi-conscious fever of composition more than anything of the kind since I wrote the first of the three in Pharais one night of storm when I was alone in Phenice Croft… In a vague way not only you, Mona, Edith and others swam into my brain, but I have never so absolutely felt the woman-soul within me: it was as though in some subtle way the soul of Woman breathed into my brain – and I feel vaguely as if I had given partial expression at least to the inarticulate voice of a myriad women who suffer in one or other of the triple ways of sorrow.*"[2]

While Fiona was developing and making quite an impression on the British Victorian public William Butler Yeats in Ireland was becoming increasingly interested in her and her writings but for a different reason. He had been working on a magical level for some time in an attempt to revive the ancient Celtic mysteries and to come up with a new Celtic Rite that would be relevant for the modern day. About the time Fiona was producing her mystical and spiritual interpretations of woman, Yeats and his friend and fellow writer Arthur Symons had a common mystical vision that Fiona would later imply she had shared. This was of great significance to him and encouraged him to believe they were psychically linked and were all playing an important role in the revealing of the Celtic Mysteries.

Yeats and Symons had gone to the Aran Islands in Galway Bay, Ireland, for three days on August 5th 1896. On return they visited their friend Edward Martyn at Tillyra Castle where they stayed for several days. During the eve-

*Mary Sharp*

ning or night of 14th August Yeats had a vision that he described in a letter to William thus, "*I invoked one night the spirits of the moon & saw between sleep & waking a beautiful woman firing an arrow among the stars. That night she appeared to Symons who is staying here, & so impressed him that he wrote a poem to her[3], the only one he ever wrote to a dream, calling her the fountain of all song or some such phrase. She was the symbolic Diana.*"[4] Diana is also connected with Lake Nemi, Fiona's birthplace. Yeats also sent a separate letter, now lost, to Fiona on other matters in which he repeated his description of this vision for her benefit. At this time he did not know that she and William were one and the same.

Many years later in his autobiography Yeats elaborated more on this vision when he said, "*I decided that it was there I must make my invocation of the moon. I made it night after night just before I went to bed, and after many nights – eight or nine perhaps – I saw between sleeping and waking… a galloping centaur, and a moment later a naked woman of incredible beauty, standing upon a pedestal and shooting an arrow at a star… Next morning… Arthur Symons [told me]… he had dreamt the night before of a woman of great beauty, but she was clothed and had not a bow and arrow. When he got back to London he found awaiting him… a story by Fiona Macleod and called,*

*I think, The Archer. Some one in the story had a vision of a woman shooting an arrow into the sky and later of an arrow shot at a faun... Some weeks later I too was in London, and found among Mathers' pupils a woman whose little child... had come running in from the garden calling out, 'Oh mother, I have seen a woman shooting an arrow into the sky and I am afraid that she has killed God.' I have... a letter from a very old friend describing how her little cousin – perhaps a few months later – dreamed of a man who shot at a star with a gun and that the star fell down, but 'I do not think,' said the child, 'it minded dying because it was so very old.' Had some great event taken place in some world where myth is reality and had we seen some portion of it?"* [5]

Yeats was so struck by his own vision and the fact that one of his magical associates had similar visions at the same time, that he mentioned it to Dr. Wynn Wescott, one of the founders of the Golden Dawn. Wescott listened to his description and then showed Yeats two drawings that related to magical grades higher than Yeats had attained while a member of that group and, therefore, he would not have previously seen. One was of a woman shooting arrows at a star and the other was of a centaur, both images that appeared in his vision. In the Golden Dawn system of magic these images relate to the Qabalistic sephiroth of Tiphareth and Yesod. Yesod is the moon, Tiphareth the sun and behind them are the stars. Another symbol of Tiphareth is the Holy Grail. At exactly the same time as these visions and symbols were being revealed to Yeats and Symons a Dr. John Arthur Goodchild, whom we shall meet in the next chapter, was also receiving visions and Otherworldly vocal instructions concerning an ancient glass bowl

*Inscription from the reverse side of photo of Mary*

that some would later claim to be the Holy Grail. Yeats was correct when he asked, *"Had some great event taken place in some world where myth is reality and had we seen some portion of it?"* We shall learn more of that great event soon.

Later Yeats and Symons learned that Fiona had also experienced a vision but hers was slightly different. In a letter to Yeats she said, *"I had a strange vision the other day, wherein I saw the figure of a gigantic woman sleeping on the green hills of Ireland. As I watched, the sun waned and the dark came and the stars began to fall. They fell one by one, and each fell into the woman – and lo, of a sudden, all was bare running water, and the drowned stars and the transmuted woman passed from my seeing. This was a waking dream, an open vision: but I do not know what it means, though it was so wonderfully vivid. In a vague way I realise that something of tremendous moment is being matured just now. We are on the verge of vitally important developments. And all the heart, all the brain, of the Celtic races shall be stirred. There is a shadow of mighty changes. Myself, I believe that new spirits have been embodied among us. And some of the old have come back."* [6]

Note that the last half of this statement echoes Yeats' ponderings on whether some great event had taken place. Keeping in mind that Fiona was Faery, what we have here is a first-hand account of a vision by a Faery occurring in the Faery realm. This opens up all sorts of questions and possibilities for those working on a magical level with Faery and, again, emphasises the importance of the Fiona Macleod writings for anyone wishing to broaden their knowledge of those realms. The last two sentences of this letter are important. Fiona, a Faery, is telling us that new spirits have been embodied among us. She was clearly one such embodied spirit but who were the others? Have we recognised them yet? Are they still among us? The reference to some of the old spirits having come back could be her first pointer towards the character she would call Dalua. Again, there must be others that we may yet need to identify. Once more, simultaneously, Dr. Goodchild was unconsciously picking up on all of this as the next chapter will show.

Was this a once-and-for-all opening between Faery and our world in which new and old spirits crossed the divide? Was it the first or just one of many? Have there been any more since then? Whatever the answers may be the important point is that Fiona made it clear that the desire to cross the divide <u>came from Faery</u>, not from our world. Today many people working with the Faery tradition see it as a one-way street – we have a desire to cross over and meet them but they remain static as far as coming to see us is concerned. Here it is clear that they, the Faeries, not only had the desire to cross over and meet with us but also the need to cross over and <u>live among us</u>. These were indeed important times, the ramifications of which are still being felt and discovered to this day.

Although the visions differ somewhat in detail they are all symbolically the same in that Yeats and Fiona both concluded they heralded something of great importance taking place within the Celtic Mysteries. There is an addendum to Yeats' story where he says that later he described the vision to a psychic friend in an attempt to find out what it meant, "*She went once more into her trance-like meditation and heard but a single unexplained sentence, 'There were three that saw; three will attain a wisdom older than the serpent, but the child will die.' Did this refer to myself, Arthur Symons, to Fiona Macleod, to the child who had feared that the archer had killed God?"* [7] Yeats never fully understood what this oblique sentence meant. It is possible though that the reference to the child that will die was a reference to Fiona Macleod. William often referred to her as their "child" and he totally believed that should the secret of her real identity be revealed she would die. It was not too many years after this event that William passed away, the secret was revealed and Fiona did indeed die.

Fiona used much of Yeats' vision as a basis for a similar visionary scene in the story called *"The Archer."* This short tale had started life many years before as *"The Last Phantasy of James Achanna"* and preceded Fiona's first published book *"Pharais."* Fiona had offered it to the *Scots Observer* who declined to publish it but returned it with such a complimentary letter that Fiona, in deference to their kind words, decided never to offer it for publication to anyone else. [8] In the original version the story ends with the death of one of the male characters but with no mention of an archer or stars. However when it eventually appeared in *"Re-issue of the Shorter Tales of Fiona Macleod, Rearranged with Additional Tales"* (Patrick Geddes, 1897) it had been extended to include the same character having visions just before he dies of an arrow being shot at a fawn whose heart is ripped out and pinned to a silver birch tree, and a vision of a female archer shooting arrows at the stars. This was the version Yeats read some months after his August vision. He was convinced that Fiona had written the complete tale before she received his letter to her (and William) outlining his vision. If this was the case then this apparently synchronistic event of Fiona having the same vision at the same time but in another place meant a very great deal to him. He was looking for other psychic and sympathetic people to join him in setting up his Celtic Mysteries and here was clear proof that Fiona Macleod was just such a person. The truth of the matter is that none of this was as synchronistic and spontaneous as Yeats believed.

Fiona had written the original version of the story at least two years before this incident and had made alterations to it while on holiday that year in Tarbert with no mention of an archer. While still in Tarbert, and after she had completed her story, she received Yeats' letter describing his archer vision in August 1896. It was only then, after she had read his letters to her and William, she renamed her story *"The Archer"* and added the final part with the fawn and the woman shooting arrows into the sky. This is the version that was eventually published in *"The Dominion of Dreams."* William mentioned this in the letter to Elizabeth, quoted above, *"I have also done the Savoy story 'The Archer'..."* This letter is dated September 23rd 1896, some weeks after receiving Yeats' account of his vision. When he said he had 'done' it he meant added the final archer incident that was not in the original story completed some time earlier. This is not just another example of Fiona taking someone else's work and adapting it to her own ends for artistic purposes, such plagiarism is bad enough, but this was more. It was a deliberate act of deception. She wished to impress Yeats as to her psychic abilities in order to get closer to him and to work with him on a magical level and by successfully convincing him that they were psychically attuned she succeeded in this. In so doing she bolstered his belief in not only her psychic prowess but also the fact that he was on the right track magically and was clearly working with competent comrades who could help him along the magical way. Happily the effect of all this turned out to be very positive in that Yeats, Symons, William, Fiona et al did go on to produce some groundbreaking magical work. A substantial amount of important writings evolved from all of this and Fiona achieved her goal of being accepted by this group of literary and magical allies and Yeats was encouraged to push on with his goal of recreating the ancient Celtic Rites.

However the real driving force behind this deception was not Fiona but was William. Note that in the letter of September 23rd he says "he", not Fiona, had finished *The Archer* story. He needed to impress Yeats and the others more than Fiona did but for different reasons. William's motive for constructing an archer vision was not deceptive but was to bring forward the inevitable and the necessary – that he, Fiona and Yeats should start to work together magically as soon as possible. But what was more important to him right then was the unhappy realisation that his own literary work was being ignored in favour of the new literary work under the pen of Fiona Macleod. He was, in short, jealous of Fiona's greater literary ability and the fact that Yeats wanted to work with Fiona, not him. At the time this whole archer vision affair was playing out William employed another deceptive device – he implied to Yeats that although there was a real woman called Fiona Macleod who put pen to paper, it was he who was the inspiration and creator of all that she actually wrote. This was the only way he could convince Yeats that he too was worthy of consideration without revealing the real truth regarding Fiona. Yeats accepted this – he had no reason not to - and from then on treated Fiona and William as equals. The fact that it was William who instigated the whole archer vision deception was made clear many years later when William (not Fiona) showed some signs of guilt and remorse when the story came up for republication. In this revised version he removed the whole fawn and archer section and restored the story to its original form. As a piece of literature it is stronger without the final visions. With this revision the previous title of *The Archer* did not make any sense so he changed the title again and it became "*Silis,*" the name of the central female character in the story. This name in Gaelic means 'tear-drop.'

Putting aside magical co-workers and deceptions for a moment it is interesting that Fiona chose to add Yeats' archer vision onto this particular story. It could as easily have been appended to almost any other of her short stories from that time or been woven into an entirely new essay. If we look at the plot of her original story we may find a clue as to why Fiona and William felt this one to be so relevant. The tale involves two fisher friends, one of whom is married to the woman Silis whom he loves. The husband discovers his friend is in love with her too. They agree that only Silis can decide who she wishes to be with and they ask her to choose. She chooses her husband although she is really in love with the other man. It is the rejected lover who has the vision of the fawn and the female archer and eventually dies. This story is semi-autobiographical with the two men being William and Frank Rinder and Silis being Edith, whom William believed loved him but who chose to remain faithful to her husband only because of the social attitudes of the day. At this time Yeats did not know that William was the author of all the Fiona Macleod stories or that he was so romantically involved with a married woman, so he would have interpreted the story differently and from his own perspective. He would have persoanlly related to the rejected lover in the story because the object of his own desires, Maud Gonne, had rejected him as a lover and in Fiona's story it was the rejected lover who had the archer vision, just as he had. This would have served to further strengthen his belief that Fiona was a powerful magical ally. Here was more evidence that she was intuitively expressing in her stories the things that were utmost in his mind at this juncture, not only his archer vision, but Maud Gonne's rejection of him as a lover. How else could she have known all this other than through a psychic link and a powerful intuitive bond between them?

Fiona may not have felt guilty about usurping Yeats' vision but she certainly managed to avoid answering in detail any questions about her own alleged visionary experience. When Yeats asked her in a letter for more information about this she replied, *"Alas, a long pencilled note (partly apropos of your vision of the woman shooting arrows, and of the strange coincidence of something of that kind on my own part) has long since been devoured by a too voracious or too trustful gull – for a sudden gust of wind blew the quarto-sheet from off the deck of the small yacht wherein I and my dear friend and confrere of whom you know were sailing, off Skye."* [9] How convenient!

Whether the trio of Yeats, Symons and Fiona did or did not share a common vision does not matter. Its effect was to confirm to them that they were on the right track together and to inspire them to new efforts in their goal of revealing the Celtic Mysteries through their public writings and in seeking deeper occult and mystical knowledge through their private magical studies and experimentation. It does though show that once again the understanding of what is right and acceptable to the Faeries is far different in many instances from our standards of acceptability. To us it is bad enough to steal someone's idea and incorporate it into a book and claim it as your own, but to then maintain the falsehood of having shared an event that was clearly important to this same person, when in fact you did not, is unacceptable. It must be said Yeats does seem to have shown a remarkable eagerness to <u>want</u> to believe that they all shared the vision. It would have been easy for him to check his dates, correspondence and so forth and realise that Fiona <u>had</u> received his letters prior to changing the ending of *"The Archer."* But he didn't, thankfully. Instead he allowed his trust in Fiona to strengthen and to turn to her for advice and comment on his own progress in the magical arts.

A personal aside: I finished writing the above section on the archer vision in February 2008. The day that I decided it was 'good enough to go' happened to be the day of a full Lunar eclipse. I closed down my computer and took a walk in the cold evening air to view the darkening of the moon. It was spectacular. The moon was in the east and as it lost its light I turned westward to see if the stars were now more visible. I gazed at the glittering points of light and I noticed one that was moving fairly rapidly across the sky. I remembered that day on the radio there had been much talk of an American spy satellite that was slowly falling back to Earth and that it would be visible that night, this was clearly it. I watched for some ten seconds or so and then it suddenly vanished, totally disappeared, yet the sky was cloudless and the object had been very bright. Next morning I learned that the US Navy had successfully shot down the rogue satellite with a missile fired from a ship in the Pacific. I immediately thought of the child who had dreamed of a man shooting at a star with a gun and it had fallen from the sky. My written thoughts and comments on the archer vision had been concluded by my own visual experience of exactly the same phenomenon.

Yeats shared this whole episode with Maud Gonne and both of them looked forward eagerly to each of Fiona's new publications. They both had the knowledge to read between the lines of her work and glean a great deal from it. In one letter to Yeats on June 24th 1899 Maud expressed concern that Fiona's writings were perhaps revealing too much of the occult nature of the Celtic Mysteries when she said, "*Thank you so much for Fiona's book. I wonder is she right to even thus far give to the world the sacred symbols?*" [10] The book in question was "*The Dominion of Dreams*" (May 1899, Messrs. A. Constable & Co.) in which the longer version of "*The Archer*" appeared. The book initially does not appear to reveal anything of sacred symbols, unless, that is, you learn to read it from a Faery perspective, then it starts to reveal much. In the Epilogue to this book Fiona herself comments on this subject, "*Symbols: yes. To some, foolish; to others clear as the noon, the clearness that is absolute light, that is so obvious, and is unfathomable.*" [11] Several of the tales in this book centre on the character Dalua. He is a god from the mythology of the Faeries and a rather shadowy, sinister one at that. Maud was right in her desire for caution not to reveal too much, at least as far as Dalua is concerned. See Appendix 4 for more on Dalua.

It is important to remember when dealing with all this that the present day plethora of magical and mystical books explaining in great detail the nuts and bolts and practical workings of any magical system you care to study were not available at the end of the 19th century. The few books that were available were couched in such heavy symbolism and allusion they were virtually impossible to decipher without an already substantial amount of background knowledge. Fiona's writings <u>do</u> reveal an enormous amount of practical and effective information for those who can open their hearts and souls to the beauty, mystery and wonder of the place where she lived, the realm of Faery. Yeats and Fiona were right in that great mysteries were being revealed, and continue to be revealed, and we today are enjoying the fruits of the seeds that were planted well over a century ago.

Although Yeats was now convinced that Fiona was capable of visions and linking psychically with him he was still not sure of William's prowess in these matters despite William's claim to be the inspiration behind all that Fiona wrote. When they met in Paris after the archer vision episode Yeats put William, unknowingly, to a psychic test. Yeats later recounted this incident as, "*When he stood up to go he said, 'What is that?' pointing to a geometrical form painted upon a little piece of cardboard that lay upon my window-sill. And then before I could answer, looked out of the window saying, 'There is a funeral passing.' I said, 'That is curious, as the Death symbol is painted on the card.' I did not look, but I am sure there was no funeral. A few days later he came back and said, 'I have been very ill; you must never allow me to see that symbol again.' He did not seem anxious to be questioned.*" [12] Unpleasant as it had been, William had passed the test. Yeats made quite a habit of giving his friends unknown psychic tests and he would test William again in an equally furtive manner some time later.

After leaving Tarbert in the summer of 1896 William went back to London to rejoin Elizabeth. She notes that, "*No sooner had W.S. returned to London than he fell ill with nervous prostration, and rheumatism. It was soon obvious that he could not remain in town, and that for a short time at any rate he must cease from pen-work.*" [13] This is one more example of William being in good health and spirits and writing freely as Fiona when away from Elizabeth but immediately on returning to her his health breaks down again and he cannot write. They decided that he needed to go to New York to attend to business matters. The American publishers of Fiona's books, Messrs. Stone & Kimball, had failed and there was quite a complicated mess to sort out. Plus he would take the opportunity while in the States to look up old friends and make new acquaintances in the literary world. He arrived in New York on Hallowe'en, his wedding anniversary, and the start of the Celtic New Year, and also right in the middle of U.S. election fever. Two million people had come to the city to watch an enormous political rally and parade, the passing of which took seven hours. This must have been challenging to William who hated cities and especially crowded cities. While on his visit to New York, Fiona's story "Green Fire" was published in Britain. This is an unusual story for Fiona in that much of it is set in Brittany. Edith published much material taken from Breton sources; perhaps she influenced Fiona in this area too. The structure and handling of it differ from Fiona's usual style. Later William acknowledged it was not Fiona's best work and he left specific instructions with Elizabeth that after his death he did not want "Green Fire" to be reprinted, at least not in its entirety.

The problem with *"Green Fire"* is that it was an experimental collaboration between William and Fiona – and it did not work. He may have felt inspired to try such a joint venture with Fiona following the success of his collaboration with Blanche Willis Howard on *"A Fellowe and His Wife"* but writing jointly with Fiona turned out to be a very different situation. The plot and characters are all from William's mind but the main impetus for the story in the first place was from Fiona. The descriptive passages, particularly those describing the Green World, which were Fiona's forte, were a joint effort between the two writers and the beauty and flowing style of Fiona is not there. This attempt at partnership was a deliberate experiment on the part of both Fiona and William to see how well, if at all, they could work together. The result showed that, at best, they could only produce mediocre work and the experiment was never repeated. Yeats, however, found parts of *"Green Fire"* interesting and wrote to Fiona to tell her so. He also wrote to his friend George Russell about the book and this in turn prompted Russell to write to Fiona. From the contents of his letter it is clear that both he and Yeats were looking to involve her in a serious magical Order working on the ancient Celtic rites, *"He* [Yeats] *talked much of reviving the Druidic mysteries and vaguely spoke of Scotland and you… Some time when the power falls on me I'll send a shadow of myself over seas just to get the feeling of the Highlands. I have an intuition that the 'fires' are awakening somewhere in the North West. I may have met you indeed and not known you. We are so different behind the veil… And if I saw you your inner being might assume some old Druidic garb of the soul, taking that form because you are thinking the Druidic thought… I sat beside a friend and while he was meditating, the inner being started up in Egyptian splendour robed in purple and gold… I write to you of these things… that your inner nature preserves the memory of old initiations, so I talk to you as a comrade on the quest. You know too I think that these alluring visions and thoughts are of little import unless they link themselves unto our humanity. It means only madness in the end."* [14] The last two sentences are important. Russell got it right when he said that all magical work must have as its ultimate goal a beneficial change to the human realm. Without such an earthing (literally) of power it is pointless and brings only illusion and delusion.

These early contacts from Yeats and Russell must have been encouraging to William and Fiona, not only to be recognised by two of the literary luminaries of the day but also two who were seriously attempting to revive the neglected Celtic mysteries and develop a working magical and spiritual system. Unfortunately Yeats and Russell's initial enthusiasm for Fiona and her writings did not last and the final years of the 19th century and the first few years of the 20th century were spent in sometimes bitter acrimony and accusations between them and Fiona.

It is likely that in May of 1897 William divulged more of the secret of Fiona to Yeats, at least in part. He had already claimed collaboration with Fiona after the archer vision episode but now he was more specific and elaborated on this by telling Yeats that the Fiona name was indeed a pseudonym but not his own. It was to conceal the identity of a woman of great beauty with whom he was in love and with whom he was collaborating on all of the Fiona Macleod writings. This was true as far as it went. He was in love with a woman of great beauty, and she may or may not have collaborated with him, but she certainly did inspire Fiona Macleod. From 1897 onwards it is noticeable that Yeats would often enclose the name Fiona Macleod in quotation marks whenever he wrote of her in private correspondence.

William's reason for this further revelation was an attempt to impress again upon Yeats that he was the true creator of all the Fiona Macleod writings that Yeats found so inspiring and of such great beauty and value to his own spiritual and magical work. William was conscious of becoming completely overshadowed by the public reaction to Fiona as his own importance and status as a writer diminished rapidly. He was trapped. He could not come out and say to the public at large that he was Fiona Macleod and enjoy the adulation he so craved because he knew to do so would result in the death of Fiona but nonetheless he needed some sort of recognition for his substantial input. By at least telling Yeats that yes, the pieces were all written by a real woman, but under his guidance and with his collaboration, would be enough to impress this important figure in his literary and magical life. William had sworn Yeats to secrecy on this matter and he later also revealed the truth to George Russell. From then on in their own correspondence to each other Yeats and Russell would often refer to "*MacSharp*" whenever they talked of either Fiona or William.

As well as working magically on the Celtic mysteries Yeats and Russell were both involved in Irish politics and were very concerned about Irish social and political reform. In the case of Yeats however this was done more to please Maud than from personal motivation. The big problem they faced when dealing with Fiona, whoever she happened to be, was that it soon became clear to them she was not political enough, not Celtic enough and not grounded enough to fit in with their needs and expectations. It is understandable that they would see her this way as they were still working on the assumption that she was a living, breathing human being. However because her true nature was Faery, the ideals of the politics and culture of this world meant nothing to her. She was incapable of understanding such things. By way of compromise to her Scottishness it had been agreed at an early stage that all references to their magical work would be that it was Celtic, not specifically Irish. In reality though it was Celtic in name only and completely Irish in content. This did not cause any problems for Fiona but the fact she rarely referred to anything of a political nature, Irish or Scottish, in her public writings and in her private correspondence started to irritate the Irish members of the Celtic mystery group, including Maud Gonne and even MacGregor Mathers with his pseudo-Scottishness.

Throughout his life William commented about the political and military situations in Turkey, France, Russia and so forth. He even contemplated joining some of these foreign armies to fight against the injustices he saw being carried out in these regions, a ridiculous concept considering his chronic poor health. Yet he and Fiona made very few references to the starvation caused by the potato blight in Ireland and Scotland or to the on-going injustices and barbarity of the Highland Clearances that were occurring in the very places Fiona so often claimed to be travelling through. Many of the cleared Highlanders were being forced to move to the slums of Glasgow and to work in the dreadful manufactories. Fiona did touch on this obliquely in a letter of June 8th 1899 to her friend John Macleay, *"Yet, on the face of it, there must surely be more likelihood of spiritual beauty where life is attuned to the great natural influences and where simple natures have more depth and scope. There is moral and spiritual beauty in the slums – but not the same in degree, I suppose: at any rate, we have overmuch literature pointing out all this in slum-life and the like – a little pharasaically it seems to me."* [15]

In her tale *"The Anointed Man"* the character Alison Achanna has been touched by the Faeries and can now only see beauty no matter where he is or what he is gazing upon. As they walk along they pass a field where the potato crop has failed and the putrid remains of the plants cover the ground but Alison can only comment on how beautiful it is. His father eventually gets so angry with him that he sends him to *" ... the towns, and see there the squalor and sordid hideousness wherein men dwelled. But thus it was with me: in the places they call slums, and among the smoke of factories, and the grime of destitution, I could see all that other men saw, only as vanishing shadows. What I saw was lovely, beautiful with strange glory, and the faces of men and women were sweet and pure, and their souls were white."* [16] Note that in the original version of this story, as given in *"The Sin-Eater,"* the Anointed Man is called Alison but in all subsequent reprintings of the tale his name is given as Alasdair. *"The Sin-Eater"* was dedicated to the writer George Meredith, who Fiona described as *"The Prince of Celtdom"* and he once told her that he read this story of Alison Achanna almost every day. [17]

She did touch upon this subject one other time in more detail in the essay *"The Four Winds of Eirinn,"* where she said, *"Can any Gael honestly say that Ireland, that the Highlands, that the Isles are in the deep sense nearer true wellbeing now than they were half a century ago, twenty years ago, ten years ago? Depopulation, the decay of the old language, ... the cancer of racial hatred in Ireland, the levelling and crushing curse of a growing materialism in Scotland; the paralysing selfishness of both native and alien landowners ... has made, and is making, the passing of the old order bitter and tragic ... If I and others of my generation feel this, how much more must those who feel it whose memories go far back; who remember the homeless glens, when the smoke of many hearths rose in peace; the deer-forests, where the hillside crofts held a contented people; the islands where now the flocks of the capitalist sheep-farmer are the only inhabitants?"* [18] Although these comments are strong and heartfelt they are but a tiny fraction of the total written corpus of both William and Fiona, especially compared to the very vocal and literary outpourings of the Irish activists of the day on the same subjects. Considering their context they also convey a sense of not coming purely from her heart but rather of being added in for the sole purpose of bowing to the pressures of her more militant Irish colleagues to make some political statement or other. They also come from a relatively late date, 1903, by which time Faery Fiona had become more sensitive to the passions and concerns of her human friends and colleagues.

---

[1] Memoir, page 267

[2] Memoir, page 267

[3] Symons' poem is entitled "To a Woman Seen in Sleep" published in 1923 in the collection "Love's Cruelty"

[4] Yeats Annual, Vol 13, page 78-79

[5] William Butler Yeats Autobiography, page 248

[6] Memoir, page 272

[7] William Butler Yeats Autobiography, page 249

[8] Rea, "Fiona Macleod", "The Critic", May 1906, page 461

[9] Memoir, page 270

[10] Jeffares, The Gonne-Yeats Letters, page 108

[11] "The Dominion of Dreams", page 320

[12] William Butler Yeats Autobiography, pages 227

[13] Memoir, page 272

[14] Memoir, page 277

[15] NLS, Edinburgh

[16] Collected Works of Fiona Macleod, Vol. 3, page 297

[17] Rea, "Fiona Macleod", "The Critic", May 1906, page 462

[18] "Fortnightly Review", February 190

# Chapter 8
# The Celtic Mystical Order and More Secrets

*'Never more,' he told us, 'would he tamper with certain forces, for such tampering might mean destruction.'*

There was a long period from the late 1890s up until 1901 when William, Yeats, Russell, Mathers and others got together whenever they could, wrote, swapped ideas, occasionally smoked hashish, took mescaline, and carried out various magical rites and ceremonies. Although Fiona was often invited to the Paris gatherings she always managed to excuse herself either by claiming ill health or that she was travelling. For example, in a letter to Lady Gregory from Paris dated April 25th 1898, Yeats said, *"I am buried in Celtic mythology and shall be for a couple of weeks or so. Miss Gonne has been ill with bronchitis. One of her lungs is affected a little so that she has to rest. She is unable to do any politics for the time and looks ill and tired. She comes here tomorrow to see visions. Fiona Macleod (this is private as she is curiously secret about her movements) talks of coming here too, so we will have a great Celtic gathering."*

Despite her necessary non-appearance she did stay in regular touch, mainly with Yeats, by frequent and lengthy letters. In a letter to Fiona, Yeats said, *"I have just finished a certain speech in 'The Shadowy Waters', my new poem, ... I think it would be very possible to get up Celtic plays ... they would be far more effective than lectures and might do more than anything else we can do to make Irish, Scotch and other Celts recognise their solidarity ... If we have one or two short, direct prose plays, of (say) a mythological and folklore kind, by you and by some writer ... I feel sure we could get the Irish Literary Society to make a start."* [1] This makes it clear that he was keen to collaborate with Fiona and had realised the power of visual imagery in the form of stage plays to influence a mass audience. Fiona would take up this idea but not for some time. Her play *"The Immortal Hour"* would incorporate many of Yeats' ideas and suggestions and would become extremely influential later in operatic form. Unfortunately this very play, motivated in part by Yeats' comments, was a

167

contributing factor in the split between the Irish school and Fiona when Yeats and Lady Gregory rejected it from being staged in the Irish theatre, not because it was too Scottish or not sufficiently Irish but because both of them believed it frankly plagiarized Yeats' "*The Shadowy Waters*."[2] There may be some truth in this but see Appendix 3 for a full discussion on "*The Immortal Hour*."

Differences in political points of view had first become obvious back in 1896 by comments William had made in the compendium of Celtic poetry "*Lyra Celtica*." Here William did not express any political or social comments as such but did ruffle many Celtic feathers by saying that these Celtic writers were, basically, English. Part of this commentary says, "*It is noteworthy that the two most convincingly poetic of all our younger poets... are predominantly Celtic; W.B. Yeats and John Davidson – and noteworthy, also, that both are too wise, too clear-sighted, too poetic, in fact, to aim at being Irish or Scoto-Celtic at the expense of being English in the high and best sense of the word... In the world of literature there is no geography save that of the mind.*"[3] Fiona would repeat this assertion several times over the next few years, particularly in an article in the "*Contemporary Review*" of 1900 called "*Celtic: An Essay*." What William and Fiona were trying to say was that the poetry was in the English language therefore it had to be considered as English poetry. Technically they are right but their naivety is surprising considering that it was this very point, the perceived anglicisation of everything Celtic in the native Celtic countries by the in-coming English, that these other poets were fighting so strongly against. Perhaps Fiona can be excused considering her Faery origin and outlook but William could plainly see the offence and hurt he was causing to his own friends and comrades by continuing with the insistence it was all English and, anyway, what did it matter. This attitude verges on smugness and an attitude of 'I'm right and you're all wrong.'

This subject was brought up again and again over the next few years and it weighed on Fiona's mind. She dealt with it as late as 1901 in "*The Winged Destiny*" where she set out very clearly her view that, "*I am not English, and have not the English mind or the English temper, and in many things do not share the English ideals; and to possess these would mean to relinquish my own heritage. But why should I be irreconcilably hostile to that mind and that temper and those ideals? Why should I not do my utmost to understand, sympathise, fall into line with them so far as may be, since we all have a common bond and a common destiny? To that mind and that temper and to those ideals do we not owe some of the noblest achievements of the human race, some of the lordliest conquests over the instincts and forces of barbarism, some of the loveliest and most deathless things of the spirit and the imagination?*"[4]

William's magical work with Yeats and others over 1896-97 was so much a part of his daily life that despite her reticence Elizabeth had to mention it, albeit briefly, in her memoir. All she said was, "*The prolonged strain of the heavy dual work added to by an eager experimentation with certain psychic*

*phenomenon with which he had long been familiar but wished further to inves-*
*tigate, efforts in which at times he and Mr. W.B. Yeats collaborated – began to tell*
*heavily on him, and to produce very disquieting symptoms of nervous collapse.*
*We decided therefore that he should pass… December and January in the South*
*of France."* [5] So in December of 1896 he made the journey to Provence to
stay with the Janviers. Years later Catharine Janvier recalled, "*While with us*
*strange moods possessed him; and, perhaps because of these, strange things hap-*
*pened. At times it was as though he struggled against an evil influence; was forc-*
*ing back a dark tide ever threatening to overwhelm his soul. Warring pressures*
*were about him, he thought; and he believed that these must be conquered even*
*at the risk of life. The culminating struggle came, and through one winter night*
*my husband watched over him as he battled against some unseen but not unfelt*
*influence. The fight was won, the dark tide stemmed, but at great cost of vitality,*
*his victory leaving him faint and exhausted. 'Never more,' he told us, 'would he*
*tamper with certain forces, for such tampering might mean destruction.' "* [6]

However the decision was no longer his and, as subsequent events
proved, Fiona would not let him rest magically. Despite this close call on the
magical front, once he was home from Provence, he immediately fell back
into his experimentations. Elizabeth claims that his only diary entry for the
whole of 1897 was one brief entry for January 1st. We have to take her word
for it but I am sure he kept careful notes of all his magical work that year,
none of which she deemed suitable for inclusion in her memoir.

There was a basic and fundamental difference between Fiona and William's needs for magical practice that needs to be recognised in order to understand why William carried on experimenting despite the negative effect it
had on his health. William was <u>seeking</u> a system of magical progression and
development, whether it be through the Golden Dawn or the Celtic Mystical Order, which required a great deal of active effort and energy on his part.
Fiona, on the other hand, was not seeking anything – she <u>already knew</u> her
magical system, her indigenous Faery tradition. Her struggle was much more
passive and much less energy consuming. Her main problem was not in coming to an understanding of the Faery tradition but rather how to lay it out in
her writings in a way that others could read and understand. These two totally
different approaches to the study and use of magic were what caused most of
William's difficulties when attempting any practical magical work.

This though brought with it another problem that became more and
more noticeable as they both progressed along their divergent magical ways.
This was William's difficulty in separating out who was William and who
was Fiona, and what was a real event and what was a magical event. This was
exacerbated by his already sensitive psychic state and on several occasions
it became heightened to a dangerous level. Many years later Yeats recalled
one such incident from the time he and William were working magically
in Paris. William described the incident to Yeats as, "*I had two rooms at my*
*hotel… As I passed the threshold of the sitting room, I saw a woman standing by*

*the bureau, writing, and presently she went into my bedroom... when I went to the bureau I saw the sheet of paper she had seemed to write upon, and there was no writing on it. I went into my bedroom and found nobody... I went down the stairs to see if she had gone that way. When I got out into the street I saw her just turning a corner, but when I turned the corner there was nobody there, and then I saw her at another corner. Constantly seeing and losing her like that I followed till I came to the Seine, and there I saw her standing at an opening in the wall, looking down into the river. Then she vanished, and I cannot tell why, but I went to the opening in the wall and stood there, just as she had stood, taking just the same attitude. Then I thought I was in Scotland and that I heard a sheep-bell. After that I must have lost consciousness, for I knew nothing till I found myself lying on my back, dripping wet, and people standing all around. I had thrown myself into the Seine."* [7] Yeats did not believe this story, partly because by that time he had heard many fantastic tales from William. It is interesting that William would imagine the woman in his hotel room, where Edith would normally be although she was not with him on this trip, and that the whole episode ended in a near-drowning incident; water, death and drowning all being strong Fiona themes.

Ignoring the confusion and dangers, he continued with his magical experiments and explorations on return to England, but, as always, he was pushing himself too far too quickly and the effects of this concentrated magical working eventually necessitated yet another spell of recuperation away from writing and magic. He returned to France but avoided Paris and instead went south where he travelled and stayed for a while once more with Catharine Janvier. She gave a nice little vignette of this time that describes a much more, relaxed, composed and peaceful William Sharp from the one she described during his earlier visit. She said, *"There was an interest in watching, as sometimes we could do, the growth of a Fiona Story. In Saint-Remy, during his visits to us there, Mr. Sharp wrote and read to us some of Fiona's work... He was fond of working in the open air; and, when the mood seized him, he would sit for hours just outside of the cottage (which had no garden in front), with people passing to and fro, calmly writing—generally with pencil—on a pad of green or of blue paper. Should one of us approach him, either a restraining hand repelled us, or he beckoned us to come near. When his writing was finished, we listened to the Fiona tale or poem or essay. We women commonly had little to say except in praise, but the two men often wrangled hotly over word or form of sentence... Yet the true Fiona mood or inspiration could not be compelled. It was a wind of the spirit that came and went as it listed."* [8]

The period of rest and recuperation was beneficial physically. This brought with it a rekindling of his passion for Edith and this in turn brought about a new vitality and optimism that had been absent for some time. Early in 1897 he wrote to Stedman, *"I have very happily relapsed into my Pagan ship, and the Sunbeam flies again at the peak. My mate in this delectable craft smiled at my attempt, and now laughs joyously that I am myself once again... Two days ago I was by the sea, with F.M. In mind and body I am ten years younger, with that joy and delight."* [9]

By April he was finishing his recuperation in St. Margaret's Bay, England and Elizabeth went to Paris to review the Salons. From there it was her turn to stay with the Janviers in St. Remy before returning to England. Her birthday fell during her time away from William and she records, *"On the early morning of 17ᵗʰ of May the waiter brought me my coffee and my letters to my room as usual, and told me gravely that a large packet had arrived for me, during the night, with orders it should not be delivered to me till the morning. Should it be brought up the stairs? The next moment the door was pushed open and in came the radiant smiling unexpected apparition of my Poet! In a little town an event of this sort is soon known by everyone, and that evening when he and I went for a walk, we found we were watched for and greeted by everyone, and heads were popped out of windows just to see 'les amants'."* [10] Despite his ill health and at times seemingly thoughtless treatment of Elizabeth he did on occasion show a much softer, loving and tender side to his wife.

Fiona also took on a more relaxed attitude early in 1897 as reflected in her private correspondence. Although she rarely gave away anything of herself, even in private communications, she did 'let her guard down' more than normal that year. On April 9ᵗʰ 1897 she wrote to an American correspondent, *"There are some writers who dwell apart in every sense of the word: and I am one of these... even those who know me say that I am a survival from a remote past, and not a proper modern at all. This is not quite true, for I believe in one intensity of emotion above all others, namely the intensity of this brief flame of life in the heart and brain, an intensity no one can have who does not account the hours of every day as the vanishing pawns in that tragic game of chess for ever being played between Time and Eternity. All the same, I have ever mentally been impassioned for the past and so it is that I find myself, both in the inner and outer life, much aloof from my fellows. I find in the close and intimate communion with nature, which is so much more possible away from towns—and I live truly only when I am in the remote isles or the mountains of Argyll—a solace and inspiration which come to me much attenuated through the human medium. Perhaps this is because, though young in years, I have a capacity for sorrow and regret which has come to me through my Celtic ancestry out of a remote lost world: because, indeed, I have myself walked the blind way between Joy and Sorrow and been led now by one now by the other. But do not think I am a melancholy person. I am not, in the ordinary sense. I am young and life has given me some of her rarest gifts, and I am grateful: and, when my hour comes, shall be ready, having lived. Not even in my vision of life am I melancholy. All the same, I am, as you discern, saturated with the gloom and strangeness of life from one vital point of view: and am ever aware of the menace of the perpetual fugitive shadow of Destiny. It is summed up in a dream I had once, lying among the grassy dunes in Iona: a dream wherein I heard a voice saying in Gaelic that the three Dominions or Powers were "The Living God, the Dying World, and the mysterious race of Man", and that behind each gleamed the shadowy eyes of Destiny.* "[11] This letter contains some of the very few references Fiona ever made to her age, twice she states that she is young, a subject that she rarely broached anywhere else. The little quotation from her visionary voice heard on Iona contains a great deal of Faery lore that would repay deep meditation. Her careful choice of words is significant.

However despite William and Fiona's joint relaxed demeanor at this time, William was having difficulty differentiating between his own thoughts and personality and those of Fiona. To complicate matters further, it was becoming clear that a third, composite being was emerging. In acknowledgement of this he adopted the habit of signing letters to his close friends who knew the secret "*Wilfion*," a composite name made from William and Fiona. In a letter to Elizabeth he said, "*I am longing to be regularly at work again – and now feel as if at last I can do so ... More and more absolutely, in one sense, are W.S. and F.M. becoming two persons – often married in mind and one nature, but often absolutely distinct. I am filled with a passion of dream and work ... Friendship, deepening into serene and beautiful flame, is one of the most ennobling and lovely influences the world has ... Wilfion*" [12] and later he revealed a little of his inner communion with Fiona when he said, " *'Where God is, there is Light,' it is one of the three Spiritual Moralities of which you know two already, 'The Fisher of Men' and 'The Last Supper.' In another way, the same profound truth is emphasised as in the other two – that Love is the basic law of spiritual life. 'The Redeemer liveth' in these three: Compassion, Beauty, Love – the three chords on which these three harmonies of Fiona's inner life have been born ...* " [13] The stories "*The Fisher of Men*" and "*The Last Supper*" can be found in "*The Washer of the Ford*" and in the Collected Works Vol.2. As the names imply they are based on the life of the Christ but are set in the Highlands and Islands. "*The Fisher of Men*" concerns an old lady who meets Christ and shortly thereafter peacefully passes away. "*The Last Supper*" is a particularly evocative short story with the Last Supper being witnessed by a young boy who sees more than is told in the Biblical version. The handwritten manuscript for this piece has very few changes or corrections in it whereas nearly all the other extant Fiona Macleod manuscripts show extensive revisions and rewriting. It clearly came to her ready made and needed little revision or change. Yeats was impressed by this short story and suggested to her it could be adapted into a play for the new theatre they hoped to open in Ireland although nothing ever came of this suggestion.

In the summer of 1897 William made his first visit to Ireland where he met the more important Irish writers and visionaries of the day including George Russell, Standish O'Grady, Dr. Douglas Hyde, Lady Gregory and Edward Martyn. He stayed for a while at Tillyra Castle, the place where Yeats and Symons had had their archer vision experiences. In her diary for September 1897 Lady Gregory wrote of her first encounter with, "*William Sharp, an absurd object, in velvet coat, curled hair, wonderful ties – a good na-*

*tured creature – a sort of professional patron of poets – but making himself ridiculous by stories to the men of his love affairs & entanglements, & seeing visions (instigated by Yeats) – one apparition clasped him to an elm tree from which he had to be released."* [14] After William's death Yeats would recall this meeting slightly differently when he touchingly said that he, *" ... never properly used or valued him. I allowed the sense of comedy, taken by contagion from others, to hide from me my own knowledge. To look at his big body, his high colour, his handsome head with the great crop of bristly hair, no one could have divined the ceaseless presence of the fluidic life."* He also gave a specific example of the visions he instigated mentioned by Lady Gregory. He would say to himself, *"When we come to the third bush, ... a red spirit will rush out of it."* And when they got to the third bush William declared, *"Some red thing has come out of the bush."* He related the elm tree incident as well, *"I once took him to a faery rath and evoked, but when I tried to speak to him I got no answer. He was entranced with his arm around a great elm tree. When he awoke he declared that his soul had flowed in the sap through the elm."* [15] Yeats never felt he was as capable of visionary work as the others he worked with magically and this led him to constantly challenge and test information and people. His test of William in Paris with the Death Card and now in Ireland with the vision of the red spirit are just two examples of his need to confirm and evaluate.

William was in his element and enjoying every moment of his Irish explorations. His euphoria though brought with it a certain lack of caution and indiscretion. Yeats recalled one of the ridiculous stories of his love affairs of which Lady Gregory clearly disapproved. He must have raised a few eyebrows with this tale that he told to the assembled Irish gentlemen, as recalled by Yeats, *"He had been somewhere abroad when he saw the sidereal body of Fiona enter the room as a beautiful young man, and became aware that he was a woman to the spiritual sight. She lay with him, he said, as a man with a woman, and for days afterwards his breast swelled so that he had almost the physical likeness of a woman."* [16]

He travelled extensively along the western coast of Ireland and may have visited the Aran Islands. In letters back to Elizabeth he frequently mentioned meeting local people who had regular encounters with the Faeries, who recognised drawings of individual Faeries made by George Russell and who, like himself, accepted the existence of the Sidhe without question or doubt. He had many plans for writings under his own name and drafted several such works, none of which would ever be written thanks to the dominating ambitions of Fiona. In December of 1897 Fiona's book *"The Laughter of Peterkin"* was published for the children's market but it proved to have great appeal to her adult readers as well. This book was well received by the critics and the public alike and several friends encouraged Fiona to write more for children but, again, the pressure of other work debarred this from ever happening. The prologue to this collection of three old Celtic tales concerns the young Peterkin sneaking out of the house for a midnight meeting with the Faeries under a large white poplar tree. This part is autobiographical and echoes some of the statements made by Elizabeth concerning William's peculiarly magical childhood and his early encounters with Faeries. From a literary point of view this introduction is superfluous and the book would stand up and be strong enough on its own without it. It seems Fiona added it on for no other reason than to show her new Irish friends that she too was familiar with the ways of the Faeries.

William accepted that the demands of Fiona had to be met despite the fact they often conflicted with his own desires and needs. The methods of expression employed by the two writers were very different and consequently it was impossible for him to switch easily from one to the other. This frequently resulted in stories, usually William's, being left unfinished and planned projects never materialising. As already mentioned, the main difference in styles was that Fiona wrote intuitively from the heart. Her impulses and impressions needed to be written down and recorded immediately without thought or censorship. Only when a piece was written in full would she revise it and make any necessary corrections or changes. William, however, wrote logically from the mind. As a result he was much slower, more methodical and gave much thought to everything he wrote before ever setting pen to paper. His whole approach was much more detached, almost clinical, and very different from Fiona's. By the late 1890s he was doing this deliberately in an attempt to make his writings as different as possible from those of Fiona, all in an effort to conceal the secret.

William still felt the strong need to continue producing more of his own work in order to maintain the reputation he had worked so hard to achieve. These powerful inner pressures, coupled with his permanent condition of psychological stress, resulted in a depression that caused severe disruption to the Sharps' day-to-day life. He could not settle anywhere, he felt the need to be constantly on the move and he needed to be alone for long periods of time. Maintaining her job in London put considerable strain on Elizabeth who was holding the fort as far as their finances were concerned. It goes without saying that yet again his health broke down to such a degree that there was real concern for his life and sanity. The cure, as in the past, was for him to find some quiet, seaside resort where he could stroll wind-swept beaches and still his disturbed and chaotic mind.

To this end he spent much of the earlier part of 1898 travelling leisurely through the southern coastal towns and villages of the English Channel. Some of the time Edith was with him, with Elizabeth's blessing. In her memoir she simply says, *"He was much alone, except for the occasional visit of an intimate friend; for I could go to him at the weekends only."* [17] The company and watchful eyes of the two women had the desired effect. He was eventually able to clear his mind and come to terms with his position and state of health. He wrote to Catherine Janvier, *" ... I am skirting the wood of shadows. I am filled with vague fears—and yet a clear triumphant laughter goes* *through it, though whether of life or death no one knows. I am also in a duel with other forces than those of human wills—and I need all my courage and strength. At the moment I have recovered my physic control over certain media. It cannot last more than a few days at most a few weeks at a time: but in that time I am myself..." * [18] This makes it clear that he was not just fighting off a mental condition caused by strain and overwork but also a psychic condition caused by his magical practices. Although he was used to frequent bouts of ill health his recent heart attacks and this current breakdown seem to have given him quite a shock. He later commented that he believed he had at one point reached "the Iron Gates" of death. None of this stopped him from seeking visions and dreams; indeed ill health was the catalyst for many such manifestations. He wrote to Elizabeth, *"The other night, tired, I fell asleep on my sofa. I dreamed that a beautiful spirit was standing beside me. He said, 'My Brother, I have come to give you the supreme gift that will heal you and save you.' I answered eagerly, 'Give it me—what is it?' And the fair radiant spirit smiled with beautiful solemn eyes, and blew a breath into the tangled garden of my heart—and when I looked there I saw the tall white Flower of Sorrow growing in the Sunlight."* [19]

This is classic Fiona Macleod, despite being written under William's name. Sorrow in many manifestations is an almost constant presence in her writings. From this dream it would appear that he literally took sorrow to heart. Not in a morbid or depressing sort of way but rather in a positive way by acknowledging the powerful emotions sorrow invokes. Through his magical workings he had come to learn that emotion is a form of energy without positive or negative aspects—it just is. The cause of this energy can certainly be positive or negative but by understanding its true nature any energy thus generated can be used in whatever way the will of the magician directs. Fiona used this technique a lot in her writings, emphasising the negative in order to stir the emotions and then allowing the reader to see the beauty thus created. This is why her writings were so popular; they 'spoke' to the reader at a deep, emotional level in a way that the intuition can understand but the logical mind cannot.

Although he was growing closer to Fiona and becoming more familiar and comfortable with her, he was simultaneously drawing away from his friends and companions in this world. His extended periods away from Elizabeth highlighted this condition and he even commented to her—his wife, the woman who loved him, carried the burden of their financial responsibilities and wanted to be near him - how beneficial it was for him to be alone. In a letter from the English Channel he said, *"The isolation, with sun and wind, were together like soft cream upon my nerves... To be alone 'in the open' above all, is not merely healing to me but an imperative necessity of my life—and the chief counter agent to the sap that almost every person exercises on me, unless obviated by frequent and radical interruption... O how weary I am of the endless recurrence of the ordinary in the lives of most people—the beloved routine, the cherished monotonies, the treasured certainties… There is a fever of the 'green life' in my veins – below all the ordinary littlenesses of conventional life and all the common place exterior: a fever that makes me ill at ease with people, even those I care for, that fills me with a weariness beyond words and a nostalgia for sweet impossible things."* [20] In the same letter he also recalled his happy days when a youth with the band of European gypsies, *"I wished, ah I wished I were a youth once more, and was 'sun-brother' and 'star-brother' again – to lie down at night, smelling the earth, and rise at dawn, smelling the new air out of the East, and know enough of men and cities to avoid both…"* [21]

It is clear from letters, diary entries, notes scribbled on pieces of paper and the statements of third parties, that William did genuinely love and care for his wife, as he demonstrated by his surprise appearance in France on her birthday. However he very often seems to have put his own needs and desires first, and occasionally made thoughtless statements that must have hurt her, even though she knew they were unintentional. Fiona, on the other hand, never had this problem because she was not married and paid little heed to the emotional exchanges of the people around her. She certainly understood them however, thanks to Edith's tutoring, as she used just such human emotional interchanges as a basis for many of her fictional characters and plots.

In December 1898 William and Edith returned for a few days to the Pettycur Inn near Edinburgh. This brought with it a sudden upsurge of Fiona-energy and as her individual personality became clearer, more defined and stronger day by day, it was proving to be very different from that of William Sharp. Not only was she continuing to write her romantic poetry and fiction but now she started to write personal commentaries on the whole issue of the Celtic revival. This was a start in leaning towards the direction Yeats and Russell had criticised her for ignoring but her wording was still too vague, ethereal and non-political for them. In *"The Fortnightly Review"* for January 1899 she published a long discussion on the Celtic writers of the day. In places she touched upon the general theme of what is Celtic and what is not and drew lengthy comparisons between the mind-set of the Celt and that of the Anglo Saxon. By our modern standards of acceptability and political correctness, in places it comes close to being what we would consider racist in its terminology. But we must read such things in context and in the accepted norms of the day. The reason why Yeats and co were still not satisfied with her statements can be seen from the following extract, *"There has been of late too much looseness of phrase concerning the Celtic spirit, the Celtic movement and that mysterious entity Celticism… What is called 'the Celtic Renascence' is simply a fresh development of creative energy coloured by nationality, and moulded by inherited forces, a development diverted from the common way by accident of race and temperament… All that the new generation of Celtic or Anglo-Celtic (for the most part Anglo-Celtic) writers hold in conscious aim, is to interpret anew 'the beauty at the heart of things', not along the line of English tradition but along that of racial instinct, coloured and informed by individual temperament.*" [22] These sentiments received favourable criticism from the general Irish reader, but the Irish writers to whom she was referring did not like the emphasis on being Anglo-Celtic. Neither did they appreciate the emphasis on the ethereal qualities of beauty and tradition at the expense of immediate social and political injustices being suffered by the common people. But that was the nature of Fiona.

"*The Dominion of Dreams*" was published by Messrs. Constable & Co. in April 1899 and Fiona was clearly pleased with it and wrote many letters to friends commenting enthusiastically on various pieces within her new book. Of one of the stories, "*The Distant Country*," she said, "*... there is nothing in The Dominion of Dreams, or elsewhere in these writings under my name to stand beside 'The Distant Country'... as the deepest and most searching utterance on the mystery of passion ... It is indeed the core of all these writings... and will outlast them all.*" [23] This is an extremely romantic piece, difficult to understand, based on passionate and unrequited love, death and sorrow. To say that it was the core of her writings and would outlast them all showed very clearly that her heart still lay in the misty Highlands, amongst lovers torn apart and men being driven mad by the power of beauty and solitude. It also reflected much of what was going on within William at that time anent Edith. In a very real sense a small piece of this story did outlast them all. Part of the epitaph on William's headstone reads, "*Love is more great than we conceive, and Death is the keeper of unknown redemptions*" which is a direct quotation from the final chapter of "*The Distant Country*" and that headstone is literally in a distant country, being on the slopes of Mount Etna, Sicily.

Towards the end of the century William and Fiona became involved with Yeats' plan to create a new magical group, the Celtic Mystical Order. Yeats' own later accounts of the Celtic Mystical Order reveal just how important this episode in his life had been, "*An obsession more constant than anything but my love itself was the need of mystical rites – a ritual system of evocation and meditation – to reunite the perceptions of the spirit, of the divine with natural beauty ... I was convinced that all lonely and lovely places were crowded with invisible beings and that it would be possible to communicate with them. I meant to initiate young men and women in this worship, which would unite the radical truths of Christianity to those of a more ancient world...*" [24] He also noted that, "*The Irish peasant has invented ... a vague, though not altogether unphilosophical, reconciliation between his Paganism and his Christianity.*" [25] All of these sentiments echo William and Fiona's thoughts and beliefs precisely – the desire for union with the natural beauty of the world, the ubiquitous presence of the Faery realm and the need to unite the spiritual truths of Christian and pre-Christian beliefs. Even though he acknowledged that for some ten years it had been his obsession, the notes and manuscripts that survive show much more practical magical work being carried out than he ever alluded to then or later. Neither did he make clear how many other people were actually involved. Apart from Maud Gonne, Fiona and William, the list of regularly working members included Moina and MacGregor Mathers, Florence Farr, Dorothea and Edward Hunter, George Pollexfen (Yeats' uncle), W.F. Kirby, Ada Waters, Mary Briggs and the support of Annie Horniman, all of whom were, or had at one time been, members of the Golden Dawn.

The practical side of the new Order involved a great deal of inner visionary work as well as intuitive, psychic work, all in an attempt to retrieve more information concerning the Four Jewels of the Tuatha De Danann that were the basis for the Order's degree structure. Initially Maud Gonne performed much of this practical magical work. Early in their relationship Yeats discovered she was very psychic although he put this down to her frequent use of chloroform, which she took to help her sleep, and her occasional use of hashish. When under the influence of either of these drugs her astral body would separate and sometimes appear many miles away to friends, two recorded cases being during a concert at the Albert Hall in London and another time on a boat sailing to France. She did not particularly like the side effects of these drugs, which she found to be very draining. She eventually stopped using them as they were taking time away from her political activities which were always more important to her than her psychic or magical practices. Moina Mathers carried on a lot of astral work for the Order during 1897-98 and Yeats, who was always looking for confirmatory signs, was impressed that she recorded much magical work with the character from the ancient Irish legends known as Connla at the same time, although unknown to her, that he and other members of the Order had been working intensely on the Connla's Well inner visions as discussed in Appendix 3. By late 1898 however Moina and MacGregor Mathers had lost interest in Yeats' Celtic group and were concentrating on their own reconstruction of the Egyptian Cult of Isis.

By August 1899 Yeats felt that their work had produced enough detail for him to prepare written drafts of what he intended would become the main rituals to be used in the new Celtic Mystical Order. The next couple of years were spent working on these drafts in an effort to perfect them. However, as early as June 1899, three months before Yeats issued his prepared drafts, William indicated that he was not happy with the way things were going. He said in a letter to Yeats, "*Serious illness (in France I had to have a doctor) has still left me so down, mentally and bodily, that I find myself unable to do anything just now involving deep concentration or spiritual intensity. Therefore the rite waits. But I feel something moving within me. (I do not think what you sent can stand, i.e. can do no more than spiritually indicate a direction: I'll explain later).*" [26] If he did explain later the letters have not survived. A month later he wrote again on the same subject saying, "*I have read and carefully consider the rite but I think it calls for something more definite in visionary insight and significance, for spiritual recasting, so to say.*" [27]

This need for 'recasting' may have been influenced by Fiona's growing belief that Yeats' eclectic interest in all things magical resulted in a neglect of sufficient focus on his own Celtic tradition. In a lengthy essay called "*A*

*Group of Celtic Writers"* that appeared in the January 1899 issue of the *Fortnightly Review* she praised Yeats' literary work of the period but said, "*I could wish for him that for a year or two he might neither read nor think nor hear of other mystics, and above all that the Rosicrucian cult and everything to do with esoteric mysticism might be put aside from him; and that in this interval he would set himself vigorously only to the determinable, the measurable, the attainable. There is enough mysticism for him in the old legends and myths of the Gael, profoundly symbolic as much of these are... In these old myths and legends is an older wisdom still... I mistrust those medieval systems which beleaguer the citadel of the spirit with secret avenues of thought, occult byways of expression, and obscure passages of outworn and arbitrary symbol.*"[28] It is clear from this that William and Fiona felt that there was too much outside, non-Celtic influence creeping into an Order that was, after all, calling itself the Celtic Mystical Order, an Order that was actively attempting to revive the Celtic spiritual tradition. Many years later Yeats would reflect on this period in his autobiography and agree with Fiona's sentiments when he said, "*To that multiplicity of interests and opinion, of arts and sciences, which had driven me to conceive a Unity of Culture defined and evoked by Unity of Image, I had but added a multiplicity of images, and I was the more troubled because, the first excitement over, I had done nothing to rouse George Pollexfen from the gloom and hypochondria always thickening about him... I was lost in that region a cabalistic manuscript, shown me by MacGregor Mathers, had warned me of; astray upon the Path of the Chameleon.*"[29]

By July 1901 things were clearly coming to an end as far as William and Fiona's involvement in the new Order was concerned. Fiona wrote to Yeats on July 26th 1901 suggesting, "*a complete reconstruction of the Rite, as for some reason we* [Fiona and William] *both still feel either an inveterate hostility or an insuperable difficulty...*" and concluded by adding he should construct a new rite, "*... identical in end but wholly distinct in externals.*"[30] Unfortunately the exact reasons for this difficulty were never spelled out but Yeats did pay attention to her suggestion for revisions. By this time he and the other members working in Ireland had produced several full rituals including a set of initiations through four degrees, or Orders as they were called, known as the Initiation of the Cauldron, Initiation of the Stone, Initiation of the Wand and Initiation of the Sword. Each of these four rituals had two separate parts and all were opened with a ceremony called simply "The Opening of the Gates." There was another two-part ritual called the "Initiation of the Spirit" that also used the "The Opening of the Gates" ritual. This was to be used for initiations into a planned secret Inner Order of the Celtic Mystical Order once a full working outer group had been established.

All of these rituals were structured along the lines of existing Golden Dawn rituals but those of the Celtic Mystical Order used only Celtic god names and symbols whereas the Golden Dawn rituals employed gods, goddesses and symbolism from many traditions, especially the ancient Egyptian

and the Hebrew Qaballah. Variants of all of the Celtic Mystical Order's rituals exist and these amended versions seem to have been inspired by Fiona's
comments regarding feeling unsatisfied with the rituals of the Order as they
originally stood. Part of these changes were in terminology, for example the
original ceremonial titles of two of the officers were "The Guide" and "The
Pupil" but in the amended versions these are changed to "The Herdsman"
and "The Wayfarer" respectively, titles both taken from two of Fiona's tales.
It says a lot regarding Yeats' esteem for Fiona that he would even consider
any changes from a person who had played no part in the work of formulat-
ing the rituals in the first place. Having said all that, despite the considerable
work put in by many people over several years, the new Order never got off
the ground and there is no record of the group ever having performed any
of these rituals.

By 1901 the Celtic Mystical Order was struggling and the original
Golden Dawn to all intents and purposes no longer existed. This was partly
because it had come to light that some members had joined Florence Farr
in forming a secret group, known as "*The Sphere*," within the main body
of the Golden Dawn. The purpose of this group was an attempt to learn
more about the existing Golden Dawn symbols and rituals by using psychic
and astral means to delve deeper into them. When the rest of the members
discovered the existence of this secret group within the lodge there was an
outcry. Despite the lessons to be learned from this, Yeats and Florence Farr
planned to form an inner, secret group within the Celtic Mystical Order that
only select members of the outer group would be invited to join, hence the
preparation of the higher degree rituals detailed above.

But back to the reasons why both William and Fiona suggested revising
the Celtic Mystical Order rituals, rituals they had not even helped to formu-
late the first time round. These were in an advanced stage and William hoped
that his suggestion that they now needed to be totally reworked would <u>not</u>
be accepted. This may seem a little confusing but he did this as a first stage
in stepping back from the Order before finally quitting for good as he had
decided he no longer wanted to be associated with it or the Golden Dawn.
He was sure that Yeats would not agree to totally reconstructing the rituals
just because he and Fiona felt unhappy with them and that would give him
the legitimate excuse of resigning on the grounds of magical incompatibility.
Despite his years of effort to convince Yeats of his own magical powers and
ability, and despite the frequent trips to Paris to work on the setting up of
the planned Order, he had now come to the reluctant conclusion that he had
to distance himself from this and all other magical groups but in a way that
would maintain his friendship with Yeats.

There were several reasons why he felt compelled to do so, none of which
were of a magical or spiritual nature. One was the emphasis within the Order
on Ireland and the Irish despite the fact it was called the "Celtic" Mystical
Order. The heavy Irish bias came from the motives of the two main found-

ers, Yeats and Maud Gonne. Maud believed that the Order would bring about a new, specifically Irish, religion that the people of Ireland would turn to instead of Roman Catholicism. She saw the power of the Catholic Church as being just as repressive as the power of the landlords and this new religion could be used for political ends in the Irish Home Rule struggle.[31] Yeats however saw other potentials in the new Order. He believed it would help unify the various Irish political activists who although all struggling for the same cause were also continually fighting with each other. He also earnestly hoped it would inspire a revival in traditional Irish culture and the arts as he believed there could be no unified Ireland until this first step had been achieved. This strong emphasis on Ireland and all things Irish to the exclusion of Scotland and the other Celtic countries only exacerbated the existing tensions being felt by Fiona and William on this already touchy subject.

Only a purely personal level, however, in the early days of the Order Yeats believed he could use it to bring about a fuller union between himself and Maud. He saw working with her as his magical partner as an opportunity to bring them closer together emotionally, possibly to the extent that their combined magical work would result in a third manifestation, a spiritual child. It is unlikely that William ever mentioned his unpublished sonnets about he and Edith producing a spiritual child but the desire and belief expressed by both men is identical. Ithell Colquhoun in *"Sword of Wisdom: MacGregor Mathers and the Golden Dawn"* points out several other close similarities in the private lives of many of the characters involved in the Golden Dawn and the new Celtic Mystical Order. Many of these similarities revolve around sex, marriage partners and children or the lack there of. I have already commented on William and Elizabeth's failure to produce offspring and it is possible that their marriage was never consummated. Moina and MacGregor Mathers never had children and, according to Moina herself, never had physical sex. Yeats at this time had not had sex with Maud Gonne and they would never produce any offspring together although they did with other partners. Other key and important Golden Dawn members such as Allan Bennett, Florence Farr, Annie Horniman, Gerald Kelly and, possibly, W. Wynn Westcott were all without issue. Other common factors that Colquhoun points out are the loss of one or both parents at an early age; chronic or frequent ill-health; Celtic descent; the constant need to travel, and frequent financial problems[32], all factors applicable to William Sharp and, by extension, to Fiona Macleod.

At the time Yeats was attempting to woo Maud through the Celtic Mystical Order he was unaware of her earlier long-standing love affair with a gentleman in France called Lucien Millevoye. Yeats certainly did not know that Maud and Millevoye had produced a son, Georges Gonne, who was born on January 11th 1889 but died of meningitis on August 31st 1891. Maud was devastated by his death. Her slight knowledge at that time of magical and spiritual matters led her to believe that the spirit of her little boy would soon be reincarnated. In an attempt to bring him back to this world again in her own family she and Millevoye went to Georges' mausoleum in the cemetery at Samois-sur-Seine, Paris where they made love in the hope that she would conceive and that Georges' spirit would enter into the body of this new child. She did not conceive at that attempt but later she and Millevoye did have another child, a daughter Iseult who was born on August 6th 1894, although there is no evidence to suggest she believed her daughter to be a reincarnation of Georges. Throughout the rest of her turbulent and unsettled life Maud kept Georges' little pair of booties with her and they were eventually buried along with her in her coffin when she died on April 27th 1953. It had been her hope that Georges would become the new King of Ireland once Ireland had become independent from Britain. [33] Her legitimate son to her husband John MacBride, Sean, took up his mother's ideals and became very active in the Irish Republican Army although he eventually went on to work for the United Nations Organization.

Maud did not reveal the secret of her affair with Millevoye and their son and daughter to Yeats until December 8th 1898. He was dumbfounded. It is noticeable that his poetry dealing with his love and passion for Maud changed in tone from that time on. When he did refer to her he would often use the name PIAL, her Golden Dawn magical name *"Per Ignem ad Lucem."* It is clear he was no longer writing about the real Maud Gonne but a perfected image of what he had hoped she would be. The shock of her revelation of her affair with Millevoye spurred Yeats on to channel his energies into the work of the Celtic Mystical Order and away from what he now realised was a futile attempt to win Maud's heart. This on-going but unsuccessful attempt at a love affair had been obvious to the other members of both the Golden Dawn and the new Order and it did not meet with their approval. One Golden Dawn and Celtic Mystical Order member, Dorothea Hunter, later wrote, *"Through all the time I knew him his barren love for Maud Gonne was tracing its icy scroll, hardening and deepening his work I believe that but for it he would not have been drawn into politics, but his love for Ireland would have been centred as was AE's on the work of building up a nation so filled with the things of the spirit & of so great a culture that no material power could dominate it."* [34] Two months after Maud revealed her secret, Yeats visited her in Paris on Feb 4th 1899 with the intention of working with her magically on the new Order but he found she was now disinterested in the whole idea and was unusually cold towards him. Five days later she left Paris and the Celtic Mystical Order in order to concentrate on her social and political work with the evicted Irish peasants.

A second and by far more important motivation for William to distance himself from the Order was much more practical and, in the short term at least, more urgent. This was to do with the amount of unsavoury publicity that was creeping into the popular Press at this time regarding the Golden Dawn and the goings-on of some of its members. One such incident had personally involved Yeats and had nearly ended up in a court case some months before.

Yeats was still active in the Golden Dawn in 1900 and had been sent to deal with a young upstart in the Order who was causing some trouble. This was Aleister Crowley. The background to this incident began in Paris when MacGregor Mathers accused Florence Farr of attempting to create a schism in the Golden Dawn, partly through her formation of the secret Sphere group. He also charged Dr. Wynn Westcott with having forged the very documents on which the Order was founded. Enraged by the setting up of a committee to investigate these charges rather than taking him at his word, Mathers had sent Crowley to take possession of the Order's London premises and to secure the documents of the Order for himself. Not only had Crowley taken occupancy of the Golden Dawn Vault as instructed, but he had taken the outrageous step of reconsecrating it according to his own magical system and was refusing the other legitimate members of the Order admittance. Eventually the landlord of the building called the police. Just when the constable arrived Yeats and another Golden Dawn initiate, Edmund Hunter, were allegedly manhandling the struggling Crowley down the stairs and out of the building. Furious, Crowley took legal action against them on the grounds of assault and a trial was set for April 28th 1900 at the Hammersmith Police Court. It never came to anything as Crowley's legal counsel advised him not to proceed. Yeats had already ensured through his solicitor that his name would not be brought up, and therefore avoided mention in the Press, and the whole affair fizzled out.[35] It is possible that William may have made the acquaintance of Crowley as indicated by Ithell Colquhoun who says, " ... *many other Golden Dawn personalities – J. W. Brodie-Innes, Aleister Crowley, G. C. Jones, Charles Rosher, William Sharp – used to foregather in a tavern, since vanished, opposite to the British Museum.*"[36] If this was so, Elizabeth certainly did not – and would not – mention Crowley in her memoir, and after the repercussions of the above incident I doubt if William would have continued to meet with him in taverns or anywhere else.

Although William was not involved in the schism in the Golden Dawn, he was nonetheless well acquainted with MacGregor Mathers, having been involved with him and Moina on a magical level on several of his trips to Paris. But over the years their relationship grew sour and very distant due to a clash of their incompatible personalities. Compare the sentiments expressed in the following excerpt from a letter Moina Mathers sent to Yeats on May 29th 1899 where she said, "*We have been much delighted to meet William Sharp, who was over here. It is impossible to say how much we liked him – We felt great sympathy – He is a very remarkable being I think – in every respect, & so strangely psychic.*"[37] to the observation Yeats made some time later, "*I notice that MacGregor Mathers considers William Sharp vague and sentimental, while Sharp is repelled by Mathers' hardness and arrogance. William Sharp met Mathers in the Louvre, and said, 'No doubt considering your studies you live upon milk and fruit.' And Mathers replied, 'No, not exactly milk and fruit but very nearly so'; and now Sharp has lunched with Mathers and been given nothing but brandy and radishes.*"[38]

Despite William and Mathers falling out, Yeats himself still had some sympathy for Mathers, "*Once when I met him in the street in his Highland clothes, with several knives in his stocking, he said, 'When I am dressed like this I feel like a walking flame.' And I think that everything he did was but an attempt to feel like a walking flame. Yet at heart he was, I think, gentle, and perhaps even a little timid. He had some impediment in his nose that gave him a great deal of trouble, and it could have been removed had he not shrunk from the slight operation; and once when he was left in a mouse-infested flat with some live traps, he collected his captives into a large bird cage, and to avoid the necessity of their drowning, fed them there for a couple of weeks. Being an unscholarly, though learned man, he was bound to express the fundamental antithesis in the most crude form, and being arrogant, to prevent as far as possible that alternation between the two natures which is, it may be, necessary to sanity. When the nature turns to its spiritual opposite alone there can be no alternation, but what nature is pure enough for that?*" [39]

The Crowley eviction was only one of several petty and rather pathetic cases but there were a few more serious ones such as the sordid case involving the Golden Dawn and a gang of professional confidence tricksters. These people, Mr. And Mrs. Theo Horos and a Dr. Rose Adams, had tricked the rather naïve MacGregor Mathers into giving them some important magical documents on which he had been working in Paris. The three tricksters duly turned up in London and, using the stolen documents, managed to convince eager seekers after membership of an occult lodge that they had something to offer. However things turned very nasty and in December of 1901 they were charged and convicted with not only fraud but also the rape of minors. Although nobody from the Golden Dawn was involved with this case the name of the Order was brought up in court and, needless to say, the Press had a field day and the implications were made that all occult groups were no more than a cover for such sordid and criminal behaviour.

William Sharp was a well known and well respected public figure in London and Paris at that time, he was very image and class conscious, and he knew that any hint of scandal or association with undesirables would be severely damaging to his hard-earned reputation. It was easier for him to allege incompatibility on a magical level and quietly withdraw from the Golden Dawn and the Celtic Mystical Order than it was to tell Yeats to his face that he was embarrassed by all the tawdry incidents he and his Golden Dawn fraters and sorors were being dragged into and that he wished no part of it. Fiona and William still felt Yeats was a literary genius and wished to remain his friend and associate but they strongly felt he should be more careful in his magical aspirations and associations. I also believe that Elizabeth encouraged William to distance himself from his magical associates. She never partook in his 'psychic experimentations' as she quaintly called his magical work and she was clearly disapproving of the whole thing. Her memoir demonstrates clearly how conscious she was of the importance of class, good breeding and a decent upbringing, by the way she names all the right names and makes frequent connections between her husband and several of the upper class families of the day. She took steps to carefully remove all evidence connecting her husband to anything so potentially damaging to his good reputation, as is reflected in how her memoir makes no reference at all to any of the above incidents.

The third and final reason for this voluntary withdrawal from magical and mystical Orders was yet another heavy secret that William and Elizabeth did not want revealed to the outside world, a secret that remained concealed until long after both William and Elizabeth were dead. On March 1st 1901 William's sister, secretary, and the pen of the Fiona Macleod correspondence, Mary Sharp, gave birth to a boy, Douglas, in a London hospital. The birth certificate names Mary Beatrice Sharp as the mother, of no occupation; the name of the father is not given. The baby was immediately taken for adoption and the whole affair was successfully hidden from friends, correspondents and their wide social circle. Mary continued to live in Edinburgh with her mother but frequently visited her eldest sister, Agnes Sharp, in London where she died on January 24th 1934 from a heart condition. She is buried in the same grave as Agnes in Croydon Cemetery, London. Agnes died in 1943. Mary never saw her son Douglas again after the birth. He spent his early years in an orphanage but was eventually adopted by an English family who did not reveal to him his true identity. In later life he decided to immigrate to Canada. When he applied for his passport his adopted parents had to give him his real birth certificate and he found out the truth regarding his mother. On arrival in Canada he changed his name to Sharpe. At the time of writing, his son still lives in Ontario and is aware and proud of his grandmother's role in the Fiona Macleod affair. I was happy to be able to send him a copy of the photograph I have of his grandmother.

William and Elizabeth spent the first half of 1901 helping Mary through her pregnancy and with caring for her when she left hospital following the birth. This was an emotional and financial strain for them with which they could just cope but another and more important birth took place that year that had a much deeper affect. On July 26th 1901, the same day Fiona wrote the letter to Yeats expressing difficulty and hostility to the Celtic Rite, Edith Wingate Rinder gave birth to a daughter, Esther Mona Rinder. The physical, emotional and spiritual strain that this put William under almost crushed him. Needless to say, Elizabeth ensured there was not the slightest hint of either of these children in her memoir. Being aware of these facts helps to explain the substantial deterioration in William's emotional and physical health from 1901 on. It was also clearly the main reason, perhaps the only true reason, for his complete withdrawal from the Celtic Mystical Order and his many magical co-workers. It may also account for his apparent permanent state of living on the bread line despite the fact Fiona's books were selling well, he was still producing his own books and Elizabeth was still generating income from newspaper work.

Esther Mona Rinder was raised by her mother and Frank Rinder in St. John's Wood, London, and eventually married a man called Ramsay Harvey in the early 1930s. They had two sons, one in 1934 and the other 1937 who, at the time of writing, are both still alive and living in England. Esther died in 1993 at the age of 92. Her mother, Edith Wingate Rinder, died in 1962 at the age of 98.

With his already delicate health troubling him greatly it was clear that William could not possibly remain an active participant in the setting up of the Celtic Mystical Order with the added responsibilities he now faced. He had to withdraw and hope these new, deeply personal secrets would never be revealed and cause the scandal he and Elizabeth so feared. In this matter they were successful even long after Elizabeth's death in the 1930s.

From Yeats' point of view, and particularly the point of view of the more militant Irish activists, this distancing by William and Fiona was a relief and was actually welcomed and, in the end, suited both parties. Putting aside scandals and innuendos, there had been a definite change of attitude by the Irish from welcoming a new colleague on the Celtic magical and political scene to that of expressing hostility to an ex-comrade. Much of this change in attitude can be found in the surviving correspondence. For example, on August 5th 1900 Russell said of Fiona in a letter to Yeats, *"Every time she bobs her head out of the Astral light I will whack it, at least so long as it bobs up in connection with Irish things."* [40] By the start of the 20th century William and Fiona were persona non grata regarding the Celtic Mystical Order and the Celtic rituals they had all been working on. Russell publicly pursued and criticised her in the *"New Ireland Review"* for unsound ideas and derivative pseudo-Celticism. His attack was given extra ferocity as he now knew that it was William Sharp who was behind Fiona's statements and he, being a real person and a Celt, should have known better.

The surviving correspondence from this time on is interesting. William had taken great care and made a successful effort to distance himself from his magical associates for the reasons detailed above and his brief correspondence with Yeats from hereon deals purely with literary matters. Fiona, on the other hand, continued to write regularly to many of the Irish activists asking for reconciliation and for a chance to patch up their differences. She was not as sensitive to scandal and public opinion as William was and she desperately tried to remain involved in the work of the Celtic Mystical Order. This shows how strongly, how overwhelmingly, her individual desires and preferences had become. The fact that they were totally contrary to those of William was irrelevant and he could not stop her. This increased even further the enormous strain Fiona was already putting William under. To make matters worse for both of them the response from Ireland was still cold and distant despite her frequent and eloquent pleas for reconciliation and forgiveness.

The resentment and accusations went on for many years and Fiona consistently made efforts to resolve their differences by pointing out the many uniting factors they all shared in common. In a letter to Russell, undated apart from 1905, Fiona said, "*You will have read the letter I have written to Mr. Rolleston. I have only this to add (forgive a pencilled line, as I am not well) – will you not help me to bury any resentment or misunderstanding for the sake of what we both have so passionately at heart. We have both no other goal or aim than the Quest, and so far as in us lies the furtherance of spiritual beauty: to be revealers and interpreters. I want to go with you, not apart from you. Will you not believe this, and let us both do things in his or her own way according to his or her inward star.*"[41] In some ways this displays the very thing that angered Russell and the rest – her continued Otherworldliness and apparent total lack of understanding of the real, physical and emotional problems of this world. But not being a creature of this world it is not surprising that she only related to things of an Otherworldly nature. This was her strength in writing but her downfall in dealing with the day-to-day matters and relationships of the world in which everyone else lived.

It was in late 1899 that Fiona started working on what would eventually become one of the few plays she ever wrote – "*The Immortal Hour.*" This is typical Faery Fiona, set in a gloomy forest and involving lost lovers, death, solitude and madness. The madness however is in the form of the Faery being Dalua, and the whole play is anything but grounded in this world. It was never performed as a play during her lifetime. Later though it would be set to music and become an opera. In this form it was hugely successful and achieved more fame in the first quarter of the 20th century than any of her other writings did. It was and still is responsible for introducing many people to the Faery and Celtic traditions. This was the great value in her romantic, solidly Faery writings – they made the general public aware of this aspect of Celticism. Yeats and the members of the Irish National Theatre had been trying to do the same thing but their heavy emphasis on portraying the political and social abuses being suffered by the native Irish, the very thing they accused Fiona of ignoring, was turning people away from anything to do with Irish or even Celtic nationalism. The view of the common people was that to proclaim allegiance to the Irish cause was to proclaim yourself to be an agitator and an anarchist fighting to break down the established social and class structures of Victorian and Edwardian British society. Yeats and his allies were very astute at bringing the reality of being a Celt to the public awareness, but the public did not like this confrontational aspect of it. Fiona, on the other hand, had found a way of making people long for a Celtic twilight that was fading away. People wanted to preserve this ideal, even if only in their dreams and fantasies, but at least they accepted it to heart.

By the end of the 19th century Elizabeth had taken on another newspaper job in London, Fiona was steadily producing magazine articles and various pieces that would eventually be combined into books and William started on an ambitious project that would be published in the summer of 1900 as "*The Progress of Art in the Century.*" He claimed he did this purely for financial reasons but it was also to ensure his name was being kept alive in the public's mind and to show that he was still capable of producing literature and art criticism, and art history in a substantial form; plus there were two babies on the way.

---

[1] Memoir, page 280

[2] Foster, W.B. Yeats: A Life; 1. The Apprentice Mage, page 237

[3] "Lyra Celtica", page 399

[4] "The Winged Destiny", page 177

[5] Memoir, page 282

[6] Janvier, "Fiona Macleod and her Creator", "North American Review", April 1907, page 722

[7] William Butler Yeats Autobiography, page 227-228

[8] Janvier, "Fiona Macleod and her Creator", "The North American Review", April 1907, page 726

[9] Yeats Annual 14, page 171

[10] Memoir, page 286

[11] Private letter to a Mr. Moore, sent from The Outlook Tower.

[12] Memoir, page 285

[13] Memoir, page 287

[14] Pethica, Lady Gregory's Diaries, page 154

[15] William Butler Yeats Memoir, page 128-129

[16] William Butler Yeats Memoir, page 129

[17] Memoir, page 292

[18] Memoir, page 293, emphasis in original

[19] Memoir, page 296

[20] Memoir, page 297, emphasis added

[21] Memoir, page 297

[22] Memoir, page 304

[23] Memoir, page 310

[24] William Butler Yeats Memoir, page 123

[25] Kalogera, page 293

[26] Finneran, Letters to WB Yeats, Page 51

[27] Kalogera, page 200

[28] "Fortnightly Review", January 1899, page 41

[29] William Butler Yeats, Trembling of the Veil, page 180

[30] Ellmann, Yeats – The Man and the Masks, page 125

[31] A few years after leaving the Order, Maud married John MacBride on Feb 21st 1903 in Paris and very soon after converted to Roman Catholicism. The marriage only lasted until 1905, during which time their son Sean MacBride was born.

[32] Colquhoun, Sword of Wisdom, pages 54 and 176-177

[33] For a full account of this episode see "Georges Gonne and the Soul of the King of Ireland" by Conrad A. Balliet, Yeats Annual No. 9

[34] "The Music of Heaven: Dorothea Hunter" by Warwick Gould, Yeats Annual No. 9, page 157

[35] For a full account of this episode see "The Music of Heaven: Dorothea Hunter" by Warwick Gould, Yeats Annual No. 9, pages 162-165

[36] Colquhoun, Sword of Wisdom, page 118

[37] Greer, Women of the Golden Dawn, page 226

[38] William Butler Yeats, Trembling of the Veil, page 232

[39] William Butler Yeats, Trembling of the Veil, page 227

[40] Foster, W.B. Yeats: A Life; 1. The Apprentice Mage, page 197

[41] NLS, Edinburgh. Note – the word 'resentment', second sentence, has been written over the original word "anger"

# Chapter 9
# A New Century, an Old Bowl

*As to the past, it is because of what is there, that I look back:*
*not because I do not see what is here today,*
*or may be here tomorrow.*

The last year of the 19th century saw William pull off one of his most subtle ploys in maintaining the illusion of Fiona Macleod being a real person. In 1899 he managed to obtain an entry for Fiona in *"Who's Who,"* the important annual directory of the famous and influential. Originally this had only listed members of the royal household and court plus ambassadors and senior clergy but in the 1890s it was expanded to include prominent writers, artists and people of higher social standing. The entry that William managed to have inserted for Fiona reads, *"Macleod, Miss Fiona; author. Publications: Pharais, A Romance of the Isles 1894; The Mountain Lovers 1895; The Sin-Eater 1896; The Laughter of Peterkin 1897; and (in verse) From the Hills of Dream 1896. Collective Edition of the Celtic Tales from The Sin-Eater and Washer of the Ford, with others added, in 3 Volumes, Spiritual Tales, Barbaric Tales and Tragic Romances 1897. Forthcoming: an Historic Jacobite Romance; a new volume of short tales; and The Children of Danu (three prose Celtic dramas). Recreations: sailing, hill-walking, listening. Address: c/o Miss Rea, The Columbia Literary Agency, 9 Mill Street, Conduit Street, W."* Her recreation of 'listening' is rather odd but that is the nature of Fiona Macleod. *"Who's Who"* continued to publish an entry for Fiona Macleod every year up to and including 1905. They were all basically the same with the exception of the titles of her new publications being added each year.

William Sharp's own first entry was in 1898, only one year before Fiona, which may have prompted him to concoct an entry for her the following year. His entry is extensive as it lists all of his own publications up until that time. His recreations in this first entry were, *"Sailing etc in West of Scotland."* He too maintained an entry until 1905 with his writings under his own name being added annually. The only other small changes were his recreations being expanded to, *"Frequent change of scene and environment; in summer roaming, sailing and swimming and cycling in Scotland"* plus his membership of various clubs – Grosvenor, Omar Khayyam, Authors and Pharos – were listed. From 1899 Elizabeth Sharp also had her own independent entries, again with her list of publications and club memberships being given and expanded annually. Her inclusion would have greatly pleased Elizabeth who was very conscious of class and social status.

The first year of the new century saw the publication of Fiona's book, *"The Divine Adventure: Iona: By Sundown Shores"* by Messrs. Chapman & Hall. This was a collection of some new pieces added to some older articles that had appeared in magazines over the preceding two years. Fiona was pleased with it and like many of her other works believed it contained some fine, strong pieces, and implied to her personal correspondents that many contained more information than just the obvious theme. She said in a letter to the Breton writer, Anatole Le Braz, *"It seems to me that in writing the spiritual history of Iona I am writing the spiritual history of the Gael, of all our Celtic race. The lovely wonderful little island sometimes appears to me as a wistful mortal, in his eyes the pathos of infinite desires and inalienable ideals – sometimes as a woman, beautiful, wild, sacred, inviolate, clad in rags, but aureoled with the Rainbows of the west. 'Tell the story of Iona, and you go back to God, and end in God.' (The first words of my 'spiritual history')"* [1]

In a letter dated December 30th 1899 to Frank Rinder William said, *"Just a line, dear Frank, both as dear friend and literary comrade, to greet you on New Year's morning, and to wish you health and prosperity in 1900. I would like very much for you to read some of this new Fiona work, especially the opening pages of 'Iona', for they contain a very deep and potent spiritual faith and hope, that has been with me ever since, as there told, as a child of seven, old Seumas Macleod (who taught me so much – was indeed the <u>father</u> of Fiona) – took me on his knees one sundown on the island of Eigg, and made me pray to 'Her.' I have never written anything mentally so spiritually autobiographical. Strange as it may seem it is almost all literal reproduction of actuality with only some dates and names altered. But enough about that troublesome F.M.!..."* [2] This is interesting for several reasons. First, he is talking about a Fiona Macleod book yet he, William, clearly states it is his biography, not Fiona's. He is very clear on this point whereas with the rest of Fiona's output he is equally clear that it all came from her and was her biographical material. So who wrote this book? Was it by William but published under the Fiona name or was it by Fiona but William was confused during the writing of this letter? Who did what is not important; the book is strong enough in itself but the confusion of who was who simply shows the constant problem of identity, or perhaps we should say identities, that William Sharp now needed to deal with.

Second, it is interesting as it is a letter from William to Frank Rinder, husband of the woman with whom he had been having a love affair for several years. The opening salutation implies there was little, if any, tension between them but things must have been difficult at times with Edith in the middle. This was no doubt complicated at times by William's frequent confusion between Fiona and Edith. Is this why the final sentence concludes by describing Fiona as 'troublesome'?

Third, from the Faery point of view the important part of this letter is the way William emphasised the word 'father' when describing Seumas Macleod. I discussed in Chapter 5 Fiona's lineage and this letter is more confirmation of what William, Fiona and I believe regarding that matter.

On a more down to earth level though this is one of the few instances where he gives a specific location, the Isle of Eigg, for his meeting with Seumas, and that this was when he was only seven years old. I would be very surprised if William's father took the family on holiday to the Isle of Eigg at that early time, if at all. Even today the Isle of Eigg is difficult to get to from Central Scotland but in 1862 in would have been well nigh impossible, especially for a family with several babies in tow. His brother David was born in June of that year and would literally have been a baby in arms, and his sister Margaret would only have been one year old. Either he and his father were travelling alone, which does not seem to have been their habit, his memory was inaccurate, or he is allowing some artistic licence here in order to paint a more romantic picture.

At the time William claimed to have been there a Dr. Hugh Macpherson had just purchased the Isle of Eigg from the Chief of Clan Ranald. Macpherson subsequently leased out large portions of the island, containing many of the tenant farms, to a Lowland Scot called Stephen Stewart. He detested the Gaelic Highlanders and started a new and extensive series of clearance evictions. It is on record that eleven families from Eigg arrived, literally in rags, at Nova Scotia in the 1850s having been cleared by the previous owner the Chief of Clan Ranald. The island records show that evictions were still being carried out under the new owner and Stephen Stewart into the late 1860s. Visitors were not welcome on Macpherson and Stewart's island kingdom. Even if somehow William and his family were allowed to stay, the idyllic scene of him sitting on the old fisherman's knee while watching the sun dipping into the western ocean does not ring true knowing the social unrest there at that time. This dreadful situation of evictions and hostility to visitors was prevalent in most of the Western Isles in the mid to late 19th century. In the end, of course, it does not really matter where this incident actually took place, assuming it took place at all. For the time being it is important to note the recurrence of the confusion between himself and Fiona and the further reference to Seumas Macleod and his influence.

It was at this time in his life that another important and influential person appeared on the scene who unwittingly happened to involve himself and William in a revival of the Grail tradition in the public mind. For a few years prior to the publication of "*The Divine Adventure*" Fiona and William had been in correspondence with a Dr. John Arthur Goodchild. Elizabeth mentions him in her memoir and reproduces excerpts from some of the correspondence but she does not make clear how influential this gentleman was on William and Fiona, nor does she make clear the long term ramifications of some of the incidents they were jointly involved with. When she first mentions him she describes him as "*an unknown correspondent, Dr. John Goodchild, poet mystic and archaeologist.*" The fact is he was hardly an unknown correspondent. Both William and Fiona had been in regular correspondence with Goodchild for several years before William died; they were both members of the *Authors' Club* in London; they had mutual close friends in Mr. & Mrs. Grant Allen, he and Goodchild had met on at least one occasion, probably more, at Glastonbury and also in Italy; they had experimented on several occasions with various magical techniques together, and both became involved in some powerful magical work the consequences of which were still being played out long after William's death. Hardly an 'unknown correspondent' but this demonstrates once again Elizabeth's constant efforts to gloss over the true extent of her husband's magical work.

We do not know much about John Arthur Goodchild. What we do know is that he was born in England on February 26th 1851, studied medicine and qualified as a doctor in 1873. He started a practice in Cannes, France, serving the large British community who wintered there each year to avoid the dreadful smog of the big English cities. When he returned home each spring he stayed either with his father in Hampstead, London, or periodically at the Francis Hotel, Bath. From there it was an easy journey west to Glastonbury or east to London. The French authorities started to make things difficult for the large number of British doctors appearing every winter in their country and so, to avoid possible legal difficulties, he moved his practice to Bordighera, Italy, in 1877 where he continued to cater to the large British community for the next thirty years.

In his biography of the writer George MacDonald, William Reaper states, "*Dr. Goodchild, a friend of George MacDonald, and, like him, a mystic; he lived at Casa Grazia, and had his consulting-room in the same house, then occupied by Mr. & Mrs. Jameson. He was an eccentric being, and an unfortunate quarrel with another doctor, in which the sympathy of the English Colony was almost entirely with Dr. Goodchild, nevertheless re-acted upon him so strongly that he suffered from a nervous breakdown and gradually lost his practice.*" Reaper also mentions that MacDonald testified on behalf of Dr. Goodchild in court during the year 1896. Elizabeth makes no mention of George MacDonald at all in her memoir yet it is almost certain that the Sharps would have had contact with him in Italy.

Goodchild was greatly interested in religion and spirituality and in particular finding the truth behind all religions and beliefs. His main fascination though was in attempting to prove that the root of the true spiritual tradition was to be found in the west. The 'mystical east' was all the rage at this time thanks mainly to the doors on the east having been opened by the Theosophical Society but Goodchild felt that it was a grave error to ignore the spiritual heritage of the west. He also had a passionate belief that the Divine was feminine and that the spiritual revival of the western hemisphere would be led by a woman or a group of women. He wrote on this subject at length which may be why Reaper described him as 'a mystic' and 'an eccentric being.' He was also a published poet and managed to impress even the great Tennyson. (His other titles include, "*Somnia Medici*" 1884, "*Chats at St. Ampellio*" 1888, "*A Fairy Godfather*" 1890, "*My Friends at Sant Ampellio*" 1890, "*Lyrics*" 1893, "*Tales in Verse*" 1893, "*The Two Thrones*" (Drama) 1895, "*The Book of Tephi*" 1897, "*The Light of the West*" 1898)

In February 1885, in Bordighera, a friend happened to mention having seen an interesting looking glass bowl and platter in a tailor's shop. Goodchild was intrigued and went with his friend to see them for himself. The bowl was quite simple but had floral designs of intertwining colours, blue, green and amber, within the glass. All the tailor could tell him was that they had been discovered in a bricked-up wall in an old vineyard in the village of Albegna. Nobody had any idea of their age but Goodchild knew that various archaeological finds from an early 4th century Christian community had already been found in that area. He was convinced that they were from this same place and period, if not older. He duly purchased the two pieces for three Pounds Sterling and on return to England that spring he took them to a glass expert at the British Museum. All that he was able to establish was that they were indeed old but how old, and where from, he could not say. He added that none of the glass experts he consulted could understand what technique had been used to create the subtle floral motifs within the thick glass of the bowl. Goodchild took them home to his father's house and placed them in a cupboard where they remained for the next ten years, untouched and forgotten.

In 1898 Kegan Paul, London, published his book "*The Light of the West: Part 1, The Dannite Colony.*" In this volume he laid out his reasons for believing in the feminine aspect of divinity and, in particular, how a Celtic warrior queen had brought the true spiritual beliefs of the west to Britain and the rest of Europe from Ireland. It runs to some 115 pages and the contents are:-

Chapter 1 – Introductory
Chapter 2 – The Dannite Settlement in Erin
Chapter 3 – Notes on the Historic Materials from the Last Chapter
Chapter 4 – Landmarks during 12 Centuries
Chapter 5 – Further Landmarks
Chapter 6 – Miscellaneous Notes

He was familiar with the works of Fiona Macleod by then as he mentions her a few times in the book, although he spelled her name "Fionna," and he sent her an unedited proof copy of this book in the hope that she might respond. She did, very favourably, and from then on the two stayed in touch by letter, realising they were kindred spirits with the same beliefs and aspirations.

Fiona was probably attracted to this book by sections like, "*The Light of the West is the beauty of womanhood. It inculcates the hatred of warfare, and of empires established by the greed of nations or rulers. It preaches woman's desire for the empire of Love. Let man, indeed, be manly in defence of wife and child; but if uncalled to such warfare, let him apply himself to the knowledge of God and his works. God will give him out of such knowledge defence, and if he wrong no man, empire also.*"[3] However the book rambles on a great deal about Ireland and the Celts' importance in the spiritual traditions of the world but his mystical commentary ends up pointing out the importance of babies learning the nursery rhyme-type names for their toes – and then they can suck on them! This odd suggestion may be partly explained by a comment he made in a later letter, "*I have dimly guessed all my life how folly might be better than the wisdom of wise men, and remembering dimly how much wiser I was myself as a child than after I had grown up, I have incessantly desired a return to that state of childish thought, and tried to learn from children, when I had the chance, the secrets of their folly which carried them so near to divinity, if they were not hurried away from their vision by those about them.*"[4]

The letter quoted earlier in Chapter 7, "*This is going to be a strange year in many ways: a year of spiritual flames moving to and fro, of wild vicissitudes for many souls and for the forces that move through the minds of men. The West will redden in a new light – the 'west' of the forlorn peoples who congregate among our isles in Ireland – 'the West' of the dispeopled mind. The common Soul is open – one can see certain shadows and lights as though in a mirror...*" had been sent by Fiona to Goodchild which shows that Fiona was in regular touch with Goodchild while at the same time attempting to gain the favour of Yeats with their combined archer vision. It is interesting everyone intuitively picked up and commented on important things being in the offing. She was clearly keeping her two magical acquaintances apart as Yeats never knew anything of Dr. Goodchild and as far as I am aware she never mentioned anything of her contact with Yeats to Goodchild. Goodchild was important to her as a close, intimate magical friend and ally with whom she could work at a deep level whereas her liaison with Yeats was much more a matter of prestige and influential contacts rather than one of a real sympathetic spiritual ally.

In early 1897 Goodchild was staying in the St. Petersbourg Hotel in Paris where he had a powerful psychic experience; Fiona had correctly predicted this would be a strange year in many ways. He suddenly found that he was paralysed, unable to stand up or even speak. He then heard a clear, distinct voice explain to him that the long-forgotten bowl still sitting in his father's cupboard was a cup that had once belonged to Jesus. Note the voice did <u>not</u> say it was the cup of the Last Supper nor did it use the term Grail, it merely stated that the bowl had once been the Christ's own property, a significant provenance in itself. The voice said that it had been decided (we do not know by who) to reveal this cup now due to the many questions, assumptions and ideas that were in the public mind concerning the Grail. It went on to say that he had to take it to Bride's Hill, Glastonbury but not until after his own father had died, why this should be he was never told. He was told that further instructions would be given as to what he was to actually do once he got to Glastonbury but the eventual goal behind all this was that the bowl would come into the possession of a woman and new spiritual truths would be revealed. The last sentence the voice spoke said, *"Later, a young girl will make a pure offering of herself at that spot where you lay down the Cup, and this shall be a sign to you."* [5] The feminine aspect of all this clearly appealed to Goodchild. The records show that William was in Paris that year but we do not know if he and Goodchild met at that time. Elizabeth does not say but that is not surprising considering how she completely plays-down the role Goodchild had in the lives of William and Fiona.

Goodchild carried on his journey to Bordighera and while there, a few weeks later, he received news that his father had died. He wrote to his sister and instructed her to bring the bowl and platter to him in Italy. She duly complied. He then sent the platter to 'a prominent Italian family' – believed to be the Garibaldi family – and kept the bowl with him until he returned to England in the spring of 1898. We do not know why he felt compelled to give the platter away while retaining the bowl. He was still corresponding with Fiona at that time but it is unlikely he specifically mentioned the bowl, the voice or anything of that nature as he was scrupulous in maintaining his silence about these events until long after the bowl was discovered. However he must have mentioned something about his beliefs in general and something about Glastonbury specifically for in a letter dated March 4th 1898 from Edinburgh, Fiona says, *"Let me say at once that your surmise is wrong: far from not interesting me your second letter interested me profoundly and not only intellectually but because of spiritual coincidence… I have long believed in the arising of the Woman Redeemer: and that she will be born in the west, perhaps in Ireland, perhaps in Iona of the prophecy… Let me thank you again for your long and interesting letters and diagrams. I must try and go to Glastonbury. If you feel inclined to write further on this strange problem I hope you will do so."* [6] Frustratingly we do not know what this strange problem was or what his diagrams were meant to represent.

Goodchild was unable to get to Glastonbury until August of that year but he eventually made it there, with the bowl, and awaited the promised further instructions. It was not until the first Monday in September that once again the disembodied voice spoke, telling him to take the bowl across the fields to where he would find a stream. He was to deposit it there, leave it untouched and tell no one of what he had done. He followed the directions the voice had given him and duly found the stream beside an old thorn tree bearing offerings of ribbons and scraps of paper with prayers from local people. He wedged the bowl in a hollow he discovered under a large rock beneath the water and returned home to Hampstead without telling anyone what he had done. He returned to Glastonbury every year from 1899 until 1906 except 1905, coincidentally the year William died. He did not go to see if the bowl was still where he had left it but instead he remained in the village and kept his eyes and ears open for any local news or gossip about the bowl being found. He never heard any such stories and for all he knew the bowl was still lying in the murky darkness of Bride's Well. For the next several years he patiently awaited further communications from the voice but none ever came. Soon, though, and unbeknown to him, other people would start to receive psychic communications regarding the mysterious bowl.

In 1900 Goodchild and Fiona had an exchange of correspondence concerning "*The Immortal Hour*" only fragments of which have survived. He was clearly impressed by the play but he gave her some type of warning, the details of which have been lost, concerning something about the subject of the play. From a fragment of a letter that survives it appears Fiona did not fully understand what he was trying to convey and she asks him to be clearer on the nature of his warning. Whether he did or did not we don't know as no letter has surfaced in reply but the most intriguing part of Fiona's letter is the final sentence where she says, "*You have (I had almost said mysteriously, but why so, for it would be more mysterious if there were no secret help in spiritual comradeship) helped me at more than one juncture in my life…*" Exactly what this help was, on what occasions and how often, we do not know. It is peculiar though that Elizabeth, who was very diligent in implying that Goodchild was no more than an unknown fan of Fiona's writings, should quote that last sentence which clearly shows their relationship was much more than just an exchange of cordial letters. The version of "*The Immortal Hour*" which Goodchild would have read at that time was the original work as published in the "*Fortnightly Review*" in November 1900. When it came to be reproduced posthumously in book form in 1907 and 1908, and when Elizabeth edited the Collected Works of Fiona MacLeod in 1910, it had already been changed several times. The version which the English composer Rutland Boughton later set to music bears even less resemblance to the original as he took out large sections of dialogue and replaced them with several of Fiona's poems that were never meant to be part of the original play.

In 1904 William's already delicate health was worsening and he knew he did not have much longer to live. Writing was becoming increasingly difficult for him and the strain of living his two lives was literally killing him. This was the year that Fiona published a collection of pieces under the title of "*The Winged Destiny.*" The dedication in this book is to "J.A.G." and runs to some six and a half pages. Clearly despite Elizabeth's passing references to him as if he had played little importance in the life of her husband he had in fact been a major and long-term influence on him and especially on Fiona. Elizabeth's memoir was published in 1910 – after the bowl had been found, the public had been made aware of it, and all the subsequent 'expert' advice and Press hyperbole–yet she makes no reference at all to this highly public and unusual event nor the role her late husband had played in this, as we shall soon see. Was this another example of the reticence she expressed to Yeats about giving the full story of her late husband's life because so many people involved in it were still alive (Goodchild did not pass away until 1914) or was it to keep the memory of her husband from being connected to the whole tawdry occult scene of the decade before and after 1900?

It was on Monday August 1st 1904, a Bank Holiday and also the ancient Celtic festival of Lughnassadh, while the bowl still lay in the murky waters of Bride's Well, that William and Goodchild met in Glastonbury. Unknown to him, and just like Yeats a few years earlier, Goodchild had decided to apply a psychic test on his friend. Goodchild had decided that if William should use the word 'joy' during their time together in Glastonbury it would be a sign that he could confide in him the secret of the bowl. Shortly after their visit William described what happened in a letter to a friend, probably Edith. It is worth quoting at length. Note that the first sentence implies they had already met on several previous occasions, *As usual one or two strange things happened in connection with Dr. G. We went across the ancient 'Salmon' of St. Bride, which stretches below the hill known as 'Weary-All' (a corruption of Uriel, the Angel of the Sun), and about a mile or less westward came upon the narrow water of the ancient 'Burgh'. Near here is a very old Thorn held in great respect. He put me (unknowing) to a singular test. He had hoped with especial and deep hope that in some significant way I would write or utter the word 'Joy' on this first day of August... –and also to see if certain spiritual influence would reach me. Well, later in the day (for he could not prompt or suggest, and had to await occurrence) we went into the lovely grounds of the ancient ruined Abbey, one of the loveliest things in England I think. I became restless and left him, and went and lay down behind an angle of the east end, under the tree. I smoked, and then rested idly, and then began thinking of some correspondence I had forgotten. Suddenly I turned on my right side, stared at the broken stone of the angle, and felt vaguely moved in some way. Abruptly and unpremeditatedly I wrote down three enigmatic and disconnected lines. I was looking curiously at the third when I saw Dr. G approach. 'Can you make anything of that,' I said– 'I've just written it, I don't know why.' This is the triad:*

> *'From the Silence of Time, Time's Silence Borrow.*
> *In the heart of To-day is the word of To-morrow.*
> *The Builders of Joy are the Children of Sorrow.'* [7]

Goodchild was delighted. Not only had William used the word 'joy' but also the word 'sorrow.' This not only proved William had passed the test with flying colours but also confirmed a suspicion Goodchild had had that the fate of the bowl, which he saw as a 'Cup of Sorrow', was for it to be transformed into a 'Cup of Joy' once it had been retrieved from the waters.

At the time William wrote these lines he had no idea what they meant but they clearly stuck with him, probably because of Goodchild's 'test.' They later appeared in an expanded form as the fore piece to Fiona's book "*Bride of the Isles*,"

I

From the silence of Time, Time's silence borrow:
*This is the Ancient Wisdom of Patience.*
*Patience-Silence-Stars of the Dusk of the Spirit.*

II

In the heart of To-day is the word of To-morrow –
*As Twilight sleeps in the noon and ariseth at Even,*
*As the Wave of Midnight uplifteth the Star of the Morning.*

III

The Builders of Joy are the Children of Sorrow.
*Bitter the waters of Grief; but sweet is the Well Spring.*
*Stoop and be fearless: drink, O ye Builders of Joy.* [8]

Later, in acknowledgement of William's part in this whole affair, the triad of maidens who would eventually discover and care for the bowl included the lines, "*Hail Cup of Joy!... Bless me that I may be an instrument fitted for the holy work of turning the Cup of Sorrow into the Cup of Joy*" into one of the services they composed to celebrate the cup. Yeats would later incorporate this image of sorrow becoming joy in one of the rituals created for the Celtic Mystical Order. Part of the Initiation of The Fiery Spear says, "*The Child of the Cauldron received in Sorrow, is brought forth and becomes the Child of the Spear in Joy.*" [9]

Now confident in his new ally's discretion, Goodchild took William to where the bowl was hidden, or so he still hoped, and told him the whole story as they walked, thus making William the only person in whom Goodchild confided the secret of the bowl as it still lay in the dark waters. The well there has long had a reputation as a healing well and, as at so many of these ancient watery sites, it is the custom for people to leave brightly coloured rags or scraps of material tied to nearby trees and bushes by way of thanks to the spirits of the healing waters. Amongst the prayers written on scraps of paper attached to the holy thorn tree there was one that caught their attention. The writer of that little prayer, Katharine "Kitty" Tudor Pole, was the sister of Wellesley Tudor Pole, a casual acquaintance of Goodchild's. They would both soon play a significant role in the story of the bowl and the realisation of Goodchild's dreams and hopes. It was this scrap of prayer that the voice he had heard in Paris referred to when it said, "*Later, a young girl will make a pure offering of herself at that spot where you lay down the Cup, and this shall be a sign to you.*" Here was the sign, now the author had to be found. William went home, Goodchild returned to Bath and for the next two years no more was said about the bowl or its purpose but all the time Goodchild was waiting for another sign or message from the disembodied voice to give him further instructions.

Then on August 26th 1906, while staying at a hotel in Bath, further signs were revealed. Goodchild had a vision of a sword suspended in the eastern sky. He did not know what it meant but he kept note of it. Just over a week later, on September 3rd, he had another vision this time of a cup in the western sky with balls of light forming a pattern in the sky above it. He felt compelled, he did not know why, to send a drawing of the sword vision to his friend Wellesley Tudor Pole in Bristol, which he did, and asked that it be passed on to the 'two pilgrims' who had recently been to the well in Glastonbury. The two pilgrims were friends of Tudor Pole, Janet and Christine Allen, who had been instructed by him to go to Glastonbury as a voice and psychic vision had earlier revealed to Tudor Pole that there was something of great importance buried there. We do not know, and probably never will, exactly how Goodchild knew that the Allens had made a visit to Glastonbury, the important thing is that he was correct.

Tudor Pole passed on Goodchild's letter containing his description of his vision to the Allen sisters who in response visited him at his hotel in Bath on 26th September. They recounted how their friend Wellesley Tudor Pole had had a psychic communication saying that they should go to the well in Glastonbury and search in the waters for something. They did this some three or so weeks before this meeting, which would be at roughly the same time Goodchild had had his visions, and they had found the bowl. They sensed its great power and sanctity and, not knowing what to do with it, they put it back in the stream, returned to Bristol and told Tudor Pole what had occurred. On September 29th Wellesley and his sister Kitty also visited Goodchild in Bath and he told them the whole story of the bowl from when he found it in Bordighera right up to date although he did not mention his psychic communication in Paris. The bowl at this point was still in the well so on October 1st Kitty went alone to Glastonbury, recovered it from the waters and took it back to Bristol.

It was placed in a special room in their home in Clifton, Bristol, and soon the Allen sisters and Kitty Tudor Pole, who were convinced it was the Holy Grail, were carrying out services and ceremonies in its presence. Goodchild was extremely happy as he could see his beliefs unfolding before him that women would start a new order of spirituality in the west. Wellesley Tudor Pole was also delighted, as he had long held the belief that a triad of maidens would one day find the Grail and revive the ancient Grail Church in England, and here they were, Christine Allen, Janet Allen and Kitty Tudor Pole. Goodchild tried to play down the belief that the glass bowl was the Holy Grail but the Allens and Tudor Poles were nonetheless convinced it was. At this stage it was not too important whether it was or whether it was not as none of this had been made public. Occasionally friends and guests were allowed to see the bowl and attend the services and soon reports of miracle cures and uncanny feelings of intense power emitting from the bowl inevitably started to circulate. Goodchild kept a close watch on the proceedings in Bristol but never interfered. He was happy to let the women carry things along. In one communication he said, *"Remember this, it is probable that at the present moment the Oratory at Clifton, is the one church in which the Name and Number of the Master, are exhibited and taught openly. I gave this word on Sharp's authority to KTP and her brother, before she went over for the Cup. OPEN! Is a hard word, but there are keys which will open all doors..."*[10]

This is very strange and ambiguous. Goodchild was very interested in the study of Gematria (the magical study of numbers), hence his reference to the 'Number of the Master,' and it is possible that he had been introduced to this subject by William. A book on this controversial subject, *"The Canon,"* had been published in 1897 and soon after Yeats had been given a large number of notes and manuscripts on the subject from the family of the author who had committed suicide. This was at the time when William and Yeats were working on the new Celtic Mystical Order and it is almost certain Yeats would have shown William these papers. Wherever he got his knowledge of Gematria from is irrelevant. Surviving letters from Goodchild show he employed its techniques frequently. But, in this case, William had been dead for almost a year before Kitty went to retrieve the cup, so when did he give Goodchild 'this word?' Goodchild's wording seems to imply that 'this word' had only just been revealed to him. If so, then it must have been done so psychically or through the service of a medium. If not, it implies that William intuitively knew that at some later date the event described would take place and 'this word' would need to be made known. Another possibility is 'this word' was a word of power given to Goodchild by William at some time in the past and he knew that it was now relevant to the retrieval of the bowl. Whatever he meant in this letter it does show that he still valued his friendship with William and that by revealing 'this word' William had played an important part in the whole story of the bowl.

It is interesting to note that for the period the bowl was hidden in the waters of Bride's Well, 1898 until 1906, this group of people – Janet and Christine Allen, Wellesley and Kitty Tudor Pole, William Sharp, Fiona Macleod, several others who played a later role in the events of the bowl, plus many independent mediums and psychics, all had visions and prophetic dreams that something of great importance was either buried in Glastonbury or would soon be revealed there. All believed that whatever this thing was would be of immense significance to the spiritual needs of Glastonbury, Great Britain and, in its fullest sense, the religious faiths of the Victorian and Edwardian world. It is as if the bowl, lying quietly in the murky waters of the well like a growing embryo in the amniotic fluid, was sending out psychic signals that sensitive people picked up on. This, in itself, demonstrates the incredible power and, it seems, intelligence that this ancient piece of glass had.

Soon though the word got out about the existence of the bowl and the goings-on in Bristol. The girls continued to tend to the now public services and to the safe keeping of the bowl while Wellesley took it to anyone and everyone whom he thought could explain something of its history, interpret its strange appeal and power or, generally realise and accept the basic fact that here was a thing of great spiritual importance. Likewise, important visitors started to travel to Bristol for an audience with the bowl. Almost invariably every one of them came away saying that just being in the presence of the bowl had had a profound effect on them. It was about this time, 1907-08, two years after William had died, that the bowl started to be referred to in the media as The Holy Grail. This was encouraged by the fact Wellesley called it such and several eminent people of the day to whom he had shown the bowl similarly declared that it was indeed the Holy Grail. It must be noted that throughout his lifetime Goodchild stressed over and over again that as far as he was concerned this was not the Grail, i.e. the actual cup used by Christ at the Last Supper, but was clearly a Grail in the sense of what The Grail symbolises and represents on a spiritual level. The more sensational newspapers in particular were eager to use the term Holy Grail. This greatly annoyed Goodchild who eventually wrote to *The Daily Express* to correct a rather inaccurate account of the bowl's history. In his letter he said, "*In 1899 the late William Sharp published The Divine Adventure, which contains his own vision of the Thorn. On August 1st, 1904, he paid his first visit to Glastonbury in company with myself. In the clyce* [sluice] *we found a small token left there by Miss Tudor Pole, and returned it next day with such tokens of thanks as we deemed suitable.*" [11]

In 1909 the Bristol services ceased. Kitty had moved with her family to the new, experimental garden city of Letchworth and Christine and Janet were making frequent and often distant journeys, Constantinople and Rome being but two of their many destinations, as a result of information given by psychics that these, and other, places held carvings, documents, parchments etc, which would reveal the true history of the mysterious bowl. None of these journeys produced any of the hoped for clues or answers. As a result it was becoming impossible for the triad to get together as regularly as they wished and the services were closed down. From 1909 through 1912 Goodchild stayed in regular communication with the girls and maintained an interest in the bowl and its effects but, as always, he never directly interfered. He was still carrying on his medical practice, wintering in Bordighera and was still having the occasional book published. For details of what finally happened to the Allens, Tudor Poles and the bowl see Appendix 6.

As said above, Goodchild, who did not know the secret of Fiona's identity, had sent her a copy of "*The Light of the West*" which deals with the subject of Celtic spirituality in a very mystical way. The contents of this book, and the doctor's ideas and suggestions, struck a chord with Fiona. In a letter of 1898, addressed from Outlook Tower, she thanked him for the book and went on to say how significant Iona and St. Columba are to the modern Gael and to the development of Celtic spirituality. She added, "*When I wrote certain of my writings (e.g. 'Muime Chriosd' and 'The Three Marvels of Iona') I felt, rightly or wrongly, as though I had in some measure become interpretative of the spirit of 'Colum the White.' I have long had a conviction... that out of Iona is again to come a Divine Word, that Iona, the little northern isle, will be as it were the tongue in the mouth of the South.*"[12] Here we have not just the highly romantic reveries of a young Victorian woman writer but another important piece of authentic Faery lore. The Faeries obviously hold Iona in as much esteem as ancient and modern mystics do.

In her lengthy dedication to Goodchild in "*The Winged Destiny*" she touches on the accusations still being hurled at her by Yeats, Russell and company of not paying attention to the misdeeds of this world while living permanently in a diminishing Celtic Otherworld twilight. About this she says, "*... while it is true that certain ideas monopolise my imagination, I do not wilfully ignore the lesser nor even the ignoble things of life; above all, I do not dishonestly seek to seem unaware of or to hide them. It is only that I have no time to attend to them, being otherwise busy... You who know the way of the wind in my mind know that I do not, as some say, 'dwell only in the past,' or that personal sorrow is the one magnet of my dreams. It is not the night-wind in sad hearts only that I hear... but, often, rather an emotion akin to that mysterious Sorrow of Eternity in love with tears... As to the past, it is because of what is there, that I look back: not because I do not see what is here today, or may be here tomorrow. It is because of what is to be gained that I look back; of what I supremely worth knowing there, of knowing intimately: of what is supremely worth remembering, of remembering constantly...*"[13]

The importance of Goodchild's work to Fiona cannot be overstressed yet Elizabeth and others who have examined and written on the life of William Sharp have ignored it. The one exception to this is Patrick Benham who in his excellent book "*The Avalonians*" spells it all out. They clearly shared common spiritual and magical beliefs, aims and ideals. They met on several occasions, they both influenced a large number of important people in many ways, and they both firmly believed in the imminent arrival of a female redeemer who would place Celtic spirituality back in the public eye and spirit. In her Edinburgh letter to Goodchild she said, "*I have considered as well as read your letter, and more and more I am impressed by the strangeness of the fundamentally identical spiritual ideas which come to many minds... There is a strange and obscure prophecy in the Hebrides upon which I had meant to write a long study... I have in my mind, however, all but finally thought out (my way of work) a spiritual study called 'The Second Coming of St Bride' which will give utterance to this faith in a new redeeming spiritual face, – a woman who will express the old Celtic Bride or Brigit (goddess of fire, song, music). The first modern saintliness of woman (<u>Bride-nan-Brat</u> St Brigit of the Mantle; <u>Muime-Chriosda</u> Christ's Foster Mother; Mary's Sister etc). The Virgin Mother* *of Catholicism; Mary of Motherhood; Mary, the Goddess of the Human Soul; Mary, Destiny; Mary, the Star-Kindler: for Destiny is but the name of the starry light hidden in each human soul: Consolatrix: Genetrix: the immortal Sister of Orchil, the Earth Goddess, at once Hera, Pan and Demogorgon: The Daughter of God: The Star of Dreams; The Soul of Beauty: the Shepherd of Immortality. In the short story called 'The Washer of the Ford'... there is a hint of this in another way—that of the conflict between the Pagan and the early Christian ideals of the Mysterious Woman, whether a Celtic Fate or a Mary Bride of God: as again, in another way, in a story called 'The Woman With The Net' in the Pagan section of my forthcoming book, 'The Dominion of Dreams'."* [14]

Note once again her emphasis on Brigid the goddess and Brigid the saint and the long listing of yet more names for this important Celtic and Faery deity. Brigid was clearly of great personal importance to Fiona. Today there is discussion amongst occultists as to whether Fiona may even have been a manifestation of Brigid herself. The above letter is a good example of the ease with which Fiona discussed pre-Christian beliefs alongside Christian beliefs and tenets as if they are one and the same. She never actually stated this nor commented directly on it but the letter above shows this quite clearly. This theme of pre-Christian and Christian beliefs and personages mixing freely without animosity or bias is common throughout the great work "*Carmina Gadelica.*" I have already commented on how Carmichael believed Fiona had stolen, or at least borrowed without acknowledgement, a lot of material from his original manuscript but by 1900 it seems William and Carmichael were back on good terms with each other. In a letter dated November 30th that year he said in part, "*At one time there was a chance that I might be near Taynuilt, and I looked forward greatly to see Mr. Alexander Carmichael again. He is a splendid type of the true Highlander, and of a nature incomparably sweet and refined—and I have the greatest admiration of him in all ways... A remarkable family, and I would to Heaven there were more such families in the Highlands now. Yes, what a book Carmina Gadelica is!*" [15] From this important collection of stories, songs, prayers and runes it is clear that the Gaels of the Western Isles were sincerely and faithfully practising Christianity but in a form that did not completely separate the early Pagan material from the later Christian teachings. Because Fiona claimed to be from this same area of Scotland it would be perfectly natural for her to feel comfortable with mixing two traditions that even today most people find difficult to mix. But, as we know, she was not from that part of Scotland at all. She was from Faery where the concepts of Pagan, Neo-Pagan, Christian, pre-Christian or whatever mean nothing. The above letter reveals a first-hand account of the Faery understanding of spirituality couched in terms we can relate to. She revealed much of this Faery spirituality in her published stories, poems and plays but her correspondence, which was considerable, often gave away even more.

Unfortunately this equality of Christian and pre-Christian added more strain to the tension and animosity expressed by her Irish colleagues who were trying so hard to revive the Celtic tradition and use it to show the injustices of 19th century Ireland. Many of those injustices were levelled at the iron-grip of the Catholic Church over the peasantry. They believed that for the peasantry to ever be truly free and in charge of their own lives both physical and spiritual it would be necessary for great changes to be made in the control exerted by the Catholic Church. Fiona never expressed this point of view. The subtle underlay of tolerance of both spiritual traditions in her writings was a thorn in the side of those who wished her to come on board and back the Irish cause and publicly decry the power of the Catholic Church. Dr. John Goodchild, however, clearly shared and inspired Fiona's viewpoint.

It was during her period of correspondence and meetings with Goodchild that Fiona wrote her two plays for the stage. This was a new venture for her and was an opportunity to experiment with a new, three-dimensional form of expression. The first of these, "*The House of Usna,*" was based on an old Irish legend that would have been more familiar to her Irish readers than it would to her English, Welsh, Breton or Scottish fans. In his role as literary critic and biographer William had occasion to dip into the world of the theatre. A diary entry from as early as May 18th 1893 notes that he had lunch that day with Bram Stoker. Stoker is remembered most today as the author of "*Dracula*" but he was an important person in the world of the London theatre in the 1890s and would have been an influential contact for William to have. The Stage Society in London, of which William was the first chairman, was the first to produce "*The House of Usna.*" The premiere was at The Globe Theatre on April 29th 1900. It first appeared in print in July 1900 in "*The National Review*" and was eventually published in book form in 1903 by the American publisher Thomas Mosher under the title "*Deirdre and the Sons of Usna.*"

One edition of this book, limited to 100 on Japan vellum and 925 on Van Gelder hand-made paper and published in 1903, contains a lengthy dedication to Esther Mona Rinder, his daughter by Edith Wingate Rinder who, at that time, was only two years old. In part it says, "*Little girl, when you grow to maidhood and womanhood, it is a hope of mine that you will love these old legendary tales, of which Deirdre and the Sons of Usna is one.*" and after commenting on the romantic nature of the old Gaelic legends Fiona goes on to so, "*And I... I shall have bent above the fading warmth, and have risen at last, cold, and gone away, when that little wondering heart of yours shall have become a woman's heart: and so I do not know whether, if I were to look in it, I should see beyond the shaken reeds of the mind the depth-held star of the old passion of beauty, the old longing, the old enchantment. But I hope so. Are you not the child of her, that friend to whom I inscribed my first book; of whom, in its prefatory words, I wrote 'we have loved the same things and in the same way... take, then, out of my heart, this book of vision and dream.'*" This touching dedication ends with, "*So, little one, come in time to love these things of beauty. Lay your child's heart, that is made of morning joy and evening longing, to that Mother-heart; and when you gather years, as now you gather the little white clan of the grass, it shall be well with you. And you, too, when your time is come, and you in turn pass on the mystery of life to another who will look up from your breast with eyes of still wonder and slowly shaping thought, forget not to tell the other to lay its child's heart of morning joy and evening longing against a more ancient and dream-filled heart than that of any woman, that mother-heart of which I speak to you, the Heart of Beauty."* This attempt by William to reach across time to speak to his daughter long after he knew he would be dead only ever appeared in this limited edition printing by Mosher. This was as public as he dared put it into print. [16]

William was clearly enthralled with the medium of the theatre and attended the rehearsals and assisted with production and direction of the play enthusiastically. He was so wrapped up in all the theatrical excitement that he seemed to forget that the author was not William Sharp but Fiona Macleod. He came dangerously close to accidentally revealing the secret of the author's true identity. He did not seem care. He was happy to see the work that had taken months to complete finally being presented to the public. It was only moderately successful. One critic said, *"It had beauty and it had atmosphere, two very rare things on the stage, but I did not feel that it quite made a drama, or convince, as a drama should, by the continuous action of inner or outer forces. It was, rather, passion turning upon itself, and with no language but a cry."* This is exactly the sort of statement that you would expect to be attributed to anything by Fiona. It also echoes the criticisms of the Irish revivalists. But it again displays the very real differences between this world and the world of Faery. Fiona was indeed writing from her heart, her Faery heart, but this did not translate into human understanding in a way that the literary and theatre critics could grasp. All would-be magicians who wish to successfully negotiate with Faery would do well to pay heed to this.

The second play that year was *"The Immortal Hour"* and it was quite a different matter altogether. Fiona had planned these plays to be part of a series that she referred to variously as *"The Theatre of the Soul"* or *"The Psychic Drama."* Other titles planned for the series but never completed were *"Nial the Soulless"*, *"The King of Ys"*, *"Drostan and Yssul"*, *"The Veiled Avenger"*, *"The Enchanted Valleys"* and *"The Book of Dalua."* The *"Book of Dalua"* would have been a very interesting book had she ever completed it. *"The Immortal Hour"* was never performed on the stage during William's lifetime but later became hugely successful as the opera composed by Rutland Boughton.

As already noted, Fiona and Goodchild corresponded on his impressions of *"The Immortal Hour."* It is clear from Fiona's questions and answers that she felt this piece to be of particular significance and that Goodchild's acceptance and understanding of it was important to her. In one letter dated November 15th 1900 she asked Goodchild, *"... and what do you think of Dalua, the Fool, here and elsewhere..."* to which he replied, *"As regards Dalua, I know nothing of him by name except what you have written yourself."* [17] As far as the Celtic mythology of this world is concerned Dalua does not and never did exist. But Fiona clearly believed he did and was keen to hear what her knowledgeable correspondent and friend had to say on the matter. Once again Fiona was unable to distinguish between the mythology of this world in which Goodchild dwelt, and the mythology of the Faery realm where she and Dalua dwelt. Elizabeth include this letter in her memoir but she was still at pains to distance her husband from the good doctor when she said again described Goodchild as, "... *his unknown correspondent...*"

It was at this time that the rift between the Irish Celts and the other Celtic nationals, Scottish, Welsh, Manx, Cornish and Breton, became more public. Letters were being written to newspapers and so forth voicing the Irish Celts' desire for political as well as cultural independence but that the Scottish, Welsh, Manx, Cornish and Breton Celts were ignoring this topic in favour of a Celtic revival that concentrated too much on literature and the arts. Several Celtic and pan-Celtic movements and organisations sprang up with pamphlets and magazines being published, and conferences and meetings being held regularly in Dublin and elsewhere. Elizabeth notes in her memoir that William took an interest in these new ventures, even subscribing under both his own and Fiona's names to some of their publications. But she states, "*F.M. deplored the uniting of the political element to the movement—and naturally had no inclination towards any such feeling.*" [18] This shows that even Elizabeth, who knew the secret longer and more intimately than anyone, recognised Fiona as being separate from her husband and capable of independent thoughts and desires. By now she had also come to realise that Fiona, being a Faery, "*naturally had no inclination towards any such feeling.*" She goes on to say, "*William Sharp's great desire was that the Celtic spirit should be kept alive, and be a moulding influence towards... yearning after spiritual beauty, whether expressed in Gaelic or in the English tongue.*" He was greatly concerned that the language, ways, songs, stories and perhaps the entire Gaelic culture would be lost in no more than two generations if people like Fiona did not continue to focus on the literary, artistic and spiritual side of the culture, even if it meant expressing such things in the English language. Clearly Fiona had to write in English, the language of her readers, but she used the Gaelic idiom whenever quoting direct speech. This is quite different from English and helped add to the ephemeral, romantic mien of her tales.

Although William spoke Gaelic he was not a native speaker. He learned most of his Gaelic as a child from his Hebridean nurse Barbara and then practiced as much as he could during his frequent trips to the Gaeltacht especially when he met up with Fiona's father Seumas Macleod. It was this that helped him glean so much lore and myth from the Gaelic speakers of the Highlands and Islands. His diaries and personal notebooks are full of one-liners, quotes, runes and verses in Gaelic as if copied from various sources or picked up during conversations with Gaelic speakers he met on his travels.

Fiona used Gaelic a lot in her writings, mainly in the form of Gaelic sayings or expressions, sometimes entire poems. Some of those we know were definitely borrowed from Carmichael's *"Carmina Gadelica"* (the original edition of this was bilingual) but many were original to her work. However several Gaelic scholars of the day expressed surprise at how poor her Gaelic was considering that this was coming from a young woman who was supposedly born and raised in the Gaeltacht where, in those days, Gaelic would have been her first language.

William tended to ignore these comments as much as he could but sometimes he could not avoid dealing directly with them. For example, in a letter to his friend John Macleay dated February 18th 1896 he says, *"Although I did not know it was noticeable, I am not surprised at Mr. Macbain's noting the Irishicism of Miss Macleod's Gaelic. As, of course, there is good reason for this, of a private kind! But over and above this Mr. Macbain may not know that the Gaelic spoken in Arran and Iona, two islands where Miss Macleod spent years as a child, before she lived further west, is full of Irish words and idioms. On the whole, Iona Gaelic is probably the least pure in the whole west. There is a marked difference between it and that of Tiree and Coll even. And between an Inverness man and an Iona man there is as much dialectical divergence as between a Yorkshireman and a Devonian. I dare say Mr. Macbain knows this: but you might bring his attention to this."*[19] William also asked Mr. Macleay to tell the Mr. Macbain not to write directly to Fiona again as she was ill and had been advised by her doctor to take a complete rest. Clearly he wished to avoid any further in-depth discussion on the Gaelic language.

What he says about the Arran and Iona Gaelic being close to Irish is still true but would have been more so in the late 19th century, standardised Gaelic being a late 20th century development, but what did he mean by, *"there is good reason for this, of a private kind!"*? Perhaps this was just one more red herring deliberately put out there to make tracing the real Fiona Macleod all the more difficult. Or perhaps it is something to do with the way Faeries use language. What is their language? Indeed, do they speak to each other in the way we do or do they communicate on a more subtle level? If the Faery Fiona had the Gaelic language herself then she would not have relied upon William's inferior, non-native version for her writings. This opens up some very interesting areas of research for those who wish to learn more of the Faery realm and particularly Faery language.

But back to the schism between Irish and Scot: the Irish approach was much more militant, anti-English and very caught up in a struggle for national independence. The debate and at times animosity was also being carried on out of the public eye in correspondence between Fiona, Sharp, Yeats, George Russell, T.W. Rolleston and others. Ironically what none of these Celtic writers seemed to spot was that their very in-fighting and disagreements are a large part and parcel of the Celtic soul. To this day Celt can agree with Celt on trivia and on the bigger picture of things. But when it comes to the important area in-between, the details, the nuts and bolts, the hows and whys of any given matter, we still fall into passionate and at times protracted and heated disagreements. Fiona's approach had always been to use suggestion, as contained in literature, rather than outright political action or statements. William too preferred this approach and as early as 1877 he had made this point to Elizabeth when he said he believed, *"People won't be preached to. Truth can be inculcated far better by inference, by suggestion..."* [20]

There was one subtle facet to the Irish struggle that was probably lost on William and Fiona. Ireland has always been, and especially at that time of renewed nationalism, symbolised by a goddess figure whose role is as the great mother, Mother Ireland. So strong was this matriarchal spiritual connection that Yeats and virtually all other nationalist Irish writers used it in their prose, poems and plays. The suffering peasants were seen as the hopeless children of a brave and strong mother who was fighting for them against the English and against all odds. Maud Gonne was particularly strong on this concept and saw herself in that role. She wrote, *"We were both held by the mysterious power of the land. To me Ireland was the all-protecting mother, who had to be released from the bondage of the foreigner, to be free and able to protect her children..."* [21] This emotional connection with the spirit of the land has never been expressed in these maternal terms in Scotland. William and Fiona both fought for the freedom and rights of real, physical mothers but they did not see the nationalist struggle of the Celts in the terms of a great Mother and her children. Perhaps if they had things would not have become so hostile.

This theme of Mother Ireland became so over-played in some activists minds that after Ireland actually won its independence from Britain the term fell out of favour. The I.R.A. activist Mairead Farrell, who was killed by the British S.A.S. Regiment in Gibraltar in 1988, said while in Armagh jail, *"It became a standard joke in there, this mother image, and we would joke about it and we would say, 'Mother Ireland get off our back.'"* She concluded with, *"It didn't reflect what we believed in, and it just doesn't reflect Ireland... Today we've moved away from that and we're not going to go backwards, we're moving forwards."* [22] The reason why Farrell called this a joke is because there is a pun in the Gaelic language that is lost in English. The old poetic name for Ireland is Erin but in modern Irish this word means a burden or an oppressive weight.

However more mundane and pressing matters were making themselves known, namely in the form of William's health. It was clear that the British climate was once again taking its toll on him. He was frequently sick and it took him longer and longer to recuperate from each bout. So, true to past habit, they once again packed up their belongings and on October 12th headed off first to France and then on to Italy. He was still very productive during this period, producing many William Sharp articles and criticisms for several magazines. They stayed in the Provence region until Christmas and were soon socialising with the local writers and poets, some of not insignificant renown, and striking up new and lasting friendships. William also planned a romance based in Provence, to be called "*Gypsy Trail*" which was inspired by the spiritual connections the gypsy people have with Provence. This was to have been a vehicle for him to recall his early experiences while living with the gypsies in Scotland during his teen years. It was never written.

By the start of the new century the Sharps were enjoying the wintry sunshine of Sicily. William's correspondence to friends from there is long, flowery, ecstatically happy and with very little mention of any writing projects. He was clearly enjoying the health-giving relaxation he had hoped to find. While there the news came from England that Queen Victoria had died. The large British community held a memorial service that Elizabeth described as impressive. At the service William and Elizabeth were introduced to the Hon. Alexander Nelson Hood, Duke of Bronte, with whom they immediately became close and dear friends. Indeed, William would later die at the Duke's Sicilian estate on the slopes of Mount Etna. Curiously, the old Coat of Arms for one branch of the Clan Macleod shows an erupting volcano. In the courtyard to the Duke's large home was a large Celtic cross carved in lava, a memorial to Lord Nelson with whom one of the Duke's ancestors had sailed. Only a few years later another Celtic cross carved in lava would be erected close by. The Duke's father, Viscount Bridport, had been Victoria's Lord in Waiting for forty years and entertained his guests with his personal reminiscences of life at the Royal Court, the Queen and, no doubt, of her devoted Scottish servant John Brown who, in his lifetime, had also been charged with neglecting his Celtic heritage in favour of an outlook that was considered by his critics as being too English. Here is another Arthurian connection: the Hood family came from the village of Butleigh which is near Glastonbury. They were great sailors and ranked high in the Royal Navy. For services to his country one of them was given the title Lord Hood of Avalon.

Before leaving in March for England Fiona wrote a letter to Edith that concluded with these words, "*But do not speak of the spiritual life as 'another life': there is no 'other life': what we mean by that is with us now. The great misconception of Death is that it is the only door to another world.*" [23] More Faery philosophy and an indication that death was on William's mind.

Once back in London both William and Fiona picked up on their respective writing projects and correspondence. In America the publisher T. Mosher had been printing versions of several of Fiona's books. These differed in some instances from the original British editions. Fiona sent a copy of one of these American editions to Yeats who, eventually, sent her a long reply. In it he made it clear that he preferred her prose to her poetry but, even then, he preferred when she allowed the myth to speak for itself rather than when she tried to put too many words of her own into the story. The letter is by no means negative or overly critical but rather the well-considered words of a true friend and one who was amply qualified to comment on prose and poetry. He ended this letter with some criticism of himself, "*To some extent I have an advantage over you in having a very fierce nation to write for. I have to make everything very hard and clear, as it were. … You have in the proper sense far more imagination than I have and that makes your work correspondingly more difficult. It is fairly easy for me, who do so much of my work by the critical, rather than the imaginative faculty, to be precise and simple, but it is hard for you in whose mind images form themselves without ceasing and are gone as quickly perhaps. But I am sure that I am right. When you speak with the obviously personal voice in your verse, or in your essays you are not that Fiona who has invented a new thing, a new literary method. You are that Fiona when the great myths speak through you.*" Note the first two sentences of the above quotation highlight the basic difference he and the other Irish writers felt they had to deal with in their work, restrictions which they felt clearly did not apply to Fiona's Scottish based writings. Note also that in the final two sentences Yeats unwittingly acknowledged the fact that our myths are nothing less than the factual history of Faery.

To the credit of Yeats I would like to point out that the above letter, complimentary and helpful in content, was sent by him during the time that there was real animosity between the Irish activists and Fiona. Yet he was able to totally separate his literary mind from his political mind and acknowledge honestly and sincerely the good work of a fellow wordsmith without reverting to the accusations of other correspondence. This ability and clarity would serve him well in his later political and diplomatic career in the newly independent Ireland.

In December 1901, five months after Esther was born, Fiona wrote to Goodchild and said, "*I had hoped by this time to have some definite knowledge of what I am to do, where to go this winter … Our friend* [William]*, too is kept to England by the illness of others … What long months of preparation have to go to any writing that contains life within it … We, all of us who live this dual life of the imagination and the spirit, do indeed mysteriously conceive, and fare thereafter in weariness and heaviness and long travail, only for one small uncertain birth.*" (Memoir, page 338) Note the frequent use of terms relating to pregnancy and delivery, 'long months of preparation,' 'contains life within,' 'mysteriously conceive,' 'long travail,' 'one small uncertain birth.' Was the 'illness of others' actually his need to be with Edith and Esther during those important first few months?

By the end of 1901 the British winter once again proved too strenuous for William and he left alone for Italy. He claimed the reason for travelling alone was that Elizabeth's mother required her constant presence due to a serious illness, but perhaps the real reason was that she was helping Edith and baby Esther. Prior to leaving England Fiona had again been writing to Goodchild and William went to Bordighera to be near him. We have no record of what happened or what intriguing things they got up to but I am sure they did not just lie back and enjoy the sun. From there he eventually went on to spend the rest of the winter with the Duke of Bronte. Elizabeth joined them in February of 1902 and, as in their previous visit, little writing was produced by either of them.

The summer of 1902 was spent back among the Scottish islands of Arran, Colonsay and Lismore. Here both William and Fiona were once again writing furiously and were fully back into the swing of things. Most of William's work was literary criticism for various magazines, all of which was published, but much of Fiona's considerable output for this period was never published. Amongst the pieces written were "*The Four Winds of Eire*," "*The Magic Kingdoms*" a long piece which William described as, '... one of the best things F.M. has ever written,' "*Sea Magic*," plus two pieces that were published, "*The Lynn of Dreams*" and "*Seumas*." At this section in her memoir Elizabeth relates one of the very few incidents in her book that did not involve William or Fiona. It is a small vignette but worth repeating. The ferryman with whom they were lodging on the little isle of Lismore would not speak the Gaelic when she was present as he thought she was English. When she explained she was actually Scottish his attitude changed completely and he opened up to her. He would take her rowing and she recalled, "*One day when we were out on the loch at sundown, and an exquisite rosy flush lay over the hill and water, he stopped rowing and leant over his oars, silent for a time, and at last murmured in his slow Highland English 'Tis the smile of God upon the waters.'*"[24]

Despite being happily settled back in his beloved Western Isles, and despite the obvious amount of creative energy he was expounding, his health was becoming more and more frail, to the extent that his friends became gravely concerned for his future. The Hon. Alexander Nelson Hood and Alfred Austin, with the backing of George Meredith, Thomas Hardy and Watts Dunton, approached the Prime Minister of Great Britain, Mr. Balfour, with a view to having William Sharp added to the Civil Pension List.[25] This would not alleviate his health conditions but would guarantee him a sufficient income upon which to live and thereby at least remove that constant worry from his mind. Alex Hood suggested that Balfour would need to be told the secret about Fiona, as a claim from William Sharp on its own would probably not be accepted. William agreed but stressed that the Prime Minister could only be told the full story verbally and in confidence.

It was not so easy. The conditions for application to be added to the Civil List stated that, "*A statement of entire claims to consideration should be laid upon the table of the House of Commons for the inspection of members.*" This was impossible as clearly to do so would result in the whole world knowing the Fiona Macleod secret. Alex Hood wrote to William to explain this and left the decision up to him whether to go ahead with the claim or not. In a very sensitively worded letter he said in part, "*If you will sacrifice your unwillingness to appear before the world in all the esteem and admiration which you are due, then, (I may say this), perhaps you will obtain freedom—or some freedom—from anxiety and worry that will permit you to continue your work but unhampered and with a quiet mind."*[26] Here his friend has shown how obvious it was to all who knew the truth about Fiona Macleod, that William's obsession with keeping it secret was utterly destroying his life. William replied from Edinburgh on August 21st 1902 and made it clear in a very long letter that he was not going to divulge the secret now after all he and Fiona had achieved. To quote part, *"I have not made many sacrifices just to lay them aside when a temptation of need occurs... rightly or wrongly I believe that this* [his spiritual life] *depends upon my aloofness and spiritual isolation as F.M. ... how much more must I feel it now, when an added and greater responsibility to others has come to me, through the winning of so already large and deepening a circle of those of like ideals or at least like sympathies in our own country, and in America. As to 'name and fame', well, that is not my business... that being so, my concern is not to think of myself or my 'name' or 'reward', but to do (with what renunciation, financial and other, may be necessary) my truest and best. Elizabeth will, I know, wholeheartedly endorse my decision"* [27] His comment about 'an added and greater responsibility to others has come to me' refers to Esther who at that time was less than a year old.

Alex Hood took this letter, in confidence, to Balfour and made the secret known to him only. Balfour agreed that he could not lay out all this information to the House in order to award a Civil List Pension but he was so impressed when he heard the whole story that he personally authorised a grant that would meet William's immediate financial needs, allowing him to once again over-winter in Sicily. Balfour may have been so easily swayed as he had at one time been President of the Society for Psychical Research and was no doubt personally interested in the whole Fiona Macleod phenomenon now that the secret had been revealed to him. Once again Fate arranged for money to come his way when he needed it most. Well done, Mr. Balfour. I wonder how many times a British Prime Minister has knowingly awarded public money to a Faery in her time of need?

This letter also contains an insight into how William saw the whole phenomena of Fiona Macleod, a subject he did not usually address in any depth. Following the disclosure of the secret after his death there was much written by others on this subject. They basically fell into four camps, or a mixture of the four. These were a) it was a case of dual personalities, b) Fiona Macleod was a previous incarnation of William Sharp, c) William was being used a channel or medium for a feminine entity from some other plane or sphere of existence, or d) it was nothing more than a literary hoax. In his letter William said, *"Rightly or wrongly, I am conscious of something to be done – to be done by one side of me, by one half of me, by the true inward self, as I believe – (apart from the overwhelmingly felt mystery of a dual self and, a reminiscent life, and a woman's life and nature within, concurring with and oftenest dominating the other) – and, rightly or wrongly, I believe that this, and the style so strangely born of this inward life, depend upon my aloofness and spiritual isolation as Fiona Macleod... I am glad and content to be a 'messenger', an interpreter, ... In a word, and quite simply, I believe that a spirit has breathed in me, or entered me, or that my soul remembers or has awaked."* [28] In a nutshell what he is saying is even he did not know. He considers that all of the first three options a), b) and c) were possibilities, but settles in the end on option c) he was a channel for a feminine entity other than of this world. Note that option d) a literary hoax, does not even enter into his consideration. It did not matter to him what Fiona 'really' was. All he knew for certain was that he felt strongly that '*something* [had] *to be done.*' This was the driving force and this was all that mattered. So with his Faery-grant from the British public he was once more off to Sicily.

The modern science of the study of DNA has recently thrown up another possibility. More and more people are being discovered who are "DNA Chimeras." This basically means that for some reason they have two complete sets of DNA within their body. Up until recently medical science was unaware of this phenomenon because DNA samples were normally only taken from one source on the body, the blood or a cheek-swab for example. Now however it has been discovered that taking multiple samples – from blood, hair, cheek, tissue, saliva etc – occasionally reveals different sets of DNA within the physical body of an individual person. Clearly this is opening up a minefield as far as DNA evidence in legal cases is concerned but it is also opening up discussion on the causes of certain mental and emotional problems such as dual or multiple personalities and may eventually shed more light on the esoteric subject of the existence of mixed human and Faery bloodlines.

The tone of his letters from Italy and Sicily show that he was soon back in high spirits and revelling in the romantic beauty that he devoured all around him. He again attacked his neglected work with a new energy but mixed his time with excursions, sightseeing and socialising. On one trip into the surrounding countryside his companion Alex Hood spied two armed bandits hiding in the undergrowth ahead ready to ambush the two foreigners. Instead of turning and fleeing Hood ran at them, revolver in hand. The two bandits were so astonished by his reckless action that *they* fled. One got away but William and his friend managed to capture the accomplice. In his defence he insisted his he had meant them no harm and that his weapon was merely a protection against wolves. William was experienced enough to be able to tell fact from fiction and he was duly handed over at the next village and arrested by the local Carabinieri.

As always when their spirits returned, William and Fiona engaged in lengthy correspondences with admirers, friends, publishers and other writers and poets. In February 1903 he wrote to Catharine Janvier, "... *letters are now my worst evil to contend against ... it is almost impossible to get anything like adequate time for essential work ... I have continually to put into each day the life of two persons – each with his or her own interests, preoccupations, work, thoughts, and correspondence. I have really ... to live at exactly double the rate in each day of the most active and preoccupied persons. No wonder, then, that I find the continuous correspondence of 'two persons' not only a growing weariness, but a terrible strain and indeed perilous handicap on time and energy for work ..."* [29]

He made a trip from Sicily to Greece via Albania to obtain background material for a travel piece he intended to write as William Sharp. His correspondence to Elizabeth and friends from this trip is full of adventures, lengthy descriptions of Albanians, gypsies, Greek peasants and so on. He described Albania as *"lost Eden"* and when he arrived in Athens he commented, *"This lovely place is wonderful. It is a marvellous <u>homecoming</u> feeling I have here. And I know a strange stirring, a kind of spiritual rebirth."* [30] Note that all of these gushing, enthusiastic descriptions of new places and peoples, and especially comments on the spiritual effect they had, always came from William, never Fiona.

The return trip from Italy and Greece in the spring took them via France to see friends and, eventually, back to England. William had been a good friend with the writer George Meredith and in June of 1903 he paid a visit to him at his home in Box Hill. Meredith was very sick and both men knew they would probably never meet again in this life. William was saddened by his friend's condition. As always, he commented on this visit at length in correspondence to other writers and friends. In one letter to Edith he commented, *"I could (selfishly) wished that he had known a certain secret: but it is better not, and now is in every way as undesirable as indeed impossible."* [31] From other comments in this same letter it is clear that Meredith held Fiona in the highest esteem making it even more difficult for William to reveal the truth. Even after keeping the secret so well for a decade William was still troubled by the deception he was imposing on old and dear friends. He and Elizabeth commented many times on the terrible strain this placed him under, as witnessed with the Civil List application, and both knew it was a large contributing factor in his continued ill health.

As if to emphasise this, that summer while visiting friends in Scotland, William became so ill that it was necessary for him to retreat to a health spa in Wales to take the waters. His frail health did not stop his continuous correspondence, under both names, but he did lay aside his and her writings. He also seems to have been facing up to the possibility that his own death was not too far away. This was probably aggravated by Meredith's recent demise as well as his own obvious bad health problems. He commented in a letter to Ernest Rhys, *"Fortunately, the eventuality does not trouble me, either way: I have lived, and am content, and it is only for what I don't want to leave undone that the sounds of 'Farewell' has anything deeply perturbing."* [32] In that year he underwent three days of painful surgery. Catharine Janvier was concerned for him and he wrote to her from London saying, *"You are not to worry yourself about me. I'm all right, and as cheerful as a lark—let us say as a lark with a rheumatic wheeze in its little song-box or gout in its little off-claw... Anyway, I'll laugh and be glad and take life as I find it, till the end. The best prayer for me is that I may live vividly till 'Finis', and work up to the last hour."* [33] He did.

William was working on a series of travel essays he called '*Literary Geography*' for the Pall Mall Magazine. He planned such an essay on Greece, hence his first visit to that country the previous winter, and now, with the winter of 1903 approaching, he and Elizabeth were preparing yet again to pack their bags and take the steamer to Sicily. The first part of the voyage was plagued by severe storms and his ill health made things even worse for him. In what must be one of his greatest understatements he commented that during the terrible voyage, "*I was very unwell, partly from an annoying heart attack.*" [34] Fortunately the annoying heart attack did not prove fatal and they eventually arrived in Italy.

In her memoir Elizabeth reveals that William had developed a technique which helped him cope with unpleasant physical conditions or times of severe ill health, by mentally creating an inner landscape which was much more pleasing and acceptable than the circumstances he was actually in. He would then set down in writing, usually in verse, a vivid description of what he was seeing. He was able to mentally create these pacific inner landscapes during times of extreme stress so well that he became oblivious of his true physical condition or circumstances and could, literally, weather the storm in the tranquillity of his own mind until outer conditions returned to normal. Nowadays we would probably call these practices 'guided meditations' or 'pathworkings.' William had a distinct advantage when it came to visualising an inner landscape. Not only had he been through a formal magical training but he was also intimate with a woman of the Faery realms who could easily unlock the doors to her homeland and let him roam free there when the need arose.

When they arrived in Athens they stayed at the interestingly named Maison Merlin and immediately fell in with the ex-patriot British community as well as the local Greek writers and artists. There is an undated scrap of paper in the Sharp Collection, Bancroft Library, Berkeley which has the following written on it in William's hand:-

**By Fiona Macleod**
**A Daughter of Merlin**

i. A Daughter of Merlin
ii. The Dark Mill of Achnacarry
iii. The Wrath Fire
v. The Sin-Eater
iv. The Leannan-Sithe
vi. Andromeda of the Isles

Note that the numbering is out of sequence. The other side of this scrap of paper says:-

*The Celtic Sorrow*
*(Notes and Episodes from the Isles of West Highlands)*
*by Fiona Macleod*

Apart from "*The Sin-Eater*" none of these were published, and were probably never written. Fiona did not write much about the Arthurian Romance at all despite its size and popularity. It is an interesting concept though, a daughter of Merlin. I wonder where Fiona would have gone with <u>that</u> possibility? Only one poem, "*The Last Fay*" (Poems and Dramas, page 272) deals with Merlin, and Arthur is only mentioned in the essay "*Beyond the Blue Septentrions*" (Where the Forest Murmurs, page 379 et seq) with regard to his mythological link to certain ancient star lore. In the 1902 Tauchnitz edition "*Wind and Wave*" there is a short tale entitled "*In Avalon*" which is actually the opening section of a longer story called "*The Birds of Emar*" that appeared in "*The Dominion of Dreams.*" The opening of this tale is set in the Scottish Isle of Arran whose old Gaelic name is linked linguistically to the name Avalon but the tale itself has no connection to the Avalon of King Arthur.

His health improved somewhat but he was clearly not able to recuperate back to full health. Each summer in Britain affected him worse than the previous and each winter in Italy and Greece produced less of a return to full health than the previous year had. It was clear to everyone who knew him that his time was running out. Despite his increasing frailty he did enjoy Greece enormously and wrote enthusiastically of his daily experiences to many of his friends back in Britain and France.

---

[1] Memoir, page 315

[2] Memoir, page 316, emphasis in the original

[3] Goodchild, The Light of the West, pages 104-105

[4] Memoir, page 320

[5] Benham, The Avalonians, page 17

[6] NLS, Edinburgh

[7] Benham, The Avalonians, pages 37-38

[8] "Bride of the Isles", T.N. Foulis, 1914

[9] Kalogera, page 192

[10] Benham, The Avalonians, page 52

[11] Benham, The Avalonians, page 80

[12] Memoir, page 317

[13] "The Winged Destiny", page ix

[14] NLS, Edinburgh

[15] Memoir, page 325

[16] "Deirdre And The Sons Of Usna", Thomas Mosher, Portland, Maine, 1903, limited edition, pages v - xii

[17] Memoir, page 319

[18] Memoir, page 321

[19] NLS, Edinburgh

[20] Memoir, page 26

[21] Gwynn, Scattering Branches, page 20

[22] Cullingford, "At the Feet of the Goddess: Yeats's Love Poetry and the Feminist Occult", "Yeats Annual, No. 9", page 50

[23] Memoir, page 332

[24] Memoir, page 344

[25] Before the introduction of automatic welfare benefits and pensions to all UK citizens the government could award a payment or series of payments from the state purse to individuals in certain circumstances. These names were then placed on the Civil List.

[26] Memoir, page 346

[27] Memoir, page 346

[28] "Fortnightly Review", Nov 1919, page 781

[29] Memoir, page 362

[30] Memoir, page 365, emphasis in original

[31] Memoir, page 367

[32] Memoir, page 369

[33] Janvier, "Fiona Macleod and her Creator", "The North American Review", April 1907, page 731

[34] Memoir, page 373

# Chapter 10
# Last Days ... and More

*I have never heard Will more brilliant
than he has been tonight.*

Instead of heading straight for Italy that winter they decided to go via New York in order that Elizabeth could become acquainted with the people William had met on his previous visits to the States. During this time Fiona had been writing a series of nature essays for serial publication in the popular magazine "*Country Life.*" These were eventually collected together and published posthumously in 1906 to much critical acclaim under the title "*Where the Forest Murmurs.*" These short essays contain less of any deep spiritual significance regarding Celtic or Faery lore in comparison to her earlier work but they do still contain fragments of lore, hints at useful meditative symbols and general pointers as to the aspects of nature we should be paying attention to. From a purely literary point of view they also display that she was still capable of producing the romantic and sometimes dramatic descriptive passages that so defined her earlier work. One critic in "*The Contemporary Review*" summed up with "*Where the Forest Murmurs*" with, "*Fiona Macleod's prose baffles description. It is perhaps hardly prose at all. It is melody in words suggesting scenes as much as by sound as by the passage of ideas ... But it is ... something quite alone: pure music of a strange and curious quality that is neither prose nor poetry, but thrilling with the pain and passion of a Gaelic chant. It conveys to the mind and heart the scenes and sounds of nature with almost magical accuracy.*" [1] This critic hit the nail on the head by describing its 'almost magical accuracy' considering that it all came from the mind and heart of a Faery.

The comment on the musical quality of her choice of words is interesting as several others had noticed this effect too. In 1902 the American composer Edward MacDowell was inspired to write a piece he called the "*Keltic Sonata*" because, "*Your poems have been an inspiration to me and I trust you will accept a dedication of music that is yours already by right of suggestion.*

*By this I do not mean that my music in any way echoes your words but that your words have been a most powerful incentive to me in my music and I crave your sympathy for it."* [2] The Scottish-American composer Helen Hopekirk set several of Fiona's poems to music, much to the delight of Fiona, William, Elizabeth and, no doubt, Edith. Just before leaving for New York in 1904 Fiona wrote to the American music critic Lawrence Gilman and thanked him for some favourable references he had made to her writing in one of his books on music. On their previous visit to the Duke of Bronte another guest, Maud Valerie White, urged William to compose a short poem in commemoration of their happy time together. This he did and Miss White set it to music based on a Sicilian air. However the *piece de resistance* to all of these musical connections was when the British composer Rutland Boughton set Fiona's play "*The Immortal Hour*" to music with unexpected results.

The visit to New York went ahead as planned and Elizabeth was delighted to finally meet the correspondents with whom William and Fiona had been engaged for the past few years. However the winter weather there came in earlier, stronger and colder than they had expected and so for the sake of William's health they cut short their U.S. visit and took a steamer direct from New York to Naples. They arrived in Italy in time to spend Christmas with "*friends at Bordighera,*" probably 'the unknown correspondent' Dr. Goodchild. From the surviving correspondence and from Elizabeth's comments in her memoir it is clear that this time the stay in Italy did not have the re-energizing or rejuvenating influences previous ones had. Fiona wrote to her American publisher T. Mosher and apologised for her tardiness in writing and commented on the fact that despite being in the warm and healthy atmosphere of the Mediterranean she was still too weak and too tired to start any serious writing projects. In part she said, "*The days go by and I say 'at night'—and every night I am too tired or listless, and say 'tomorrow': and so both the nights and the morrows go to become thistles in the Valley of Oblivion.*" [3]

The winter was spent pleasantly enough with the usual social functions, afternoon teas and society dinners but by spring 1905 they were, again, back in the U.K. William's correspondence noticeably lightened up from now on and he seemed to be happier back in England and Scotland, despite the poor weather and his ill health, and his humour had certainly returned. While visiting the island of Lismore near Oban, Scotland, with his sister Mary, he sent the following card to a friend, "*Awful accident in a lonely Isle of the West. A distinguished stranger was observing the vasty deep, and had laid a flask-filled cup on a rock beside him when a tamned gull upset it and at the same time carried off a valuable Indian cheroot. Deep sympathy is everywhere expressed, for the distinguished stranger, the lost cheroot, and above all for the spilt cup and abruptly emptied flask. A gloom has been cast over the whole island.*" [4] Lismore was the birth place in 1832 of Alexander Carmichael, collector of the runes and sayings that he published as "*Carmina Gadelica.*"

While on Lismore he listened with fascination to a local fisherman who told tales of a Maighdeann Mhara (literally 'maiden of the sea,' a mermaid) who had very recently been seen and heard sobbing in a cavern on the island. He and Mary attempted to get to the cave but the weather was too windy and cold and they abandoned their attempt. They stayed that night with this same fisherman and he and William swapped horror tales of the sea and sea creatures late into the night to the point that Mary abruptly excused herself and crept off to bed in a state of fright. This was the sort of stuff that his nurse Barbara had raised young William on and it was the very essence of Fiona's earlier writings. Clearly he still felt the excitement of these tales and alleged sightings of mythical beasts and still cherished the company of the local people of the islands.

On April 20th 1905 William wrote to Elizabeth from Lismore to say he had just learned that Fiona had been made an honorary member of the French League of Writers. He was delighted with this news and finished the short letter to his wife by saying, "We're glad, aren't we, you and I? She's our daughter, isn't she?"[5] Was his emphasis on Fiona being their daughter due to the fact that he had his own daughter, Esther, with Edith and that Elizabeth regretted they had never had any children of their own? The existence of Esther must have been very hard for Elizabeth who had learned to accept the presence of Edith in William's life as being necessary but I am sure neither Elizabeth, William or Edith had expected a child to appear.

After all those same years his personal life was still being affected by the need to keep Fiona's identity a secret. Sadly for William she would never be able to give a public acceptance speech to the French League of Writers. Not only was maintaining the secret still affecting his need for caution in words and comments but it was also curtailing his freedom of movement. In a letter sent a few days later he commented to Elizabeth that he had abandoned his original plan to leave Lismore and go on to Iona because he had learned he would be the only stranger there and he knew it was a place where a lookout was being maintained for any sightings of Fiona. He dared not arrive on the island in company with his sister Mary and risk facing a barrage of questions from the zealous members of the Press who were all hoping to be the one to get the first pictures and interview with the elusive Miss Macleod.

In the same letter he said, "However, it is isolation plus 'atmosphere' I want most of all—and I doubt if there is any place just now I could get so much good from as Lismore... And I have got much of what I want—the 'in-touch' above all, the atmosphere: enough to strike the keynote throughout the coming year and more, for I absorb through the very pores of both mind and body like a veritable sponge."[6] Although this letter was from William the description of how he gained inspiration by absorbing the atmosphere of the quiet little island clearly relates to Fiona. His winters in Italy were necessary for his own physical health but his springs and summers in the Highlands and Islands were just as necessary for Fiona's creativity to continue and remain fresh. Fiona had commented on her 'use' of the Western Isles in a letter to John Macleay on June 8th 1899 where she said, "*But I don't 'go to the isles' for beauty. The isles—the past—the pagan wonder and mystery—come to me! It is what a writer receives that makes him or her. All art is from within. It is from what dies into one, and is reborn.*"[7] This helps to explain her constant references in correspondence to traveling from island to island, or small fishing village to small fishing village, the length and breadth of the Western Isles. These were rejuvenating and inspirational journeys rather than business or social obligations. Even a Faery can feel homesick and in need of the familiar and comfortable.

On April 25th William left Lismore for the mainland. While traveling by train from Oban he wrote a short letter to Elizabeth. The handwriting is very shaky because of the movement of the train but probably also due to his ill health. He said, "*Yes, I was sorry to leave Lismore. It may be my last time in the Gaelic West. I don't say this 'down-ly'—but because I think it likely; and, in a way I'll explain later, am even glad. There is much that I want, and now, need to do and that I realise must be done abroad where alone can I keep well—mentally even more than physically.*"[8] Elizabeth quotes an edited version of this letter in her memoir but omits the comment about being glad that this may have been his last trip to the Gaelic West. Was this a premonition of his death that would occur less than eight months later? Why was he glad at the thought of never going back to the Gaelic West, the place he loved above all others? If he did explain later, as he stated in his letter he would, Elizabeth did not give the explanation in her memoir and none of the surviving correspondence or diaries refer again to this comment. The work that he felt he needed to do abroad may have been connected with Dr. Goodchild in Italy, and with his bowl that was still lying in the murky waters at Glastonbury. Whatever he meant, things were certainly changing for him.

Predictably the cold of the Western Isles had badly affected his health, to the point he had to journey to a clinic in Neuenahr, Germany for treatment and recuperation. From his letters it is clear that his condition had been very serious and he had been closer to death than he had ever been before. In typical fashion he made light of it, explaining it thus, "*It has been a 'narrow squeak.' Briefly, after a hard tussle at the brink of 'Cape Fatal' and a stumble across 'Swamp Perilous' I got into the merely 'dangerous condition' stage—and now at last that's left behind..*"[9] He was in touch with Dr. Goodchild while in Germany who was amazed that William did not seem to understand just how seriously ill he had been. William replied, "*... these physical troubles meant little to me... and might be healed far more by spiritual wellbeing than by anything else: also that nature and fresh air and serenity and light and warmth and nervous rest were worth far more to me than anything else... Why should I bother about either living or dying? I shall not die before the hour of my unloosening comes. I want to be helped all I may be—but all the waters in the world can only affect the external life, and even that only secondarily very often...*"[10]

His health did improve considerably at Neuenahr and his humour started to reappear. For example he described this lovely little vignette in a letter home to Elizabeth, "*Then I got up to come in and write to you ... but first stopped to speak to a gorgeous solitary dandelion. I stroked it gently, and said, 'Hullo, wee brother, isn't the world beautiful? Hold up your wee head and rejoice!' And it turned up its wee golden nose and said, 'Keep your hair on, you old skidamalink, I'm rejoicing as hard as ever I can. I'm always rejoicing. What else would I do? You are a rum old un-shiny animal on two silly legs!' So we laughed, and parted—but he called me back and said gently in a wee soft goldy-yellow voice, 'Don't think me rude, Brother of Joy. It's only my way. I love you because you love me and don't despise me. Shake pinkies!'—so I gave him a pinkie and he gave me a wee golden-yellow pinkie-petal ...*"[11]

His improving health and his sense that his end was near seem to have had the effect of drawing him emotionally nearer and closer to Elizabeth than he had been for several years. He had never neglected her even though he was still passionately in love with Edith but neither had he been very expressive to her in any tender, loving way. However on June 16th he wrote to Elizabeth from Germany, "*Darling.... this is not keeping to Drs' advice about writing as little as possible. But what's the use of a darling wife if I can't write to her when I want—and hear from her often too I hope. Dearest love to me, Dearest One. Wilf.*"[12] Note that he used the composite name Wilf(ion) even though this is a most personal letter from William to his wife. All of his correspondence during the last year or so of his life shows a significant amount of confusion between his own personality and that of Fiona. Wilfion, the combination of the two, was certainly the dominant force from now until his death.

Despite his confusion of personalities his physical and mental health had improved as a result of his German sanatorium visit. However on July 30th 1905 he wrote a very curious and rather disturbed sounding letter to Dr. Goodchild in which he said, "*... August is always a 'dark' month for me—and not as a rule, I fancy, a good one: at any rate an obscure and perhaps perilous one. But this time I fancy it is on other lines. I believe strong motives and influences are to be at work in it perhaps furtively only: but none the less potently and far reachingly. Between now and September-end (perhaps longer) many of the Dark Powers are going to make a great effort. We must all be on guard—for there will be individual as well as racial and general attack. But a great Unloosening is at hand.*"[13] What on earth did he mean? Note that the overall tone is calm and sincere, not paranoid ravings, and he clearly felt comfortable talking to Dr. Goodchild about such dark matters. Elizabeth makes no comment nor gives any explanation for these psychic impressions and troubled feelings of dark foreboding but simply goes on to say, "*We therefore went to Scotland to say goodbye to his mother and sisters ...*"[14] Did Elizabeth interpret these comments as William having a premonition of his own death, which is why she included them in her memoir? To my mind it was something much more important and sinister than his own demise. He had already made clear to several people over the years that his death was not a thing he feared and the comment that there will be individual as well as *"racial and general attack"* shows clearly that these attacks by Dark Powers would be on more than him as an individual. This note to Dr. Goodchild, although not fearful in content, was certainly intended to be a sincere warning to his friend and magical ally of great dangers ahead.

Throughout her memoir Elizabeth drops in these little references to his magical work and psychic powers but without comment or analysis. It is as if she added them reluctantly because she knew that if she omitted all references to his magical interests she would not be doing justice to his memory. She did not feel comfortable with this aspect of her husband's interests and did not actively participate in any of his magical work. She did make a final direct comment on all of this in the conclusion to her book where she said, *"I have said little concerning my husband as a psychic; a characteristic that is amply witnessed to in his writings. From time to time he interested himself in definite psychic experimentation, occasionally in collaboration with Mr. W.B. Yeats; experimentation that sometimes resulted in such serious physical disturbance that he desisted from it in later years... the psychic, visionary power belonged exclusively to neither* [William or Fiona]; *it influenced both, and was dictated by laws he did not fully understand... I remember from early days how he would speak of the momentary curious 'dazzle in the brain' which preceded the falling away of all material things... I have been beside him when he has been in trance and I have felt the room throb with the heightened vibration. I regret now that I never wrote down such experiences at the time."* [15]

Her comment that in later years he desisted from psychic experimentation is true in part. He had distanced himself from the Golden Dawn and from Yeats' Celtic Mystical Order but he was still active with Dr. Goodchild and his experimentation. This withdrawal from active magical group work would explain the fact, noted earlier, that Fiona's later writings noticeably moved away from the allegorical, symbolic tales of her earlier work that contain much Faery lore of a unique and powerful kind to more descriptive nature-based essays and commentaries containing practical Faery knowledge on the ways of the weather, the mysteries of the seas and oceans and the habits of the flora and fauna. All useful stuff and key to understanding the deeper aspects of the Faery tradition but certainly not with the spiritual depth and magical insight of her earlier work. Elizabeth defined the noticeable different stages of Fiona's work when she said that she, *"... passed from the youth in 'Pharais' and 'The Mountain Lovers', through the mature manhood of 'The Barbaric Tales and Tragic Romances' to the greater serenity of later contemplative life in 'The Divine Adventure,' 'The Winged Destiny' and 'Where the Forest Murmurs.'"* [16] I would concur with this as it also points out that Fiona Macleod had gone from conception on January 3rd 1891; to birth at Phenice Croft in 1892; to youth with her first two novels; to the action and determination of maturity with the bulk of her writing; to the serenity and assuredness of later life. She had packed an entire lifetime into thirteen short but extremely fruitful years.

Although Edith Wingate Rinder has not been mentioned for a while and may seem to have disappeared from the picture she and William were still in touch and enjoying the occasional short liaison although much less frequently than before. After his return from Germany William wrote to her on September 15th 1905, three days after his fiftieth birthday, and said in part, *"I have been away, in the Isles, and for a time beyond the reach of letters. I wish there were Isles where one could also go at times, where no winged memories could follow. In a Gaelic folk-tale, told me by an old woman once, the woman of the story had only to burn a rose to ashes and to hold them in the palms of her hands and then to say seven times 'A Eileanain na Sith,' 'O Isles of Peace'! and at once she found herself in quiet isles beyond the foam where no memories could follow her and where old thoughts, if they came, were like phantoms on the wind, in a moment come, in a moment gone. I have failed to find these Isles, and so have you: but there are three which lie nearer, and may be reached, Dream, Forgetfulness, and Hope. And there, it may be, we can meet, you and I... But you will understand me when I say that you must not count on our meeting – at any rate not this year. I too stand under obscure wings."* [17] These comments to Edith, and his touching little note from Germany in June to his 'darling wife' Elizabeth, show that he was slowly drawing away from Edith and returning his affections to Elizabeth. Certainly he and Edith would never meet again after this letter was sent although of course at that time neither of them knew this. It may also have been the case that he and Edith had decided that now Esther was four years old he should stay in the background and allow the young girl to grow up recognizing Frank Rinder as her father.

As Elizabeth's memoir draws to its inevitable conclusion she fills out the last chapter with excerpts from letters that have little bearing on the events in William's rapidly declining life. Many of these correspondents were well known members of Edwardian society and by naming these people Elizabeth wanted the world to know the extent of her late husband's influence and social circle. One such example she gives is a lengthy letter and poem that Fiona sent to the Duchess of Sutherland. She gives no comment on why Fiona and the Duchess were in correspondence in the first place nor does the content of the letter seem relevant to the text of the memoir preceding or succeeding it. It is ironic though that Elizabeth included the Duchess of Sutherland in her name-dropping as it was this same family that was responsible for some of the most brutal and well documented Clearances of the early to mid 1800s. With the benefit of hindsight today it would seem better had she not included this letter at all.

Elizabeth states that whenever she and William spoke of Fiona they always did so in the Third Person, as if she were a physical being, so that they would not be caught out if either of them became engaged in conversation with anyone who did not know the secret. They would be less likely to accidentally use the First Person in such cases. She also states that it was William's habit on the occasion of his birthday to send two birthday cards. One was from him to Fiona in which he would comment on her work over the preceding year and the other was from Fiona to himself in which she criticized his work. On his last birthday, September 12th 1905, just before they left for the winter in Sicily, he received his two birthday cards. The one from him to Fiona is written in English but he wrote the address in Gaelic, "*Gu Fionaghal nic Leoid, Sliabhean n'an Aisling, Y-Breasil (na Tir-fo-Tuinn)*" which means 'To Fiona Macleod, Hill of Dreams, Y-Breasil (by the Land under Wave)' and it reads,

> "*Dearest Fiona,*
>
> *A word of loving greeting to you on the morrow of our new year. All that is best in this past year is due to* you, *mo caraid dileas: and I hope and believe that seeds have been sown which will be reborn in flower and fruit and may be green grass in waste places and may even grow to forests. I have not always your serene faith and austere eyes, dear, but I come to much in and thro' my weakness as you through your strength. But in this past year I realise I have not helped you nearly as much as I could: in this coming year I pray, and hope, it may be otherwise. And this none the less tho' I have much else I want to do apart from* our *work. But we'll be one and the same* au fond *even then, shall we not, Fiona dear? I am intensely interested in the fuller development of the Celtic Trilogy – and shall help in all ways. You say I can give you what you have not: well, I'm glad indeed. Together we shall be good Sowers, Fionaghal mo run: and let us work contentedly at* that. *I wish you Joy and Sorrow, Peace, and Unrest, and Leisure, Sun, and Wind, and Rain, all of Earth and Sea and Sky in this coming year. And inwardly dwell with me, so that less and less I may fall short of your need as well as your ideal. And may our 'Mystic's Prayer' be true for us both, who are one.*
>
> *Ever yours, dear,*
> *Will*"[18]

Fiona's card to William is also in English, including the address, "*Hills of Dream, Y-Breasil*" and is of quite a different tone,

> "*My dear Will,*
>
> *Another birthday has come, and I must frankly say that apart from the loss of another year, and from what the year has brought you in love and friendship and all that makes up life, it has not been to your credit. True, you have been in America and Italy and France and Scotland and England and Germany – and so have not been long settled anywhere – and true also that for a month or two you were seriously and for a few months partially ill or 'down' – but still, after all allowances, I note not only an extraordinary indolence in effort as well as unmistakable laziness in achievement. Now, either you are growing old (in which case admit dotage, and*

*be done with it) or else you are permitting yourself to remain weakly in futile havens of ignoble repose or fretful pseudo rest. You have much to do, or that you ought to do, yourself: and as to our collaboration I see no way for its continuance unless you will abrogate much of what is superfluous, curtail much that can quite well be curtailed, and generally serve me loyally as I in my turn allow for and serve you. Let our New Year be a very different one from the last, dear friend: and let us not only beautifully dream but achieve in beauty. Let the ignoble pass, and the noble remain.*

*Lovingly yours, dear Will,*

*Fiona*"[19]

This kindly worded but nonetheless rather stern letter displays again the fact that those of the Faery race do not have the same sensibilities or expectations that we mere humans do. Although she acknowledges that, *"for a month or two you were seriously and for a few months partially ill or 'down',"* she does not address the fact that William was <u>chronically</u> sick and was rapidly getting worse and worse. She then goes on to instruct him that he must work harder in their coming year for their collaboration to remain successful. This constant pressure to do more and more, coupled with the unbearable burden of maintaining the secret for over a decade, was literally killing William. His premonitions and the several comments to friends concerning his own death show that he was aware of this but his resigned acceptance to his imminent fate are puzzling. At no time did he ever say to Fiona, "Stop!" and at no time did he ever try to reason or argue with her for alternative courses of action. Surely it would have served him, Fiona and their joint collaboration better if he was to live longer, write more under both names and continue to reveal to the human world the important messages of Faery rather than burn out in an explosion of writing that only scratched the surface of this huge subject? This though, like so much else in William Sharp's life, is a mystery and must remain so.

By October they were once more off to Sicily but it was already clear that William's health was never going to return to normal. He was weak and frail but despite the rigors and hardships of the long journey from England to Sicily it was necessary. The alternative of remaining in the cold, damp, fog-strewn London winter was not acceptable. They stayed with their friend Alex Hood, the Duke of Bronte, at his estate Castello di Maniace on the slopes of Mount Etna. It had been William's intention to use the peace and quiet of this very English household on the slopes of Etna to finish off a piece he had already started called *"Greek Backgrounds,"* a drama entitled *"Persephonaeia, or the Drama of the House of Aetna"* as well as a drama by Fiona entitled, *"The Enchanted Valleys."* However, despite the warmer climes and the conviviality of his host and surroundings, for the first few weeks he did not have the strength to tackle these projects let alone commence anything new. He did however manage to summon up enough strength to write long letters to Edith in England detailing all his travels and adventures but which, contradictorily, complain of not having the will or the energy to commit to any serious writing. It seems his priority was to stay in touch with Edith at the expense of his and Fiona's literary reputations and livelihood but this is understandable, as he would no doubt wish to enquire after Esther while away from her.

By December the weather had turned cold and stormy but he started to write more than he had up until then. The few diary entries for early December list the completion of Fiona's *"At The Turn of the Year"* plus several other smaller projects under both names. The inclement weather and his need to work did not stop him from venturing out whenever the opportunity arose to experience all he could of wintry Sicily. Elizabeth was clearly concerned for his health and would encourage him to leave the mountainside and return to Maniace whenever the wind and snows would suddenly blow up. He had become noticeably much more frail and it was obvious to everyone that he did not have long to live. William was aware of this and his words and actions showed he was saying goodbye and preparing himself for his death. He had already commented in his letter from Lismore that he felt he would never see the Gaelic West again, and when he and Elizabeth left Scotland for Italy he commented that he thought he would never see the country of his birth or his mother and sisters again. On December 6th during a trip up the slopes of Etna he stopped at some old oak trees and, touching them gently, said, *"Ah dear trees of the North, dear trees of the North, goodbye."* Elizabeth had to coax him to leave the trees and return to the carriage out of the rain. It is curious that he called them the trees of the north – was he confusing Sicily with Scotland?

His diary entries stop on December 8th 1905. This final entry says, *"A fine morning but very doubtful if yet settled. Went out and was taken by Beek to see the observatory instruments and wind-registers and seismographs. Then took the dogs for a walk, as 'off' work today. Wrote a long letter to Robert Hichens, also to R.L.S. Also, with poem 'When Greenness comes again' by W.S. to C. Morley Pall Mall Magazine. In the afternoon we had a lovely drive up above the Alcantara Valley along the mountain road toward Cesaro."* [20] Elizabeth gives more detail about the afternoon drive by adding that on the way home the wind changed direction, coming off the snow-clad volcano, and for much of the way William was exposed to the full icy blast. Despite this, that evening before dinner, he said to Elizabeth, *"I am going to talk as much as I can tonight. That dear fellow Alec is rather depressed. I've teased him a good deal today; now I am going to amuse him."* [21] He was in fine spirits and entertained his friend and host Alex Hood with his fantastic tales and fond reminiscences into the small hours. On retiring for the evening the Duke commented to Elizabeth, *"I have never heard Will more brilliant than he has been tonight."* [22]

The next morning William complained of increasing pain. The doctor was summoned but by midday it was clear he was dying, nothing more could be done. The doctor stayed in the house and did what he could to make him comfortable. He lay in increasing pain for three days until the 12ᵗʰ December, a day of wild storm, wind, thunder and rain, when he realised that his end, the 'White Peace' to use the Gaelic expression he was so fond of, was imminent. This seemed to give him some new strength, a sense of eagerness and anticipation. He knew now that he would finally experience the greatest transformation of all. At 3 o'clock in the afternoon, with Alex Hood and Elizabeth by his side, he suddenly leaned forward, his eyes sparkling brightly, and exclaimed, "*Oh, the beautiful 'Green Life' again!*" He sank back into his devoted wife's arms, sighed, and quietly said, "*Ah, all is well.*" With those final words William Sharp and Fiona Macleod passed for the last time into their beloved Dominion of Dreams. Elizabeth later recounted to W.B. Yeats that on the morning of William's death she had heard what she described as "*visionary music.*" Her only comment on a personal psychic experience.

He was buried two days later in a woodland graveyard on the slopes of Etna within the sound of the running water of a little stream, much swollen by the recent storm. The Duke of Bronte read Fiona's "*Invocation of Peace*" and, later, a simple Celtic cross, made of Etna lava, was placed by his head. On it were the words that he had decided many years before should be his epitaph:-

> *Farewell to the known and exhausted,*
> *Welcome the unknown and illimitable*
>
> *Love is more great than we conceive, and*
> *Death is the keeper of unknown redemptions.* [23]

The last two lines of the inscription are taken from Fiona's "*The Divine Adventure,*" (page 83) a long allegorical tale of the Body, Mind and Soul discussing what life and death means to each of them individually but how all three of them are interconnected due to the mortality of the Body. The Body finally dies and the Will says, "'*... see, he is already clay. What word have you to say to that, to me who likewise am already perishing?*' [the Soul says] '*This – do you remember what so brief a while ago we three as one wrote – wrote with my spirit, through your mind, and the Body's hand – these words: Love is more great than we conceive, and Death is the keeper of unknown redemptions... it was true there: it is true here. Have I not ever told you that Love would save?*'"

I am glad that he was laid to rest so close to water. He and Elizabeth had first met as children beside a sea loch in Argyll, it was beside a pool that he first encountered his Faery Lady of the Sea, his early mentor was Seamus Macleod, a fisherman, Fiona was born at Lake Nemi and his love for Edith Wingate Rinder blossomed on that same spot, he and Fiona spent many happy days sailing the waters between the many islands of the Hebrides, and both had written many words concerning the sea and sea-creatures.

It is fitting that when he finally left this life he was in the arms of his devoted wife Elizabeth. Edith was not present. During his life he needed Edith's presence and inspiration to allow Fiona to come through and write, but he needed Elizabeth more to support him as William Sharp. With his passing went the passing of Fiona Macleod. Edith was no longer needed. Sadly, but typically, Elizabeth made no mention of her own emotions and feelings on the loss of her husband. As for Edith, she passed away in 1962 at the age of ninety-eight years. Never during her long life did she ever write or comment on her own experiences of Fiona Macleod, her relationship with William Sharp nor her feelings on his early death.

In 1932 when Elizabeth died two packages were found amongst her papers that were marked to be destroyed unopened on the occasion of her death – they were. Ithell Colquhoun, amongst others, believes these may have contained William's Golden Dawn magical diaries, as it was customary practice for members of the Golden Dawn to leave such instructions. Considering William's peripheral role in the Golden Dawn I think this unlikely. It is much more likely that these two packages contained the dozens of private letters between William and Edith Wingate Rinder that Elizabeth never wished to be made public, even after her death. They would also have contained as much evidence as she could gather and hide away concerning William's relationship to Edith's daughter Esther Mona Rinder. This would explain why so very few letters between the two lovers have ever surfaced and why Esther's children have no material evidence of her paternity other than one of the sons bearing a striking resemblance to William Sharp, his grandfather.

\* \* \*

... and More

In his usual thorough and detailed fashion, William had left specific instructions on what was to be done on the instance of his death. His first and foremost priority was to finally throw off the heavy and burdensome cloak of secrecy and tell the world that he was indeed Fiona Macleod. To this end on the day of his death Elizabeth sent telegrams from Sicily to the London newspapers informing them that William Sharp, the well-known man of letters, had died while abroad and that he wished it to be made known that he was the author of all of the works under the pen of Fiona Macleod. At the same time she sent a separate telegram to Edith Wingate Rinder informing her of William's passing. Edith then sent out several personal telegrams to William's more intimate friends and acquaintances. Edith's telegrams were all the same, taken from her original copy,

> 21, Woronzow Road,
> St. John's Wood, N.W.
> Dec. 14, 1905
>
> Dear Sirs,
>
> I deeply regret to inform you that from a telegram received in the night from Mrs. William Sharp I learn that Mr. William Sharp died quietly on Tuesday last, while on a visit to Castello di Maniace, Bronte, Sicily. Mr. Sharp's health has caused concern for a long time, and for the past six winters he has been abroad. Mrs. William Sharp further ex-

*pressly authorizes me to disclose that Mr. Sharp was the author of all the works which have appeared under the name of Fiona Macleod. I beg that you will regard this communication as private until to-morrow morning, when notices will appear in the papers.*

*Yours truly,*
*Edith Wingate Rinder* [24]

The letter has been typed although the signature is in her handwriting. The *"Dear Sirs"* is typed apart from the final 's' which has been written in by hand. There is no addressee on the letter, giving the impression it was intended to be copied and sent to several recipients. William, Elizabeth and Edith had already agreed upon this plan of action following his death and Edith had a list of the intended recipients of this more personal letter. I have already stressed that Elizabeth and Edith worked closely and in harmony to tend to William during his lifetime and now, at the hour of his demise, this shows they were still willing collaborators in carrying out his final wishes. But it does raise the question why did they agree to this two-tier way of contacting people? Elizabeth could easily have sent out all of the telegrams to newspapers and friends alike without the involvement of Edith at all. Very few people knew of William and Edith's romance during his lifetime so why involve her in spreading the news of his death to his close and intimate friends? Surely this in itself would have raised the question why was Mrs. Wingate Rinder, not Mrs. Elizabeth Sharp, sending such a personal notification of William Sharp's death? Did William feel that he not only had to relieve himself of the secret concerning Fiona but also had to divulge his other great secret, his affair with Edith? Perhaps this was why, five years later, Elizabeth gave a nod to this wish by giving the final comment in her memoir to Frank Rinder despite the fact she barely mentions him at all in the text. In part, he said, *"I can but bear testimony to the ever-ready and eager sympathy, to the sunny winsomeness, to the nobility of the soul that has passed. William Sharp was one of the most lovable, one of the most remarkable men of our time."* [25]

But Elizabeth and Edith's telegrams were not the only posthumous communications William had planned. He knew that some special friends would feel hurt when they read in the newspapers that he had indeed been Fiona Macleod, despite his repeated sincere denials to them. For these close friends he had prepared a personal note that said,

*"This will reach you after my death. You will think I have wholly deceived you about Fiona Macleod. But, in an intimate sense, this is not so, though (and inevitably) in certain details I have misled you. Only, it is a mystery. I cannot explain. Perhaps you will intuitively understand or may come to understand. 'The rest is silence.' Farewell.*

*William Sharp.*

*It is only right, however, to add that I, and I only, was the author—in the literal and literary sense—of all written under the name of 'Fiona Macleod.'"* [26]

As Flavia Alaya succinctly put it, "*The price exacted for that death-bed revelation was high, as Sharp must have known it would be. His wife and friends were forced by it to endure both the sorry private jokes about his female proclivities and the ready public accusations of charlatanism. There is only one purpose for which he could have wanted them to pay such a price: to be judged by posterity as the author of all his work.*" [27] This was certainly one of his motives but in my opinion not the only one. The main reason was to finally come clean and tell his dear, special friends, the truth he could never reveal during his lifetime. Fiona Macleod was in great part responsible for driving William Sharp to an early grave and for weighing him down so heavily with the burden of a secret he could not, dared not, reveal. The finality of the grave removed that burden and gave him the peace of mind and the clarity of conscience that he never had during the final years of his life. It was a very difficult thing for him to do from a purely personal point of view. As Lilian Rea said, "*I should explain Mr. Sharp's unbroken reticence on this point by a certain delicacy which he felt in acknowledging his belief to the world at large that a woman's soul really lived within himself in dual unity with his distinct man's nature.*" [28] which confirms what Flavia Alaya said above.

His dear and close friend Catharine Janvier saw some humour in the revelation when she said, "*... the sudden revelation of the identity of William Sharp and Fiona Macleod surprised many people; and, most of all, Fiona's numerous correspondents. Women, I take it, were not displeased to find that they had been writing to a man; but for men, I fancy, it was an unpleasant shock to discover that Fiona was one of themselves.*" [29] William would have been amused by this thought but I wonder how the poor, heart-broken suitor mentioned earlier took the news! Catharine had been one of first to know the secret and had in her possession many letters and papers from William that disclosed the secret. The last time she saw William was in New York on November 25th 1904 and she asked him then what to do with all these documents. After thinking for a moment, he replied, "*Keep all these papers. Who knows what may happen after my death? These letters and papers–should proof ever be needed–are proof positive that I am Fiona Macleod.*" [30] His concern that proof might be needed turned out to be well founded as was displayed when people started to refute the obituaries containing the revelation that William and Fiona were one and the same.

For example, during William and Fiona's writing careers the editor of the respected literary journal "*Bookman,*" Dr. Robertson Nicoll, had argued several times that William Sharp could not be Fiona Macleod as the writing styles were so different it was impossible for him to accept they came from the same source. He was so strong in this belief that even after the death-bed confession he still refused to accept they were one and the same person. His reason was, "*Fiona Macleod's best work discloses knowledge and power which Mr. Sharp did not possess.*" [31] Here was the final paradox of the confusing life of William Sharp. During his lifetime he had spent a vast amount of time and energy denying that he was Fiona Macleod. Now that he was dead and the secret had been revealed his friend's and acquaintances found themselves having to take the opposite stance by trying to convince unbelievers of the truth that, yes, he truly was Fiona Macleod.

William's death proved what he had believed all along that should the secret ever get out then Fiona would die. As soon as the secret was told to the world people stopped buying the Fiona Macleod books. Sales plummeted and since 1905 almost none of her works have been reprinted. Maud Gonne asked an interesting question to W.B. Yeats shortly after hearing the news in December 1905, "... – *tell me about Fiona Macleod, is Sharpe's* [sic] *death the end of her as well as of his writings?"* Towards the end of William's life Maud knew the secret but this question shows that she also understood that Fiona Macleod was much more than a figment of his mind or was a mere literary ploy. I do not know how Yeats answered but it is still a question worthy of consideration, was William's death the end of Fiona's writings? If Fiona had been capable of writing 'through' William could she not find another host and to carry on writing with? I think not. The relationship between William Sharp and Fiona Macleod was so intimate, so personal and so spiritually entwined that I do not believe the Faery who called herself Fiona Macleod could ever repeat the relationship with any other human being.

Soon after William died Elizabeth started to attend séances, despite her objections to her late husband's 'psychic experimentations,' and believed that she managed to communicate with his spirit. I do not know what these communications revealed, if anything, but she was not the only one to have beyond the grave messages from William. In 1969 an American gentleman by the name of Konrad Hopkins was attending a séance one evening when a spirit communicator spelled out the name Fiona Macleod. None of the other sitters had ever heard of Fiona Macleod but Konrad had. He asked the spirit communicator, "*Are you William Sharp?"* and the spirit replied, "*Yes.*" It also claimed that, "*Fiona is no more.*" The spirit of William Sharp remained in psychic communication with him over the next several years. In 1976, and unbeknown to Konrad Hopkins, a British medium by the name of Margo Williams started to receive clairaudient messages from William Sharp. She too had never heard of William Sharp or Fiona Macleod. Konrad learned of this purely by accident when in 1979 he read a magazine article about Margo's extraordinary psychic powers. The magazine article mentioned her communications with a Scottish writer called William Sharp so Konrad immediately got in touch with her. Over the following years William communicated with Margo frequently and during these communications he recited many new poems that he had composed since 'passing over.' Konrad collected these together and published them in 1980, along with an explanation of their peculiar source, in a little book called "*The Wilfion Scripts.*" Throughout their years of communication however William was at pains to make it clear that Fiona is no more, which answers Maud's question above. Make of it what you will.

Maud Gonne had always held a deep respect for Fiona and clearly wished to draw closer to her and get to know her better and more intimately. This desire was partly prompted by the fact that the only other woman involved in the Irish movement was Lady Gregory who did not like Maud and kept her at a distance as she felt she was a bad influence on Yeats. Maud's concern for the non-existent Fiona is highlighted in an old letter to Yeats responding to his news that Fiona was ill, "*I am so sorry what you say about Fiona. Curiously I was thinking of her a great deal lately & I knew she was ill—I am so sorry for her—I believe she COULD be cured, but I don't think she would—I wish I knew her, I might be of use to her.*" [32] She kept the last letter she ever received from William Sharp in an envelope together with the last letter she ever received from William Butler Yeats. [33]

Despite their political differences Yeats too was affected by William's death. On January 6th 1906 he wrote to Elizabeth, "*Thousands will feal his loss with a curious personal regret … a strange mystery and also a dear friend. To talk with him was to feal the presence of that mystery, he was very near always to the world where he now is and often seemed to me to deliver its messages. He often spoke to me of things of my personal life that were unknown to him by the common channels of sense … that one who was so often as it seemed out of the body which he had, cannot have undergone any unrecognisable change or gone very far away.*" [34]

Following the announcement of the death of William Sharp there was a flood of obituaries and letters from friends in the newspapers and literary journals but there was nothing from his mother, sisters or surviving brother. Several writers expressed genuine astonishment at the revelation of the secret as the authors claimed to have met Fiona Macleod in the flesh. For example, a letter in the "*Glasgow Evening News,*" arguing that William could not possibly have been Fiona, said, "*More remarkable is the fact that portraits of a lady said to be 'Miss Macleod' have been shown to some people, and that one man at least—now a Professor in Toronto—was introduced to a lady called 'Fiona Macleod' by the very gentleman who invented the name and sustained the fiction of her real existence.*" We know that this was Edith Wingate Rinder but why did Elizabeth not specifically comment on this in her memoir and clear up this final mystery once and for all? The closest she got to telling all was when she said in the conclusion, "*He purposely did not dispel the idea of a collaborator, an idea which grew out of the half veiled allusions he had made concerning the friend of whom I have written, whose vivid personality appealed so potently to a phase of his complex nature, and stirred his imagination as no one else had done.*" [35] Although you would need to look carefully far back in Elizabeth's memoir to figure out who this friend was, by then, five years later, it was not exactly public knowledge but his affair with Edith had been known to a few close friends. It had also been strongly implied to others by the personal telegram they received from Edith following William's death. Why not just give the whole story, including the fact that Edith played the part of Fiona when necessary, in the memoir? The answer has to do yet again with the close friendship between Elizabeth and Edith that survived William's death. Edith and Frank Rinder were still a happily married couple, now with a young daughter. If Elizabeth had laid bare the details of not just Edith's inspiration on Fiona's writings but also the details of William's love affair with her, the scandal that would have followed such a revelation in Edwardian times would have been disastrous for all concerned. Such a full disclosure would also undoubtedly have caused some close friends to put two and two together and realise just who Esther Mona Rinder's father really was.

It was the occasion of William's death and the revelation of the secret that finally prompted Frank Rinder to make his one and only public statement on William's life and his dual identity. I have stressed throughout this book that had it not been for Elizabeth's understanding and tolerance of her husband's relationship with Edith Wingate Rinder then things would have turned out very differently for all concerned. The same must also be said for the silent witness to this whole amazing story, Frank Rinder. He too knew of William and Edith's affair and he as the 'wronged husband' could easily have caused enough disruption to draw the whole thing to a rapid close. But he did not; he too knew the great importance of this wonderful thing that was Fiona Macleod. His genuinely warm and affectionate tribute was published very soon after William's death in the February 1906 issue of "*The Art Journal.*" It conveys a real sense of the loss of a dear friend and a person who he clearly admired. I make no apology for quoting him at length, "*There was a vivid charm, a freshness, a magic potency in his touch that surprised into pleasure... The beauty, which as a spiritual energy, was his comrade, he distilled from all things, animate and inanimate, on the earth, in the sky, in the deeps of the human heart... He was overflowingly handsome, with the shock of hair, silvered latterly, leaping up to crown the great, proud head. A breath of spring, a shaft of sunlight, entered the room with him. How inspiring, too, was his manner, blent of boyish irresponsibility, unfaltering zest, tender courtesy, flaming more and more from the love that understands. Eagerly he leapt forth towards life; in turn, life to him was prodigal. As a friend has well written: "He lived, thought, felt, enjoyed, suffered as much in one hour as others in a year;" indeed, a moment was often an eternity, for in his dream-scheme of the cosmos—nearer to the heart of the truth than most of our 'realities'—so many of the limitations of time and space were swept away... William Sharp had an astonishing memory, and few possessed in approximately equal measure his ability to vivify material, his adaptability, his capacity for work—and for play. Inertia was the one thing he found it hard to tolerate... He was, again, a prince of raconteurs, no matter what the theme, of letters, writers. Even one of his exquisite scraps—penned, spaced and set on the page as though design were the sole end—resolved for the recipient his mood of the moment; it may be buoyant as some gossamer of the air, deliciously irresponsible, radiantly happy or perplexed.*"

His only comment on Fiona Macleod was, "*Now the world knows that deep in the heart of William Sharp dwelt Fiona Macleod; and I have full authority to state, emphatically and unmistakably, that he, and he only, wrote every word under that pseudonym...* "*I will set my face to the wind, and throw my handful of seed on high*" *wrote Fiona. Now the wayfaring spirit is with the* "*Wind, Silence and Love, friends who have taught me most.*" *It was, surely, the nostalgia for a wider, subtler sphere of usefulness that caused the cloud to vanish, the seer to go onward to the finer illumination which is peace. And for us everything remains. Not in vain was thrown on high the handful of seed. The harvest—our heritage—is not only in the wonderfully wrought Romances, Poems, Prayers, charged with so sweet and strangely insistent a music for others than the Gael, but also in the memory of that life which, winged and sunward-looking, earned the right to be a bearer of joy to many, a stricken spirit that before had hardly known compassion—earned the right, in a word, to go forth into the* "*Divine Adventure.*"" It is unlikely that any readers of "*The Art Journal*" realised the full truth of his first sentence, "*... I have full authority to state, emphatically and unmistakably, that he, and he only, wrote every word under that pseudonym...*"

In the end William's friend Ernest Rhys came the closest to revealing what he knew, although he too stopped short of naming names. In a short memoir he expressed these sentiments, "*The gate shut on one of the most vital spirits and one of the most imaginative men of our time, at the death of William Sharp. I have called him a great illusionist, and it may be thought that 'Fiona Macleod' was the greatest of his illusions; but she was real, and very real to him. He wrote her letters every birthday, and I remember going with him once to buy an antique silver and ebony crucifix for her in Holborn. Moreover, through him, she did many mysterious, kind services and gave secret gifts; and her apparition certainly once appeared on an island of the British coast while he was apparently far away on the Southern Mediterranean, She was not, then, as some of his critics think, only a part of that 'blue mist of youth and love and romance' which he described in one of his 'Spiritual Tales.' She was a real woman, who really entered into his life and counsels and inspired him. And for the rest, let us recall his own words, where he says, 'I write not because I know a mystery, and would reveal it; but because I have known a mystery, and am today as a child before it, and can neither reveal nor interpret it.*" [36]

---

[1] Memoir, page 393

[2] Memoir, page 389

[3] Memoir, page 394

[4] Memoir, page 396

[5] Memoir, page 398

[6] Memoir, page 399

[7] NLS, Edinburgh

[8] NLS, Edinburgh

[9] Memoir, page 399

[10] Memoir, page 400

[11] Memoir, page 401

[12] NLS, Edinburgh

[13] Memoir, page 403

[14] Memoir, page 403

[15] Memoir, page 424

[16] Memoir, page 423

[17] Memoir, page 405

[18] Memoir, page 410

[19] Memoir, page 411

[20] Memoir, page 418

[21] Memoir, page 418

[22] Memoir, page 419

[23] In William's notebooks from the mid 1890s there is an entry that reads,
> "I should like inscribed on my tomb
>> Farewell, then, to the known and the exhausted:
>> Welcome to the unknown and the unfathomed.
> The passage from Fiona Macleod ("The Distant Country")
>> Love is more great than we conceive, and
>> Death is the keeper of unknown redemptions."

Note that this is slightly different from the final inscription. NLS, Edinburgh

[24] William Sharp Collection, Bancroft Library, UC Berkeley, California

[25] Memoir, page 427

[26] Le Gallienne, "The Mystery of Fiona Macleod", "The Forum", February 1911, page171

[27] Alaya, William Sharp – 'Fiona Macleod,' 1855-1905, page 7

[28] Rea, "Fiona Macleod", "The Critic", May 1906, page 460

[29] Janvier, "Fiona Macleod and her Creator", "The North American Review", April 1907, page 725

[30] "Fiona Macleod and her Creator", "The North American Review", April 1907, page 724

[31] Rea, "Fiona Macleod", "The Critic", May 1906, page 460

[32] Jeffares, The Gonne-Yeats Letters, Page 104

[33] Jeffares, The Gonne-Yeats Letters, Page 527

[34] Foster, W.B. Yeats: A Life; 1. The Apprentice Mage, Page 345

[35] Memoir, page 421

[36] Rhys, "William Sharp and Fiona Macleod", "The Century Illustrated Monthly Magazine", May 1907, page 117

William Sharp
From a photograph taken by the Hon. Alex. Nelson Hood, 1903.

# Appendix I
# Main Works of Fiona Macleod and William Sharp

The original titles and publication dates of Fiona Macleod's main works are given below but it should be noted that most of them were reprinted several times in different combinations during William's life and for several years after his death. Several foreign publishers also published many editions and these are often different from their British originals. Not only were the collections of tales in each volume switched from one to another but the text of many of them was also edited and amended on subsequent editions resulting in a confusing mixture of editions and versions.

*Pharais: A Romance of the Isles* Frank Murray, Derby, 1894. Reissued by T.N. Foulis, Edinburgh, 1907.

*The Mountain Lovers* John Lane, London, 1895. Second edition John Lane, London & New York, 1906.

*The Sin-Eater and Other Tales* Patrick Geddes & Colleagues, Edinburgh, 1895. Reissued David Nutt, London, 1899.

*The Washer of the Ford and other Legendary Moralities* Patrick Geddes & Colleagues, Edinburgh, 1896. Reissued David Nutt, London, 1899.

*Reissue of the Shorter Tales of Fiona Macleod* Patrick Geddes & Colleagues, Edinburgh, 1896. Reissued David Nutt, London, 1899.
    *Volume 1 - Spiritual Tales*
    *Volume 2 - Barbaric Tales*
    *Volume 3 - Tragic Romances*

*Green Fire: A Romance* Archibald, Constable & Co., Westminster, 1896.

*From The Hills of Dream: Mountain Songs and Island Runes* Patrick Geddes & Colleagues, Edinburgh, 1896.

*The Laughter of Peterkin: A Retelling of the Old Tales of the Celtic Wonderland* Archibald, Constable & Co., Westminster, 1897.

*The Dominion of Dreams* Archibald, Constable & Co., Westminster, 1899. Reissued Constable & Co., 1909.

*The Divine Adventure: Iona: By Sundown Shores: Studies in Spiritual History* Chapman and Hall, Ltd., London, 1900.

*Wind and Wave: Selected Tales* Bernhard Tauchnitz, Leipzig, 1902.

*The Winged Destiny: Studies in the Spiritual History of the Gael* Chapman and Hall, Ltd., London, 1904.

*The Sunset of Old Tales* Bernhard Tauchnitz, Leipzig, 1905.

*Where the Forest Murmurs: Nature Essays* Georges Newnes, Ltd., New York, 1906.

*From the Hills of Dream: Threnodies and Songs and Later Poems* William Heinemann, London, 1907.

*The Immortal Hour: a Drama in Two Acts* T.N. Foulis, London, 1908.

*A Little Book of Nature* T.N. Foulis, Edinburgh and London, 1909.

*The Works of "Fiona Macleod"* Uniform Edition, London, Heinemann, 1910. Arranged by Mrs. William Sharp.
   *Volume 1 – "Pharais: The Mountain Lovers"*
   *Volume 2 – "The Sin-Eater: The Washer of the Ford"*
   *Volume 3 – The Dominion of Dreams: Under the Dark Star*
   *Volume 4 – The Divine Adventure: Iona. Studies in Spiritual History*
   *Volume 5 – The Winged Destiny: Studies in the Spiritual History of the Gael*
   *Volume 6 – The Silence of Amor: Where the Forest Murmurs*
   *Volume 7 - Poems and Dramas*

## Main Works of William Sharp

The original titles and publication dates of William Sharp's main works are given below. Although many of them were reprinted they were not as heavily rearranged or edited as were the works of Fiona Macleod.

*The Human Inheritance; The New Hope; Motherhood* Elliott Stock, London, 1882.

*Dante Gabriel Rossetti: A Record and a Study* Macmillan & Co., London, 1882.

*Earth's Voices: Transcripts from Nature; Sospira and other Poems* Elliott Stock, London, 1884.

*Life of Percy Bysshe Shelley* Walter Scott & Co., London, 1887.

*Romantic Ballads and Poems of Phantasy* Walter Scott & Co., London, 1888.

*Life of Heinrich Heine* Walter Scott, London, 1888.

*The Sport of Chance* 3 Volumes, Hurst and Blackett, London, 1888.

*The Children of To-morrow: A Romance* Chatto and Windus, London, 1889.

*Life of Robert Browning* Walter Scott, London, 1889.

*Sospiri di Roma* La Societa Laziale, Rome, 1891.

*The Life and Letters of Joseph Severn* Sampson Lowe, Marston and Co., London, 1892.

*A Fellowe and his Wife* James R. Osgood, MacIlvain & Co., London, 1892, with Blanche Howard Willis.

*Fair Women in Painting and Poetry* P.G. Hamerton, London, 1894.

*Vistas* Frank Murray, Derby, 1894.

*Madge o' the Pool: The Gipsy Christ and other Tales* Archibald, Constable & Co., Westminster, 1896.

*Ecce Puella and Other Prose Imaginings* Elkin Matthews, London, 1896.

*Wives in Exile: A Comedy in Romance* Grant Richards, London, 1898.

*Silence Farm (A Novel)* Grant Richards, London, 1899.

*The Progress of Art in the XIX Century* W. & R. Chambers, Ltd., London & Edinburgh, 1902.

*Selected writings of Williams Sharp* 5 Volumes, William Heinemann, London, 1912, arranged by Mrs. William Sharp.
 *Volume 1 – Poems*
 *Volume 2 – Studies and Appreciations*
 *Volume 3 – Papers Critical and Reminiscent*
 *Volume 4 – Literary geography and Travel Sketches*
 *Volume 5 – Vistas and Other Prose Imaginings*

William Sharp and Fiona Macleod both contributed essays, poems, criticisms and articles to many of the literary and art journals, anthologies and magazines of the day. Included in these are *The Canterbury Series, Camelot Classics, The Art Journal, The Academy, The Literary World, Literature, The Realm, The Young Folks' Paper, The Glasgow Herald, The Athenaeum, Modern Thought, Harper, The Fortnightly Review, Good Words, New York Independent, Atlantic Monthly, Nineteenth Century, Pall Mall Magazine, Century, Country Life, Theosophical Review, Dome, Contemporary Review* and *The North American Review*. In the second volume of her two-volume set *William Sharp (Fiona Macleod) A Memoir* (William Heinemann, London, 1912) Elizabeth Sharp gives full details of all of these pieces, many of which were never reprinted anywhere else.

## Appendix II
# Brief Biographies of Friends and Acquaintances

I have only included in this appendix those people who are mentioned in the text but who are probably not so well known today. I have not included William's many other more famous friends, such as W.B. Yeats, MacGregor Mathers, George Russell, Rossetti etc, as sufficient biographical material on them is readily available elsewhere.

### RUTLAND BOUGHTON

Although not an acquaintance or inspiration for either William or Fiona, Rutland Boughton is included here because of the work he did with Fiona's play "*The Immortal Hour*." He was born on January 23rd 1878 in the little English town of Aylesbury. He showed evidence of being a gifted musician from an early age but his father, the owner of a small grocery business, could not afford to pay for music lessons. While working as an apprentice to a London concert agency he taught himself music and composition and managed to spend a brief period at the Royal College of Music. For much of his early adult life he lived in poverty and this experience encouraged him to adopt strong socialist ideals that remained with him for the rest of his life. In 1905 he took up a post at the Midland Institute of Music, Birmingham, where his compositions developed and started to attract favourable criticism. He envisaged what he called "*Choral Drama*" as a specifically English form of opera to counteract the domination of the Italian, German and French composers. He also advocated artistic communities of artists and musicians living and working together. On August 4th 1914 war was declared in Britain and on August 5th he and several friends held the first meeting of the Glastonbury Festival in the Assembly Rooms of that small Somerset town. Three weeks later on August 26th 1914 his operatic version of Fiona's "*The Immortal Hour*" was performed for the first of three performances. It went on to become the longest running popular opera ever written. He also spent many years working on a cycle of five musical dramas based on the legends of King Arthur – "*The Birth of Arthur*," "*The Round Table*," "*The Lily Maid*"

"*Galahad*" and "*Avalon.*" He composed and performed many other pieces, wrote several provocative essays and books and was outspoken in his support of socialism. He died on January 25th 1960.

## MONA CAIRD

Alice Mona Alison was born on May 24th 1854 on the Isle of Wight, England. Her father John Alison was an inventor and landowner. She married James Alexander Henryson-Caird on December 19th 1877. He was eight years older than her, Scottish and wealthy. They lived between their Scottish estate, a house in London and a country home in England. Mona, as she preferred to be called, was a friend of Elizabeth Sharp from a young age. She was a very vocal supporter of women's rights and for true sexual equality. She was not opposed to marriage as such but did express strong views, including that for marriage to be a truly happy institution for both parties it was necessary for the woman to have her own independent income, a radical view in the 1870s. Her husband agreed with this and she made a successful career as a writer. She travelled a lot abroad without her husband. This was a common theme amongst William's female friends, Mona, Edith, his own wife and Catharine Janvier. She was a member of the Independent Anti-Vivisection League and as well as caring for the welfare of animals she also wrote passionately for the under privileged everywhere. Her literary out put was considerable; much of it dealing with marriage and women's rights issues, and received much favourable critical acclaim. She was optimistic regarding the future of women as she saw the 20th Century dawning and attitudes slowly changing. She was a forerunner and founder for the burgeoning women's movement of that century. She died on February 4th 1932 in London.

## RICHARD LE GALLIENNE

Despite his French sounding name he was born in England in 1866. He was a writer of minor importance in the late 19th century and a contributor to the popular publication of the time known as the "*Yellow Book.*" He moved to the United States in the late 1890s and continued to write, although not profusely, until his death in 1947. He was best known as being an associate of the major writers, artists and poets in the late Victorian period.

## EDITH MAUD GONNE

Although Maud Gonne spent virtually her entire adult life fighting for Ireland and its people she was actually born to a wealthy high-ranking officer in the British Army on 21st December 1866 in Surrey, England. The family moved to Ireland when she was two years old but later moved back to London and from there to the South of France. She lived in Dublin with her father from age sixteen until she was twenty-six and it was during this time she developed her passion for the plight of the Irish peasantry and, ironically, her hatred of the English and military rule. She was a frequent speaker at public rallies but according to Yeats, not a very good one. He believed the crowds were drawn more by her striking appearance; she was 6 feet tall and very beautiful. Throughout her life she was plagued by ailments of the lungs. While she was living in France she met the married, but separated, Lucien Millevoye, with whom she had two children. The first, a son, Georges, was born on January 11th 1890 but died of meningitis on August 31st 1891. Her daughter, Iseult, was born on August 6th 1894. She first met Yeats on January 30th 1889 and the two would remain friends, although Yeats craved a closer relationship, for the rest of their lives. She was initiated into Golden Dawn on November 16th 1891 mainly due to Yeats' coaxing. On February 21st 1903 she stunned everyone, especially Yeats, when she converted to Roman Catholicism and married an army officer John MacBride. Their son Sean was born on January 26th 1904. He would go on to become a commander in the Irish Republican Army, be awarded the Nobel Peace Prize in 1974 and eventually work for the United Nations organization. Not long after Sean's birth Maud filed for divorce on February 25th 1905 on the grounds of her husband's drunkenness and physical cruelty. In the summer of 1917 Yeats had given up proposing marriage to Maud so, instead, he proposed to her daughter Iseult. Not surprisingly she too rejected him. Even after Ireland gained its independence from Britain she was still an advocate for the common people. She died on April 27th 1953 in a home near Dublin. Georges' little booties were placed in her coffin along side her.

## KATHARINE HINKSON - SEE *KATHARINE TYNAN*

## NORA HOPPER

Nora Hopper was born on January 2nd 1871 in Exeter, England. Her father Harman Baillie Hopper, a captain in the 31st Bengal Native Infantry, was Irish and her mother, Caroline Augusta Francis, was Welsh. Despite her strong Celtic background she lived most of her short life in London. However it was her Celtic background that gave her a love of Celtic mythology, particularly Irish Celtic mythology. She also studied Icelandic folklore. From an early age she began writing prose and poetry and her first published work appeared when she was only sixteen years old. She became acquainted with William Butler Yeats and Katharine Tynan and started to produce a considerable amount of writing, mainly poetry based on Irish themes. This brought her a certain amount of public attention but most of it was not favourable. Throughout her career accusations of plagiarism followed almost all of her publications and she was never taken as seriously as perhaps she should have been. It is true that much of her work does bear a strong resemblance to that of Yeats, and he acknowledged this, but she was capable of producing poems that were clearly her own unique work. She married the critic Wilfred Hugh Chesson on March 5th 1901 who edited her collected works after her death on April 14th 1906. We know from entries in Lady Gregory's diaries that Hopper and William Sharp were acquainted. It is ironic that she should have suffered under the accusation of plagiarism as Fiona Macleod, who was also subject on occasion to the same accusation, may have borrowed heavily from one of Hopper's poems when she composed "*The Immortal Hour*." It is mainly due to her connection with Yeats that she is remembered at all today.

## CATHARINE JANVIER

Catharine Ann Drinker was born in Philadelphia, U.S.A., on May 1st 1841. Her mother was Susannah Budd Shober and her father was the splendidly named Captain Sandwith Drinker who spent most of his sailing career trading in the East Indies. Because of her father's occupation she spent much of her early life in the Far East and Hong Kong. She was an intellectually gifted child and excelled in mathematics and languages. Her father died in Macao in 1857 and her mother decided to return with the family to the States. At one point in the long crossing to Baltimore young Catharine took over the navigation of the ship as the captain was drunk and the First Officer was not proficient enough in reading the charts. Her mother died in 1858 and she became the sole support for her brother and sister. She later studied art and proved herself to be a talented artist. She married Thomas Allibone Janvier on September 26th 1878 and they travelled extensively especially in Mexico, England and France where they eventually settled in Saint-Remy, Provence. They first met William Sharp in New York in 1892 and they remained close friends until his death. William and Elizabeth stayed with them in Provence on several occasions and Catharine was one of the first people to know the secret of Fiona Macleod. During her time in France she translated several major French works into English and wrote several of her own. She died on July 19th 1922.

## THOMAS JANVIER

Thomas Allibone Janvier was born in Philadelphia. USA on July 16th 1849. He was from an old Huguenot family. His father Francis de Haes Janvier was a writer and poet and his mother Emma Newbold was a published author of children's books. It was from his literary parents that Thomas took his love of writing. During his lifetime he produced an impressive number of novels, short stories, essays and, especially, travel guides, all written from first hand experiences. He loved old New York and wrote of its secret places and many interesting characters. He married Catharine Ann Drinker on September 26th 1878 and after a period of traveling in Mexico and Europe they settled in Provence close to where his family had originally come from. He died in New York on June 18th 1913.

## WALTER HORATIO PATER

Walter Pater was born in East London on August 4th 1839, the son of a surgeon of Dutch descent. His father died while he was still a child and an aunt raised him. He started adult life as a devout Christian but this waned soon after he started at Oxford University. He made his mark by proposing that the current critical style and moral attitudes to art were wrong and outdated and a new, more flexible approach was needed. He wrote several essays on the Old Masters, amongst others, and was a regular contributor to many art and literature magazines, including "*The Fortnightly Review*." His outspokenness and well-written articles and novels brought much criticism from the establishment critics and editors but the new romantic artists and writers of the day took keenly to his new approach to art. His health had never been good and he died of a heart attack on July 30th 1894.

## Sir Joseph Noel Paton R.S.A., LL.D., D.L.,

Joseph Paton was born into a family of weavers in Dunfermline, Scotland on December 13th 1821. He worked for a while in the family damask trade but his real talent lay in art. His was of the Pre-Raphaelite style and his subjects were mainly of a religious or Faery nature. These massive works at first seem dreamy and typically 'fairy' in appearance but a closer look at the many details in background and foreground reflect the more sinister aspect of Faery that the Victorian's firmly believed in. His talent was soon recognised to much critical acclaim and his work was hung in many major galleries and at the Royal Scottish Academy. In 1858 he married Margaret Ferrier. They had two sons. In 1865 he was appointed Queen Victoria's Limner for Scotland. He died on December 26th 1901 in Edinburgh.

## Ernest Percival Rhys

Although born in London on July 17th 1859 Ernest Rhys was raised in the town of Carmarthen in Wales and later in Newcastle-upon-Tyne, North England, both industrial, working class areas. He worked for a spell in the coal industry. From 1886 he worked as an editor on the popular "*Camelot Series*" of reprints and translations. After five years of this he started to write his own essays, short stories, plays, poetry and novels. In 1890 he helped found the "*Rhymer's Club*" in London and the following year he married his wife, Grace. In 1906 he started the "*Everyman*" series of classic reprints through the publisher J.M. Dent. The idea was to issue 1,000 titles. This feat was accomplished in 1956. He did not live to see this as he died on May 25th 1946.

## Katharine Tynan

Katharine Tynan was born on January 23rd 1861 in Clondalkin, Ireland. Her parents Andrew and Elizabeth Tynan were comfortably off but not rich. At an early age she developed a serious eye complaint that resulted in near blindness for the rest of her life. Her mother and sister both died while she was still young and at the same time her father's business began to fail. Being the eldest child she was taken away from school in order to look after her siblings. Despite these considerable difficulties she managed to read avidly and started to produce her own writings. For the rest of her life she was a prolific writer producing dozens of books, poems and articles. She came to the attention of the new writers in Ireland, particularly Dublin, at the time and regular visitors to her home included the then relatively unknowns William Butler Yeats, George Russell and Douglas Hyde. It is mainly thanks to these personal connections that she remains relatively well known today. In 1893 she moved to London with Henry Albert Hinkson whom she married at the home of Wilfred and Alice Meynell. He qualified as a barrister in 1902 and they remained in London for twenty years. In 1912 her husband became the resident magistrate in Castlebar, Co. Mayo, Ireland and Katharine now found herself back in rural Ireland, a move that did not please her after the comfort and cosmopolitan life of London. Her husband died in 1919 and from then on she led an almost itinerant life, without much money, but continuing to produce an enormous output of writings of minor importance. Throughout her life she relied heavily on her Catholic faith to see her through times of trouble. Although she was considered a radical in her day due to her comments on the role of women in society, she held the belief that the best way a woman can show her true femininity was by being a daughter, a wife and a mother. She died on April 2nd 1931.

# Appendix III
# The Immortal Hour

I have referred to the importance of the play "*The Immortal Hour*" several times throughout the book and here I wish to give what is in reality no more than a mere hint as to why. As you will see from the following analysis of the play and its content there is a great deal more embodied in the script than the superficial story gives away. There is still much more that can be deciphered than I am unable to give here due to limitations of space. This same analytical technique can be used on almost all of Fiona's writings to elucidate much that is hidden in the text of what are often rather uneventful and apparently insignificant short stories or essays. I have also given a comparison between the two main scripts of the play and the later libretto composed by Rutland Boughton. I do this to show that these allegorical works are capable of expansion and meaningful adaptation by those with the inner knowledge to so do. They are not set in stone and only capable of revealing one interpretation. Like all else in Faery they are fluid and malleable and will change and shift according to the understanding of the interpreter and also to the morals and acceptable social standards of the times in which the interpretation is being made. This is important. This play, like many of Fiona's other more important pieces, is a mirror of the reader and the public attitudes of any given time. Its content is organic, growing and capable of development just as each individual reader is and just as each period of social change is.

One important introductory comment – "*The Immortal Hour*" being a play and an opera is meant to be spoken aloud. It is meant to be heard by the ears as well as read by the eyes. Making the vocal sounds that pass through the medium of the air is in itself an important magical act as anyone who has read the script for a ritual and then spoken those same words in performance can attest. This applies to all of Fiona's work, especially her poetry. Read it, analyse it, interpret it and mull it over, but at some point read it aloud. Breathe life into it and let it once again take to the air.

* * *

251

First we need to take a look at the period of social development in which the work first appeared. By the late 1890s the Celtic movement in Ireland was making some headway mainly under the influences of Yeats and Lady Gregory. They had already decided upon the need to have a national Irish theatre to express their hopes and aspirations and to inspire others to join them. They were both writing plays and looking for works by other Celtic writers that could be adapted to the stage. In a long letter from Paris in January 1897 Yeats wrote to Fiona and broached this subject with her, "*Have you ever thought of writing a short play? Our Irish literary & politico-literary organizations are pretty complete now… and I think it would be possible to get up celtic* [sic] *plays through these societies. They would be far more effective than lectures and might do more than anything else, we can do, to make the Irish, Scotch, & Other, Celts recognise their solidarity… If we had two or three short & direct prose plays, of (say) a mythological and folk lore kind, by you and by some Irish writer… I feel sure we could get The Irish Literary Society to make a start… My own theory of poetical or legendary drama, is that it should have no realistic or elaborate, but only a symbolic and decorative setting. A forest for instance should be represented by a forest pattern not by a forest painting. One should design a scene which would be an accompaniment but not a reflection of the text… It would give one's work the remoteness of a legend. The acting should have an equivalent distance from common reality.*"[1] He suggested Fiona's "*The Last Supper*" (from '*The Washer of the Ford*') or "*Morag of the Glen*" (from '*The Dominion of Dreams*') as being the type of short story that could be successfully adapted to the stage. Fiona took this suggestion on board but decided rather than adapt any of her existing work she would compose new plays from scratch.

Unfortunately she was not quick enough in coming up with the goods and by the time she had two plays ready for production, "*The House of Usna*" and "*The Immortal Hour*," the atmosphere in Ireland had changed considerably. Elizabeth stated that she could not remember exactly when Fiona started to write "*The Immortal Hour*" but she could recall William reading it to her at Ballycastle, Ireland in the summer of 1899. It first appeared in print in the November issue of "*The Fortnightly Review*" in 1900. This was at least a full two years after Yeats' initial suggestion. In between times the theatre had changed from being the *Celtic Literary Theatre* to the *Irish Literary Theatre*. On this change of name and emphasis Lady Gregory said, "*I think the word 'Celtic' was put in for the sake of Fiona Macleod whose plays however we never acted.*"[2] By 1900 the rift between Fiona and the Irish movement had become irreparable and she was not welcome in Ireland. This is rather ironic as the two plays she had written are both based on specifically Irish themes, employed the type of scenery, dialogue and presentation that Yeats' had suggested and were totally suited to the new theatre whether it declared itself Irish or Celtic.

It was not the quality or subject of the plays that caused them to be rejected, it was the identity of the author. By then Yeats, Russell and Gregory knew that William Sharp was behind all the Fiona Macleod writing. That made producing the plays even more difficult as he, being a real person and a Gaelic speaking Celt, should have been more vocal and militant in the Irish and Celtic cause. Also, on a more practical level, as Lady Gregory pointed out, "... *we used to amuse ourselves by thinking of the call for 'author' that might follow one, and the possible appearance of William Sharp in place of the beautiful woman he had given her out to be, for even then we had little doubt they were one and the same person.*" Lady Gregory also felt that "*The Immortal Hour*" blatantly plagiarized Yeats' own play "*The Shadowy Waters.*" Although the subject matter is very different they are very similar in their presentation with a dreamy, un-worldly, setting; the use of characters and voices off-stage; the main character in each play being obsessed with a quest; an almost total lack of realistic scenery and an ending that does not fully explain who the characters were, how they came to be where they were and what happened next. What Lady Gregory seems to have missed is that all of these qualities that she accused Fiona of stealing from Yeats are the very ones that he himself had suggested Fiona should employ.

I have been unable to find any specific comment or reaction from William or Fiona on being rejected by the Irish theatre but it must have been a sad blow. Fiona had taken to Yeats' suggestion with enthusiasm and had planned a whole series of plays that she referred to as "*The Theatre of the Soul*" or as "*The Psychic Drama.*" Other titles planned for the series were "*Nial the Soulless,*" "*The King of Ys,*" "*Drostan and Yssul,*" "*The Veiled Avenger*" and "*The Book of Dalua*" but none of these were ever completed. Perhaps Fiona lost heart after the rejection of her first two plays in the series.

"*The House of Usna*" was performed during William's lifetime, he being the director, but only in London, never in Ireland. "*The Immortal Hour*" was never staged anywhere during his lifetime. Like so many of her other works Fiona was constantly editing and amending it with every reprint, and today we are left with two main versions. Both are very close in style and content to each other but the impression we get is that Fiona was never quite satisfied with it. It was a work in progress for several years right up to William's death. Even then he left instructions to Elizabeth concerning how the collected works of Fiona Macleod should be edited and amended in any posthumous reprintings. As Elizabeth said, "'*The Immortal Hour' was altered and rewritten several times. I cannot recall when it was begun, but my husband read it to me at Ballycaslte, Ireland, in the summer of 1899. The original form, as printed in 'The Fortnightly Review', lacked the present opening, and finished with a short epilogue; this forepart was specially revised and printed separately as 'Dalua,' and thus described by the author: 'A fragment, as 'The Immortal Hour' itself is, of the as yet unwritten 'Book of Dalua' or 'Book of the Dark Fool,' of whose fulfillment the author sometimes dreams.' 'The Immortal Hour' was published posthumously in America by Mr. Mosher, in 1907, and in England by Mr. T.N. Foulis in 1908.*" This bibliographical note is taken from Volume VII of *The Collected Works of Fiona Macleod,* edited by Elizabeth Sharp, where the play appeared again in 1910. Since 1910 it has been performed a few times over the decades mainly by William Sharp/Fiona Macleod enthusiasts but never on a large scale.

It was edited and rearranged yet again as a libretto and set to music by the English composer Rutland Boughton who transferred it into a very successful opera. This is a good example of my point regarding the play reflecting the society of the day. Fiona wrote it during the final years of the 19th century while Queen Victoria was still on the throne and when Victorian society was very set in its ways, was immoveable in its attitude as to what was right or wrong, what was moral or immoral, and was very unbending. It was over a decade into the 20th century when Boughton came to study it and make his alterations. Victoria had been dead for several years, King Edward was on the throne and a very different set of rights and wrongs, morals and immorals, were in place. The wording of the opera had to reflect this. We shall come to this important version of "*The Immortal Hour*" after we have studied the original play. By then we shall be able to make comparisons between the two main versions of the play and the opera.

## THE PLAY

"*The Immortal Hour*" is more than a psychic drama. It is a lengthy and extremely important magical ritual. Like all rituals it involves physical movement, the use of props, lines that need to be spoken by the correct person at the right time, all of which work together to build a powerful atmosphere. The participants in any ritual will hold a full dress rehearsal and go through all of these movements, check the props, know when to say their part and generally ready themselves for the ritual proper once it commences. In a play all the actors and actresses similarly go through a dress rehearsal and the important stage directions provide the instructions on movement, the use of props, who says what, where and when. The stage scenery is important in giving visual clues to the audience that helps build the atmosphere and these too are in the directions.

All plays have a meaning or purpose, even if that purpose is just to make the audience laugh. Similarly all rituals must have a purpose and this purpose should be known to all the participants and stated clearly at the commencement of the working. At the conclusion of the ritual a similar statement of completion of purpose must be said. The purpose behind the ritual played out in "*The Immortal Hour*" is to demonstrate the psychological and spiritual effects of initiation. The characters, their movements, their words to each other and the settings in which this plays out, are all intended to give the audience an in-sight into the practical effects of working magically and spiritually with the Faeries. This, as noted earlier in this book, was the sole purpose of virtually all of Fiona Macleod's writings.

The version of the play in "*Poems and Dramas*" Volume VII of the Collected Works of Fiona Macleod has become the standard for performance, is the one Boughton based his opera on, and is the one I intend to examine here. It is slightly different from the first published version, in the "*Fortnightly Review*" November 1900, and I shall point out the small but important changes Fiona made to this version as she reworked the play over the following years. It is prudent to pay attention to the stage directions throughout the play. Understandably most people go straight to the spoken parts to eke out the valuable lore and often completely overlook the stage directions but these are of value too, as we shall see.

Dramatis Personae

**EOCHAIDH**  High King of Ireland.
**ETAIN**  a Lost Princess, afterwards Eochaidh's Queen.
**MIDIR**  A Prince of the Hidden People.
**DALUA**  The Amadan-Dhu.
Two peasants, **MANUS** and **MAIVE**, and Harpers, Warriors, etc.

In the 1900 version the two peasants are given as **TEIG** and **GRANEY**, otherwise the Dramatis Personae are the same.

### ACT I SCENE I

The script for the play starts with the following stage direction, "*A forest glade at the rising of the moon. In the background is the hazel-shadowed pool of a wide waste of water. As the moonshine falls upon an ancient oak to the right, the tall figure of DALUA is seen leaning against the bole. He is clad in black, with a small black cap from which hangs a black hawk's feather.*" The overall effect is one of remoteness, a place away from human habitation, gloom, stillness, slightly eerie, with a sense of expectancy. This all directly reflects Yeats' suggestion in his 1897 letter, "*... it should have no realistic or elaborate, but only a symbolic and decorative setting. A forest for instance should be represented by a forest pattern not by a forest painting. One should design a scene which would be an accompaniment but not a reflection of the text... It would give one's work the remoteness of a legend.*"

The specific reference to the hazel tree should be noted. From a scenic point of view the exact species of tree is irrelevant, any tree, even a generic 'tree' would fit the bill. Indeed Yeats suggested that it should not be realistic at all but purely symbolic, yet here Fiona deviates from his idea by being very precise. The original stage directions in the 1900 version are the same except for the second sentence which reads, "*In the background is the tree-shadowed curve of a mere.*" It is clear that in reworking the play Fiona decided that the tree in question had to be a hazel tree. This was intentional and the choice of a hazel tree was deliberate as this in itself contains a mass of symbolism and lore, Faery and otherwise.

Much of the magical work that Yeats' Celtic Mystical Order had been doing centred on retrieving information from the Faery realm by the use of inner journeys using the visual imagination. 'Pathworkings' to use the modern terminology. These journeys of the imagination started with the group building up an inner image of Connla's Well, a forest pool mentioned in several ancient Irish legends, from where the free-form imagery would start. According to these ancient legends a hazel tree overhung this pool. The nuts of this tree would drop into the water where a great salmon would eat them. This salmon was known as the Salmon of Wisdom because the hazel nuts contained all the knowledge of the world and the salmon, by ingesting them, knew everything and everyone. Anyone who swam in the pool or ate of the flesh of the salmon would likewise gain all this knowledge. Just by changing *'tree-shadowed'* to *'hazel-shadowed'* Fiona made it much clearer that this is a powerful place, a place where great knowledge can be obtained and it is a portal to the Otherworld, the realm of Faery.

The reworked directions further define this pool as a *"wide waste of water"* as opposed to the 1900 version that describes simply the *"… curve of a mere."* This new direction gives more of an impression of a lake spreading out from the small pool of Connla's Well. As has been noted elsewhere, lakes in these legends are often the doorways to the world of Faery and are the places where initiates of the Faery Tradition are educated. By simply defining the hazel tree and describing the water in more detail Fiona is telling us that this opening scene is taking place in a very ancient and very important Otherworld site, the inference being that all characters and events located in this place are also of great importance. We can also see how her reworking involving the changing of a few words makes very little difference to the effect of the stage scenery but does reveal a great deal more magical and mythological symbolism.

Immediately another tree is mentioned, the oak. This one is no more than a prop being used by Dalua to rest against. Again the specific species is irrelevant from a stage-craft point of view, any tree or even a boulder or wall would suffice. Why be so specific in naming the oak? As before the answer lies in ancient Celtic legend. Many people today associate the oak with the Druidic order, thanks mainly to a comment made by Julius Caesar when he was in Gaul, but in Ireland the Druids favoured the yew tree while the oak tree was connected more specifically with the High King. The fact Dalua is leaning against this oak tree draws our attention to it and infers a connection between Dalua and the High King. The role of the Celtic High King was a spiritual one, not a legal or political one. He was the physical embodiment of the spirit of the land, to such an extent that should he suffer sickness or injury the land, the very fertility of the soil, would similarly be impaired, as shown in the character of the Fisher King from the Arthurian tradition. All life ultimately depends on the fertility of the land so the choice of the correct High King was crucial. His body and character had to be without injury, scar

or blemish. Dalua, by leaning against the oak tree, is assuming this responsibility. Just by naming two trees and opening the play in a forest next to a
pool and a lake Fiona has told us a great deal about the mysterious black-clad
figure who is on stage even though not a word has been spoken yet.

There is a footnote in the 1900 version that is not in the script or directions for the later version of the play. This explains quite specifically a
small piece of this obscure symbolism. What Fiona said in this footnote was,
"*Dalua: The Amadan-Dhu, or Dark Fool, the Faery Fool, whose touch is madness or death for any mortal, whose falling shadow, even, causes bewilderment
and forgetfulness. The Black Hawk or Eagle alluded to in first 'direction' preceding text is the Iolair-Dhu, which on the first day of the world launched itself
into the darkness and has never yet caught up with the dawn, though its rising
or sinking shadow may be seen over the edge of dark at night-dusk or morning
twilight. It should be added that with the ancient Gaels (and with the few Gaels
of to-day who have not forgotten or do not disdain the old wisdom) the hidden
people (the Sidh or Shee) were great and potent, not small and insignificant beings. 'Mab' long ago was the terrible dark queen, Maive (Medb, Medbh, Mabh);
and the still more ancient Puck was not a frolicsome sprite, but a shadowy and
dreadful power.*" By simply giving Dalua a hawk/eagle feather in his cap she
opened up yet another area of ancient symbolism and legend.

In the *Collected Works* version of the play Dalua slowly moves out of the
moon shadows and starts to speak. This opening dialogue is not in the1900
version of the play. What this extra dialogue reveals is that he is confused and
does not know where he is or how he got there. As he muses aloud he is answered by unseen voices from the wood. This does not startle him nor does
he seek to identify their source, instead he strikes up a long conversation
with them. What we are hearing is a conversation between Dalua's thoughts
and the intuitions of his Higher Self. At one point he says to these unseen
voices, "*My lips have lost the salt of the driven foam, howbeit I hear no more the
long dull roar of the long grey beaches of the Hebrides.*" By identifying the Hebrides as the place Dalua has come from Fiona gives a clear link to our human
physical world, but it is still vague enough to be mysterious, uncertain. The
Hebrides is a long archipelago with many different islands all with unique
characters – from which one has Dalua come? We do not know and it does
not matter. All we need to know is that he was recently in the same physical
world we inhabit but he is now in some other, as yet unknown, location.
Fiona used this connection with the Hebrides in a short story "*When Dalua
Was A Prince Of This World*" that implies there is some specific reason why
Dalua is associated with these Scottish islands.

The voices continue by saying that despite what he thinks he has not
travelled far at all. They say, "*You have come but a little way who think so far
the long uncounted leagues to the world's end; and now you are mazed because
you stand at the edge where the last tangled slope leans over the abyss.*" He replies, "*You know not who I am, sombre and ancient voices. And if I tread the*

*long continuous way within a narrow round, not thinking it long, and fare a single hour thinking it many days, I am not first or last, of the Immortal Clan, for whom the long ways of the world are brief and the short ways heavy with unimagined time."*

The voices respond with, *"There is no first or last, or any end."* The voices are correct; he has not come far, at least in the physical world terms of kilometres or miles, but he has shifted from our own physical world to the Faery realm represented by Connla's Well and the Lake. This is not a long way at all, indeed it is often said that the Faery world sits invisibly alongside our own, it is no distance, it is here. Note the last part of his comment, *"I am not first or last, of the Immortal Clan, for whom the long ways of the world are brief and the short ways heavy with unimagined time,"* which points out his realisation that the conditions of our world are reversed and distorted in the Faery realm. So by the simple stage directions regarding scenery, clothing, and the poetic dialogue between one character on-stage and several off-stage, Fiona has introduced a great deal of linked symbolism and lore and set the scene and the character fairly and squarely in a very important part of the Faery realm.

None of this was in the 1900 version and Fiona obviously felt that more detail was needed to explain how Dalua got where he was. Again this addition makes little difference to the overall effect of the play but it does reveal more from a magical ritualistic point of view. The 1900 version now joins the *Collected Works* version with Dalua saying,

*I have come far, led here by dreams and visions,*
*And know not why I come, or to what end,*
*Or wherefore 'mid the noise of chariot wheels*
*Where the world crashed along the starry ways*
*The Voice I know and dread was one with me,*
*As the uplifted grain and wind are one.*

The *Collected Works* version now has more dialogue between Dalua and the unseen voices that describes a whole array of Faery and Celtic gods and goddesses that is not in the 1900 version. It is in the opera but not in *Act 1 Scene 1*. Boughton moved this dialogue to *Act 2* as we shall see when we come to look at the libretto. The details of this conversation are given there along with some further comment. Both versions of the play follow on with further conversation between the unseen voices and Dalua that is almost identical with just a few minor changes. Then in both versions Dalua suddenly realises that someone is approaching through the trees. He instinctively withdraws to the side of the oak tree and in the 1900 version says, *"Voices, be still! One comes: And I have that within me which can tell when idle feet or fateful feet draw near."* The *Collected Works* version has him say, *"Voices be still! The woods are suddenly troubled. I hear the footfall of predestined things."* Note this curious expression – he does not hear the footfall of a person but of 'predestined things.' This change has the effect of lifting his premonitions to a higher level. He does not simply hear idle or fateful feet approaching but realises that the approaching person is playing out some great, predestined things that will affect everyone and everything throughout the rest of the play.

The stage directions in both versions now say, *"Enter ETAIN, in a coiled robe of pale green, with mistletoe intertwined in her long, dark, unloosened hair. She comes slowly forward, and stands silent, looking at the moon-shine on the water."* Etain is described in the Dramatis Personae as *"A Lost Princess, afterwards Eochaidh's Queen."* The fact she is dressed in green indicates she is of the Faery. Green has long been connected by tradition with the Faeries and many people in the Gaeltacht of Scotland and Ireland will not wear anything in the colour green, as they believe this will anger the Faeries. My own mother had such an inhibition and as children my three brothers and myself never possessed any green coloured clothing and, in deference to my mother's wisdom, I should add none of us were ever attacked by angry Faeries. The mistletoe entwined in Etain's hair gives her a symbolic connection with Druids, and therefore deep knowledge, and the fact her hair is unloosened gives her a rather wild and seductive mien.

The name Etain means 'tin' in Old Irish. This is significant. The metal tin was important to the early Celtic people not just for the manufacturing of weapons and utensils but also for trading. Much of this tin was mined in Cornwall, a Celtic area of southwest England closely connected with the Arthurian legends, and earlier, with the coming to Britain of Joseph of Arimathea who by tradition brought with him the young Jesus. Fiona would have been aware of all of these symbolic connections, especially after William's meeting with Dr. Goodchild in Glastonbury. By simply giving this character the name Etain and by directing that she should wear green and have mistletoe in her hair, Fiona opened up all these mythological and symbolic connections for those who understand the symbolism.

Etain, who has not yet noticed Dalua standing in the shadows, walks to the water's edge and stands staring into the lake. What this simple act suggests is that Etain is scrying, or gazing into the Otherworld gateway of the lake, for guidance. She too is lost and confused as to how she got there. Her opening lines are not spoken but are sung to a slow monotonous air. This reinforces the fact she is Faery and from a place that is often described in the legends and folklore as being full of music and song. Dalua comes forward and there follows a lengthy dialogue between them. As Etain struggles to recall who she is and how she got there Dalua does not physically touch her but does allow the shadow of his hand to fall on her. This brings with it total forgetfulness. Dalua tests this by making several references to Faery but Etain can remember nothing. He goes on to say that once he loved her and she loved him but Etain is only further confused by this revelation. He makes much of his old love for her but she says, *"...And if you love me thus, why is there neither word nor smile nor glance of love, nor any little sign that love shakes like a windy reed within your heart?"* Dalua's sombre reply is simply, *"I am Dalua."*

Here is a very clear warning that Dalua can and does manipulate people through his powers of forgetfulness. He does not show any emotion when he does this nor is he ever reprimanded or punished for such enforced mind control. It is all very functional and lacking in emotion. Etain's question to him about his statement of his old love for her but his total lack of any display of love also warns us that he does not share the same emotional responses that she does or, importantly, that we humans do. He then goes on to warn Etain that his kiss would be fatal and that, "… *We are sheep led by an unknown Shepherd, we who are the Shee, for all we dream we are as gods, and far upgathered from the little woes of men.*" This tells us that even they, the Faeries, who think themselves so godlike and unconcerned with the affairs of humans, are not in control of their own destiny. Somehow making this statement causes Dalua to suddenly realise why they are both there.

He tells Etain that a 'king of men,' a human being, is approaching and that this king is searching for true love with a passion and the conviction that he will find it this night. A blast from a hunting horn is heard off-stage and Dalua once again touches Etain with the shadow of his hand so she will forget even this recent conversation. He says, "*Now go. The huntsman's lodge is near. I have told all that need be told, and given bewilderment and dreams, but dreams that are the fruit of that sweet clay of which I spoke.*" Etain puts her hand to her head and, looking bewildered, resumes the singing with which she entered the scene. She has forgotten everything.

### END OF ACT 1 SCENE 1

Superficially not very much has happened in this opening scene at all. Two people have had a mysterious conversation about who they are and how they got there but without elucidating answers to either of these questions. A few off-stage voices have added a further air of mystery and then one character realises what is about to happen next and the scene closes. From the comments I have made above with particular reference to the stage directions though it is clear that Fiona wrote a great deal more into this first scene than many people would be aware of. Such was most of her work.

### ACT 1 SCENE 2

This scene opens in the same place. Etain has left the lakeside and Dalua awaits the arrival of the king of men. The dialogue in the two versions is virtually identical for the whole of *Scene 2*. The stage directions say, "*DALUA stands, waiting the coming of EOCHAIDH the king. The king is clad in a leathern hunting dress, with a cleft helmet surmounted by a dragon in pale findruiney.*" The name of the king, Eochaidh, is not an uncommon one in Old Irish legends and it can be translated as either 'horse warrior' or 'yew warrior.' This gives the bearer of the name aspects of both a warrior in battle and of a Druid, due to the previously noted yew associations with Druidry in Ireland. The Dramatis Personae describes him simply as '*High King of Ireland.*'

Comment has already been made on the spiritual significance of the High King. The subtle description of him having a dragon atop his helmet is noteworthy. The dragon is an ancient symbol of the powers of the Green World, the energies of nature. This ties in nicely with the intermediary functions of the High King who must mediate those same energies for the benefit of his people and of the land. Again though it hints at a possible Arthurian connection due to one of King Arthur's titles being 'Pendragon' meaning the 'Head of the Dragon.' These connections with King Arthur are not to be found in any ancient Irish legends but they serve to again demonstrate my point of how these magical allegories change and adapt with the times. The late 19th century saw a great flowering in interest in all things Arthurian. Fiona's simple stage directions reflect this contemporary interest. You can begin to see how there are many visual clues in this play that lead onto much diverse mythology and symbolism. When these visual clues are supplemented by a detailed examination of the entire dialogue an astonishing wealth of information is revealed. It is beyond the scope of this present work to provide such an in-depth analysis of the entire script but a synopsis of both versions of the play and the later opera continues with some of the more obscure but nonetheless important details pointed out.

Dalua greets Eochaidh graciously and calls him king. Eochaidh is surprised to see anyone in these dark woods but more surprised that this person recognises him as king. He asks the stranger his name and Dalua replies almost exactly as he did to Etain, "*I am called Dalua.*" The king seems to remember the name from somewhere, vaguely, perhaps in a dream, but Dalua touches him lightly and he instantly forgets everything including who he is and that he is king. The stage directions then say, "*Suddenly a fountain rises in the mere, the spray rising high in the moon-shine.*" Dalua says, "*Look, O King!*" but despite looking in the right direction Eochaidh sees nothing. The stage directions then say, "*Plucking a branch from a mountain-ash, and waving it before the king's face,*" Dalua repeats, "*Look!*" Now Eochaidh can see the fountain and he replies, "*I see a Fountain and within its shadow a great fish swims, and on the moveless wave the scarlet berries float: dim mid the depths the face of One I see, most calm and great, august, with mournful eyes.*"

There is a great deal going on here. The scene is set in the same place as the opening scene but now things have moved to a higher level. Dalua is no longer dealing with a lost queen of Faery but with the spiritual High King himself. The symbolism has gone up a notch. Note that in *Scene 1* the mere fall of Dalua's shadow was enough to make Etain forget everything but here in *Scene 2* Dalua has to physically touch the High King with his hand, an action which in the physical world would bring death, but here on the higher levels only produces forgetfulness. A third tree is introduced, the mountain ash, also known as the rowan tree or quicken tree. The mountain ash occurs in several Old Irish legends and Fiona used this same motif, especially in connection with water as here, in several of her own stories. William also used this imagery in his important poem "*The Swimmer of Nemi.*" This tree has long been associated with powerful magic and, in later folklore, with witches. It is a tree that can grow further up mountainsides than any other and is therefore symbolically closer to the spiritual realms. Its profusion of spiritual knowledge-giving red berries is a 'higher' version of the clusters of wisdom-giving nuts of the hazel. The wisdom that the hazel gives is of the affairs of this world, the wisdom that the mountain ash bestows is of a spiritual nature. It is only when the mountain ash branch is shaken over Eochaidh that he can see the great fountain spouting forth from the centre of the lake. This fountain is symbolic of an eruption of great spiritual power and knowledge bursting free from the realms of Faery and spraying its energies and wisdom high into the human world. Eochaidh sees the Salmon of Knowledge being carried aloft in its gushing and recognises within its spray the ancient goddess of the Fountain, a figure who also appears in the Arthurian legends. We know from Yeats' records of workings performed by the Celtic Mystical Order that on Dec 29th 1897 he and several others had an inner vision of Connla's Well sending a fountain of water high into the air. [3] William was not present at this working but would have been informed of it by Yeats later. A footnote to the record of this magical working says, "*The magic well of Connla lies at the foot of a mountain ash. Those who gaze therein may, if they can find a guide, be led to the Fountain of Perpetual Youth. The ash berries fall into the waters and turn them to fire. Connla, the Druid, is the Guardian of the Well.*" [4]

This whole scene is from the original Old Irish version of Connla's Well from which the goddess Boyne erupted forth in a great fountain of water and created the river in Ireland that still bears her name (in some versions the river is the Shannon). As noted at the start of this commentary, this legend was used by the members of Yeats' Celtic Mystical Order as the starting place for their inner journeys and Fiona was a member of this order. Perhaps Yeats was reluctant to stage this play for the reason that it gave away too much symbolism that up until then he had considered secret and esoteric. Maud Gonne had expressed similar reservations regarding Fiona's earlier prose. But this was Fiona's mission, to reveal as much as she could of the Faery mysteries.

Dalua asks Eochaidh what it is that he most wants and he answers, "The word of wisdom. O thou hidden God: show me my star of dreams, show me the way!" The dialogue continues but Dalua keeps silent while "A Voice" from off-stage takes over the conversation with Eochaidh. Eochaidh does not seem to notice that Dalua is no longer the one who is speaking and asks again about his dreams. In response the invisible voice tells him emphatically several times to return. This voice is that of his own Higher Self warning him he has already gone too far. His desire to achieve his dreams, or his desire for initiation into higher realms of knowledge and service, are driven solely by personal desire, his physical desire for Etain. No one seeking such initiation into the higher realms of magic can be accepted if their desire is driven by no more than human emotion. The unseen voices tell him he must forget his dreams and return to this world. Then the king realises it is no longer Dalua speaking. He looks around for him but discovers he is alone. The teacher has withdrawn, now the student must learn for himself. This is a crucial stage in magical and spiritual progress. Until now a teacher has been giving out information and guidance but this has ceased, the teacher can do no more. The student's Higher Self takes over and its words of wisdom are a dire warning to stop and go back. The point has been reached where neither the teacher nor the Higher Self can do any more. The student must now stand on his own two feet and be responsible for his own decisions and actions. The king cries to the voice that he will not go back, he cannot return, as he must follow his dreams. He has made his decision. When he mentions his dreams again, Dalua's mocking laughter is heard coming from the shadows and he says, "*Follow, O follow, king of dreams and shadows!*" to which Eochaidh falteringly replies, "*I follow. ...*"

### END OF ACT 1 SCENE 2.

This scene ends on an uncertain and perhaps dangerous note for the High King but he is clearly determined to pursue his dreams at all costs. There is much more to this scene than just a simple moral warning regarding the wisdom or otherwise of chasing dreams. Fiona has given out many important powerful symbols as well as much practical magical information in a scene that is less than half the length of the first. Again though much of this information is hidden in the easily missed stage directions and descriptions of the scenery.

### ACT 1 SCENE 3

This scene opens with another important shift in level, this time fully downwards. The action moves from the higher spiritual realms, symbolised by the gloomy Faery forest, to our mundane physical world, symbolised by the interior of a rustic dwelling. The directions for the *Collected Works* version say, "*The rude interior of the cabin of the huntsman, MANUS. He is sitting, clad in deerskin, with strapped sandals, before a fire of pine-logs. Long, unkempt, black hair falls about his face. His wife, MAIVE, a worn woman with a scared look, stands at the back, plucking feathers from a dead cockerel. At the other side of the hearth, ETAIN sits.*" The 1900 version has the same directions but the names of the huntsman and his wife are given as Teig Mahone and Graney. These are two very typical and common Irish names and were probably chosen by Fiona to fit in with the Irish emphasis of the Irish Theatre. Using such everyday names also helped to emphasise the shift from the higher Faery realms to literally back down to earth. They were changed for the *Collected Works* version as Fiona was no longer writing to impress the Irish theatre and, on a more practical level, they were unfamiliar and unpronounceable to most English speaking readers. Manus and Maive are much simpler. Now the emphasis has shifted from a vague, gloomy, ethereal stage setting to one that emphasizes two very basic humans in their rough, ungraceful home. Manus and Maive represent the basic human instincts and emotions and also, on a more subtle level, they are the ancestors, those who have gone before us. Etain has found her way to their humble cabin and is given shelter from the storm raging outside by the poor huntsman and his wife.

Manus starts the dialogue by saying, "*I've seen that man before who came to-night. (pause) I say I have seen that man before.*" Maive nervously replies, "*Hush Manus beware what you say. How can we tell who comes, who goes? And, too, good man, you've had three golden pieces.*" This lets us know that someone has already been at their home earlier that evening, someone who was generous enough to give them three gold pieces and predict that others were yet to come. This was Dalua. We know this because at the conclusion of *Act 1 Scene 1*, after his shadow falls on Etain for the second time, he says to her, "*Now go. The huntsman's lodge is near.*" The three gold pieces are for "*... her who stays with us to-night ... the other was for any who might come, asking for bite or sup. ... The third for silence.*" These three gold pieces are not referred to again. Was this an idea, a sub-plot that was never developed by Fiona?

The conversation that follows amongst Manus, Maive and Etain introduces for the first time expressions of fear and nervousness. So far all the characters, Dalua, Etain and Eochaidh, have accepted without fear or trepidation their unfamiliar, moonlit woodland setting and their communal loss of memory. They are curious about these things but are not fazed or unsettled by their circumstances. Now that the action has shifted to our own mundane level, fear and nervousness are abundant. Maive in particular is reluctant to discuss the identity of their night visitor and gets anxious when Manus speaks of the Faeries. This says a lot about the basic emotional differences between human and Faery. I wonder if nervous Faeries caution their partners not to speak of the humans? They also speak much of two ancient gods whom they will only refer to as Grey Feathers and Blind Eyes. They are in fact the forces behind the wind and the rain. They obviously hold them in awe and a certain amount of fear. These are two ancient deities from the times of the early ancestors and bring with them the ancient ancestral emotions of fear of the unknown and the need to placate the hostile elements, such as wind and rain.

Soon Eochaidh arrives at their rude home and asks for shelter from the storm. Manus lets him in and marvels at the fact neither Eochaidh nor his clothing are wet despite the downpour taking place outside. This is a common motif in folklore and Faery stories to alert the reader to the fact that this person has come from the Faery realm. This puts Maive into an even higher state of fear and she pleads with Eochaidh to have pity and do them no harm. Eochaidh asks Manus if anyone else is expected that night. In the 1900 version he replies, "*No one, fair lord.*" But the *Collected Works* version says, "*No one, fair lord. The wild gray stormy seas are doors that shut the world from us poor island-folk.*" This is the first mention that they are on an island – the Hebrides from where Dalua came? There is no further mention of being on an island in either version of the play or in the opera. This is the only point in *Act 1 Scene 3* where there is a divergence in the script between the two versions of the play.

Etain invites Eochaidh to sit with her by the fire while Manus and Maive withdraw to the shadows in the back of the cabin. Eochaidh immediately realises that Etain is the woman of his dreams and starts to woo her passionately. She responds to his advances and thinks she can vaguely remember Eochaidh from some long distant time in the past. She recalls fading memories of the Faery realm as the night wears on and the fire dims. Eochaidh has now found contentment and peace through Etain and he speaks, "*The years, the bitter years of all the world are now no more. We have gained that which stands above the trampling feet of hurrying years.*" Exactly at that moment "*a brief burst of mocking laughter is heard*" and Eochaidh turns and asks angrily of Manus and Maive, "*Who laughed? What means that laughter?*" Manus replies that no one laughed. Etain says, "*None laughed. It was the hooting of an owl. Dear lord, sit here. I am weary.*" Eochaidh settles down, forgets the laughter and resumes his wooing of Etain. She though seems far away in dream and once again starts to sing her ancient song of the beautiful Faeries and their domain.

## END OF ACT I

### ACT 2 SCENE I

This is the first anniversary of Etain and Eochaidh's meeting. All the events from now on in both versions of the play and in the opera take place in the banqueting hall at Tara. The directions say, "*A year later. In the hall of the Royal Dun at Tara. The walls covered with skins, stag's heads and boar's heads, weapons: at intervals great torches. At lower end, a company of warriors, for the most part in bratta of red and green, or red and green and blue, like tartan but in long, broad lines or curves, and not in squares, deerskin gaiters and sandals. Also harpers and others, and white-clad druids and bards. On a dais sits EOCHAIDH the High King. Beside him sits ETAIN, his queen. Behind her is a group of white-robed girls.*" All this is clearly in our world, no longer the world of Faery, and we are given a specific physical world location, Tara in Ireland. There are many more characters on stage and there is much more sound, colour and light than in Act 1.

The scene opens with the assembled company singing the praises of Eochaidh towards the end of the feast celebrating Eochaidh and Etain's first anniversary. It is late in the evening and Etain excuses herself as she is very tired. Eochaidh tries to persuade her to stay a little longer but she says she is too tired to stay awake. Eochaidh then confesses he does not want to be left alone as for the previous three nights he has had disturbing feelings, bad dreams and premonitions and has again heard the invisible mocking laughter he heard a year before in Manus' cabin. Etain then discloses that she too has seen strange visions and heard music but all of her experiences were pleasant, non-threatening and reminded her of the Faery world. She eventually leaves and Eochaidh dismisses the rest of the assembled company. The directions say, *"Raising a white hazel-wand, till absolute silence falls."* So the hazel crops up again but now Eochaidh has a wand of this wood at his command implying he has gained some of the wisdom of the Salmon of Knowledge, he is now more capable of controlling the powers of this world. He bids a good-night to all but then the directions say, *"The warriors, bards, minstrels troop out, leaving only the harpers and a few druids, who do not follow, but stand uncertain as a stranger passes through their midst and confronts the king. He is young, princely, fair to see; clad all in green, with a gold belt, a gold torque round his neck, gold armlets on his bare arms, and two gold torques round his bare ankles. On his long curling dark hair, falling over his shoulder, is a small green cap from which trails a peacock-feather. To his left side is slung a small clarsach, or harp."*

This is a classic description of a Faery that could have been taken from any one of many ancient Celtic legends. Note the profusion of green, the Faery colour, and the opulence of the amount of gold. One old name for the Faeries was 'the Shining Ones' and the person being heavily adorned in shimmering and shining gold often represents this in legends. His cap is decorated with a colourful peacock feather. Compare this stranger's dazzling appearance with the sombre opening description of Dalua, clad all in black with a black cap adorned by a hawk's feather. Dalua appears like the mere shadow of this beautiful stranger. Note also how the bards and druids simply stand aside and watch as this total stranger walks directly towards their lord, the High King. They seem mesmerized by his appearance and unable to move to defend their king.

The stranger apologises for arriving late to the feast but asks the High King for a boon anyway. Rather rashly Eochaidh agrees to this despite the fact he does not yet know exactly what this boon might be. Before the stranger can name his boon Eochaidh goes on to lament the fact that he too desires a boon, one that nobody can give him. His most earnest desire is to know for certain that the joy of his love for Etain will never fade and that she will always be with him. The stranger then says that his own boon is much simpler – he wishes to play the High King at chess. Eochaidh says it is late and that his chessboard is in the room where Etain is now sleeping. The stranger says this is not a problem and pulls from beneath his cape a small ivory chessboard with gold pawns. The workmanship is exquisite and Eochaidh has never seen anything like it. They start to play chess accompanied by the soft sound of one of the court minstrels playing his harp.

**END OF ACT 2 SCENE 1**

## ACT 2 SCENE 2

It is the same place but many hours later. The script of both versions is almost identical for the rest of the play. They have been playing chess nearly all night and now the stranger has finally beaten Eochaidh. In good spirits he asks the stranger what he would claim as his prize. He says all he wishes is to be allowed to kiss the queen's hand and sing her a song he has composed in her honour. The queen is sent for and when she appears she is wearing the same green dress she wore when she first met Eochaidh in the cabin and once again she has mistletoe intertwined in her long loose hair. Eochaidh is surprised by this but explains what has happened and what the stranger has claimed as his prize. The directions say, *"ETAIN looking long and lingeringly at MIDIR, slowly gives him her hand. When he has raised it to his lips, bowing, and let it go, she starts, puts it to her brow bewilderingly, and again looks fixedly at MIDIR."* She tells him to sing his song. It is the same song that she herself sang the night she and Eochaidh met in Manus' cabin. She looks confused and bewildered and Midir continues to sing of the beauties of the Faery realm. Note that after this brief kiss on the hand Midir does not touch or attempt to touch Etain again. He has to encourage her to come to him by singing the Faery song in the hope of jogging her memory of who she really is. This is because he is from the Faery realm, a higher level than Eochaidh's physical world fortress, and he cannot force any physical being to return to Faery with him. She must come of her own desire.

She slowly starts to walk towards Midir. Eochaidh discovers that he cannot move but can only watch helplessly as Etain draws closer and closer to the singing Midir. Now Midir is singing in the language of the Faeries and part of his song reminds us again of where this story started,

*Among the nuts*
*on the hazel tree*
*I sing to the Salmon*
*In the faery pool.*

*What is the dream*
*The Salmon dreams,*
*In the Pool of Connla*
*Under the hazels?*

*It is: There is no death*
*Midir, with thee,*
*In the honeysweet land*
*Of Heart's desire.*

*. . .*

*The Salmon of Knowledge*
*Hears, whispers:*
*Look for it, Midir,*
*In the heart of Etain.*

Eochaidh pleads, "*Etain, speak! What is this song the harper sings, what tongue is this he speaks? For in no Gaelic lands is speech like this upon the lips of men. No word of all these honey-dripping words is known to me. Beware, beware the words brewed in the moonshine under ancient oaks white with pale banners of the mistletoe twined round them in their low and stately death. It is the Feast of Samhain.*" Etain answers dreamily that she cannot hear him, he sounds too far away. She now claims that she can no longer understand the words that Eochaidh is saying, and that she is going from dark to light. Next, she starts to excitedly relate all the sounds she can now hear coming from Faery while Midir encourages her all the time to keep walking towards him. Suddenly she asks who laughed and she knows that Dalua is near. Midir tries to convince her that Dalua is not there. Part of his speech includes the following, "*... on a quicken* [the mountain ash], *growing from mid-earth and hanging like a spar across the depths, Dalua sits: and sometimes through the dusk of immemorial congregated time, his laughter rings: and then he listens long, and when the echo swims up from the deeps he springs from crag to crag, for he is mad, and like a lost lamb crieth to his ewe, that ancient dreadful Mother of the Gods whom men call Fear... Even the high gods who laugh and mock the lonely Fairy Fool when in his mortal guise he haunts the earth, shrink from the Amadan Dhu* [the Dark Fool] *when in their ways he moves, silent, unsmiling, wearing a dark star above his foamwhite brows and midnight eyes.*"

Etain eventually draws alongside Midir and the directions say, "*Slowly ETAIN, clasping his hand, moves away with MIDIR. They pass the spell-bound guards, and disappear. A sudden darkness falls. Out of the shadow DALUA moves rapidly to the side of EOCHAIDH, who starts, and peers into the face of the stranger.*"

### Eochaidh
*It is the same Dalua whom I met*
*Long since, in that grey shadowy wood*
*About the verge of the old broken earth*
*Where, at the last, moss-clad it hangs in cloud.*

### Dalua
*I am come.*

### Eochaidh
*My Dreams! My Dreams! Give me my dream!*

### Dalua
*There is none left but this ----*
*(Touches the king, who stands stiff and erect, sways, and falls to the ground)*

### Dalua
*... The dream of Death.*

### THE END

## The Opera

Rutland Boughton wrote the opera during 1911-12 when he was living in a cottage deep in the woods of Grayshott, England. He was inspired by the forest surroundings and his original plan was to have the opera staged in the open air with the actors and choruses entering and leaving through the natural, surrounding trees. He based the libretto on the *Collected Works* version of the play but with several of his own additions and omissions. He must have been very familiar with the general writing of Fiona Macleod as the additions he made are not his own compositions but are some of her lesser-known poems that fit seamlessly into the original script of the play.

It still holds the record for the greatest number of consecutive performances of any serious opera. It was first performed in the Assembly Rooms, Glastonbury, England on August 26th 1914. It was later brought to the Birmingham Repertory Theatre in June 1921, and scored such a success there that the composer was persuaded to try it in London. It was duly moved to the Regent Theatre, King's Cross, London on October 23rd 1922 where it proceeded to run for 216 consecutive performances. A revival on November 17th 1923 brought another 160 consecutive performances, and major revivals followed in 1926 and 1932. Since then the opera has seen several smaller revivals. Hyperion Records Limited, London, released it on a two discs CD set in 1987, catalogue number CDA66101/2. This recording was made in June 1983 with Roderick Kennedy as Dalua and Anne Dawson as Etain, with music by The English Chamber Orchestra under the baton of Alan G. Melville.

In the booklet that accompanies the CD, Michael Hurd comments, "*For the most part he* [Boughton] *took the play as it stood, but made a number of important cuts that significantly tightened its dramatic shape. He also expanded certain lyrical moments by the insertion of appropriate poems by the same author. All in all, Boughton's version of The Immortal Hour is much more theatrically effective than the original play and much more apt for music.*" Many of the differences are small and necessary – shortening a sentence by a word or two so it fits better with the music, cutting out some of the small incidental one-word comments and replies that do not change the sense of the play but help keep the rhythm of the music and so forth as Hurd explains. However there are large sections of dialogue in the play that have been completely omitted from the opera and, conversely, there are several Fiona Macleod poems inserted into these gaps, and elsewhere, which were never intended to be part of the play. Fortunately the sleeve notes for this release give Boughton's complete libretto making it much easier to compare his additions and omissions with Fiona's original versions of the play, which we can now examine.

## DRAMATIS PERSONAE

**DALUA**, The Lord of Shadow
**ETAIN**, a Princess of the Land of the Ever-Young
**EOCHAIDH**, the High King of Eire
**MANUS**, a peasant
**MAIVE**, his wife
**MIDIR**, A Prince of the Land of the Ever-Young

A Spirit Voice, An Old Bard, Druids, Bards, Warriors, Maidens, Elemental Spirits

### ACT I SCENE I

The opera opens in the same gloomy woodland scene as in the play with Dalua on-stage. The libretto starts by following the script of the play but the section where Dalua remembers being in the Hebrides has been cut. Most of the following dialogue between Dalua and the unseen voices is as in the play apart from a long section of twenty two lines that deals with a good deal of magical and mythological lore which Boughton cut from here but reintroduces as the opening lines of *Act 2*. In this transplanted section the voices mention many Celtic and Faery gods – Orchil, Kail, Oengus, Lugh, The Dagda, Ana, Manannan, Brigid, and Midir – and give an interesting little rune:

#### Other Voices

*Oengus, keeper of the East: of Birth: of Song:*
*The keeper of the South: of Passion: and of War:*
*The keeper of the West: of Sorrow: of Dreams:*
*The keeper of the North: of Death: of Life.*

#### Dalua

*Yet one more ancient even than the god of the sun,*
*Than flame-haired Oengus, lord of Love and Death,*
*Holds the last dreadful key . . . Oblivion.*

In one of William's notebooks held in the National Library of Scotland, Edinburgh, is a slightly expanded version of this rune,

#### Angus of the Four Keys

| | |
|---|---|
| *The East: Birth: The Key of Music* | E |
| *The South: War: The Key of Passion* | S |
| *The West: Dreams: The Key of Sorrow* | W |
| *The North: Life: The Key of Death* | N |

*The Key of the East, that is also the Key of Birth, and*
*        the Key of Music*
*The Key of the South, that is also the Key of War, and*

*the Key of Passion*
*The Key of the West, that is also the Key of Dreams, and*
*the key of Sorrow*
*The Key of the North, that is also the Key of Life, and*
*the Key of Death*

Notice that this version uses the name Angus whereas the play gives Oengus. These are the same name, pronounced 'innes,' with Angus being the Scottish version and Oengus the Irish. This shows that as well as choosing an Irish theme and setting for her plays Fiona was also being politically correct in changing the spellings of personal names where appropriate. She had clearly originally wanted the Irish theatre to produce them. Both of these versions have come from an old Gaelic rune that William's nurse Barbara related to him, given on page 272, Volume IV, of the Collected Works of Fiona Macleod,

### The Four Stars of Destiny

*Reul Near (Star of the East), Give us kindly birth;*
*Reul Deas (Star of the South), Give us great love;*
*Reul Niar (Star of the West), Give us great age;*
*Reul Tuath (Star of the North), Give us Death.*

William and Fiona used the theme of 'four' several times with four keys, four cities, four coloured winds, four gods and goddesses etc appearing in the prose and poems as well as in William's personal notebooks. The Golden Dawn system of magic also made much use of fours – the four directions, four quarters, four Archangels, four magical tools and so forth. Yeats' Celtic Mystical Order's main focus was in retrieving knowledge concerning the Four Treasures of the Tuatha De Danann – the Sword of Nuada, the Spear of Lugh, the Cauldron of the Dagda and the Lia Fail or Stone of Destiny. Anyone today familiar with group magical working will be aware of the importance of these groups of four. They are worth noting when you come across them in Fiona or William's writings. Yeats also came up with an association concerning trees that I have never seen anywhere else. He placed the Apple in the East, the Rowan in the South, the Oak in the North and the Hazel in the West. Students of the ancient Celtic tree alphabet known as Ogham may make something of this.

The opera and play coincide for several more lines but then the opera omits a short statement by Dalua that is crucial to understanding his complex character better. In the play he says, "*I am but what I am. I am no thirsty evil lapping life.*" But in the opera a chorus of voices crying hail to Dalua has replaced this statement. This one small line from the play makes it clear that Dalua has no control over his powers of forgetfulness and death and he is no more than a pawn of Fate. Knowing this fact changes our understanding of Dalua significantly. He is not evil, malicious or scheming. He is no more than a tool, a servant to a higher force. But this in itself makes him dangerous. He is unpredictable and it is pointless trying to argue or reason with him. His actions are not the result of his own personal desires or whims. It appears Boughton deliberately wished to change our understanding of Dalua by omitting this line. I shall say more on this when we come to the end of the opera which likewise contains a small change by Boughton that infers Dalua <u>was</u> deliberately malicious and evil.

At this point in both the opera and play Etain is heard approaching. In the *Collected Works* version of the play Dalua makes his strange comment about hearing the footfall of *'predestined things'* but this has been cut from the opera and the libretto goes straight to Etain coming on-stage singing her slow Faery song. Another small change follows here in that she does not gaze into the lake while singing as she does in the play. Her attempt to recover memory or information from the Otherworld lake has been cut out. Dalua's important act of touching Etain with his shadow of forgetfulness is included but then the whole following section, fifty-eight lines, where Dalua recounts his old love for Etain, has been removed completely from the opera. This removal significantly changes the operatic audience's understanding of the relationship between Dalua and Etain and, as above, implies that all of Dalua's actions were intentionally evil. By not explaining that Dalua and Etain were at one time lovers we must assume that Dalua has no personal emotional connection to Etain or what she does. We know from the play that this was not the case and was not what Fiona had originally intended The dialogue between Etain and Dalua then picks up again as in the original script up to the point where she leaves the stage, being the end of *Act 1 Scene 1,* and Eochaidh enters, being the beginning of *Act 1 Scene 2*. In the opera there is no change of scene. Etain exits, Dalua remains on stage, Eochaidh enters and they start their dialogue. This means that the important shift in level of consciousness, made clear in the play by the ending of one scene and the start of the next, is lost in the opera. From a magical point of view this is significant but from a purely operatic point of view Boughton's rearrangement is much better.

Boughton omitted some minor interchange between the High King and Dalua during the beginning of their conversation but it does not affect the sense of what is happening. Things do change though between the play and the opera after Dalua touches Eochaidh in order to clear his memory. In the play there is an exchange where Dalua tests Eochaidh's memory of who he is and why he is there. From his confused responses it is clear that Eochaidh remembers nothing. This has been cut from the opera but this is not important. Next both the opera and the play have the scene with the fountain suddenly erupting from the lake. In the play this is an important part where Eochaidh cannot see the fountain until Dalua uses the branch of mountain ash to give him inner vision. In the opera Eochaidh sees the fountain immediately and the mountain ash is never mentioned. Once again this makes an important difference from the magical point of view but Boughton was unaware of these deeper, symbolic meanings and was merely editing to better fit the score and the libretto.

Now comes the part where Eochaidh tells Dalua of his dreams and the higher voice is heard from off-stage urging him to return. Dalua has disappeared but his laughter is heard and he mockingly tells the High King to follow his dreams if that is what he really wants. The scene closes with Eochaidh's faltering assertion, "*I follow. ...*" Up to this point the libretto is the same as in the play but in the opera the scene does not end here as it does in the play. Boughton has added on a completely separate Fiona Macleod poem called "*Dalua.*" The libretto reads,

### Eochaidh

*I follow ...*
*I have heard you calling, Dalua, Dalua!*
*I have heard you on the hill,*
*By the pool-side still,*
*Where the lapwings shrill Dalua ... Dalua ... Dalua!*
*What is it you call, Dalua, Dalua!*
*When the rains fall,*
*When the mists crawl,*
*And the curlew call Dalua ... Dalua ... Dalua!*
*(Eochaidh goes off into the wood)*

*Dalua (in another part of the wood)*
*I am the Fool, Dalua!*
*When men hear me, their eyes*
*Darken: the shadow in the skies*
*Droops: and the keening woman cries Dalua ... Dalua ... Dalua!*

This addition does not change the sense of what is happening, fits in seamlessly and adds to the content of the opera. It shows Boughton was sufficiently familiar with Fiona's work to be able to add so appropriately one of her own poems rather than resorting to composing his own. We also know from Elizabeth's later comments on the changes Fiona made to the play that she had used this same poem in the original version but there it appeared at the very end of the play, after Eochaidh's death.

### END OF ACT I SCENE I

### ACT I SCENE 2

This is *Act 1 Scene 3* in the play. The libretto follows the script for most of this entire scene. There are several small cuts, which do not change the sense of what is happening, but they do make for a better operatic production. The one section that has suffered most from omissions is where Maive expresses her fear of the Faeries and her superstitious belief that it is unlucky even to speak of them while Manus tries to hush her. Again this is not very important and would have been difficult to add to the libretto without lengthy and tedious repetition. The most significant change in this whole scene however is at the end. In the play Etain sings her Faery song to herself as she sits by the fire and Eochaidh woos her but in Boughton's version Etain is silent and it is the unseen voices that sing her song.

### END OF ACT I SCENE 2

### ACT 2

The script for the play has *Act 2* spread over two scenes but Boughton has amalgamated them into one. It opens with the same setting, the banqueting hall at Tara, but immediately the libretto is different. Instead of the three-line salutation of the Chorus of Bards in the play, the opera opens with first Druids, then Maidens, then Warriors singing praises to the land of the Faeries and to Eochaidh. The Druids opening song is Fiona's poem "*The Rune of the Four Winds*" that is given exactly as Fiona wrote it but with one small change. The poem has three lines, repeated twice, that say,

> *That Man knoweth,*
> *That One dreadeth,*
> *That God blesseth –*
> but Boughton changed the last line to,
> *That Man knoweth,*
> *That One dreadeth,*
> *That Lu blesseth –*

He then added to this poem the section that he cut from *Act 1 Scene 1* where the unseen voices sing of the Faery and Celtic gods but the order in which the gods are named has been rearranged and this makes a better libretto.

Once the Druids have finished their opening song the Maidens take over with another song of praise that is not in the play. This is Fiona's poem "*The Bells of Youth*" which is reproduced as per the original except for a repeated line that in the poem says,

> *Spring has risen with a laugh, a wild rose in her mouth,*
> *And is singing, singing, singing thro' the world.*
> which in the libretto has been changed to,
> *Spring has risen with a laugh, a wild rose in her mouth,*
> *And is ringing, ringing, ringing thro' the world.*

Finally the Warriors sing another poem that is not in the play, this one being "*The Song of Ahez the Pale*." When they have finished, Eochaidh lifts his drink and proposes a toast, as in the play, but then Boughton has added in another verse, sung by the Bards, Warriors and others, that says,

> *Green fire of Joy, Green fire of Life,*
> *Be with you through the stress and strife;*
> *Be with you through the shadow and shine,*
> *The immortal Ichor, the immortal wine!*

> *Drink deep of the immortal wine,*
> *It gives the laughter to the strife;*
> *Drink deep, and through the shadow and shine*
> *Rejoice in the Green Fire of Life!*

The libretto then follows the script of the play up to the point where Eochaidh asks Etain not to leave as he has been troubled for the past few nights by visions and the same strange laughter he heard in the wood and in Manus' cabin when they met. Here Boughton has added on to Eochaidh's plea Fiona's poem *"The Lords of Shadow"* which fits perfectly as it concerns the actions of Dalua. Etain leaves and the stage directions for the play read, *"ETAIN leans and kisses the king. He stoops, and takes her right hand, and lifts it to his lips. Warriors raise their swords and spears, as ETAIN leaves, followed by her women."* The directions for the opera however contain a subtle change, *"She gives him her hand. He kisses it tenderly but looks over his shoulder as if startled by some unseen phantom. Etain repeats her gesture of weariness and bewilderment. She rises up and steps down from the throne."* The warriors then repeat the *"Green Fire"* chant as above. By adding the poem *"The Lords of Shadow"* to Eochaidh's speech and by giving Etain a glimpse of a phantom, Boughton has strengthened the importance of Dalua at this point in the opera in a way that is missing from the play. The Druids and Bards then repeat the chant of the old gods cut from *Act 1 Scene 1* but used earlier at the opening of this Act.

Now things change considerably between the script and the libretto. In the play Midir asks the King to play him at chess, there is some minor dialogue, and they then sit at the table and start the chess game. This brings *Act 2 Scene 1* of the play to a close and *Act 2 Scene 2* opens with the same stage setting but later in the night when Midir has just won the game. In the opera there is no chess game and no change of scene. The omission of the chess game works better in the overall running of the opera but it is a significant loss from a magical point of view. Chess games occur frequently in the old Celtic legends, especially in the Welsh and Irish, and it is clear that when such a scene crops up more than just a game of intellectual challenge is being played. The word 'chess' is of course the English translation of either the Welsh or Old Irish words for the game, "Gwyddbwyll" and "Fidchell" respectively, but neither of these words means chess. The Irish word translates literally as 'wood-knowledge' that indicates the game was

based on a detailed knowledge of the Old Irish Ogham alphabet.[5] The legends describe this game as being played on a square, checkered board with
both players having movable pieces of various complexity. The early transla-
tors understandably took this to be chess and hence we are stuck with this
mistranslation.[6] In short this is an important magical and ritualistic game
and its inclusion in the play is of significance with regard to the on-going
development of the magical and Faery lore and symbolism Fiona deliberately
wove into the script and stage directions.

Boughton replaced the 'chess' game with a considerable amount more
poetry that is not in the script. This starts with Midir singing "*The Love Song
of Drostan*" which Fiona described as being "*From 'Drostan and Yseul,: an
unpublished drama.*" Just before Midir starts to sing the last verse Eochaidh
interrupts by taking over the singing and sings,

> *Hear us, Oengus, beautiful, terrible, Sun-Lord and Death-Lord!*
> *Give us the white flame of love born of Aed and of Dana…*
> *Hearken, thou Pulse of hearts, and let the white doves from thy lips*
> *Cover with passionate wings the silence between us,*
> *Where a white fawn leaps and only Etain and I behold it.*

the last line of the original poem says,

> *Where a white fawn leaps and only Yseul and I behold it.*

When Eochaidh sings this last line the stage directions for the opera say,
"*Midir regards him lightly. A look of fear comes into the eyes of Eochaidh. He
half-ashamedly tries* to cover it." Which implies the Eochaidh knew the original version of the song but altered it to reflect his own love for Etain.

Once Midir has finished singing, Eochaidh asks what is his boon and
Midir replies he wishes to kiss the hand of the queen and sing her his song.
From here until the end of the play the libretto follows the general sense of
the plot – Etain is called and appears dressed as she was when she first met
Eochaidh; Midir sings the Faery song and she starts to remember who she is
and who Midir is; Eochaidh tries in vain to prevent Midir singing and Etain
from leaving but he is rooted to the spot. The remaining dialogue has been
moved around somewhat and much of the singing of the Faery song comes
from unseen voices rather than directly from Midir. One cut in the opera is
the part where Etain hears Dalua's laughter but Midir persuades her he is not
there despite the fact he goes on to recite his long poem about Dalua.

The final few lines of the libretto have been changed from those of the
script and these changes are important. The script says that as Etain leaves
Tara with Midir a sudden darkness falls, Dalua moves rapidly to Eochaidh's
side, Eochaidh sees and recognises him and pleads, "*My Dreams! My Dreams!
Give me my Dream!*" whereupon Dalua says to him, "*There is none left but
this— [touches the High King and he dies] … the dream of Death.*" Boughton
however has it that Eochaidh is unaware of Dalua's presence. As the unseen

voices finish their song, and as Etain and Midir finally disappear, Eochaidh cries his plea for his dreams. The operatic directions say, "In the darkness and unseen by Eochaidh, Dalua moves in swiftly. He touches Eochaidh with the gesture made before Etain in the wood. Eochaidh momentarily stands stiff and erect, then falls. Dalua, the *Lord of Shadow, draws himself up to his full, regal height.* " The unseen voices sing,

> *They play with lances*
> *And are proud and terrible,*
> *Marching in the moonlight*
> *With fierce blue eyes.*

and the curtain falls.

Boughton's changes to this last brief scene alter the role of Dalua significantly. The way Dalua avoids being seen by Eochaidh and does not speak to him are the actions of a stealthy assassin. Once he completes his assassination the final direction, "*Dalua, the Lord of Shadow, draws himself up to his full, regal height.* " gives him an air of triumph, of superiority in victory, which insinuates that personal vengeance was behind all of Dalua's final actions. However, as the play makes clear, Dalua is not responsible for his actions and has no feeling, positive or negative, about his powers of forgetfulness and death.

These same changes, Eochaidh not seeing Dalua before he deals his fatal touch and Dalua not speaking to him, renders the ending incomplete from a magical point of view. From this stance the original ending of the play is much more important. In any ritual openly stating the purpose and intent of the working is vital. Actually speaking these words not only makes it clear to all participants what is going on and what is expected of them but also sets up conditions in the Faery realm to help make such changes occur. In the play having Dalua specifically tell Eochaidh that there is no dream left for him other than Death clearly and precisely concludes the ritual and closes down the connections that have been set up between the characters and between the human world and the Faery world. It would be very messy and unsafe not to do so from a magical perspective. This final statement by Dalua also lets us know that Eochaidh, who is now dead to this world, now knows that death is but a dream and he lives on in the Otherworld. There he finally achieves his dream of being reunited with Etain in the Faery realm. This happy ending is not clear from the opera.

Finally I should point out that despite his brief appearances on stage, this play is very much about Dalua. It is easy to miss this fact, as most of the story seems to revolve around Eochaidh and Etain. Dalua appears in many of Fiona's stories and poems and he is key to understanding the complex mythology of Faery. For more information on him see Appendix 4.

## THE PECULIAR DEATH OF NETTA FORNARIO

It is impossible to comment on "*The Immortal Hour*" without mentioning the curious story of Netta Fornario. Norah Marionetta Fornario was born in 1897, the daughter of an Italian father and an English mother. She was estranged from her father, a doctor, who had returned to Italy and with whom she seems to have had little or no contact. She was a member of the 'Arts and Crafts' movement of the early twentieth century, making her own woolen or silk clothing, following a vegetarian diet and wearing her hair in two long plaits. She was gifted intellectually and studied astrology, ritual magic, occultism and psychic healing. She became a member of the Golden Dawn's Alpha and Omega Temple in London and was a friend of Dion Fortune the well-known occultist and founder of the Society of the Inner Light. Dion referred to her affectionately as 'Mac.' In 1929 she was living with a Mrs. Varney in lodgings at Mortlake Road in Kew, London. Later Mrs. Varney would say that Netta did not believe in doctors but preferred to cure herself and others by telepathic means. She was a cheerful young lady if somewhat unorthodox for the time in her beliefs and appearance.

While living in London she saw the opera of "*The Immortal Hour*" twenty-three times and wrote a lengthy explanation of its inner meanings. Part of this says, "*Visitors to the Regent Theatre may be roughly classified as follows; students of mysticism and folk-lore who are able to understand the great truths concealed behind this gossamer curtain of faery; (a small clan, but they come frequently and every time discover some new aspect of illuminating significance), a large number of people who think the play beautiful but sad; and many for whom the whole drama is so elusive and incomprehensible that they irritably demand of each other "what on earth the fellow can be getting at," and are frankly bored: and there is a fourth class who, while keenly appreciating the artistic beauty of the performance, also sense the existence of a deeper meaning, but are hopelessly baffled by their inability to interpret the intricate symbolism employed.*" [7]

In August of 1929 she suddenly decided to move to the little island of Iona, still a remote destination in those days. She clearly intended to make her stay there a permanent one as she took with her all her furniture and several large packing cases containing all of her belongings. She first took lodgings at the east end of the island but soon moved to a house towards the west of the island. A Mrs. MacRae, who fascinated Netta with her tales of Hebridean folklore and tales of the Faery people, owned this house. This was the same house in which William Sharp lodged on his frequent visits to Iona some thirty years before. It was also the same house that was rented for a while by Christine Allen, then newly wed to the artist John Duncan, a member of Geddes' College in Edinburgh and contributor to "*The Evergreen.*" Christine was one of Dr. Goodchild's triad of women administering to the sacred bowl he had taken to Glastonbury. It is likely that Netta knew of these important connections and it had probably been her intention all along to set up home in this important little cottage, hence her sudden change of accommodation shortly after arriving on the island when a room became available in Mrs. MacRae's home.

Netta spent most of her days either walking on the beach attempting to communicate with the Faeries and spirits of the island or meditating on a small hill, near her accommodation, which was known locally as the Fairy Hill. At night she would stay in her room and go into a trance either to telepathically heal someone or to further attempt spirit communication. Mrs. MacRae had been given strict instructions that should she ever find Netta in a trance under no circumstances was she to call a doctor.

In November she had sent a letter to her old landlady in London and in it she said, "*Do not be surprised if you do not hear from me for a long time. I have a terrible case of healing on.*" Then late on a Sunday afternoon, she came down from her room in a very agitated state and told her landlady she had to leave the island immediately, that night. This was impossible, as the ferry did not sail on the Sabbath. At first she rejected this and went to the pier anyway but eventually accepted she would not be able to leave that night and returned home. She went to her room in a state of distress but reappeared some time later, calm and steady, and announced she was just going out for a while. She did not come home that night. By mid afternoon on the Monday a search was started but it was Tuesday before her body was found lying on the slopes of Fairy Hill. The descriptions of the scene on Fairy Hill now differ. The popular story today is that her naked body was lying inside a large cross that had been cut into the ground with a large ceremonial knife that was found lying close by. The soles of her feet were badly scratched and bloody but the heels were unharmed as if she had been running fast and hard over the rough ground in bare feet. Round her neck a silver cross and chain had turned black. Her clothing was never found. However, the contemporary report, later confirmed by Calum Cameron, who was twelve years old at the time, lived in the house and remembered Netta vividly, was quite different and much less sensational. The first published account of the incident was from the "*Glasgow Bulletin*" newspaper that said, "*The body was lying in a sleeping posture on the right side, the head resting on the right hand. Round the neck was a silver chain and cross. A few feet away a knife was found. Miss Fornario had left the farm (about a mile away) sometime during Sunday night. The island was bathed in moonlight and a keen frost prevailed. The doctor who was called gave it as his opinion that death was due to exposure. With the exception of a few scratches on the feet, caused by walking over the rough ground, there were no marks on the body.*"

Calum added that the 'ceremonial knife' of later accounts was no more than a normal table knife, taken from the kitchen. There was no cross cut into the turf but Netta had told him a few days before that she had been trying to dig into the hill in order to make contact with the Faeries. The silver round her neck had not turned black and the look on her face was one of peace and contentment, as if asleep. Her father was duly traced and contacted but he seemed to be completely uninterested in the sad fate of his daughter. Touchingly, when the islanders on Iona heard of this, they contributed what money they could and paid for her to be buried on Iona. She now rests in the small graveyard next to Oran's Chapel.

What was the terrible case of healing that she had embarked upon? Was it something to do with this that had terrified her to the point of needing to leave the island immediately? Why was her body naked in the middle of a freezing November night and what happened to her clothes? Keeping in mind her interest (obsession?) with "*The Immortal Hour*," and with her own warnings about it being dangerous, one wonders if she came a little bit too close to Dalua. Whatever happened, she is now at rest on Iona with the Faeries she so dearly longed to be with. She finally achieved her dreams, just like Eochaidh.

---

[1] Yeats Annual, No. 13, page 97

[2] McHugh, Our Irish Theatre, A Chapter of Autobiography, By Lady Gregory, page 20

[3] Kalogera, page 120

[4] Kalogera, page 76

[5] see my "Celtic Tree Mysteries, Secrets of the Ogham", Llewellyn, St Paul 1997, for details.

[6] For a full and detailed examination and explanation of Gwyddbwyll I recommend "Merlin's Chess" by Mike Harris obtainable from www.ritemagic.co.uk

[7] Visit www.servantsofthelight.org for the complete text of this lengthy critique.

## Appendix IV

# Dalua – a Faery God

**THE CHARACTER**

Fiona's writings are usually vague regarding location and timeless regarding exactly when in history the narrative is played out. They tend to be set on remote islands or in romantic Highland glens and there is rarely mention of any detail that gives an indication of the year, decade or even century in some cases. It is this very vagueness, as if everything is viewed through some misty Celtic twilight, which gives them a great deal of their fascination. Because of the lack of specific locations and dates it is very hard to pin down exactly when and where the stories are meant to be set, indeed if the reader is meant to be able to pin them down at all. This is not important to the casual reader. The stories make sense and stand up in their own right as vignettes of a vanished or vanishing Celtic and Gaelic way of life, but it can be very frustrating to the researcher into Celtic and Faery lore hoping to glean some new and valid information. At first glance her writings appear to offer a wealth of such material with pieces of folklore, traditions and rituals sprinkled throughout the tales. She quotes ancient sayings and chants that have a ring of authenticity about them but often such pieces of practical information are given without any verifiable source. Instead she gives her source as, for example, "*an old fisherman,*" or gives an even more vague comment like "*as they say in the Isles…*" Such sources are indeed valuable and Yeats too recognised this when in his semi-autobiographical novel "*The Speckled Bird*" he said, "*The fishermen of today talk of the same things shepherds talked of before there was a town in all Europe.*" Fiona's vagueness is in keeping with her style of writing but it is challenging for the researcher trying to separate genuine old Gaelic and Celtic lore, of which there is actually a great deal, from her personal Faery lore that she mixes in without discrimination or separation. Both sources are of great value but it is important to be able to identify which is which. They are not the same and it is important to recognise this.

One way to achieve this is to pay close attention to the names she uses. Most of her characters have fairly ordinary personal and family names that you still come across in the Highlands and Islands today but others have decidedly odd, unusual and in some cases unique names. This applies not only to her fictional characters but also to the frequent references to gods and goddesses that she often identifies as being from the old Celtic mythology. Many of them are indeed from old Celtic sources but there are a good many others that are purely Faery. It is important to identify clearly which is which before attempting any magical or Inner work with either of these. The following comments should help in this matter.

The most important of the Faery gods that Fiona revealed to us is Dalua. This character appears in several of Fiona's works under his own name and under titles such as Master of Illusion, the Amadan-Dhu (the Black Fool), the Secret Fool, the Accursed of the Everlasting Ones, God of Enchantment, and the Haughty Father. He is said to be the dark brother of Angus Og and his wife is the deadly Bean-Nimhir (The Serpent Woman) who is herself the dark aspect of St. Brigid. Angus Og and St. Brigid, or the goddess Brigid, are from the Celtic tradition. By giving them dark twins who are from the Faery tradition Fiona is hinting at a link between these two traditions that many believe exists but few have ever tried to ascertain. A study of Dalua will help point out the links between the Faery tradition and the Celtic tradition and therefore, by extension, between Celtic mythology and human spiritual understanding.

Fiona's first story specifically about Dalua is entitled, appropriately, "*Dalua*" and appeared in *The Dominion of Dreams*, 1899. This story opens with a poem that later appeared separately in "*Poems and Dramas.*" It reads:

> *I have heard you calling, Dalua*
> > *Dalua!*
> *I have heard you on the hill,*
> *By the pool-side still,*
> *Where the lapwings shrill*
> > *Dalua ... dalua ... dalua!*
>
> *What is it you call, Dalua,*
> > *Dalua!*
> *When the rains fall,*
> *When the mists crawl*
> > *Dalua ... dalua ... dalua!*
>
> *I am the Fool, Dalua,*
> > *Dalua!*
> *When men hear me, their eyes*
> *Darken: the shadow in the skies*
> *Droops: and the keening-woman cries*
> > *DALUA ... DALUA ... DALUA*

After the poem, the narrative starts with Dan Macara going home after a night of drinking with friends. It was late, rainy and the moon gave an eerie glow to the bleak moor. Dan noticed a man ahead of him, playing the pipes, and with a flock of sheep following him. The sheep made no noise. The pipe music was wild and unfamiliar to Dan who was confused and frightened by it. He tried to catch up with the piper but never seemed to get any closer. He turned off the track to follow the stream home but the piper's tune suddenly changed to a soft, delicate air. Dan paused to listen and as he did so the rain stopped and just for a moment the cold, dark moor became like a paradise but quickly returned to normal. Then he caught up with the piper and saw that the silent sheep were no more than shadows, but not shadows of sheep. They were of everything the piper had passed during the day – shadows of trees, plants, cattle, mice, a woman at a well, a dead man in a pool, a boy playing etc. Then he saw his own dark shadow. He lunged at the piper but went straight through him, as if he too was shadow, and struck his head against a cold granite boulder. When he came too a moment later he walked off looking for his shadow but eventually fell asleep in the heather. Dalua then appeared beside him and took the shadow of a reed-flute and played it. A curlew flew by and Dalua took its shadow and played it into the mind of Dan Macara. Then Dalua touched him. At that Dan awoke and forever after was mad. He feared nothing except shadows and spent his days walking the hillsides and calling like a curlew.

This introduces all the main themes and symbols of Dalua – madness, illusions and shadows, the playing of hypnotic music, a touch that brings madness or death and the curlew. There is also the subtle but important point that Dalua brings death or madness for no obvious reason. In this story Dan Macara has done nothing wrong, is not an evil man, has not slighted Dalua and seems to be the victim of an unprovoked attack by the Dark Fool. Why? It is all rather pointless as it stands. This is the way of Dalua. He is not responsible for his actions and he has no feelings for them, good or bad. He does what he has to do and moves on. The warning is that Dalua can appear to anyone, anywhere and at any time.

The same book, *The Dominion of Dreams*, contains the tale "*By Yellow Moonrock*" in which Dalua is only referred to as the Amadan Dhu, not specifically as Dalua. This tale was shortened in subsequent reprints but in its original form it concerns an itinerant piper by the name of Rory McAlpine who had disgraced himself when drunk in the village of Dalibrog and had vowed never to return. However, a year or so later, word came that his foster brother's wife had delivered their first child and he wanted Rory to play at the christening which would be on St. Bride's Eve. He decided to go. During the celebrations he confided to an old woman that he had been having a recurring dream of St. Bride. She would appear to him by a local landmark, a great boulder out on the moor known as the Yellow Moonrock, where she would pick up what he at first thought was an adder but then realised it was a flute and play the most beautiful music for him. The old woman listened to his description of the woman with the flute and said it was not of St. Bride that he had been dreaming but of the *Bean-Nimhir*, the Serpent Woman, who can suck the soul out of a man through his lips. She is the wife of the Amadan-Dhu–Dalua. Rory did not like this interpretation and went back to heavy drinking and playing his pipes for the dancers. Eventually he passed out and was put to bed.

Three times during the night he awoke to the sound of beautiful music drifting over the moors. He decided to find whoever was playing the music and walked out into the darkness, hoping it was the beautiful woman in his dream, St. Bride, ignoring the warning about the Serpent Woman given earlier. A poor tinker was sleeping out in the open close by and he could make out Rory talking to someone else who the tinker could not see. Soon Rory started to rant and rave loudly and started dancing a wild, flailing dance that terrified the tinker. He heard a soft, sweet music but could not see who was playing it. Suddenly Rory started to shout, *"Let me go! Let me go! Take your lips off my mouth! Take your lips off my mouth!"* Then he suddenly fell silent. The tinker ran terrified to the village where he told his tale. Next day at daybreak a search party returned to the Yellow Moonrock. There they found the body of Rory McAlpine, his clothes in tatters, his pipes smashed, and his lips blue and swollen. A drop of black blood was on his throat. One of the men said, *"It's an adder's bite."*

This story is similar to the first in that Rory has done nothing to deserve such a horrible end and is the victim of a premeditated and unprovoked attack. In the earlier part of the story Fiona gives a good deal of information regarding the lore and customs connected with the celebrations of St. Bride's day by the Highlanders. Part of this includes an invocation to the adder. Rory's dream of St. Bride picking up an adder that becomes a flute, and the old woman's interpretation of this as being the Bean-Nimhir, all point out the fact that St. Bride and her dark half, the Serpent Woman, are one and the same. These dark aspects are not mentioned or discussed by the Church or by other Celtic and Gaelic folklorists but come directly from the Faery tradition. Looking upon Dalua and the Bean-Nimhir in this light starts to raise many, deep questions regarding the links between Faery and Christianity. It also challenges us to take a look at our basic understanding of the Christian saints and the Christ Himself–do they, can they, really have these dark sides? If so, how do we interpret them and, more importantly, how do we bring them into our personal belief system regarding the very nature and purpose of the Incarnation? Fiona spent a great deal of time and effort trying to explain these esoteric teachings to us in a way that we might understand, hence her use of the character Dalua many times over throughout her entire writing career.

"*The Birds of Emar,*" also from *The Dominion of Dreams*, is the most Faery of all Fiona's stories involving Dalua. At first it seems to be dealing with several identifiable gods from the Celtic tradition but as the tale unfolds it takes on a very different form and character from any other Celtic myth. The writing style is very unusual for Fiona with many short, abrupt sentences and none of the lengthy descriptive passages that are so much her signature. Events happen very quickly and there is so much shape-shifting and swapping of places between humans and Faeries that it is difficult to follow exactly what is going on. It is clearly a story taken straight from the Faery mythology and, as such, makes for very peculiar reading. It is worth reading slowly and carefully meditating on all the gods and goddesses, heroes and heroines, mentioned as well as visualising the various actions and episodes they are engaged in. There is much to be learned from this but it takes a lot of unravelling.

In the tale she makes reference to someone identified only as '*the Haughty Father.*' This is Dalua in his aspect of the dark side of Christ. He appears in this form again in one of Fiona's better-known poems "*Invocation of Peace.*" Very often today only a few of the middle lines are quoted and it is often mislabelled as being "*Ancient Celtic*" or "*Old Irish*" or something of that vein. The full poem, and the version you will probably find today, reads,

> *Deep peace I breathe into you,*
> *O weariness, here;*
> *O ache, here!*
> *Deep peace, a soft white dove to you;*
> *Deep peace, a quiet rain to you;*
> *Deep peace, an ebbing wave to you!*
> *Deep peace, red wind of the east from you;*
> *Deep peace, grey wind of the west to you;*
> *Deep peace, dark wind of the north from you;*
> *Deep peace, blue wind of the south to you!*
> *Deep peace, pure red of the flame to you;*
> *Deep peace, pure white of the moon to you;*
> *Deep peace, pure green of the grass to you;*
> *Deep peace, pure brown of the earth to you;*
> *Deep peace, pure grey of the dew to you;*
> *Deep peace, pure blue of the sky to you!*
> *Deep peace of the running wave to you,*
> *Deep peace of the flowing air to you,*
> *Deep peace of the quiet earth to you,*
> *Deep peace of the sleeping stones to you!*
> *Deep peace of the Yellow Shepherd to you,*
> *Deep peace of the Wandering Shepherdess to you,*
> *Deep peace of the Flock of Stars to you,*
> *Deep peace from the Son of Peace to you,*
> *Deep peace from the heart of Mary to you,*
> *From Briget of the Mantle*

> *Deep peace, deep peace!*
> *And with the kindness too of the Haughty Father,*
> *Peace!*
> *In the name of the Three who are One,*
> *And by the will of the King of the Elements,*
> *Peace! Peace!*

As this stands it is a typical Gaelic-style Christian invocation to Mary, Brigid, God and Christ. But only Mary and Brigid are actually named. The other titles used, *Son of Peace* and *King of the Elements*, are found in many similar Gaelic prayers and refer to the Christ. The other reference to the *Haughty Father* has always been assumed to mean God. However there is another version of this poem with a very subtle one-word addition. The poem is otherwise identical up until the final invocation, which reads,

> *And with the kindness too of Dalua the Haughty Father,*
> *Peace!*
> *In the name of the Three who are One,*
> *And by the will of the King of the Elements,*
> *Peace! Peace!*

This gives the whole poem a totally different slant. It is clearly still Christian but with the insertion of the name Dalua it takes on a very esoteric form of Christianity, one that accepts Christ's dark side as being equally worthy of invocation. Take note of the use of the word '*kindness*' in connection with Dalua. The stories that Fiona has given us of Dalua do not reveal a kind side. Clearly there is much more to him than we realise.

I found this Dalua version of *Invocation of Peace* on the web site of a church in Massachusetts where it is used in occasional services they give under the category of Celtic Christianity. I contacted the minister of the church and asked how this unique version managed to appear on the web site but all she could tell me was that someone had copied it from an old, hand-written copy of the invocation which was now lost. I would contend that the only person who would have written such a version was William Sharp. Considering his several visits to the east coast of the United States it is possible just such a copy did exist. This is a clear example of how important it is to really study closely what Fiona says. Being able to recognise and understand the names and poetic descriptions of places and people she uses reveals an enormous amount of crucial Faery lore that is otherwise missed completely. The above discussion is also a good example of how easily and seamlessly the Christian and pre-Christian mix in the world of Faery whereas in our world we see clear lines of demarcation between them. Such lines do not exist. It is interesting though that the only place this alternative version of the *Invocation of Peace* has survived is on a web site belonging to a Christian church and that it is being used to this day in a Christian service.[1]

A personal aside: During the writing of this book my wife had occasion to purchase some file-folders from one of the country's large office supply chains. She picked up a box of twelve folders, paid for them and took them home. When she opened the box they were all shrink-wrapped together. She cut the shrink-wrap away, took out the first new folder and opened it. Inside was a sheet of paper. Instead of being the advertising for other similar products that she expected it to be, it turned out to be a copy of Fiona's "*Invocation of Peace*" nicely spaced and in a delicate font. All of the other eleven folders were empty. Other than the poem the sheet is completely blank, no name, no date, no dedication, just the "*Invocation of Peace*." How on earth did it get there and why out of the thousands of such folders all across America was she guided to pick up this one? This was almost as jaw-dropping as the meeting with Rev. M------- in Fiona's old Edinburgh home mentioned in Chapter 5.

Fiona says more on this Haughty Father aspect in a piece entitled "*The Hill-Tarn*" from "*The Silence of Amor*". (Collected Works Volume 6, page 108) The hill tarn, or pool, of the title is said to be in Ross-shire, northern Scotland and in the essay she describes the seven mountains that surround it. Of one of these she says, "*It is called Maol Athair-Uaibhreach, the Hill of the Haughty Father: I know not why. 'The Haughty Father' is a Gaelic analogue for the Prince of Darkness—son of Saturn, as he is called in an old poem: 'God's Elder Brother,' as he is named in a legend that I have met or heard of once only—a legend that He was God of this world before 'Mac Greinne' (lit.: Son of the Sun) triumphed over him, and drove him out of the East and out of the South, leaving him only in the West and in the North two ancient forgotten cities of the moon, that in the West below the thunder of grey skies and that in the North under the last shaken auroras of the Pole.*" This is deep Faery lore and takes a lot of thought and meditation to understand. It is also a good example of Fiona's vagueness when it comes to identifying sources, as discussed earlier. This is an extremely important piece of lore but all she says of its source is that it is from "*an old poem*" and "*a legend that I have met or heard of once only.*" Note that God only drove Dalua the Haughty Father out of half of the world, East and South, leaving him the West and North for his domain, coincidentally the areas of Europe where the Celts still live to this day, thus making another link between the Celtic people and the Faeries.

In "*Studies in Spiritual History of the Gael*" there is a short essay entitled simply "*A Dream.*" This piece first appeared in the *Theosophical Review* for September 1904. This may explain its very mystical style, so unusual for Fiona, as she was not writing for her usual readers but readers familiar with the writing style and teachings of the Theosophical Society. I give it in full,

I was on a vast, an illimitable plain, where the dark blue horizons were sharp as the edges of hills. It was the world, but there was nothing in the world. There was not a blade of grass nor the hum of an insect, nor the shadow of a bird's wing. The mountains had sunk like waves in the sea when there is no wind; the barren hills had become dust. Forests had become the fallen leaf; and the leaf had passed. I was aware of one who stood beside me, though that knowledge was of the spirit only; and my eyes were filled with the same nothingness as I beheld above and beneath and beyond. I would have thought I was in the last empty glens of Death, were it not for a strange and terrible sound that I took to be the voice of the wind coming out of nothing, travelling over nothingness and moving onward into nothing.

"*There is only the wind,*" I said to myself in a whisper.

Then the voice of the dark Power beside me, whom in my heart I knew to be Dalua, the Master of Illusions, said: "*Verily, this is your last illusion.*"

I answered: "*It is the wind.*"

And the voice answered: "*That is not the wind you hear, for the wind is dead. It is the empty, hollow echo of my laughter.*"

Then, suddenly, he who was beside me lifted up a small stone, smooth as a pebble of the sea. It was grey and flat, and yet to me had a terrible beauty because it was the last vestige of the life of the world.

The Presence beside me lifted up the stone and said: "*It is the end.*"

And the horizons of the world came in upon me like a rippling shadow. And I leaned over darkness and saw swirling stars. These were gathered up like leaves blown from a tree, and in a moment their lights were quenched, and they were further from me than grains of sand blown on a whirlwind of a thousand years.

Then he, that terrible one, Master of Illusions, let fall the stone, and it sank into the abyss and fell immeasurably into the infinite. And under my feet the world was as a falling wave, and was not. And I fell, though without sound, without motion. And for years and years I fell below the dim waning of light; and for years and years I fell through universes of dusk; and for years and years and years I fell through the enclosing deeps of darkness. It was to me as though I fell for centuries, for aeons, for unimaginable time. I knew I had fallen beyond time, and that I inhabited eternity, where were neither height, nor depth, nor width, nor space.

But, suddenly, without sound, without motion, I stood steadfast upon a ledge. Before me, on that ledge of darkness become rock, I saw this stone which had been lifted from the world of which I was a shadow, after shadow itself had died away. And as I looked, this stone became fire and rose in flame. Then the flame was not. And when I looked the stone was water; and it was as a pool that did not overflow, a wave that did not rise or fall, a shaken mirror wherein nothing was troubled.

Then, as dew is gathered in silence, the water was without form or colour or motion. And the stone seemed to me like a handful of earth held idly in the poise of unseen worlds. What I thought was a green flame rose from it, and I saw that it had the greenness of grass, and had the mystery of life. The green herb passed as green grass in a drought; and I saw the waving of wings. And I saw shape upon shape, and image upon image, and symbol upon symbol. Then I saw a man and he, too, passed; and I saw a woman, and she, too, passed; and I saw a child, and the child passed. Then the stone was a Spirit. And it shone there like a lamp. And I fell backward through deeps of darkness, through unimaginable time.

And when I stood upon the world again it was like a glory. And I saw the stone lying at my feet.

And One said: "*Do you not know me, brother?*"

And I said: "*Speak, Lord.*"

And Christ stooped and kissed me upon the brow.

Note that the dream starts with Dalua, the dark aspect of Christ, standing next to her and talking with her but at the end of her timeless vision her companion has become the Christ of Light. Note also that Christ calls her 'brother' – who is relating the story? Clearly not Fiona.

"*The Lynn of Dreams*," a story from "*The Winged Destiny*," is headed with an excerpt from *The Little Book of the Great Enchantment* that says, "*Ah, son of water, daughter of fire, how can ye twain be one?*" followed by a longer quotation from something called *The Ancient Beauty* – another Faery source book?- that reads, "*And lest that evil Destiny which puts dust on dreams, and silence upon sweet airs, and still songs, and makes the hand idle, and the mind an ebbing leaf, and the spirit as foam upon the sea, should take from this dreamer what he had won, the god of enchantment and illusion gave the man a broken heart, and a mind filled with the sighing of weariness.*" The main character of the story is not specifically identified but referred to only as 'John o' Dreams.' He is a master poet and wordsmith but he longs to find the source of all poetry, of all words, the true inspiration behind all verse and song. As he is dreaming on this one day he realises that Dalua is standing beside him. Dalua knows his desire and says he can take him to the pool that is the fount of all language. The poet goes with him until they reach a small pool and therein he sees more than he can possibly comprehend regarding poetry, songs, stories and language in all its many forms and manifestations. As he gazes in wonder he is suddenly startled by the sound of a plover's cry – the plover, or curlew, is a symbol of Dalua. The pool vanishes and he is back where he first met Dalua. He asks what has happened and Dalua says he gave him a drink from the Lynn of Dreams, the pool of all words and inspiration. However from that moment forth the poet can no longer compose verse, make wise utterances or even deal with the problems of every day language. He had seen too much and could not cope with it. The story ends with, "*It was all gone: the master-touch, the secret art, the craft. He became an obscure stammerer. At the last he was dumb. And then his heart broke, and he died. But*

*had not the Master of Illusions shown him his heart's desire, and made it his?"*
This final sentence concerning Dalua granting the heart's desire that brings
death with it is also the crux of the play *"The Immortal Hour."*

As well as this final salutary warning to be careful what you desire most,
Fiona also includes earlier in the text a paragraph warning of the dangers of
spending too much time in the glamour of the Otherworld, *"Dark, pathless
glens await the troubled thought of those who cross the dim borderlands. To dwell
overlong, there; to listen overlong, there; overlong to speak with those, or to see
those whose bright, cold laughter is to us so sad (we know not why), and whose
tranquil songs are to us so passing forlorn and wild; overlong to commune with
them by the open gate, at the wild wood or near the green mound or by the grey
wave; is to sow the moonseed of a fatal melancholy, wherein when it is grown and
its poppy-heads stir in a drowsy wind, the mind that wanders there calls upon
oblivion as a lost child calling upon God."* This is still good advice today. By all
means visit Faery if you can. But don't overstay your welcome, you will not
benefit from it. It is no coincidence that a common expression for someone
who has lost his or her grip on reality is that they are away with the Faeries.
Be aware and beware of this.

*"The Tribe of the Plover"* from the collection of essays called *"Where the
Forest Murmurs,"* is a lengthy essay on the folklore of many lands concerning
the birds the plover, the lapwing and the curlew. All of these birds are connected with Dalua as is made clear in the essay. Fiona illustrates that all of
this international folklore gives these birds a bad reputation and associates
them with illusions, death and madness. Perhaps any reader who is a bud-
ding ornithologist with an interest in Faery lore could make a deeper study
of the habits, preferences and lifestyles of these birds to see if further parallels
can be drawn with Dalua. Fiona put a lot of effort and research into producing this particular essay. She was trying to point out something.

In the essay *"The Rainy Hyades,"* also from *"Where the Forest Murmurs,"*
Fiona discusses at length the god Imbrifer and the constellation of Cap-
ricorn. Again she draws upon various mythologies from across the globe,
throws in the names of many gods, stars and constellations from many different countries and makes comparisons here and there. Dalua is named but
the essay does not tell us anything we do not already know about him. I
include it here for the sake of completeness.

I discuss *"The Immortal Hour"* in Appendix 3 but it is worth reiterating
a small quotation from the play in this current section. The lines in question
say, *"... on a quicken* [the mountain ash], *growing from mid-earth and hanging like a spar across the depths, Dalua sits: and sometimes through the dusk of
immemorial congregated time, his laughter rings: and then he listens long, and
when the echo swims up from the deeps he springs from crag to crag, for he is
mad, and like a lost lamb crieth to his ewe, that ancient dreadful Mother of the
Gods whom men call Fear ... Even the high gods who laugh and mock the lonely
Fairy Fool when in his mortal guise he haunts the earth, shrink from the Ama-*

*dan Dhu when in their ways he moves, silent, unsmiling, wearing a dark star above his foamwhite brows and midnight eyes."* This lets us know that Dalua walks with equal ease among humans and among the high gods of the Faeries. Fiona also points out a difference in his stature depending where he is. When he walks among us he is known as the Fairy Fool and has no power in the Faery realm for it is when he is here on earth that they Faery gods feel safe in their laughter and mockery of him. But when he is in their realm he becomes the Dark Fool and the powerful Faery gods grow silent and shrink from him. In legend and folklore we are often told that the things of this world are reversed in the Faery world. If Dalua is a mad, pathetic creature deserving pity in our world then it makes sense that in the Faery world he becomes a creature of power and stature that even the gods wish to avoid. However, as a further section in *"The Immortal Hour"* points out, he is unable to control his movements between one world and the other. He is tossed between them as some higher need determines.

This theme of loss of control of his location is brought up in another section of *"The Immortal Hour"* where Dalua realises he has suddenly been transferred from the Hebrides of Scotland to the gloomy forest where the play opens. The link between Dalua and the Hebrides is made clear in a short essay called *"When Dalua Was A Prince Of This World"* in one of the limited edition American printings of Fiona's works, *"The Silence of Amor,"* published by Thomas Mosher in 1902. I give it in full as it is not so easy to find these days:

When Dalua the King came to the Isles of the West, none but those who had hidden wisdom knew of it. No one saw him by day or by night: the wisest knew not whence he had come, or when or whither he would go. Dusk lay on whatsoever path he trod, and his feet were shod with silence. But after many days it was known to all that the Dark King was there, and all feared him.

The days slid by, like wave on wave into an ebbing tide, and perhaps the King gave no sign: but one day he would give a sign: and that sign was a laughing that was heard somewhere, upon the lonely hills, or by desolate shores, or in the heart of him who heard. And whenever the King laughed, he who heard would go from his clan to join the King in the shadow.

But sometimes Dalua the Dark King laughed in the unpeopled solitudes, only because of vain hopes and wild imaginings, for upon these he lives as well as upon the savours of death.

To-night, dreaming, I stood in a waste place, where the wind whistled in the grass, though I saw no leaf stir, no reed quiver. The wind passed, and the moon rose, and the wailing of plovers ceased. But Dalua neither heard me nor saw me, for was I not there as a phantom only, the phantom of a dream? There, in that unpeopled solitude, I knew that he went his secret way, for I heard a wild and lonely laughter in the night. Was it because of vain hopes and vain imaginings borne by that whistling wind out of bowed and broken hearts?

Answer, O heart, that so many imaginings have filled, so many hopes lifted.

Dalua crops up in another Fiona Macleod poem called,

## THE LORDS OF SHADOW

Where the water whispers 'mid the shadowy
      rowan-trees
I have heard the Hidden People like the hum
      of swarming bees:
And when the moon has risen and the brown
      burn glisters grey
I have seen the Green Host marching in
      laughing disarray.

Dalua then must sure have blown a sudden
      magic air
Or with the mystic dew sealed my eyes
      from seeing fair:
For the great Lords of Shadow who tread the
      deeps of night
Are no frail puny folk who move in dread of
mortal sight.

For sure Dalua laughed alow, Dalua the fairy
      Fool,
When with his wildfire eyes he saw me 'neath
      the rowan-shadowed pool:
His touch can make the chords of life a bitter
      jangling tune,
The false glows true, the true glows false,
      beneath his moontide rune.

The laughter of the Hidden Host is terrible to
      hear,
The Hounds of Death would harry me at
      lifting of a spear:
Mayhap Dalua made for me the hum of
      swarming bees
And sealed my eyes with dew beneath the
      shadowy rowan-trees.

In the moving dedication to his daughter Esther Mona, found only in the 1903 Thomas Mosher limited edition printing of *Deirdre and the Sons of Usna,"* Fiona says to the then two year old Esther, *"Long ago, one of the old forgotten gods, the god of enchantment and illusion, made a glory that was a glory of loveliness, an ecstasy of sound, and a passion of delight. Then he watched seven mortals approach it in turn. Three saw in it no loveliness, heard in it no ecstasy, caught from it no rapture. Of three others, one knew an inexplicable delight, and took away the wonder and the memory to be his while he lived: and one heard an ecstasy of sound, and went away rapt, and forgetting all things because of that dream and passion not seen but heard: and the third looked on that loveliness, and ever after his fellows spoke of him as one made insane by impossible dreams, though he had that in his life which rose in a white flame, and quenched his thirst at wells of the spirit, and rejoiced continually. But of the seven only one saw the glory as the god of enchantment and illusion had made it, seeing in it the spirit that is Beauty, and hearing in it the soul of Music, and uplifted by it to the rapture that is the passion of delight. And lest that evil Destiny which puts dust upon dreams, and silence upon sweet airs, and stills songs, and makes the hand idle, and the mind an eddying leaf, and the spirit as foam upon the sea, should take from this dreamer what he had won, the god of enchantment and illusion gave the man a broken heart, and a mind filled with the sighing of weariness, and sorrow to be his secret friend and the silence upon his pillow by night.*

*And I have told you this to help you understand that it is what we bring to the enchantment that matters more than what the enchantment may disclose. And, when you have been kissed by sorrow—may the darker veiled Dread pass you, dear—you will understand why the seventh dreamer who looked upon the secret wonder was of the few whom the gods touch with the hands, of the chosen keepers and guardians of the immortal fire."* The most important line in this packed little story is, *"... it is what we bring to the enchantment that matters more than what the enchantment may disclose."* This should be kept in mind during all magical and Inner work.

The only reference I have been able to find to Dalua that is not by William or Fiona is in a letter from Yeats to George Russell dated August 27th 1899, *"If you can call up the white fool and have the time I wish you could make a sketch of him, for Dalua seems to be becoming important among us. Aengus is the most curious of all the gods. He seems both Hermes and Dionysus. He had some part perhaps in all enthusiasm. I think his white fool is going to give me a couple of lines in 'The Shadowy Waters.'"* [2] The 'white fool' that Yeats is referring to had appeared psychically to Russell in 1895 when he and Yeats were staying with Lady Gregory at her estate Coole Park. At that time, and unknown to Russell, Yeats had been doing some magical work with the god Aengus using the magical image of a jester, or fool, in a white costume. Russell reported seeing just such a person walking the corridors of Coole Park. Yeats was impressed that Russell had picked up on this intuitively but in this letter it is not clear if Yeats believes the white fool to be Aengus or Dalua. He comments that Dalua is becoming important to the Celtic Mystical Order but then goes on to speak of Aengus and in the last sentence calls the white fool 'his' (i.e. Aengus's) fool.

The timing of this statement that Dalua was becoming important is significant as this was at exactly the same time Fiona was fine-tuning "*The Immortal Hour*," which centres around Dalua, and for which she was accused of plagiarism of Yeats' "The Shadowy Waters" – the very same play he states the white fool was about to give him some lines for. It is most likely that Yeats learned of Dalua directly from William because, as stated in this appendix, his name is not to be found in any other independent source. The fact that he does not crop up again in Yeats writings or correspondence implies that Dalua did not turn out to be as important as Yeats had assumed.

One of the rituals of Yeats' Celtic Mystical Order contains the following lines,

> THE GUIDE – What is that sound now, farther out on the waters?
>
> THE TEACHER – It is the searching sorrowful cry of the curlew.
>
> THE GUIDE – what is that glad laughing sound very far on the waters?
>
> THE TEACHER – That is the welcome given by the waves to the dragon's wings as they beat through them."[3]

These are clear references to Dalua for, as previously noted, two of his magical symbols are the curlew and distant laughter. I have been unable to find any more references by Yeats or any other members of the Celtic Mystical Order to Dalua. This implies that Dalua did not prove to be as important as Yeats believed he would be. If Dalua was appearing to Yeats and Fiona at the same period of time, as the date of the above letter shows, it seems Dalua dropped his contact with the Celtic Mystical Order in favour of concentrating his efforts on communicating with Fiona.

* * *

### THE NAME

All of the above helps give us an idea as to the nature, purpose and character of Dalua but what of his name? What does it mean and where did it come from? In the prologue to "*The Immortal Hour*" Fiona states, "*Of Dalua I can say but a word here. He is the Amadan-Dhu, or Dark Fool, the Faery Fool, whose touch is madness or death for any mortal: whose falling shadow, even, causes bewilderment and forgetfulness. The Fool is at once an elder and dreadful god, mysterious and potent spirit, avoided even of the proud immortal folk themselves: and an abstraction, 'the shadow of pale hopes, forgotten dreams, and madness of men's minds.' He is too, to my imagining, madness incorporate as a living force. In several of my writings this dark presence intervenes as a shadow … sometimes without being named, or as an elemental force, as in the evil music of Gloom Achanna in the tale called 'The Dan-Nan-Ron,' sometimes as a spirit of evil, as in 'Dalua,' the opening tale in The Dominion of Dreams.*"

There is a footnote to the tale "Dalua" that says, "*Dalua, one of the names of a mysterious being in Celtic mythology, the Amadan-Dhu, the Dark Witless One, or Fairy Fool.*" Here we are specifically told that Dalua is from Celtic mythology. There are many fools, madmen and evil personages scattered throughout the literature of the Celts as there are in other traditions but the specific name Dalua is not to be found in the corpus of Celtic mythology. Curiously, despite these earlier strong assertions as to his authentic Celtic origin, Fiona changes tack in the foreword to "*The Immortal Hour*" where she admits that Dalua does not exist in Celtic mythology after all. She says, "*Nor has Dalua part or mention in the antique legend. Like other ancient things, this divinity hath come secretly upon us in a forgetful time, new and strange and terrible, though his unremembered shadow crossed our way when first we set out on our long travel, in the youth of the world.*"

So where did she get this name from? If he is not to be found in Celtic mythology can we find any historical person bearing this unusual name? There is a lesser-known 7th century Irish Christian saint named Dalua. Some Leinstermen, who decided to use him as a target for spear practice, captured him but at the last moment he was saved. Unfortunately the terror of this incident left him with permanently crossed eyes. He was so grateful to God that he founded a monastery and the place became known as Cill Dalua, since corrupted into its modern form of Killaloe. The town's main claim to fame is as the birthplace of the great Irish hero Brian Boru but there are no obvious connections between the cross-eyed saint, the Irish hero who defeated the Vikings and the Amadan-Dhu of mythology to whom Fiona refers. There is also a small river in Co. Cork called the River Dalua after the saint but there are no connections between this river and the alleged Fairy Fool of Fiona's description either.

If the name Dalua cannot be found in Celtic mythology or Celtic history where else could she have taken the name? Perhaps the answer lies in the fiction of another contemporary writer on Celtic themes, Nora Hopper. In 1894, several years prior to Fiona first using the name Dalua, Nora Hopper published a book called "*Ballads in Prose.*" (John Lane, London, 1894) In this slim volume is a short story called "*Daluan.*" This piece first appeared earlier than 1894 in a magazine called "*Household Words.*" It is written in the First Person and concerns the narrator's chance encounter with a mysterious man who goes by the name of Daluan. The narrator is walking in Galway, Ireland, when a stranger, who seems to know much about him, suddenly comes alongside and accompanies him on his walk. They walk for some time and have a strained conversation, all the while the narrator feeling uneasy at the presence of this stranger. They stop at an inn for food and the serving lad is convinced that Daluan is of the Faery folk. As they leave the inn a swirl of dust blows by the door and Daluan steps into it, dancing wildly amongst the blowing leaves, dust and debris. When the air clears he is nowhere to be seen. Years later, on the eve of Samhain, the narrator and a friend go in the evening gloom to visit an old burial chamber close by the same inn. In the fading light the narrator gets lost and takes a wrong turning. He comes across what looks like a funeral with a circle of women standing around a newly made mound of turf and stones and a group of men standing back, in the shadows. The women are keening (crying and wailing in lament) for the deceased. They are crying, "*Daluan is dead–dead. Daluan is dead.*" But suddenly they give a burst of laughter and cry, "*Da Mort is King!*" Later, after the narrator and his friend are reunited, he relates his tale but is told that no funeral could have taken place because he knows for a fact nobody had died recently in the area, certainly not one with the peculiar name Daluan. They go back to the spot the next day during daylight but fail to find any trace of the turf mound or any other semblance of a grave. The narrator's friend then explains that the name Daluan is a play on Da Luan, the Irish for Monday and Da Mort is the Irish for Tuesday.

We know from Lady Gregory[4] that William heard Nora Hopper read this specific piece at a party in London on March 7th 1898 where he and Elizabeth were guests along with Yeats, Lady Gregory and others but he may have already been familiar with it from "*Ballads in Prose*" or even from the magazine "*Household Words.*" If so, then the name Daluan would have been in his mind from before Fiona started to write. Less than a year after the London party Fiona referred to Nora Hopper's story in her essay "*A Group of Celtic Writers*" that appeared in the "*Fortnightly Review,*" "*I know no story of Celtic savagery so terrible as that of 'Aonon-na-Righ,' and I doubt if there be a finer telling of an existing legend than in 'Daluan.' These seem to me Miss Hopper's finest achievement in prose.*"[5] As she says "*Daluan*" is based on an existing folk tale. This tale, common in various versions throughout Scotland and Ireland, is usually about a hunchback who one night stumbles across the Faeries singing and dancing in a ring. The song they are singing simply repeats the words, "*Monday, Tuesday. Monday, Tuesday. ...*" over and over again. Eventually the hunchback gets caught up in the monotonous rhythm and blurts out, "*... and Wednesday!*" whereupon the Faeries realise they are being watched. However they adopt this new word and find that their new song, "*Monday, Tuesday, Wednesday*" is much better and they thank the hunchback by removing his deformity. Clearly Nora Hopper's story is based on this old folktale and it is a tale William was almost certain to have heard in his childhood in the West of Scotland.

Just to confuse things there is another piece called "*Daluan,*" this one being a short poem, written by Norah Holland (1876 –1925) that appeared in her book "*Spun-Yarn and Spindrift*"

### Daluan

*DALUAN, the Shepherd,*
*When winter winds blow chill,*
*Goes piping o'er the upland,*
*Goes piping by the rill;*

*And whoso hears his music*
*Must follow where he will.*

*Daluan, the Shepherd,*
*(So the old story saith)*
*He pipes the tunes of laughter,*
*The songs of sighing breath;*
*He pipes the souls of mortals*
*Through the dark gates of Death.*

*Daluan, the Shepherd,*
*Who listens to his strain*
*Shall look no more on laughter,*
*Shall taste no more of pain,*
*Shall know no more of longing*
*That eats at heart and brain.*

*Daluan, the Shepherd,*
*Beside the sobbing rill,*
*And through the dripping woodlands,*
*And up the gusty hill,*
*I hear the pipes of Daluan*
*Crying and calling still.*

("*Spun-Yarn and Spindrift*" by Norah M. Holland, London & Toronto, J.M. Dent & Sons, New York, 1918)

This poem was written in 1918, long after Fiona's frequent mention of Dalua and long after Nora Hopper's story had been published. This character however is clearly more influenced by Fiona's Dalua rather than by Nora Hopper's folktale. For some reason though Norah Holland gave her character the name Daluan. Norah Holland was a cousin of W.B. Yeats and the very similarly named Nora Hopper was an acquaintance of the poet, which only serves to show yet again that any attempt to delve into the origins or depths of the name or character of Dalua always brings up coincidence, confusion and blind alleys. The above story and poem are good examples of how quickly and easily a name can slip into (relatively) common usage with its true origin being quickly forgotten. The name Fiona is another perfect example. The important point is that the name Dalua, and therefore his character and personality, have been 'planted' in our modern minds by Faery. There are those of Faery who wish to make his presence and purpose known, especially as the dark aspect of the Christ, and that he can be a link between the two worlds and between the Dark Christ and the Christ of Light. Understanding and developing this character is important in our world and the Faery world alike.

One other literary occurrence of the name Dalua is worth mentioning.

In 1906 the travel writer Hilaire Belloc published a little volume of short travel essays entitled *"Hills and the Sea."* In the introduction to the volume he comments on two travelling companions who roamed England and the Pyrenees together. He describes the many and varied experiences they had and in one chapter he says, *"Many things came to them in common. Once in the Hills, a thousand miles from home, when they had not seen men for a very long time, Dalua touched them with his wing, and they went mad for the space of thirty hours. It was by a stream in a profound gorge at evening and under a fretful moon. The next morning they lustrated themselves with water, and immediately they were healed."* [6]

In the same volume there is a short story entitled *"The Wing of Dalua"* in which he gives the story of these two men travelling through a mountain pass in Andorra. They get totally lost, hear mocking laughter around them, as in *"The Immortal Hour,"* suffer a terrible storm, delusions and madness, before finally stumbling into a village a full twenty-four hours later. To their surprise and horror they realise they are at the very place from which their journey started, having unknowingly come full circle during the night. Nobody in the village recognises the route they claim to have taken saying that no such place exists.

This little piece by Belloc is frustrating in that nowhere does he explain who Dalua is or was, where he got the name or idea from, if it is native to Andorra or is a name he adopted to fit the story. He could indeed have taken it from Fiona's *"The Immortal Hour"* as the play had appeared in the November 1900 issue of *"The Fortnightly Review."* Whether this was Belloc's source or not it only adds to the confusion surrounding this peculiar name and character and again emphasises his consistent connection with madness and confusion. Note also his reference to the wing of Dalua, implying Belloc was familiar with the knowledge that one of the magical symbols for Dalua is a bird, the curlew.

I have already mentioned the Irish town of Killaloe and the River Dalua as having no connection with the god but there is one physical location where the name Dalua had already quietly slipped through to our world, and that place is connected with the Faery Dalua, not the cross-eyed saint. It is a place that was very important for William and Fiona and, as her writings make clear, an important place for the Faeries too. Here is a personal aside describing how I stumbled upon it: in June of 2006 I was working as a guide and historian on a small cruise ship in Scotland. One of our regular ports of call was the Isle of Iona, a favourite haunt of William's and a place long connected with the Faeries. To get there we had to moor the ship in Craignure on the Isle of Mull and drive from there to the other side of Mull to catch the small ferry that crosses to Iona. En route to the ferry we would stop to visit the beautiful Torosay Castle, not far from Craignure. I had been there many times before but had never previously noticed in the grand entrance hallway an old map of Mull hanging on the wall next to a rather tatty case of stuffed birds. The map did not bear a date but its appearance and style was that of the late 18th century. The map was detailed enough to include the many rocky outcrops, known locally as 'skerries,' which litter the coastline of Mull and Iona making navigation hazardous. In the Sound of Iona, the stretch of water between Mull and Iona, I noticed several names that were clearly not Gaelic[7] but looked like phonetic attempts at spelling names the cartographer was unfamiliar with – "*Yl Chalua*", "*Rering*" and "*Dedym*." Then my eyes rested on one skerry, sitting off the shoreline of southern Iona, which was clearly labelled "*Dalua*."

Later that day I returned to Tobermory, the main town on Mull, and in the local bookshop looked up the present day Ordnance Survey map for that area of Mull. The skerries are all shown in great detail but none of them bear any of the names given on the Torosay map. The modern names are all in the modern Gaelic spelling and all have some definite meaning. I then asked the curator at the Mull Historical Society Museum if I could look through all of the old maps they possess covering the Ross of Mull and Iona. I was graciously given free rein to examine all that I wished but despite a thorough search of maps ranging from great antiquity up to the present day I found none that repeated the odd names to be seen on the Torosay map. Nor had any of the knowledgeable local folks at the museum ever heard of the name Dalua being used for any of the skerries. The following week I was back at Torosay Castle and I asked the owner of the house if she knew when the map in the entrance hall had been drawn. She did not. All she knew was that it had been hanging there for as long as she could remember. I kept up my searches whenever time and opportunity permitted and I eventually found another old map, the "*Blauer Map*" of 1662, that also lists the names of some of the skerries but is not detailed enough to name all of them. Two in particular are clearly labelled, one being "*Yl Chalua*," just as in the Torosay map, and the other being "*Valua*." Unfortunately the small skerry labelled "*Dalua*" on the Torosay map is unlabelled on the Blauer map but it is clear from both maps that the word-ending '… *alua*' was in common use in that area and that Dalua may well have been the name given by the islanders of Iona to the small rocky outcrop off the south coast of that little island as shown on the Torosay map.

William spent much time on Iona and liked to sit on the shore and small hills around the island to compose his and Fiona's prose and poetry. The collection of rocks known as Dalua are easily seen from the house in which he stayed while on Iona. He had an old map that he described as an, "*ancient MS. Map of Iona with all its fields, divisions, bays, capes, isles etc.*" [8] and there is a good chance that this ancient map also gave the names of the skerries. He made a point on all of his visits into the Gaeltacht to speak to as many local people as he could in order to collect stories and runes as well as local detail. During his visits to Iona he would have asked the islanders for the Gaelic names of any of the topographical features that interested him on Iona and along its shoreline. At some time he would have been given the name Dalua for the little skerry. But, of course, the important question is why did the islanders of Iona choose to give this uninhabited and uninhabitable rocky outcrop the name Dalua in the first place? Does this mean that the other similar names on the maps, Chalua and Valua, are also the names of old gods from the Faery realms? Often in Celtic mythology deities appear in threes and Fiona occasionally listed Faery gods in threes, such as Seithoir, Teithoir and Keithoir. Is Dalua part of a threesome that includes Chalua and Valua?

Another, more recent, fabrication of Celtic mythology that was claimed to be ancient also comes from Iona and from another MacLeod, no less a person than Lord George MacLeod, founder of the Iona Community. The symbol of the Iona Community is a wild goose, an image you will see frequently on the island. It was chosen to be the symbol for the community because Lord George once said it was a sacred symbol of the Holy Spirit as used by the early Celtic church, such as that founded on Iona in 563AD by St. Columba. Lord George's biographer, Ron Ferguson, looked for old references to the wild goose and could not find any so he asked Lord George what his source for this was and his short but honest reply was, "*No idea. I probably made it up.*" [9] I suppose if Fiona Macleod could pull things out of the thin air of Iona then so could Lord George MacLeod!

---

[1] The full title to the invocation is "Invocation of Peace (after the Gaelic)" which some have interpreted as meaning translated from the Gaelic but this is not the case. The poem is a Fiona Macleod original, written in English, but inspired by a similar type of poetry found in the Gaelic language. Alexander Carmichael collected many examples of this for his compilation "Carmina Gadelica." This example, taken from that book, shows the same repetitive style, and also the free mixing of Faery, Christian and pre-Christian lore that inspired Fiona to write her piece,

> "The Invocation of the Graces"
>
> I bathe thy palms
> In showers of wine,
> In the lustral fire,
> In the seven elements,
> In the juice of the rasps,
> In the milk of honey,
> And I place the nine pure choice graces
> In thy fair fond face,
> The grace of form,
> The grace of voice,
> The grace of fortune,
> The grace of goodness,
> The grace of wisdom,
> The grace of charity,
> The grace of choice maidenliness,
> The grace of whole-souled loveliness,
> The grace of goodly speech.

Dark is yonder town, dark are those therein,
Thou art the brown swan,
Going in among them.
Their hearts are under thy control,
Their tongues are beneath thy soul,
Nor will they ever utter a word
To give thee offence.
A shade art thou in the heat,
A shelter art thou in the cold,
Eyes art thou to the blind,
A staff art thou to the pilgrim,
An island art thou at sea,
A fortress art thou on land,
A well art thou in the desert,
Health art thou to the ailing.

Thine is the skill of the Fairy Woman,
Thine is the virtue of Bride the calm,
Thine is the faith of Mary the mild,
Thine is the tact of the woman of Greece,
Thine is the beauty of Emir the lovely,
Thine is the tenderness of Darthula the delightful,
Thine is the courage of Maebh the strong,
Thine is the charm of Binne-bheul.
Thou art the joy of all joyous things,

Thou art the light of the beam of the sun,
Thou art the door of the chief of hospitality,
Thou art the surpassing star of guidance,
Thou art the step of the deer of the hill,
Thou art the step of the steed of the plain,
Thou art the grace of the swan of swimming,
Thou art the loveliness of all lovely desires.

The lovely likeness of the Lord
Is in thy pure face,
The loveliest likeness that
Was upon earth.

The best hour of the day be thine,
The best day of the week be thine,
The best week of the year be thine,
The best year in the Son of God's domain be thine.

Peter has come and Paul has come,
James has come and John has come,
Muriel and Mary Virgin have come,
Ariel the beauteousness of the young has come,
Gabriel the Seer of the Virgin has come,
Raphael the prince of the valiant has come,
And Michael the chief of the hosts has come,

>     And Jesus Christ the mild has come,
>     And the Spirit of true guidance has come,
>     And the King of kings has come on the helm,
>     To bestow on thee their affection and their love,
>     To bestow on thee their affection and their love.

(Carmina Gadelica, Rune Number 3)

[2] Kalogera, page 95

[3] Kalogera, page 163

[4] Pethica, Lady Gregory's Diaries, page 176

[5] "Fortnightly Review", January 1899, page 47

[6] Belloc, Hills and the Sea, page X

[7] there is no letter 'y' in the Gaelic alphabet.

[8] Memoir, page 236

9 McIntosh, Soil and Soul, page 1

# Appendix V
# Brigid – Celtic Goddess, Celtic Saint and Faery Incarnation

This appendix examines the theory that Fiona was nothing less than a manifestation of the Celtic goddess Brigid, or the early Celtic Christian St. Brigid, working through the mind, body and pen of William Sharp. Although Fiona never specifically called herself Brigid at any time, nor did William discuss this issue, it has, nonetheless, an air of possibility to it and this gives extra importance to the whole corpus of Faery lore and mythology revealed by Fiona. Not much has been written on this subject but it is an idea that is discussed from time to time in occult groups and amongst those working magically and spiritually within the Celtic and Faery traditions. As well as drawing on her native Faery tradition Fiona also drew heavily on both pre-Christian and Christian material for use in many of her stories. This was not uncommon amongst the Gaelic speakers of both Scotland and Ireland as displayed in the hundreds of charms and sayings quoted in Carmichael's "*Carmina Gadelica*" where the two traditions mix freely and easily. This compilation also demonstrates just how important she was to the Gaelic peoples of western Scotland by the many times Brigid is named in runes, chants and songs. Some of these runes are strong and powerful invocations to Brigid such as,

*Each day and each night*
*That I say the Descent of Brigit,*
*I shall not be slain,*
*I shall not be sworded,*
*I shall not be put in a cell,*
*I shall not be hewn,*
*I shall not be riven,*
*I shall not be anguished,*
*I shall not be wounded,*
*I shall not be ravaged,*

*I shall not be blinded,*
*I shall not be made naked,*
*I shall not be left bare,*
*Nor will Christ*
*Leave me forgotten.*

*Nor fire shall burn me,*
*Nor sun shall burn me,*
*Nor moon shall blanch me.*

*Nor water shall drown me,*
*Nor flood shall drown me,*
*Nor brine shall drown me.*

*Nor seed of fairy host shall lift me,*
*Nor seed of airy host shall lift me,*
*Nor earthly being destroy me.*

*I am under the shielding*
*Of good Brigit each day;*
*I am under the shielding*
*Of good Brigit each night.*
*I am under the keeping*

*Of the Nurse of Mary,*
*Each early and late,*
*Every dark, every light.*

*Brigit is my comrade-woman,*
*Brigit is my maker of song,*
*Brigit is my helping-woman,*
*My choicest of women, my guide.*[1]

However not all the invocations to Brigid are in such high terms. She was also very much a goddess to be called upon in times of more mundane need as in this little rune begging for release from the pain of toothache,

*The incantation put by lovely Bride*
*Before the thumb of the Mother of God,*
*On lint, on wort, on hemp,*
*For worm, for venom, for teeth.*
*The worm that tortured me,*
*In the teeth of my head,*
*Hell hard by my teeth,*
*The teeth of hell distressing me.*
*The teeth of hell close to me;*
*As long as I myself shall last*
*May my teeth last in my head.*[2]

To assist the reader in drawing his or her own conclusions as to the feasibility of the possibility that Fiona was a manifestation of Brigid, and that she wished to reveal more of herself in her writings, I give here some of the more obscure references made by Fiona to Brigid and include some comments from other sources that help fill out the bigger picture on this esoteric subject.

One important statement on the idea that Brigid predates both the saint and the goddess and came originally from Faery is by the Scottish writer and antiquarian James Wilkie B.L., F.S.A. In the conclusion to his book *"Saint Bride: The Greatest Woman of the Celtic Church"* he says, *"Who and what, then, is St Bride? She is Bridget of Kildare; but she is more. She is the daughter of Dagda, the goddess of the Brigantes; but she is more. She is the maid of Bethlehem, the tender Foster Mother; but she is more even than that. She is of the race of the immortals. She is the spirit and genius of the Celtic people."*[3]

The pre-Christian Celtic goddess Brigid is associated with poetry, healing and fire. First, to state the obvious, Fiona was a poet. Second, many of her tales and much of her correspondence are taken up with healing, mainly of a spiritual nature. Third, she frequently used the analogy of fire, especially lit torches, in her correspondence when addressing the subject of either her own writings or the coming of the female Redeemer. Fire was important to her. Amongst the Gaelic speaking Highlanders and Islanders Brigid is also very closely associated with childbirth and safe delivery for both mother and child. Many old runes and sayings still exist calling on Brigid for assistance at this crucial time. Fiona's writings are full of references to child bearing, childbirth and infant mortality. Her four long poems *The Prayer of Women*, *The Rune of the Passion of Woman*, *The Rune of the Sorrow of Women* and *The Shepherd*, that Elizabeth called collectively *"From the Heart of a Woman"*[4], reflect this in its fullest.

In her story *"The Gaelic Heart"* she reveals several titles for Brigid that have never appeared anywhere else. Where did she get these names? This is one of those easily missed passages by Fiona that give out a good deal of previously unknown but important Faery lore. In this story Fiona has come across old Mary Macarthur asleep on the shore in Iona. Mary wakes and describes a dream she had of Brigid coming to her. The emphasis is on the pre-Christian Brigid and her many names. This is what Brigid said to Mary in her dream, *"I am older than Brighid of the Mantle... I put songs and music on the wind before ever the bells of the chapels were rung in the West or heard in the East. I am Brighid-nam-Bratta, but I am also Brighid-Muirghin-na-tuinne, and Brighid-Sluagh, Brighid-nan-sitheachseang, Brighid-Binne-Bheul-Ihuchd-nan-trusganan-uaine, and I am older than Aona and am as old as Luan. And in Tir-na-h'oige my name is Suibhal-bheann; in Tir-fo-thuinn it is Cu-gorm; and in Tir-na-h'oise it is Sireadh-thall."* Then the following explanations are given in a lengthy footnote, *"The other names are old Gaelic names: Brighid-Muirghin-na-tuinne 'Brighid-Conception-of-the-Waves'; Brighid-Sluagh – 'Brighid-*

*of-the-Immortal Host'; Brighid-nan-sitheachseang – 'Brighid of the Slim Fairy Folk'; Brighid-Binne-Bheul-Ihuchd-nan-trusganan-uaine – 'Song-Sweet (lit. melodious mouth'd) Brighid of the Tribe of the Green Mantle.'. She is also called Brighid of the Harp, Brighid of the Sorrowful, Brighid of Prophecy, Brighid of Pure Love, St. Bride of the Isles, Bride of Joy, and other names. Aona is an occasional and ancient form of Di-Aoin, Friday; and Luan, of Diluain, Monday. Tir-na-h'Oige is the Land of (Eternal) Youth; Tir-fo-thuinn is the Country of the Waves; and Tir-na-h'oise is the Country of Ancient Years. The fairy names Suibhal-bheann, Cu-Gorm and Sireadh-thall respectively mean Mountain-traveller, Grey Hound, and Seek-Beyond."[5]*

There are enough clues and valuable information given in these passages concerning Brigid to keep the determined seeker after Faery lore occupied for months. Note that her first statement, *"I am older than Brighid of the Mantle"* makes it clear that she predates the Celtic Saint Brigid, who was known as Brigid of the Mantle (or cloak) because she used her mantle to wrap the baby Jesus in while Mary slept. In a letter to her friend Dr. Goodchild, Fiona gave more names for Brigid and talked of her belief in the woman Redeemer who would soon arise in the west. She said, *"There is a strange and obscure prophecy in the Hebrides upon which I had meant to write a long study… I have in my mind, however, all but finally thought out (my way of work) a spiritual study called 'The Second Coming of St Bride' which will give utterance to this faith in a new redeeming spiritual face, - a woman who will express the old Celtic Bride or Brigit (goddess of fire, song, music). The first modern saintliness of woman (<u>Bride-nan-Brat</u> St Brigit of the Mantle; <u>Muime-Chriosda</u> Christ's Foster Mother; Mary's Sister etc). The Virgin Mother of Catholicism; Mary of Motherhood; Mary, the Goddess of the Human Soul; Mary, Destiny; Mary, the Star-Kindler: for Destiny is but the name of the starry light hidden in each human soul: Consolatrix: Genetrix: the immortal Sister of Orchil, the Earth Goddess, at once Hera, Pan and Demogorgon: The Daughter of God: The Star of Dreams; The Soul of Beauty: the Shepherd of Immortality. In the short story called 'The Washer of the Ford'… there is a hint of this in another way – that of the conflict between the Pagan and the early Christian ideals of the Mysterious Woman, whether a Celtic Fate or a Mary Bride of God: as again, in another way, in a story called 'The Woman With The Net' in the Pagan section of my forthcoming book, 'The Dominion of Dreams'"[6]*

One of the most in-depth discussions by Fiona on the nature of Brigid was in an article entitled *"St. Bridget of the Shores"* published in *"Country Life"* magazine that has never been reprinted or republished. This was written at a time when the Faery Fiona had become much more comfortable and capable of expressing important Faery lore in her writing and I feel that this particular essay was a deliberate attempt by her to set out much lore relating to the connections between Brigid and Faery. The complete article is long and deserves seeking out but I quote from it at length as it contains much unique lore and commentary that is not found elsewhere. This, again, begs the question how did Fiona know all these unique names that no other researcher, antiquarian or Celtic crofter ever knew? In part, she said, *"I have heard many names of St. Bridget... but there are three... many of my readers may not know. These are 'the Fair Woman of February,' St. Bride of the Kindly Fire, and 'St. Bride (or Bridget) of the Shores.'... in several of the isles – Colonsay, Tiree, the Outer Hebrides – 'St. Bride of the Shores' is not infrequent in songs and seasonal hymns... Everywhere in the Gaelic lands 'Candlemas-Queen' is honoured at this time. It is an old tale, this association of St. Bridget with February. It goes further back than the days of the monkish chroniclers who first attempted to put the guise of verbal Christian raiment on the most widely loved and revered beings of the ancient Celtic pantheon. Long before... ever the first bell of Christ was heard by startled Druids... the Gaels worshipped a Brighde or Bride, goddess of women, of fire, of poetry.*

*When, today, a Gaelic isleman alludes to Bridget of the Songs... he refers, though probably unconsciously, to a far older Brigid than do they who speak with loving familiarity of 'Muime Chriosd, [Christ's Foster-Mother] they refer to one who in the dim, far off days of the forgotten pagan world of our ancestors was a noble and great goddess... They refer to one whom the Druids held in honour as a torch bearer of the eternal light... one whom the bards and singers revered as mistress of their craft, she whose breath was a flame, and that flame song: she whose secret name was fire and whose inmost soul was radiant air, she therefore who was the divine impersonation of the divine thing she stood for, Poetry...*

*None forgot that she was the daughter of the ancient God of the Earth, but greater than he, because in him there was but earth and water, whereas in her veins ran the elements of air and fire...*

*In the moment when she died from earth, having taken mortality upon her so as to know a divine resurrection to a new and still more enduring Country of the Immortal, were there not wings of fire seen flashing along all the shores of the west and upon the summits of all Gaelic hills? And how could one forget that at any time she had but to bend above the dead, and her breath would quicken, and a pulse would come back into the still heart, and what was dust would arise and be once more glad.*

*Few remember... that she lived before the coming of the Cross: but all love her because of her service to Mary in Her travail and to the newborn Child...*

*What, then, are the insignia of St. Bridget of the Shores? They are simple. They are the dandelion, the lamb and the sea-bird popularly called the oyster-opener[7]... To this day shepherds on 'Am Fheill Brighde' are wont to hear among the mists the crying of innumerable young lambs, and this without the bleating of ewes, and so by that token know that Holy St. Bride has passed by, coming earthward with her flock of countless lambs soon to be born on all the hillsides and pastures of the world. Fisher-folk on the shores of the west and far isles have gladdened at the first long repetitive whistle of the oyster-opener, for its advent means that the host of the good fish are moving towards the welcoming coasts once more... To see the bright sweet face of the dandelion once more – 'an dealan*

*Dhe,' the little flame of God, 'an bearnan Bhrighde,' St. Bride's forerunner –
what a joy this is. By these signs is St. Bridget of the Shores known."*[8]

Fiona's longest tale concerning Brigid is her story *"Bride of the Isles"*
which is taken, as she explains in a footnote, from a popular folk-tale from
the Gaeltacht of the young Brigid being spirited off from Iona to the Holy
Land to tend to the baby Jesus while Mary rested. The commonly held folk
tale is usually rather brief and contradictory in places but Fiona's version
is much longer and contains a lot of detail not to be found anywhere else.
Once again we must ask where did she get this information from?

Her version starts with Dughall Donn, a prince of Ireland, being exiled
for allegedly fathering a child on a woman of noble birth who died during
the delivery. He denied that he was the father but none believed him. At the
time of the child's birth a poet and seer said that the girl child was Brigid of
the immortal race and Dughall could not possibly be the father. However he
and the child Brigid were banished from Ireland never to return. They sailed
north from Ireland in a flimsy little vessel that was eventually blown ashore
in a little cove on the Isle of Iona, Scotland. Many years later the similarly
exiled Colum Cille, later known as St. Columba, would be washed ashore in
this same cove. On landing on the shore, the baby Brigid, who was still too
young to speak, picked up some small shells and sang in a tongue Dughall
could not understand. He then knew that the seer had spoken truly when
she had said the child was not of the human race. He bowed his head to the
little baby and asked if she was of the Tuatha De Danann, the gods and goddesses. Brigid then spoke in the Gaelic and said,

> *I am but a little child,*
> *Dughall, son of Hugh, son of Art,*
> *But my garment shall be laid*
> *On the lord of the world*
> *Yes, surely it shall be that He*
> *The King of the Elements Himself*
> *Shall lean against my bosom,*
> *And I will give Him peace,*
> *And peace will I give to all who ask*
> *Because of this mighty Prince,*
> *And because of His Mother that is the Daughter of Peace.*

At the time this all happened Iona was home to Druids who had witnessed the boat floundering and came to help the man and the child. The
Arch-Druid questioned Dughall as to who he and the baby were and Dughall told him the whole story. The Arch-Druid accepted what he said and acknowledged that Brigid was an immortal. He told Dughall he and the child
could remain on Iona but he was never to tell anyone who he or the baby
was. Dughall, who was now called Duvach[9] to hide his real identity, took a
wife who raised the baby as her own and who gave Duvach a new son every

year for the next seven years. Brigid grew as a normal child and seemed to remember nothing of her origin nor of the day she sang in the strange tongue. Duvach questioned her on this from time to time when she was young but stopped asking when he eventually accepted she remembered nothing. One day however her closest brother came upon her sitting on a hillside and again she was singing in the unknown language, her eyes soft and distant. He reproached her for wasting her time sitting around singing and said to her, *"Idle are these pure eyes, O Bride, not to be as lamps at thy marriage-bed."* She replied, *"Truly is it not by the eyes that we live?"* and passed her hands before her face revealing that her eye sockets were black and empty. Then Duvach, her father, said, *"By the Sun I swear it, O Bride, that thou shalt marry whomsoever thou wilt and none other, and when thou willt, or not at all if such be thy will."* Then Brigid smiled, passed her hands back over her face, and once more her shining blue eyes were smiling back at him.

The passage that now follows in Fiona's version contains a wealth of symbolism and information and is a classic example of the mingling of Christian and pre-Christian belief and practice. According to Fiona it was Bealtaine, the May Day Festival, also Brigid's birthday. She went clad in white and wearing rowan berries to the only hill on Iona. On the top of the little hill three of the island's Druids were awaiting the sunrise in order to light the sacred Bealtaine fire. Although women were normally excluded from this part of the ceremony Brigid was allowed to stay. As the sun rose and the flame was lit, the druids started to chant to their own gods but all Brigid could see was the beauty of the life of the Christ (who had not yet been made incarnate) being revealed to her inner eyes. She was moved to tears by these visions and left the druidic fire and went to the Fountain of Youth, a little pool still to be found on the top of this hill, to wash her face and eyes. On the way there she came across a lamb that had managed to get itself stuck in a crevice between two boulders. A falcon was circling above it, crying excitedly, as it looked down on the potential meal. Brigid rescued the lamb and held it to her breast. It calmed down immediately and snuggled into her bosom. Brigid then looked skywards to the falcon and said, *"There is no wrong in thee, Seaobhag,* [Gaelic for 'falcon'] *but the law of blood shall not prevail for ever. Let there be peace this morn."* The falcon then flew down and landed on her shoulder and the falcon, the lamb and Brigid all knew perfect peace and harmony. The lamb's mother eventually found her lost lamb, the falcon flew off and Brigid carried on towards the Fountain of Youth.

When she arrived she found that two rowan trees had grown there where previously there had been none. She stooped to drink of the water and was startled to see the reflection of a beautiful young woman standing behind her. She turned round quickly to see the woman better but there was nobody there. The rowan trees, however, had now grown together with their higher branches forming a perfect archway. Despite it being early in the growing season the berries were full and red like clusters of droplets of blood hanging in the bright air. She walked towards this arch and as she did so it took the form of a great crown and the berries dropped from the branches like slow dripping scarlet blood. She then noticed a white merle sitting in the branches and singing, and a pure white dove slowly flew through the archway towards her. Brigid smiled, walked through the archway and was not seen on Iona again for a year and a day.

The scenes that Fiona described next are a curious mixture of desert and Gaeltacht; of the Gaelic language, names, mythology, even bagpipes and collie sheep-dogs, but all set in Bethlehem two thousand years ago. Brigid had been to the well to draw water and was making her way across the hot, parched desert as night fell. She had a vague memory of a distant island in the north, green and fertile, unlike her desert home. Her father, still called Dughall, was the inn-keeper in Bethlehem and he told her he must journey to Jerusalem where he had heard there was water to be had. He left instructions with Brigid that under no circumstances was she to allow anyone to eat or drink at the inn as there was only enough water for Brigid herself while he was away. Neither was she to offer accommodation to anyone while he was gone no matter how desperate their circumstances. The next day he loaded his camels, donkeys and asses with empty water containers and, with a piper playing a stirring march at the head of the procession, set off across the desert for Jerusalem.

Three days later an old man came to the inn with his young wife heavy with child, and asked for sustenance and shelter. Brigid looked at the beautiful young woman, radiant and fresh despite the dust and drought of their travels, and vaguely remembered a dream of seeing a reflection in a mountain top pool. She at first apologised and explained that she was under oath to her father not entertain any guests. Then the young woman on the donkey said, in the Gaelic, "*And is it forgetting me you will be, Brigid?*" whereupon Brigid remembered her dream at the Fountain of Youth in a far-off land and invited them in to share what little food and drink she had left. When they had eaten she directed them to a nearby byre where they could spend the night at peace. When she returned to the inn she found that the food and drink had been more than replenished despite the fact the strangers had eaten and drunk to their fill. Later that same evening her father returned with plenty of water from Jerusalem. As he ate and rested Brigid told him of the strangers and the fact that the food and drink had miraculously replenished itself. As she spoke they were interrupted by a noise outside – it was raining, the first rain anyone had seen in a long, long time.

Brigid and her father went to the byre to check on their new guests and as they approached in the darkness of the night they were amazed to see the byre lit with such intensity it seemed like the sun shone from within. Inside they discovered that the woman had delivered her baby and the child slept soft and sound in her arms. Dughall asked the old man who the child was and he replied, "*It is the Prince of Peace.*" Mary then handed the young infant to Brigid as she was tired and needed to sleep. Brigid wrapped the precious baby in her mantle and sang to him as Mary slept. At that moment, far, far away on Iona, Cathal the Arch-Druid died. But before the breath went from him he had a vision of joy and his last words were, *"Brigit Bride, upon her knee, the King of the Elements asleep on her breast!"* In the morning, when Mary awoke, she said, *"Brigit, my sister dear, thou shalt be known unto all times as Muime Chriosd."* The foster-mother of Christ.

Brigid fell into a deep slumber and her father left her in the byre with the couple and the Prince of Peace for the night. In the morning however he found that they had all left without a trace except Brigid who was still sleeping deeply. There was a radiance of soft light emanating from her. In her sleep Brigid dreamed of being back on Iona where she could hear the sound of bagpipes and soft harp music and she again looked upon the green, fertile Hebridean landscape. When she awoke and found the byre bare she thought that the whole thing had been nothing but her dreams. Then she saw her mantle still lying in the manger. When she lifted it she discovered that it was only half of her mantle, the other half still being with the infant Jesus. The remaining half though had miraculously become entwined with gold threads and precious jewels. When she placed it around her shoulders she found it more than covered her yet it was only half of its original length.

Her father meantime had gone through the village telling all and sundry that the Prince of Peace had been born that night in the byre behind his humble inn. Nobody believed him but still he insisted it was true. Eventually the elders of the village placed a fine on him for disrupting the peace and for spreading false rumours. The fine was three barrels of good ale, a sack of meal and three thin chains of gold each three yards long. This was a considerable sum and far beyond his means to pay. Brigid calmly told him to go into the cellar of the inn and see what was there. He did so and found more than enough ale, meal and gold chain to pay the fine in full. Next Brigid walked though the village and outside the house of Lazarus she laid her mantle on the ground. The gold threads and precious jewels took wing and became invisible birds of healing. They flew all that night over every house in Bethlehem and the next morning the entire village awoke to full health even though many had been suffering from various ailments for a long time. Later when everyone left their homes that day they found a new white robe, new sandals, plenty of food and water, a gold piece and new staff.

Brigid left Bethlehem that evening and walked out into the desert in the direction of Nazareth. In the moonlight she could see the imprints of two sets of footprints in the dewy grass, one was of a woman the other of a child. All night she followed without feeling tired or weary. The prints always seemed newly formed but never did she see the woman or the child before her. Eventually they stopped and she lifted her eyes and looked ahead. Not far away she could make out the twinkling lights of a large town, Nazareth.

As she gazed though the scene became blurred and indistinct as if it was somehow changing. She then realised that the lights of the town were in fact the first feint rays of the rising sun in the east. As she stood and watched the sunrise she was aware of the smell of heather and bracken, she could hear ewes and lambs calling to each other and close by she could hear the soft sound of gentle waves breaking on a sandy beach. Herring gulls flew over calling to each other. She was confused and did not know which way to go. She looked for the footprints to again show her the way but they were no longer to be seen. At her feet she saw in the growing light a little yellow flower. She plucked it and asked it to show her the way. Just then a little bee flew from between its petals and headed up the hill to her left. From that day forth the common dandelion was known as *an Bearnan Brighde* the Way-shower of Brigid. Just then a sea bird flew over head whistling loudly. She asked of it the same question – which way? The bird flew up the hill following the bee and ever since the oyster-catcher has been known as *an Gille Brighde* the Servant of Brigid. She followed the bee and the oyster-catcher up the hill and there found an archway of rowan branches, topped with a crown made of rowan berries and leaves. In the tree was a white merle that sang and a pure white dove flew through the arch as she followed. She walked on down the hill and saw the blue peat smoke rising from her father's house. And there was Peace.

This tale is laced throughout with much pre-Christian lore and symbolism and explains why the dandelion, oyster-catcher and lambs, mentioned in her *Country Life* essay, are connected so closely with Brigid. It is a story that is worth seeking out, reading in the full, and meditating over. It has much to say on Fiona's knowledge, perhaps First-Hand knowledge, of Brigid. William Sharp's friend and one-time colleague, the artist John Duncan who has cropped up on several occasions throughout this book, painted a wonderful scene of the young Brigid, sleeping, being carried by two angels across the Sound of Iona to the Holy Land. If you look closely at this large painting you can just make out the square-shaped outline of Iona Abbey set against the purple clouds on the far right of the horizon. The brightly coloured robes of the two angels, one female, one male, show scenes from the birth and death of the Christ, the beginning and the end, with the white-clad Brigid sleeping soundly as they fly above the waves and seals.

Fiona often referred to Brigid by name (in its various spellings) in her private correspondence and in her belief that a Redeemer would soon arise in the west and that this Redeemer would be a woman. In a letter dated October 18th 1905, two months before William died, Fiona said to the composer Helen Hopekirk, "*Wherever I am, St. Bride's Day is always for me the joy-festival of the year – the day when the real new year is born, and the three dark months are gone, and Spring leans across the often gray and wet, but often rainbow-lit, green-tremulous horizons of February.*"[10]

One of the few in-depth commentaries on the subject of whether or not Fiona was Brigid is an essay written in 1919, shortly after the conclusion of the Great War, by Ethel Rolt-Wheeler in which she discussed the possibility of Fiona Macleod being a manifestation of Brigid. In this essay she says, "*What are the qualities this distracted world most needs today? The Virgin quality of Purity; the Mother quality of Healing; the Goddess quality of Power. They are the qualities of Ideal Woman... only a few women in the whole course of history have been crowned with this triple crown of glory... Brigid is one, Virgin, Mother and Goddess...*"[11] She goes on to discuss how these qualities are to be found throughout Fiona Macleod's writings and she presents an interesting case.

As has been stressed throughout this book, Fiona dealt a great deal with sorrow in her stories and poetry. Eleanor Merry, the Anthroposophical writer and follower of Rudolf Steiner, comments in her book "*The Flaming Door*" on the sorrow that underlies so many of the thousands of Celtic tales. In connection with Brigid she says, "*Bride, who is the <u>soul</u> of the ancient Mysteries – wanders for ever in loveliness under the canopy of Heaven, wrapped in her mantle of bluest aether, and the vision of her calls every human heart away from the dark companionship of his shadow-soul, and saves every one from that sinister dominion... But she too has her shadow: the <u>forgotten</u> Mysteries. And this shadow lives in all the sadness of Celtic twilight tales, when hearts wake again to longing for the forbidden lands, or for the shining hosts of the Sidhe, or the caves of the hoary Sleepers; but it is a longing filled with dread and hopelessness and the expectation of death. And when the wanderer meets the 'shadow' of Bride, she is the Woman of Tears, or the Woman of the Crossways... 'Sometimes,' says Fiona Macleod, 'she is seen as the Washer of the Ford, a tall gaunt woman, chanting the death-dirge as she washes the shroud of him who sees her; and sometimes she may grow great and terrible, and inhabit darkness, and the end is come.' She tells too of the 'Woman of Tears' – who 'had her feet far down among the roots and trees, and stars thickening in her hair as they gather in the vastness and blackness of the sky on a night of frost.' Her form fills all the world where wisdom dwells. But she is sorrowful and terrible, for the hearts of men know her no more in her ancient loveliness.*"[12]

Later in the same book she says more on Bride, or Brigid, "*The Celtic Folk-soul is no longer the soul of a people, but the soul of a spiritual awakening of mankind. The blue banner of Bride is his banner shaken out over the expectant heavens. King Arthur will not be roused by the blast of the horn of any national egotism, though it may shake the Earth; he will awake only at the touch of the 'Woman of Beauty' who will 'come into the hearts of men and women like a flame upon dry grass, like a flame of wind in a great wood.'*"[13] Note the interesting connection with King Arthur, a connection already mentioned in Chapter 5 with reference to Lake Nemi and the Lady of the Lake. In his monumental work "*Carmina Gadelica*" Alexander Carmichael describes at length the scene in a poor crofter's home during a 'ceilidh' or social gathering. In part he said, "*One gives the songs of the chief poets, with interesting accounts of their authors, while another, generally a woman, sings, to weird airs, beautiful old songs, some of them Arthurian.*[14] The ancient Gaelic tales of Arthur have been long ignored by Arthurian researchers and writers but they contain a wealth of material not available from any of the other Arthurian sources. But that must be the matter for another book.

---

[1] Carmichael, Carmina Gadelica, Rune number 264

[2] Carmichael, Carmina Gadelica, Rune number 126

[3] Wilkie, Saint Bride, page 54

[4] "Poems and Dramas", Pages 83 - 99

[5] "The Gaelic Heart" from "The Winged Destiny" Collected Works of Fiona Macleod, Volume 5, page 209 et seq.

[6] NLS, Edinburgh

[7] Today this bird is commonly known as the oyster-catcher

[8] "St. Bridget of the Shores" from "Country Life" magazine, February 25th 1905, pages 259-262

[9] This is a play on the Gaelic word for 'sorrow.'

[10] Memoir, page 407

[11] Rolt-Wheeler, "Fiona Macleod – The Woman", "Fortnightly Review", CXII, November 1919, page 789

[12] Merry, The Flaming Door, page 249

[13] Merry, The Flaming Door, page 328

[14] Carmichael, Carmina Gadelica, page 22

## Appendix VI

# The Fate of the Bowl and the Triad

In 1909 Janet and Christine Allen, and Kitty and Wellesley Tudor Pole, became convinced that three holy sites in Britain - Avalon, Iona and a place they referred to as "the western isle" - had to be reactivated spiritually and the bowl would help them achieve this. The first of these, Avalon, they considered to be Glastonbury and as it was already well on its way to a strong spiritual revival it needed little help from them or the bowl at that time so they decided to make an attempt at spiritually reactivating Iona first. It was a long way from Bristol, the Abbey and its buildings were still in ruins and very few people visited the island but they felt compelled to make the long journey anyway. On June 26th 1909 the three girls arrived on the isle of Iona, complete with bowl, and spent several days taking it around the sacred places on the little island. By the time they had finished they felt it had been a successful venture and that an opening had been made which would greatly enhance the spiritual life of Iona. With the benefit of hindsight we now know they were right. Almost three decades after the bowl's visit to Iona, the Anthroposophist writer Eleanor Merry commented in her book "*The Flaming Door*" on the power of place. Referring specifically to Iona she said, "*How much more significance places have than we ever imagine to-day! How little we realise with what care and with what vision they were chosen, so that the living Earth should pour into the atmosphere what was needed for a particular cult – whether of moisture, or dryness, or heat, or cold, whether of iron or copper or lead or sparkling silica, or the 'magnet's invisible passion'!*"[1]

The third sacred site, the western isle, was Devenish Island in Lough Erne, Co Fermanagh, Ulster. This had been the home of the 6th century monk St. Molaise who later moved to the Holy Isle, off the east coast of the Isle of Arran, Scotland. Arran was also a favourite haunt of William's and was a place he occasionally claimed Fiona had spent her early years. It was considered by the Gaelic Celts to be the physical manifestation of the Otherworld. Its old Gaelic name is Eamhain Abhlach (Holy Hill of the Apple

Trees) connecting it symbolically with Glastonbury, the Isle of Apples, and linguistically as well in that Abhlach is pronounced '*avaloch,*' later corrupted to Avalon. However Wellesley felt that Devenish Island was not ready for reopening spiritually and that it was a difficult place because he believed it to be overrun by hostile Elementals. It may have been this belief that caused them to refer to it obliquely as 'the western isle' and never use its real name. As a result no serious effort was made on Devenish to reactivate it as had been done on Iona. One wonders if it is still a difficult place today? What this shows is that these keepers of the bowl were not just using it as an object of veneration but were actively using it as a magical tool in an effort, often successful effort, to achieve spiritual goals here on Earth. All of this must have been pleasing to Goodchild.

However in 1911 Thomas Allen, the girls' father, died. Christine decided to leave Bristol, her sister, comrades, and her work with the bowl, and move with her mother to a house in Nelson Street, Edinburgh. This effectively meant that the work of the bowl and Goodchild's dream of the new church was over. Had the Iona and Devenish sojourns been the culmination of their spiritual work and the outer work of the bowl? The split was harmonious and may actually have been a relief to all connected with the bowl. Now maybe they could let it slip from the public eye and slowly be forgotten. Kitty and Janet were now responsible for it. As far as I can tell, after her move to Scotland, Christine had no more contact with the bowl. On April 27th 1912, less than a year after moving to Edinburgh, Christine married John Duncan, the same artist who had been involved with Patrick Geddes in the Outlook Tower scheme and had accompanied William on some of his Hebridean wanderings. Duncan's stated philosophy on art was that, "*Art could find the greatest incentive in unsatisfied desire*" and that there was a "*profound and everlasting beauty in unrequited love – a beauty far more conducive to creative art than physical satisfaction that was fleeting.*" [2] Christine was aware of these sentiments and later confessed to a friend that they were not the most reassuring comments for the start of what she hoped would be a happy marriage. It is not clear how she made this surprising decision to marry John Duncan. As a child she had enjoyed a good standard of living. Her father worked for the railway and whenever they travelled by train they were treated like royalty. All ten of the Allen children received a good education and the girls were sent to finishing school in Switzerland and then on to Germany for music lessons. John Duncan was the son of a grocer and although somewhat successful in the art field was certainly not as highly educated as Christine, less travelled (although he spent nearly three years teaching art in Chicago) and had always struggled financially. It also has to be pointed out that when they were wed he was forty-five years old, Christine was only twenty-six. However, married they were, and they set up home in St. Bernard's Crescent, Stockbridge, Edinburgh where Duncan would spend the rest of his life. Despite his comments re unrequited love and fleeting physical satisfaction they did have two children, Christine Margaret, known affectionately as "Bunty," born in 1914 and Vivian Mairi in 1915. Duncan was utterly devoted to his daughters but, as time would show, he did not hold the same feelings for his wife.

They kept the house in Edinburgh but also rented a house on Iona where Christine and the girls would often stay when their father was working on a commission or new painting. Duncan loved the Hebrides, particularly the Isle of Eriskay, and Christine must have had fond memories of her bowl-work on Iona only a few years prior. The house they rented was the same house William had often used on his frequent visits to the island, and, later, was the same place that Netta Fornario would move to. When his work was complete, or when he needed a rest, Duncan would take a break from Edinburgh and join his family on Iona. He once commented to a friend, *"Iona, dear and lovely as ever... saw things that gave me the heartache. Crystalline, jewelled seas and aching sunset skies, the kind that send shivers up and down your back. And lovely clouds sailing through white cloud-drift and little fat birds tip-toeing along white stretches of sand. The Angel Hill put a spell on me. There's something not chancy about it."* [3] After one such visit he started to have spiritual visions so vivid they verged on hallucination. He wrote these down and incorporated them into much of his work. He did however make a cautionary remark when it came to working with Celtic imagery, especially that inspired by psychic vision, *"... the Celtic 'glamour' and 'twilight' is a dangerous dope."* [4] Fiona gave exactly the same warning in her story *"The Lynn of Dreams,"* as discussed in Appendix 4.

By 1916 his fortunes had changed and work was becoming less frequent due to the war that was raging in Europe and the fact that their financial burden had increased due to the needs of the two babies. A friend who visited them at that time commented on the squalor of the house in Stockbridge and the fact that Christine looked tired, haggard and at her wit's end. What a polar shift in just a few short years from being a Grail Maiden, travelling the country, holding spiritual services and being visited by the rich and famous, to becoming a worn-out housewife in a dirty and untidy artist's studio in Edinburgh. This is the exact opposite from several characters in the Grail legends of old who start off as, say, a swineherd but who eventually become elevated to Knights of the Round Table. The marriage was a loveless one that slowly deteriorated over the next ten years. Finally, in 1925, Christine could take it no longer. She told Duncan that she was taking the children to visit her sister, which was true, but this was not just a family visit or a break away from the misery of the family home. She borrowed fifty Pounds from her sister Dolly and immediately sailed with the two girls to South Africa without a word to Duncan. He was shattered at the loss of his beloved daughters and humiliated that he did not even know where they were. However, two and a half years later, one of the astonishing coincidences that peppered the lives of all the people mentioned in this book happened. A mutual friend of Duncan and Christine was visiting Cape Town in South Africa when he just happened to bump into Christine in the street. Word got back to Duncan and he immediately filed for divorce, as it was clear she had no intention of returning. From then on he continued to live in the family home and hired a housekeeper to look after him but his fame and fortune never fully returned. There was one happy time for him before he died when in the 1930s his daughter Vivian returned to Edinburgh to study medicine. During her time at university she lived with her father. He died in Stockbridge in 1945 at the age of seventy-nine.

Christine stayed in Cape Town and became involved in helping the poor. She and two other women (another female triad) started a soup-kitchen in 1935 called the Service Dining Rooms that provided good, nourishing food to the poor for a few cents, far less than the actual cost of the food provided. It was a great success and carried on long after her death. Her daughter Bunty ran it from 1976 until 1992. Christine remarried and returned to Britain on several occasions. When her old friend and spiritual comrade Wellesley Tudor Pole set up the Chalice Well Trust and bought the Chalice Well house and gardens in Glastonbury, she became it first warden, overseeing the repairs and renovations. She died from cancer in 1973.

Her sister Janet Allen remained in regular contact with Dr. Goodchild. He visited her and the bowl in Bristol several times after 1912 but commented that he felt the work of the bowl was done. Its aura, which he had been able to see clearly before, had all but gone and the atmosphere in the Oratory where it was kept had diminished considerably. On June 28th 1913, with Janet's approval, Kitty took the bowl to the new Tudor Pole home in Letchworth and it disappeared from view and from the public mind. In 1914 Janet moved to London where her mother was living after having left Bristol. Goodchild had recently died but of all the people involved with the bowl from its early days she was the only one who still sought a spiritual life. To this end she was taken into the Roman Catholic Church on January 10th 1920, taking the names Margaret Brigid, and on November 21st 1921 she entered the closed Benedictine community at Stanbrook Abbey, Worcestershire. She kept in frequent touch by letter with Kitty. She remained at the Abbey until her death on December 4th 1945.

There was another Allen sister, Mary, who certainly knew of the bowl and her sisters' belief it was the Holy Grail but she never got caught up in the glamour of it all. In fact she became a woman police officer, a very controversial organisation in those days, and rose high in the ranks. She liked the uniform and long leather boots and rarely went out in public without them. She also wore a monocle and the combined effect of this and the uniform made her appear very masculine. In the 1930s she went to Germany to train a new women's police force there and became enamoured by the up and coming Chancellor Hitler. She never expressed direct sympathy for the political, social or racial views of the Nazis but she was under the spell of Hitler himself.

The year after Christine Allen's marriage to John Duncan, Wellesley Tudor-Pole married Florence Snelling on August 17th 1912. He took up a military career and kept his interest in all things magical, spiritual and the Grail alive. During the First World War he was on active duty near Jerusalem in 1917 when Turkish snipers attacked him and his comrades. He was shot but the bullet passed through his body without damaging any major organs. As he lay on the ground losing blood he became aware of a presence near him. An inner voice told him not to move but that he would be rescued. The Turks left him for dead and eventually he was rescued and taken to a military hospital in Cairo where he made a full recovery. Following a distinguished military career he became a very successful businessman dealing in buying and selling a vast array of goods and commodities. After World War I he had taken possession of the cup from Kitty and still made attempts at discovering its origin. He kept this psychic side of his life very quiet, even his own three children were unaware of it. When hostilities broke out again in 1939 he did not reenlist but he did come up with a simple but brilliant idea that he passed on to Prime Minister Churchill in September 1940. He suggested that the BBC radio service should have a minute of silence every evening following the last stroke of nine o'clock by Big Ben that preceded the evening's news. This was to allow the nation as a whole to combine in a prayer for peace. Churchill saw what a powerful psychological weapon this would be against the Nazis and instigated it immediately. It was so successful that a minute of radio silence at nine o'clock remained in the BBC's programming until 1961.

In the 1960s he set up the Chalice Well Trust to raise funds in order to purchase the old monastery, Chalice Well House, which is situated next to the famous Chalice Well that still gushes copious amounts of red-tinged water. This venture was successful and the property and its extensive gardens are now in the care of the Chalice Well Trustees. Wellesley Tudor Pole never lived in Glastonbury. He died of cancer at his home in Sussex on September 13th 1968.

Kitty Tudor Pole stayed in the family home in Letchworth where she made a living by teaching the violin. Her spiritual needs were met when she joined the Quaker movement. She inherited the bowl following her brother's death, and in 1969 she handed it over to the care of the Chalice Well Trust, Glastonbury, where it remains to this day. She eventually passed away in 1986 at the age of 104.

The forgotten hero of this whole amazing episode is Dr. John Arthur Goodchild. It is still not clear why Elizabeth felt compelled to so play down his connections with William and Fiona and the great importance he had in the whole magical and spiritual world of the late Victorians. His name has largely been forgotten now – just like his bowl – but we modern Avalonians owe him an enormous debt for doing what he did. On February 16th 1914, Dr John Arthur Goodchild died alone at his hotel in Bath. He never married nor had any children. To the outer world his life's work was dedicated to the medical needs of his patients in Italy but to a smaller group his simple purchase of an old glass bowl in 1885 was one of the most important spiritual events of the 19th and 20th centuries.

For a complete and detailed account of this whole period and these fascinating people see Patrick Benham's excellent book, "*The Avalonians*" Gothic Image Publications, Glastonbury, 1993 with an expanded and edited version published in 2006.

---

[1] Merry, The Flaming Door, page 292

[2] Kemplay, The Paintings of John Duncan, page 59

[3] Kemplay, The Paintings of John Duncan, page 118

[4] Kemplay, The Paintings of John Duncan, page 11

# Bibliography

Alaya, Flavia *"William Sharp – "Fiona Macleod" 1855-1905"* Cambridge, Harvard University Press, 1970

Belloc, Hilaire *"Hills and the Sea"* Marlboro Press, Vermont, 1906

Benham, Patrick *"The Avalonians"* Gothic Image Publications, Glastonbury, 1993

Beversluis, Joel (ed) *"A Source Book for Earth's Community of Religions"*, CoNexus Press, Grand Rapids MI, 1995

Blamires, Steve *"The Irish Celtic Magical Tradition"* Aquarian Press, London, 1992

"      "      *"Glamoury"* Llewellyn, St Paul, 1995

"      "      *"Celtic Tree Mysteries: Secrets of the Ogham"* Llewellyn, St Paul, 1997

Bridge, Ursula *"WB Yeats and T, Sturge Moore: Their Correspondence 1901-1937"* London, RKP 1953

Caine, Hall *"My Story"*, Ballantyne, Hanson & Co, London, 1963

Cardozo, Nancy *"Lucky Eyes and a High Heart: The Life of Maud Gonne"*, Bobbs-Merrill Company, NY, 1978

Carmichael, Alexander *"Carmina Gadelica"* Floris Books, Edinburgh, 1992

Clarke, Austin *"The Celtic Twilight and the Nineties"* Chester Springs, Dufour Editions 1970

Colquhoun, Ithell *"Sword of Wisdom: MacGregor Mathers and the Golden Dawn"*, NY, Putnam 1975

Cullingford, Elizabeth Butler, "At the Feet of the Goddess: Yeats's Love Poetry and the Feminist Occult", *Yeats Annual, No. 9*, ed Deirdre Toomey, Palgrave

Denson, Alan *"Letters from AE"*, Abelard-Schuman, London, 1961

Donoghue, Denis *"Memoirs"* New York, Macmillan, 1973

"Dual Personality in the Case of William Sharp", *Journal of the Society for Psychical Research*, X pages 57-63, April 1911

Ellmann, Richard *"Yeats – The Man and the Masks"*, Dutton, New York, 1948

*"The Evergreen: A Northern Seasonal"*, 4 Volumes (Spring, Summer, Autumn, Winter), Patrick Geddes & Colleagues, Edinburgh 1896

Finneran, RJ, Harper GM, Murphy WM (eds) *"Letters to WB Yeats"* 2 Volumes, MacMillan 1977

Foster, RF *"W.B. Yeats: A Life; 1. The Apprentice Mage"*, Oxford University Press, New York, 1998

Gardner, Laurence *"The Magdalene Legacy"* HarperElement, London, 2005

Goodchild, Dr. John Arthur *"Light of the West: The Dannite Colony"*, Kegan Paul, London, 1898

Gould, Warwick "The Music of Heaven: Dorothea Hunter", *Yeats Annual 9*, ed Deirdre Toomey, London, 1992, pages 132-188

Greer, Mary K. *"Women of the Golden Dawn"* Park Street Press, Vermont, 1995

Gwynn, Stephen, editor, *"Scattering Branches"*, MacMillan, New York, 1940

Halloran, William F "W.B. Yeats and William Sharp: The Archer Vision", *English Language Notes*, June 1969, pages 273-280

Halloran, William F "W.B. Yeats, William Sharp, and Fiona Macleod: A Celtic Drama: 1887 -1897", *Yeats Annual 13*, ed Warwick Gould, MacMillan, London, 1998, pages 62-109

Halloran, William F "W.B. Yeats, William Sharp, and Fiona Macleod: A Celtic Drama, 1897" *Yeats Annual 14*, ed Warwick Gould, MacMillan, London, 2001, pages 159-208

Halloran, William F "William Sharp as Bard and Craftsman", *Victorian Poetry*, Spring 1972, Volume 10, pages 57-78

Hancock, Ian "*A Handbook of Vlax Romani*", Ohio, Slavica Publishing, 1995

Harris, Mike "*Awen*" Sun Chalice Books, Oceanside CA, 1999

Heilmann, Ann "*New Woman Strategies: Sarah Grand, Olive Schreiner, Mona Caird*" Manchester University Press, 2004

Holland, Norah "*Spun-Yarn and Spindrift*" J.M. Dent & Sons, New York, 1918

Hopkins, Konrad "*William Sharp/Fiona Macleod – a biographical sketch*" Paisley, Renfrew District Libraries, 1977

Hopkins, Konrad "*The Wilfion Scripts*", Wilfion Books, Paisley, Scotland, 1980

Hopper, Nora "*Ballads in Prose*", John Lane, London, 1894

Hunter, James "*Scottish Exodus*", Mainstream Publishing Company, Edinburgh, 2005

Janvier, Catherine "Fiona Macleod and her Creator" *North American Review*, CLXXXIV, pages 718-732, April 1907

Jeffares, A. Norman & White, Anna MacBride (editors) "*The Autobiography of Maud Gonne: A Servant of the Queen*" University of Chicago Press, Chicago, 1994

Kalogera, Lucy Shepard "*Yeats's Celtic Mysteries*" Florida State University, 1977 (thesis)

Kemplay, John "*The Paintings of John Duncan: A Scottish Symbolist*" San Francisco, Pomegranate Artbooks, 1994

Kitchen, Paddy "*A Most Unsettling Person: The Life and Ideas of Patrick Geddes, Founding Father of City Planning and Environmentalism*" Dutton, London, 1975

Knight, Gareth "*Dion Fortune & The Inner Light*" Thoth Publications, Loughborough, England, 2000

Le Gallienne, Richard "The Mystery of Fiona Macleod" *Forum*, XLV, pages 170-179, February 1911

Lochhead, Marion "*The Renaissance of Wonder*", Harper & Row, San Francisco, 1977

MacBride White, A & Jeffares, A "*The Gonne-Yeats Letters 1893-1938*", W W Norton & Company, New York, 1992

McHugh, Roger editor "*Our Irish Theatre, A Chapter of Autobiography, By Lady Gregory*" Gerrards Cross: Colin Smythe, 1972

McIntosh, Alastair "*Soil and Soul*", Aurum Press Ltd, London, 2002

Macleod, Fiona "St. Bridget of the Shores" *Country Life*, February 25th 1905, pages 259-262

Meredith, George "*The Letters of George Meredith to Alice Meynell*", London, Nonesuch Press, 1923

Merry, Eleanor "*The Flaming Door*" Rider & Co, 1936

Meynell, Viola "*Alice Meynell, A Memoir*", London, Jonathon Cape, 1929

Mikhail, E.H. editor "*W.B. Yeats: Interviews and Recollections*", MacMillan, London, Vol 2, page 352

Pethica, James "*Lady Gregory's Diaries: 1892-1902*" Oxford University Press, 1996

Rea, Lilian "Fiona Macleod" *The Critic*, XLVIII, May 1906, pages 460-463

Rhys, Ernest "William Sharp and Fiona Macleod" *Century*, LXXIV, pages 111-117, May 1907

Rinder, Frank "William Sharp – Fiona Macleod: A Tribute" *Art Journal*, LVIII February 1906, Pages 44-45

Rolt-Wheeler, Ethel "Fiona Macleod – The Woman" *Fortnightly Review*, CXII, pages 780-790, November 1919

Sharp, Elizabeth "*William Sharp (Fiona Macleod): A Memoir*" London, Heinemann, 1910

"       "       " Thoughts From The Note-Books of 'Fiona Macleod'" *The Quest*, Volume 1, January 1910, pages 354-357

Sharp, William "Garden of the Sun: 1" *Century Magazine*, LXXI, Mar 1906, pages 663-681

"       "       "Garden of the Sun: 2" *Century Magazine*, LXXII, May 1906, pages 37-54

Silver, Carole G "*Strange & Secret Peoples: Fairies and Victorian Consciousness*", Oxford University Press, 1999

Slavov, Atanas (Editor) "*Gypsy-English/English-Gypsy Dictionary*" New York, Hippocrene Books 1999

Tynan, Katherine "William Sharp and Fiona Macleod" *Fortnightly Review*, LXXVI, pages 570-579, March 1906

Walker, Hugh "*The Literature of the Victorian Era*" Cambridge University Press, 1910

Waugh, Arthur "Fiona Macleod: A Forgotten Mystery" *Spectator*, page 277, August 14, 1936

Wedeck, H. E. "*Dictionary of Gypsy Life and Lore*" New York, Philosophical Library Inc., 1973

Wilkie, James "*Saint Bride: The Greatest Woman of the Celtic Church*" Edinburgh, T.N. Foulis 1913

Yeats, William Butler "*The Autobiography of William Butler Yeats*" New York, MacMillan 1953

# Index
(Titles of publications are shown in italic)